THE

FOUR

GOSPELS

L. Thomas Holdcroft

CeeTeC Publishing
Abbotsford, Canada

The assistance of the following is gratefully acknowledged: Laurence Van Kleek who proofread the manuscript and prepared the library cataloguing information, Art Craddock who provided the cover drawings, and Sylvia Quiring who assisted in formatting the manuscript in its published form.

The Four Gospels
Third edition
Copyright © 1988, 1994, 1999 by
Leslie Thomas Holdcroft

ISBN 0-9680580-1-9

Holdcroft, L. Thomas (Leslie Thomas)
   The four Gospels / L. Thomas Holdcroft.
   3rd ed.
   p. cm.
   Bibliography: p. 257-259.
   Includes index.
   ISBN 0-9680580-1-9 (pbk.)
   1. Bible. N.T. Gospels—Commentaries. 2.
Jesus Christ. 3. Synoptic problem I. Title.
BS2555.3.H644 1999   226/.07/7

PRINTED IN CANADA

PUBLISHED BY
CeeTeC Publishing   U.S. address:
P.O. Box 466 Main   P.O. Box 1117
Abbotsford, B.C. V2S 5Z5   Sumas, WA. 98295-1117
Phone (604) 807-5831

CONTENTS

Lovingly dedicated to all past, present, and future students of the four Gospels. May your study and reflection upon these remarkable historical records of the earthly life and teachings of Jesus of Nazareth result in an unswerving lifelong conmitment to obey, honor, and serve Him.

NOTES:

1. Throughout this book, when Greek or Hebrew words are cited, their approximate pronunciation is shown phonetically. The syllable to be accented is printed in small capitals.

2. Abbreviations are those commonly found in a dictionary of abbreviations. In the index, "f" denotes "and the following page," and "ff" denotes "and the following pages."

3. When an individual identified by the dates of his or her lifespan is named more than once in a section, the dates are given only on the occasion of the first mention. If that person is mentioned again in a later section, however, the dates are repeated.

MAPS AND CHARTS

Figure

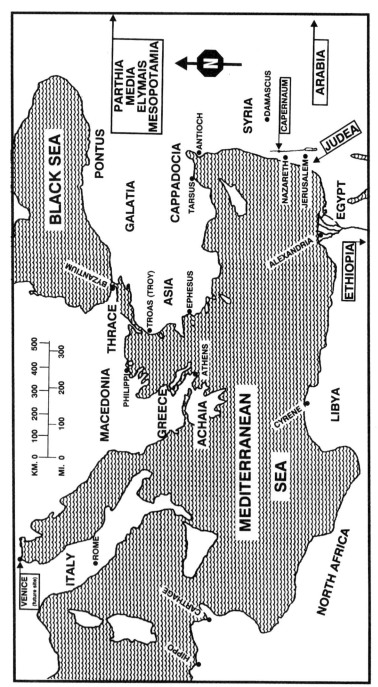

Figure 1: The world of the four Gospels

vi

ONE:

THE FOUR GOSPELS AND THEIR BACKGROUNDS

The Gospels exist because Jesus Christ lived on earth. His person and being are their center and focal point as they report His birth, His life, His death, His resurrection, and His teaching. By preserving God's record of the life and work of Jesus, the Gospels convey priceless insights that have changed the world. It has been rightly said that these four booklets, because of the One they present and the truths they convey, are more important than all other books known to humans!

Some Facts About the Gospels

The four Gospels comprise a little more than one-tenth of the entire Bible, and a little less than one-half of the New Testament —10.6% and 45.5% respectively. The total count of words in the Gospels is about 86,000. It is said that a thoughtful attentive reading of the Gospels typically requires eight hours or a little more. About this same amount of time is required to read the Gospels aloud at pulpit speed.

The Greek word for "gospel" (*euaggelion* [eu-ang-GEL-ee-on]) is also translated "good news"; modern versions often interchange these two expressions. Thus: "Jesus went throughout Galilee . . . preaching the *good news* [Gk. *euaggelion*] of the kingdom" (Mt. 4:23), or "The beginning of the *gospel* [Gk. *euaggelion*] about Jesus Christ . . . ." (Mk. 1:1). The report of the advent to this earth of mankind's Savior is truly wondrous good news.

Though there are four Gospels, Matthew, Mark, and Luke have a great deal in common, while John is markedly different. Thus, the first three Gospels are known as the "synoptics." This word denotes, "to see together" or "to look at something from the same viewpoint." The four gospel writers are sometimes called "evangelists," which is the Anglicized form of the Greek, and which acknowledges that they are messengers of good news.

Almost all scholars agree that the synoptics were not written for at least ten years after Jesus' ascension, and John's Gospel did not appear for several more decades. Soon after John was written, however, it was combined with the existing three, and the four were circulated as a collection. From about A. D. 95, almost all literary citations that refer to the Gospels are from the Gospels as we know them today. Not long after A.D. 150, Tatian's *Diatessaron* appeared. This work, known only indirectly apart from brief fragments, was a gospel harmony based on the four Gospels.

The Gospels quickly became a vital Christian resource. From the mid-second century, the four Gospels acquired a unique authority within the community of believers. In that century Justin Martyr (c. 100-c. 165) first used the term "Gospels" in the sense that we now use it. Clement of Alexandria (c. 150-c. 215) spoke of "the four Gospels that have been handed down to us." Origen, in about A.D. 230, referred to "the four Gospels, which alone are undisputed in the church of God." Though other, so-called "apocryphal Gospels" emerged, they never seriously challenged the recognition and authority of the four.

Since the late second century, when the comparison was suggested by Irenaeus (c. 130-c. 202), the four Gospels have been compared to the four-faced cherubim of Ezekiel's vision (cf. Ezek. 1:5-10). Matthew depicts Jesus as the **lion** of Judah; Mark depicts Him as an **ox** who patiently serves. Luke depicts Him as a **human** the intellectual one, and John depicts Him as an **eagle** soaring to realms above.

Why Are There Four Gospels?

In the second century, Christians began to ask this question. At that time they concluded that there are four in order to convey the message to different classes of people. Later scholars have noted God's pattern of authenticating witnesses by additional reports. (cf. "A matter must be established by the testimony of two or three witnesses" [Deut. 19:15b]). God had something so important and so precious to convey that He employed not two witnesses, but two times two.

The four gospel witnesses are not at all duplications, but four complementary accounts. The records confirm, supplement, and interpret one another. The four individual writers bring differences in observations, memories, and writing styles. Each tells of the life and work of Jesus Christ from his own viewpoint, and the harmonized outcome is a delightfully unified mosaic. Our four trustworthy messengers have left us a priceless legacy.

In Which Order Were the Gospels Written?

For many centuries scholars accepted that the order in which the Gospels were written was the same as the order in which they are placed in our Bibles. The statement of Irenaeus (c. 130-c. 200) was considered definitive:

> Matthew put forth a Gospel writing among the Hebrews in their own speech while Peter and Paul were preaching the gospel in Rome and founding the church there. After their departure, Mark, Peter's disciple and interpreter, has likewise delivered to us in writing the substance of Peter's preaching. Luke, the companion of Paul, set down in a book the gospel proclaimed by that apostle. Then John, the

disciple of the Lord, who reclined on his bosom, in turn published his Gospel while he was staying in Ephesus in Asia (*Against Heresies* 3.1.1)

Eusebius (*EH* 6:14.5)[1] quotes Clement of Alexandria as saying that Matthew and Luke were written first. He also quotes Origen (*EH* 6.25.4): "The first gospel was written by Matthew . . . and it was prepared for the converts from Judaism, and published in the Hebrew language." The conclusions of Augustine (354-430), whose teachings virtually dominated the church for 1,000 years, have been paraphrased: "The writer of the Second Gospel knew the First, the writer of the Third knew the other two, and the writer of the Fourth knew the former three."[2]

Significant challenges of this traditional belief were by Henry Owen in 1764 and Karl Lachmann in 1835. These scholars taught that Mark was written first and that it was used as a reference source by both Matthew and Luke. This view was based on an analysis of the literary relationships among the three Synoptic Gospels. Others who promptly adopted and promulgated the theory were by C.G. Wilke (d. 1854) and C.H. Weisse (d. 1866). To this day the so-called "priority of Mark" remains the dominant, but increasingly challenged, presupposition in scholarly literature concerning the Gospels. Some typical arguments supporting the priority of Mark include:

1) Mark is the shorter Gospel and the natural course of events would be to expand a shorter account.

2) Matthew and Luke differ from Mark in some details, but only rarely do they agree together against Mark. Thus they appear to have independently used Mark as their source.

3) Matthew and Luke are considered to improve upon Mark in style, vocabulary, and grammar, and they appear to be rewriting previously existing material.

4) If Matthew had been written first it would have been available to Luke. In that case the two would have had much more in common than they actually do.

5) If Matthew already existed there would have been no real reason for Mark to be written since only seven percent of its content is unique.

Though the priority of Mark is a popular view, some noted scholars oppose it. They prefer to accept the traditional priority of Matthew. They note that since Matthew was an eyewitness in the

---

1 The notable work *History of the Christian Church* by Eusebius of Caesarea preserves much of what is known about many leaders in the church during its early centuries. References to this work often use *EH* for *Ecclesiastical History*, or *HE* for *Historia Ecclesiastica*.

2 John B. Orchard, *A Synopsis of the Four Gospels*. Edinburgh: T. & T. Clark Ltd., 1983, p. xi.

circle of disciples, and Mark was not, Matthew would not have needed Mark's account as the basis of his Gospel. Many conservative evangelicals feel that the "priority of Mark" theory places too much emphasis upon the natural human composition of the content of the Gospels. Thus they assign the theory no particular role in gospel studies.

Some Unique Values of the Gospels

The four Gospels are a vitally important portion of the Holy Scriptures:

1) They bridge the Testaments.

Though the four evangelists expand the Old Testament revelation, they maintain its design, its goals, and its principles. In the Gospels, scholars count as many as 300 or more Old Testament quotations, references and allusions. The student of the Old Testament reading the Gospels for the first time finds himself on comfortably familiar territory.

On the other hand, without the Gospels, the Book of Acts, the Epistles, and the Book of Revelation would be greatly reduced in intelligibility. All of the remainder of the New Testament rests on the Gospels. The fourfold account of the manifestation of Christ is thereafter interpreted, explained, and applied to become the realization of Christ as the Lord of the church.

2) They reveal the personal nature of Christianity.

The Gospels tell about people, and they provide a new dimension in relating God and humans. The narratives shared by the evangelists portray flesh and blood humans touching God and being touched by Him. The Gospels name a total of fifty-four people associated with Jesus, and they tell of many others without naming them. The recognition of the worth of individual humans is impressed by the real-life biographical vignettes of the Gospels.

3) They reveal Jesus Christ

The purpose of the Gospels is not primarily to set forth a biography but to present a Person. The story may omit details that we wish we knew, but the living Christ is beautifully revealed in all His glorious splendor. Even if there are gaps in the biography, we have all that we need to enable us to know the Lord Jesus Christ. Each of the four gospel books is about the same Person, and when they lead us to know Him, they have fulfilled their witness.

I. THE GOSPEL ACCORDING TO MATTHEW

The New Testament begins with Matthew's Gospel because, when the Bible was being assembled, Matthew was seen as the first written Gospel. With its Jewish emphases, Matthew serves as an excellent bridge from the Old Testament to the New. The expression "according to" translates the Greek *kata* (kat-AH], and

	MATTHEW	MARK	LUKE	JOHN
Author an Apostle?	yes	no	no	yes
Traditional Symbol	lion	ox	human	eagle
Depicts Jesus as	Son of Abraham	Son of Man	Son of Adam	Son of God
Probable Place of Writing	Palestine or Antioch	Rome	Achaia or Jerusalem	Ephesus
Style of Writing	Didactic: a teacher	Anecdotal: a preacher	History: a theologian-historian	Spiritual: a theologian
To Whom Written	Jews	Romans	Greeks	Christians
Emphasis on Jesus'	dis-courses	miracles	parables	doctrines
Portion Quoting Words of Jesus	3/5	3/7	1/2	7/16
Space for Passion Week	2/7	3/8	1/4	1/2
O.T. Citations and Allusions	128	63	96	43
Parables Recorded	40	8	35	0
Miracles Recorded	20	18	20	8
Major Discourses	16	13	20	15
Of 165 Basic Events Gives	98	83	94	51
Commonalities	58%	93%	41%	8%
Uniquenesses	42%	7%	59%	92%

Figure 2: Comparative facts pertaining to the four Gospels. "Commonalities" denotes events also reported in other Gospels, "Uniquenesses" denotes events not so reported. Older terms for these categories were: "Coincidences" and "Peculiarities."

the title is simply saying that the person named is giving his report of the good news of salvation.

1. Date and Place of Writing

Two internal clues relate to the date of writing: 1) Matthew explains that the potter's field "has been called the Field of Blood to this day" (27:8) indicating that years had passed since the crucifixion, 2) Matthew records Jesus' prediction of the destruction of Jerusalem with no hint that it had occurred. Critics claim that such a vivid description could only have been written after the fact, but most evangelicals hold that Jesus' Olivet Discourse, telling of Jerusalem's destruction, was prophetic. Thus, Matthew must have written before A.D. 70, when the city was destroyed.

As we have noted, Irenaeus identified Matthew as the earliest Gospel written while Paul and Peter were ministering in Rome. Wenham dates Matthew around A.D. 40 (see Appendix), and most evangelicals place it not later than A.D. 50.

The patristic writers portray Matthew in Palestine when he wrote, and this is the traditional view, though no specific site is named. Modern critical scholars, assuming that Matthew wrote after A.D. 70 when Jerusalem ceased to be inhabited, suggest a Jewish center abroad such as Antioch or Alexandria. Since Matthew records Jesus' instructions for life in the church (18:17), Matthew may have visualized a particular local church, but Scripture does not identify it. Tradition says that Matthew ministered for fifteen years in Judea, then in Parthia (Persia or Iran), and finally in Ethiopia where he was martyred.

2. Matthew the Author

Matthew is not named the author, but usage and tradition are virtually unanimous in so identifying him. Eusebius quotes Papias, who wrote in c. A. D. 130, "Matthew composed the oracles [*logia* (LOG-ee-ah)] in the Hebrew dialect and everyone translated them as he was able." Later writers understood this statement to refer to an original work by Matthew, and they concluded that the Greek gospel of the New Testament was a translation of this Hebrew original.

As well as Eusebius (c. 260-c. 340), other church fathers endorsing Matthew's authorship include Irenaeus and Origen (c. 185-254). Apollinaris of Hierapolis, writing in c. 175, assigned Matthew's name to material that he quoted from the book. The name "Matthew" is the author's own name for himself; Mark and Luke tend to call him "Levi the son of Alphaeus" (cf. Mk. 2:14). Most scholars hold that this Alphaeus was a different man from the father of James the younger (cf. Mt. 10:3; Mk. 15:40).

In his Gospel, Matthew tells the story of his call to follow Jesus out of a background of service as a customs tax collector (i.e., a publican) (cf. Mt. 9:9-13). He marked the occasion by providing a "great banquet" (Lk. 5:29), though modestly he calls it only a "dinner." Among the disciples he identified himself as "Matthew the tax collector" (Mt. 10:3), a deliberately humble designation not used in the other Gospels. As a tax collector, Matthew was necessarily proficient in maintaining systematic records. Someone notes that of all the disciples "the only one who was a professional pen-pusher was Matthew." Thus Matthew at the outset, and later John, were the only disciples chosen to write a Gospel.

3. Matthew's *Logia*

A theory about Matthew's Gospel has resulted from Papias' statement that was quoted above: "Matthew composed the *Logia* in a Hebrew dialect . . . ." We have noted (p. 3) that in the fourth century Eusebius quoted Origen's claim that Matthew wrote in Hebrew. Also, Eusebius quoted Irenaeus, "Matthew indeed produced his Gospel written among the Hebrews in their own dialect" (*EH* 5.8.2). These citations suggest that the original version of the Gospel was in Hebrew [Aramaic], and that the usual Greek version is a translation. Many scholars supporting this view find internal evidences suggesting a Hebrew original:

1) The sentence, "You are to give him the name Jesus, because he will save his people from their sins" (1:21), is directly understandable in Hebrew but not in Greek or English. The Hebrew form of Jesus (Joshua) means "the Lord saves" and therefore only in Hebrew is it instantly clear why Mary's Son should be called Jesus.

2) Matthew's frequent use of the plural "heavens" (fifty-seven times) has been said to "make strange Greek," but in Hebrew the word is almost always plural.

3) The frequency of occurrence of certain words in Matthew would be typical in Hebrew, but unusual in Greek. Thus: *idou* (id-OO) occurs sixty-six times in Matthew and six in Mark. This word is rendered "behold" or "lo" in traditional versions and usually left untranslated or occasionally rendered "look" in newer versions; *tote* (TOT-eh) which is rendered "then" or "when" or sometimes left untranslated occurs ninety-nine times in Matthew but only six times in Mark.

As an alternate to the view that Matthew's *Logia* was the original Hebrew version of his Gospel, some suggest that the *Logia* was an earlier collection of Jesus' sayings. Matthew is thought either to have compiled this collection as a resource document to use in writing his Gospel, or to have secured it from another and then incorporated it into his Gospel. This concept merges with the claim of a source document called *Q*.[3] Views of this sort are commonly held by critical scholars and they reject any simple claim that Matthew originally wrote in Hebrew. After a survey of

---

3 For a discussion of *Q* see the Appendix.

such scholars, R.T. France wrote in the late 1980's: "Modern scholarship is unanimous that the gospel of Matthew . . . is not a translation of a Semitic document, but an original Greek work."[4]

Whatever is actually true in regard to the *Logia* remains a matter of speculation. However, two claims are widely accepted as fact: 1) the Greek version that we know today existed in Matthew's day, and 2) the supposed original and possibly more accurate *Logia* version does not exist today.

4. Matthew and the Old Testament

Matthew writes out of the riches of his Jewish heritage and the new found treasures of his Christian faith. In representing "Jewish Christianity," he addresses his Gospel particularly to Jews to whom, in at least forty references, he presents Christ who fulfills Old Testament Messianic predictions as King of the Jews. Expressions such as "so was fulfilled" or in modern versions, references to "what was said," (the so-called "fulfillment formula"), occur in Matthew at least eleven times, and four near variants increase the total to fifteen. Of 128 undisputed Old Testament references in Matthew, fifty-three are specific quotations, and seventy-five are passing references or allusions. Matthew quotes from at least nineteen Old Testament books (some counts range as high as twenty-five) and he names seven Old Testament individuals, plus many whom he mentions in his genealogies.

The exact manuscript from which Matthew quotes is usually not easy to determine. Of the eleven formula-quotations, only one is identical to the *Septuagint* version.[5] The others usually seem to be translations from the Hebrew Scriptures. By modern standards, Matthew's Old Testament quotations reflect various degrees of: "free, independent, and creative renderings." It has been suggested that Matthew quoted in this free fashion in order to suggest possible fulfillment, but to leave with the reader the task of precisely researching the reference. Most agree that he presents adequate evidence that Jesus of Nazareth and the Messiah of the Old Testament prophets are the same person.

5. Matthew and the Kingdom

Matthew frequently refers to the kingdom and it is a dominant concept in his gospel. The expression "kingdom of heaven," which occurs thirty-two times (some Greek manuscripts may vary this count) and is always written literally "kingdom of heavens," is unique (i.e., found only in Matthew) to his book. He uses

---

4 R.T. France, *Matthew: Evangelist and Teacher*. Grand Rapids: Zondervan Publishing House, 1989, p. 60.

5 This document, which is the translation of the Hebrew Scriptures into Greek, and which was completed during the third century B.C., is usually identified by the abbreviation: *LXX*.

"kingdom of God" at least four times. Scholars suggest that Matthew probably was guided by usage in Daniel 2:44: "the God of heaven [lit. "heavens'] will set up a kingdom that will never be destroyed." The kingdom, as depicted in Chapter 13, includes both believers and unbelievers (those who profess but do not possess), and thus it is not identical with the true spiritual Church. As Matthew depicts the kingdom, it is both present and also future. Though in the gospel era the kingdom was rejected by humans, it was affirmed by God.

6. Matthew and the Other Synoptic Gospels

Readers generally agree that Matthew is the most systematically structured and organized of the four Gospels. Though basically he records the life of Jesus, at times he prefers to pause and develop a topic rather than to proceed with the chronology of events in Jesus' life. The wide-ranging content of this book best meets the needs of most Christians. There are said to be at least sixty notable facts about Christ's teaching and ministry that are unique to Matthew. Because of the book's traditional pre-eminence among the Gospels, Matthew has had a major influence in determining the outlooks of mainstream Christianity.

A distinctive characteristic of Matthew is his emphasis upon the discourses rather than the activities of Jesus. McCumber comments on this book: "It is a teaching manual and, therefore, a learning tool, replete with urgent lessons and mnemonic aids."[6] About three-fifths of the book consists of the direct words of Jesus, and a total of nine chapters primarily record Jesus' sermons. To keep his book within the size limitations of a scroll, Matthew necessarily condensed some of the reports of Jesus' activities. Though we find twenty-one miracles in Matthew, only four are unique, but of the fifteen parables, eleven are unique.

II. THE GOSPEL ACCORDING TO MARK

Though it is only three-fifths of the length of the other Gospels, this Gospel possesses its own charming simplicity in its concise selection of important events. The book pictures Jesus as a man of action, it stresses His deeds more than His teachings. Thus, Mark addresses his book to the practical energetic Roman of his day.

1. The Markan Authorship

The title "according to Mark" was not added to the manuscript until early in the second century, but a virtually unanimous early tradition assigns the authorship of the second Gospel to John Mark, Writers such as Irenaeus (c. 130-c. 202), Clement of Alexandria (c. 150-c. 215), Tertullian (c. 160-c. 220), Origen

---

6   William E. McCumber, *Matthew*. Kansas City: Beacon Hill Press, 1975, p. 14.

(c. 185-c. 254), and Jerome (c. 347-c. 420), all confirm Mark's authorship. The classic statement, however, was by Papias (c. 60-c. 130) and it has been preserved for us by Eusebius:

> Mark, indeed, who had been the interpreter of Peter, wrote accurately, as far as he remembered them, the things said or done by the Lord, but not however in order. For he had neither heard the Lord nor been his personal follower, but at a later stage . . . he had followed Peter, who used to adapt the teachings to the needs, but not as though he were drawing up a connected account of the oracles of the Lord; so that Mark committed no error in writing down some of them just as he remembered them. For he had only one object in view, *viz.* to omit none of the things which he had heard.[7]

Note that Papias explains the lack of chronological sequence in Mark by the fact that the evangelist simply wrote what he remembered from Peter's discourses.

Irenaeus described Mark as "the disciple and interpreter of Peter" (*Against Heresies* 3.1.1), and he added that Mark wrote his Gospel after Peter's death. Peter's words, "my son Mark" (1 Pet. 5:13) confirm Mark's close association with him. It has been said, "The whole tone of the book reflects Peter's energetic and impulsive nature." Justin Martyr called the book, *"The Memoirs* [or Gospel] *of Peter.* Facts that relate Mark to Peter include: 1) Mark four times names Peter when the other Gospels do not in parallel events (Mk. 1:36; 11:21; 13:3; 16:7). 2) In six instances when Peter is reported commendably or honorably in the other synoptics, Mark omits Peter's name (cf. Mt. 14:28-31; 15:15; 16:17-19; 17:24-27; Lk. 22:8; 22:31-32). If Peter was the source of the data, modesty would account for the omissions.

2. Date and Place of Writing

On the basis of content, one school of thought sees Mark to have been written between A.D. 40 and 50; Wenham places it "about 45." This earlier date would accommodate a plausible solution of the so-called "synoptic problem," but the majority of scholars question it. Most prefer to hold that the comments of Papias and Irenaeus establish that Mark did not write until Peter had died. On the other hand, Mark almost surely wrote before the later months of A.D. 64, for Emperor Nero's persecution began at that time, and if a destructive persecution had been occurring, Mark would surely have reported it. These facts establish the plausibility of James Brooks' conclusion concerning the date of writing of Mark: "It must have been written shortly before the beginning of the persecution of Nero and therefore in A.D. 63 or the first half of A.D. 64."[8]

---

7   Eusebius, *EH,* 3.39.14ff.

8   James A. Brooks, *Mark.* Nashville: Broadman Press, 1991, p. 28.

Several church fathers state that Mark wrote from Rome, and this view is the generally received tradition. The claim of Chrysostom (c. 347-407) that Mark wrote from Alexandria is not supported. Mark was with both Paul and Peter in Rome when certain of their epistles were written (cf. Col. 4:10, Philem. 24, 1 Pet. 5:13 [Rome is identified by the code name Babylon]). In his final letter, just prior to his execution, Paul asked that Mark be brought to him in Rome (cf. 2 Tim. 4:11). Mark obviously was well adjusted to life in that city.

3. To Whom Written

The Gospel according to Mark is seen as a manual of the life of Christ especially suited to the busy middle class Roman. It concisely describes Jesus in such a way as to invite the reader to become His disciple. Mark favors brief hurried descriptions, an emphasis on the deeds of Jesus, direct quotations, and the present tense. His characteristic word (Gk. *eutheos* [eu-THEH-os]) occurs at least forty times and is usually rendered "straightway" in older versions, and in modern versions as: "immediately, at once, as soon as." He prefers short direct action sentences, often joined by simple conjunctions.

In Mark's own material, there are only two direct quotations from the Old Testament, although in reporting the words of Jesus he adds another eighteen indirect Old Testament quotations. The total of all Old Testament quotations and allusions in Mark is sixty-two, in contrast to Matthew's 128. Mark usually explains Jewish customs and sects for his readers, and he uses more Latin words than any other Gospel writer. He pointedly translates Aramaic quotations into Greek (cf. 5:41; 7:11; 14:36).

4. Concerning Mark the Author

John Mark is named nine times in Scripture. John is a Jewish name, Marcus (or Mark) is Latin. He was a son of the Mary whose home in Jerusalem was a meeting place for the Christians (cf. Acts 12:12), and probably the church's first headquarters. Mark was not one of the twelve apostles, but he had broad contact with the surviving eleven, and he was chosen to accompany Paul and his cousin Barnabas (cf. Col. 4:10) on their first missionary journey. John Mark's sudden withdrawal from this mission (cf. Acts 13:13) appears to have alienated him from Paul (cf. Acts 15:37-38). Later, however, Paul wrote, "Get Mark and bring him with you, because he is useful to me in my ministry" (2 Tim. 4:11).

According to a second century tradition, Mark was known by the nickname *Kolobodaktulos*. This name appears to mean "stumpy-fingered" or "ham-handed," and it suggests that Mark had unusually short fingers or perhaps a defective finger. Some relate the nickname to Mark's Gospel, and see it as a reference to its brevity of content and unadorned style of writing.

Mark is mentioned in four Epistles (Col. 4:10; 2 Tim 4:11; Philem. 24; 1 Pet. 5:13), but there is no record of his life after the gospel era. According to tradition, he ministered as head of the catechetical school in Alexandria. In that city he attained the rank of bishop, and there he suffered martyrdom. After his death, his body was taken to Venice, Italy, to be buried. In the ninth century the San Marco church was built on the supposed site of his grave to preserve what were said to be his relics.

5. Mark's Secrecy Theme

Mark characteristically emphasizes Jesus as a mystery person, not understood by His human associates. Thus, Mark appears to stress Jesus' many appeals for secrecy:

> "He would not let the demons speak" (1:34); "See that you don't tell this to anyone [to the one healed from leprosy]" (1:44); "He gave [the evil spirits who recognized His deity] strict orders not to tell who he was" (3:12); "He gave strict orders not to let anyone know about this [resuscitation of Jairus' daughter]" (5:43); "Jesus warned them not to tell anyone about him [His role as Christ]" (8:30); "Jesus gave them orders not to tell anyone what they had seen [in the transfiguration]" (9:9).

Mark may have selected instances of Jesus' appeals for secrecy because he felt that a valid interpretation of Jesus' acts required a complete insight into His life and death. For Jesus' peers to have classified Him on the basis of a single miracle would have been a deficient view. He desired that people commit to His kingdom for only the right reasons, and great crowds of mere miracle-seekers only hindered what He sought to achieve.

6. Mark's Relationship to the Other Gospels

In comparing Mark with the other gospels two sets of contradictory data emerge. On the one hand, very little of the substance of Mark is unique. Out of 661 verses, the substance of all but twenty-four is found in the other two synoptics; Matthew alone contains all of the substance of Mark except fifty-five verses. But on the other hand, Mark presents his material in his own words. One count found only two percent of Mark to be verbatim with Matthew. Thus the usual claim that only seven percent of Mark is unique is misleading: Mark's Gospel is not a mere duplicate, but a creative literary work with a particular object in view.

Although Mark is shorter than the other Gospels, what he does report is not necessarily reduced in length. Out of fifty-one events or pericopes[9] that the three synoptics have in common,

---

9 A pericope (pronounced pe-RICK-ah-pea) is "a selection out of a book." Bible scholars use the term to identify the topical segments that comprise the stories and teaching events of the gospels. (e.g. The Calling of Levi, The Feeding of the 5,000 etc.).

Mark's account is the longest twenty-one times, Matthew's eleven times, Luke's ten times, and nine times the three accounts are virtually of equal length. Mark's brevity is not because the book is an abridgment, but because he records fewer events. One-third of Mark's Gospel is devoted to the passion of Christ, and he totally omits the nativity stories and the pre-adult life of Christ.

7. The Epilogue of Mark

It is widely held that Mark 16:9-20 is a conclusion or epilogue added by another writer. Supporting this claim is the fact that the Sinai and Vatican manuscripts, which are two of the oldest known copies of the New Testament, conclude Mark's Gospel at 16:8. Also, a tradition dating back at least to the tenth century declares that the author of the epilogue was an elder named Ariston. Church Fathers who supported the verse eight ending included: Clement of Alexandria (c. 150-c. 215), Origen (c.185-c. 254), Eusebius (c. 260-c. 340), and Jerome (c. 342-420)

It is known, however, that the longer ending was in use by the time of Irenaeus (c. 130-c. 202) and until 260. Some hold that the longer ending is missing from the manuscripts because between 260 and 340 its authenticity was being reviewed, and it was temporarily removed from the book. Nothing conclusive is proved by style differences between the ending and the rest of the Gospel.

Most evangelical scholars hold that even if Mark's epilogue is withdrawn, almost none of its content is unique and what it communicates can be found elsewhere in Scripture. Also, virtually everyone admits that from a very early date the material in question was being used and cited as a valid part of the Gospel. If this is not the direct word of God, it is a centuries-old statement of how the people of God think and what they expect. This matter is discussed further on page 247.

III. THE GOSPEL ACCORDING TO LUKE

Luke's Gospel has been described as "the most literary of the gospels" and "the most beautiful book in the world." Quite fittingly, it both begins and ends with rejoicing. As the longest book in the New Testament it is more nearly a biography of Jesus than the other Gospels. Luke is said to have addressed his Gospel to the Gentiles in general, and to the Greeks in particular, since they were representatives of culture and intellectualism. The book embodies the writing style of classic Greek literature, although on occasion it reflects a Hebrew background. Thus expressions of the KJV: "he answering said" (instead of "he answered"), "it came to pass," or "before the face of" (2:31). Newer versions tend to drop such literal phrases in favor of idiomatic English.

In Luke there are more references to secular history, and to the customs, institutions, and political leaders of the time, than in the other Gospels. He writes as a man with a world outlook.

Although he was a theologian, Luke provides an authentic life of Christ that is not distorted by his theological concerns. Luke portrays Christ, not so much as the Jewish Messiah, but as the world's second Adam. His book has inspired more religious art than any other Bible book, and since he includes five songs, he has been called "the first hymnologist of the church."

1. Date and Place of Writing

Since Luke begins by stating that other records of the life of Christ already existed, he appears to be the last of the synoptic authors. The consensus of the usual datings place Luke in the early sixties. Wenham, however, holds that Luke's Gospel was well known in the mid-fifties, and therefore it was written prior to that time.

According to tradition, after Paul's death Luke ministered in Achaia and there he wrote his Gospel. An alternate modern view suggests that Luke may have written his Gospel in Jerusalem when Paul was in prison in Caesarea. During these two years, while Luke apparently waited in Jerusalem (cf. Acts 21:17, Acts 27:1), he would have had ample time to write.

2. Luke the Author

The Gospel does not name Luke, but almost all Christendom declares him the author. The Gospel is assigned to Luke by Marcion (c. 100-165), Irenaeus (c. 130-c. 202), Clement of Alexandria (c. 150-c. 215), Tertullian (c. 160-c. 220), and Origen (c. 185-c. 254), and is so listed in the Muratorian Canon (c. A.D. 170).

Marcion no doubt had other goals than to endorse the Lukan authorship. In c. 135, however, in order to promote his heretical dual-God doctrine, he published an edited version of Luke's Gospel. The document is no longer extant, but later references to it survive. This material establishes that in Marcion's time the Gospel of Luke existed, and it was considered authoritative and trustworthy. At that early date it obviously had enough prestige that a heretic would attempt to adopt it for his purposes.

Scripture gives no evidence that Luke was one of the twelve disciples, and probably he was not converted until after Jesus' ascension. He makes clear that he was not an eyewitness of the events he would describe (cf. Lk. 1:2), and he thus was the only evangelist who did not know Jesus in the flesh.[10] His name, Luke (Lucanus abbreviated), is Gentile. Other indicators that Luke was a Gentile include: 1) Eusebius' identification of him as a Greek, 2) his listing by Paul apart from the Jews who were his

---

10 Tradition chose to embellish Scripture, and by the third century it was teaching: 1) Luke was one of the seventy-(two) that Jesus sent forth (cf. Lk. 10:1-24), 2) Luke was the unnamed disciple with Cleopas on the Emmaus road (cf. Lk. 24:13-35). These claims cannot be proved, however, from Scripture.

fellow workers (cf. Col. 4:11, 14), 3) most scholars see the perspective of his Gospel to be Gentile. It is noted, however, that though Luke may have been a Gentile, he was unusually well acquainted with the Jewish Scriptures. Scholars find in Luke as many as 100 Old Testament allusions, quotations, and echoes.

The three times that Luke is named in Scripture are all in the writings of Paul (cf. Col. 4:14; 2 Tim. 4:11; Philem. 24). As Mark was associated with Peter, so Luke was associated with Paul. Some scholars suggest that Luke likely was converted under Paul. The alliance of the two is first inferred from the use of the pronoun "we" in Acts 16:10. During the second and third missionary journeys, and on the journey to Rome, Luke accompanied Paul. Thus Irenaeus called Luke "Paul's inseparable companion" (*Against Heresies*, 3:14:1). When a pastor was needed in Philippi, however, Paul left Luke in charge.

An interesting statement reflecting traditional beliefs concerning Luke is found in what is called "the Anti-Marcionite Prologue to Luke." This prologue is found in certain ancient manuscripts of the *Vulgate* that some date as early as A.D. 160:

> **Luke is a Syrian of Antioch, a physician by profession. He became a disciple of the apostles and later he accompanied Paul until his martyrdom. He served the Lord without distraction, having neither wife nor children, and at the age of eighty–four he fell asleep in Boetia, full of the Holy Spirit.**

A popular tradition identifies Luke as "the brother who is praised by all the churches for his service to the gospel." (2 Cor. 8:18). Anciently it was thought that these words concerned appreciation for the gospel-book, modern scholars interpret it as speaking of service to the gospel message. The original would allow either view.

Luke addresses his Gospel to Theophilus. The name means "lover of God," and since it is Greek, it is possible that he is addressing a newly converted Gentile nobleman. Other suggestions are: that the name generically includes all who love God, that it is an indirect allusion to Paul who was Luke's special friend, or that Theophilus was Luke's sponsor and literary patron.

3. Luke the Beloved Physician

Paul identified Luke as "the beloved physician" or "our dear friend the doctor" (Col. 4:14). Luke's outlooks, and the scientific precision with which he gathered data and reported it to others, substantiate the fact that he was a physician. Traditionally, scholars have found many medical references in Luke; the classic text in this regard is W.K. Hobart's *The Medical Language of St. Luke,* (1882). Today, however, many of Hobart's arguments, though not necessarily his premise, are rejected by some scholars. There is no evidence that in Luke's time there was a technical medical vocabulary. Thus, Luke's medical background is proved by reviewing the topics he chose and the nature of his reports, rather than primarily by analyzing his language.

4. Luke and the Other Gospels

Since Luke was probably not an eyewitness to the events of Jesus' life, he necessarily drew upon reports of others. He no doubt interviewed the eleven surviving disciples, and others who had been associated with Jesus. Perhaps he gleaned details of the nativity from Mary. Luke was efficient in his research, for more than half of his Gospel consists of the words of Jesus.

Luke and Mark were together in gospel ministry (cf. Col. 4:10, 14; Philem. 24), and they could have freely exchanged information. Luke likely wrote with Mark's Gospel before him; he reproduces about half of Mark almost verbatim. In "the great omission," however, Luke entirely omits the data of Mark 6:45 through 8:26. In "the great insertion" from 9:51 through 19:27 Luke vastly expands the account of Jesus' return journey from Galilee to Jerusalem. Parallel portions in the other Gospels are as follows: Mt. 19:2-20:34; Mk. 10:2-52; Jn. 10:22-11:57.

THE SYNOPTICS	The GOSPEL of JOHN
All three written prior to A.D. 70	Written after A.D. 85
Stress biography	Stresses doctrine
Many parables	No parables
Chiefly report the Galilean ministry	Especially reports the Judean ministry
Give account of 23 miracles	Gives account of 8 miracles
Stress public discourses	Sresses private interviews
Tell what Jesus did	Tells why He did it
A "moving picture" of Jesus	An "X-ray" of Jesus' Person
Focus on deeds	Focuses on words
Depicts Jesus' ministry as if it continued for just one year	By reporting three Passovers reveals that Jesus ministered for three years

Figure 3: Contrasts between the synoptics and John

Luke was the only evangelist who wrote a sequel to his Gospel. Apparently, it was through his travels and shared ministry with Paul that he became well enough informed about the early church to write the Book of Acts. Luke's two manuscripts (Luke-Acts) contain twenty-three percent more material than Paul's thirteen books. Thus Luke, almost surely the only Gentile writer, is the individual author who contributed the largest portion the New Testament.

IV. THE GOSPEL ACCORDING TO JOHN

John's Gospel stands apart from the synoptics, for he shares with them only eight percent of his material. Obviously, this Gospel makes a major contribution to our knowledge and understanding of the life and person of Jesus Christ. The book's message is the most universal of the four Gospels, and it addresses the entire world of Jewish and Gentile believers. Lessing described John's Gospel as "the most important portion of the New Testament," and Ernesti saw it as "the heart of Christ."

In comparison with the synoptics, John deals less with Jesus' actions, and more with His inner life. Though there are charming stories from the life of Christ, the book particularly reports Jesus' profound addresses that challenge the scholar to expound their meaning. In view of these sweeping variations of content, the book has been described as "a river in which a child can wade and an elephant can swim."

It is suggested that John wrote, at least in part, to counter the Gnostic cult that denied the reality of the incarnation. Gnosticism was a philosophy and pseudo-religion that appealed to some Christians and caused controversy in the churches (cf. Colossians, 1 and 2 John). Although John's Gospel is certainly much more than a philosophical polemic, it can be shown to refute each tenet of Gnosticism. Also, this book encouraged Christians of that era to maintain a commitment to Christ's deity and not relapse into Judaism.

1. Date and Place of Writing

Almost all agree that John's is the last Gospel. It is usually dated between A.D. 85 and 95, more than fifty years after Christ's ascension, and some time after A.D. 70 when Jerusalem was destroyed and the Jews dispersed. Though the book was written near the end of John's long and productive life, it is believed that it preceded both the book of Revelation and John's epistles.

According to later writers, John was associated with Ephesus, and it was from that city that he wrote his Gospel. Also, it was from Ephesus that he was banished to the Isle of Patmos, and apparently it was there that he returned after his release. Tradition claims that John was the only disciple who died a natural death, and, of course, he lived the longest of all the disciples.

2. John the Author

In the Gospel, John modestly kept himself nameless, but he
has long been identified as "the disciple whom [Jesus] loved" (cf.
13:23; 19:26; 20:2; 21:7; 21:20) or "that other disciple" (cf. 18:16;
19:26; 20:2, 3, 4, 8). Tradition has seen no conflict in this identification and has freely credited him with the authorship. Theophilus of Antioch (late second century) first named the apostle John
as the author of the fourth Gospel, and from his time the commitment became virtually universal. Theophilus put to rest the claim
of Papias (c. 60-c. 130) that John the author was a different person from John the apostle. Though almost a century had passed,
no one else had supported Papias' view.

Church fathers such as: Irenaeus (c. 130-c. 202), Clement of
Alexandria (c. 150-c. 215), Tertullian (c. 160-c. 220), Origen
(c. 185-c. 254), and Eusebius of Caesarea (c. 260-c. 340), as well as
Jerome (c. 347-c. 420), all testify to the Johannine authorship of
the fourth gospel. Irenaeus wrote, "Afterwards, John the disciple
of the Lord, who also had leaned upon His breast, did himself pub-
lish a gospel during his residence at Ephesus in Asia." (*Against
Heresies* 3.1.2). Some have suggested that 21:20-24 is John's
claim to authorship, but the claim in inconclusive because the
author is identified only as "the disciple whom Jesus loved."

John was "one of the best known characters of the New Testament," and an eyewitness of the events which he describes (cf.
1:14). He, and his brother James, were the sons of Zebedee and
Salome (Mt. 27:56; Mk. 15:40). In his early life, John, James, and
their father Zebedee were fishermen. As a young convert, John
possessed a quick temper, and Jesus called him "Son of Thunder."
(Mk. 3:17). After Pentecost he became a faithful worker, and he
was among those in Jerusalem "reputed to be pillars" (Gal. 2:9).
In later years, "the lion became a lamb," and traditionally, John is
known as "the apostle of love."

It is thought that John was originally a disciple of John the
Baptist and that he was the unnamed partner of Andrew (cf. Jn.
1:35-40). If this premise is true, then it was John and Andrew who
left their first master in order to follow Jesus and become His first
disciples. As we have noted, in associating with Jesus, John became "the disciple whom Jesus loved." He was one of the three
who shared the inner circle, and with Peter he prepared for the
last supper and was present at Jesus' trial. It was to John that Jesus committed the care of His mother.

3. John's Purpose in Writing

In concluding his Gospel, John noted that he had not used all
his information, but he had written with an objective in view.

> Jesus did many other miraculous signs [Gk. *semeion*] in the
> presence of his disciples, which are not recorded in this
> book. But these are written that you may believe that Jesus

is the Christ, the Son of God, and that by believing you may have life in his name. (Jn. 20:30-31).

John is saying that he has specifically presented a series of miraculous signs in order to convince his readers that Jesus is the Son of God. The term *semeion* (say-MY-on) denotes a sign that is contrary to the usual course of nature, a wonder or a miracle.

In the so-called "Book of Signs" (Jn. 2:1 to 12:50) John presents seven miraculous signs performed by Jesus: 1) Water to wine (2:1-11); 2) Royal official's son healed (4:46-54); 3) Healing at the pool of Bethesda (5:1-18); 4) Feeding the 5,000 (6:5-14); 5) Walking on water (6:16-21); 6) Healing the man born blind (9:1-41); and 7) Raising Lazarus (11:1-45). Only 4) and 5) are included in the synoptics; the others are unique to John. Although 5) is distinct from the other events in not being identified in Scripture as a sign (i.e. *semeion*), most scholars agree that it is one. Taken together, the seven miraculous signs recorded by John demonstrate that Jesus rules in all those areas that are beyond human control.

4. John and the Old Testament

Though John sought to show that Jesus of Nazareth was the Jewish Messiah predicted in the Old Testament, he avoided an obvious emphasis upon Old Testament content. His work is a universal Gospel which does not depend upon prior knowledge of what some see as a sectarian Jewish book. In John, a typical count sees only nineteen quotations from six books of the Old Testament, seven references to the fulfillment of Old Testament Scriptures, and about seventeen allusions. John undoubtedly possessed, however, deep reverence and love for the Old Testament and its content guided his interests and values. From this in-depth perspective, John did indeed freely use the Old Testament. Graham Scroggie claimed that by looking beyond the direct letter of the text, he could identify no less than 124 Old Testament references, allusions, and quotations in John. The low count of formal references perhaps tells only part of the story.

5. John and the Other Gospels

John's Gospel presupposes the synoptics and the reader's familiarity with them. Thus, in John, as Scroggie wrote, "There are no genealogy, no birth, no boyhood or growth, no baptism, no temptation, and no Gethsemane: everything is directed to the end in view to prove that Jesus was God." Nevertheless, John includes such notable details as: the lad with the five barley loaves, the crown of thorns, and the soldiers gambling for the seamless robe. About one-third of each of the synoptics concerns the passion of Christ, but in John the proportion is one-half.

John's report focuses on Jesus' ministry in Judea, while the synoptics emphasize the ministry in Galilee, Perea, and Syro-Phoenicia. John describes events on only twenty days out of the 1,200 days over which Jesus' ministry extended. Nevertheless,

John maintains the chronology of Jesus' ministry, and he shows that Jesus ministered three years while the synoptics appear to indicate only one year. He shares with the synoptics only three events prior to the last week, and in contrast with their reference to two feast days, he tells of a total of six. John mentions unclean spirits or demons only to report twice that Jesus' critics charged Him with demon possession (cf. 8:48-52; 10:20).

By the time that John wrote, people and institutions of Jesus' time had passed away. While the authors of the synoptics had to observe caution, John could freely reveal details and name names without causing problems for those still alive. Thus, for instance, where the synoptics use the word "Jew" five times, John uses the word over sixty times. Usually when John speaks of "the Jews" he refers to Jewish leaders who were opposed to Jesus. In John's time Jewish synagogues were no longer open to Christian witness. Beginning in A.D. 85 a formal synagogue prayer, recited in each service, included a curse on "Jewish Christian heretics."

Whether John wrote with copies of the synoptics before him is debated. Most scholars conclude that he did not, for had he used the actual manuscripts his quotations and references would have been more exact. It is suggested that John had read the synoptics, however, and that he had distinct memories of their content. Also, he may have read, and perhaps even possessed, non-canonical gospels. Obviously he had his own unique sources of information, and of course, the Holy Spirit was his overall guide and motivation. Thus, John's book is an essential expansion of the gospel story, and by it the church is greatly enriched.

TWO:

PREPARATION FOR JESUS' MINISTRY

Each synoptic begins with a brief literary introduction, but John moves directly to a presentation of the preexistent Christ. These introductions stand apart from the gospel harmony that is the essential core of the record, but they nevertheless contribute significantly.

1. Introduction to the Synoptic Gospels (Mt. 1:1; Mk. 1:1; Lk. 1:1-4)

Matthew begins by stating that he intends to give the genealogy of Jesus Christ and he identifies Him with both David and Abraham. The name Jesus was a personal name, but Christ was an official title meaning "anointed One." It translated the Hebrew *Mashiah* (maw-SHEE-ach) (cf. Ps. 2:2) which by way of Latin came into English as *Messiah*. In these opening words Matthew is leading up to his claim that Jesus is the Messiah. His use of the dual name Jesus Christ became popular after the ascension.

Mark declares that he will describe the gospel's beginnings, and he affirms the Lord's deity by naming Him "Jesus Christ, the Son of God." By thus identifying Jesus, Mark makes his perspective clear. He will describe the ministry of John the Baptist as the one coming to prepare the way of the Lord.

In the style of Greek secular writers, Luke introduces himself as a painstaking historian. He identifies his sources as "eyewitnesses" and "servants [or ministers] of the word"—those who had preached the gospel of Christ. In this elegant single-sentence paragraph (vv. 1-4) he notes that his account is not the first one written, and he states that he intends to produce an orderly (or logical) written account of the events in the life of Jesus.

As we have seen, Luke addressed his Gospel to Theophilus so he might "know the certainty" of the gospel (v. 4). This man may have been Luke's patron-sponsor, a new Christian, or perhaps an interested inquirer. In addition to meaning "lover of God," the name could mean "dear to God" or "friend of God." The title "most excellent" suggests that he held an important office.

2. The Eternal Divine Christ (Jn. 1:1-5, 9-14, 16-18)

John's prologue clearly establishes that Jesus Christ is the eternal Son of the eternal God. The original is in rhythmical prose

that some describe as poetry. Someone comments, "John's prologue is a summary and every statement made in it is verified in
the course of the narrative." Though the synoptics describe Jesus' human origins, John depicts Him as the eternally existing divine Word. His beginning parallels that of Genesis, but he
expands his words into a theological statement that introduces
many of his major themes. In speaking of Jesus as the "Word"
(Gk. *logos* [LOG-os]), John used a Greek philosophic term that denoted the "intelligence [or reason or ordering mind] of the universe." John thus communicated the reality of Jesus by a term
that was current among secular readers of that time.

The prologue divides into four sections. One of these is narrative (vv. 6-8) telling of John the Baptist, but the remaining three
present **fourteen** qualities and achievements of the divine Word.

THE WORD AND CREATION (vv. 1-5)

1) **eternal**—"in the beginning" (v. 1)—the Word (*Logos*) was not a
   created being, He was already there when creation began;
2) **personal**—"with God" (v. 1)—in close and intimate association
   and communion and on equal terms with Him;
3) **deity**—"the Word was God" (v. 1)—He is the image and re-
   vealer of God, for the Word and God are the same in essence
   and character;
4) **creator**—"without him nothing was made" (v. 3)—though God
   the Father is the creator, Jesus is the agent of creation and
   creation centers in Him;
5) **source of life**—"in him was life" (v. 4)—the Word is the essence of life and in Him is the principle of life; (John is characteristically concerned with life, and he uses the word
   thirty-six times; he uses the word light twenty-one times);
6) **inextinguishable light**—"the light shines in the darkness"
   (v. 5)—though there is the midnight blackness of fallen mankind that darkness cannot overcome Jesus' light.

THE WORLD'S RESPONSE TO THE WORD (vv. 9-13)

7) **universal light**—"gives light to every man" (v. 9)—God's illumination penetrates spiritual darkness, but though illumination is universal, salvation is not;
8) **unknown creator**—"the world did not recognize him" (v. 10);
9) **unrecognized Messiah**—"his own did not receive him"
   (v. 11)—fortunately, there were those who did;
10) **gateway to God's family**—"to those who believed . . . he
    gave the right to become children of God" (v. 12);

OUR WITNESS TO THE WORD (vv. 14, 16-18)

11) **incarnate logos**—"the Word became flesh" (v. 14)—for deity
    to become human flesh was a previously unheard-of concept,
    but God became Jesus of Nazareth; in this verse John reveals

that the Word is no mere abstract cosmic principle but it is the incarnate Christ. This Word dwelt—tarried, taberna-cled—among humanity;

12) **believer's provider**—"from the fullness of his grace we have all received one blessing after another" (v. 16)—fullness in-cludes the total of all that is in God;

13) **source of grace and truth**—"grace and truth came through Jesus Christ" (v. 17)—grace was revealed in His actions, truth in His words;

14) **the revelation of God**—"God the One and Only [or the Only Begotten][1], who is at the Father's side, has made him known" (v. 18).

Some of the verses mentioned above deserve further comment—

v. 1: "the Word was God" implies the trinity (or at least two dis-tinct Persons). To mistranslate this verse as "the Word was a God" would be to teach polytheism.

v. 3: Jesus is involved as a mediator in all of God's works: creation, salvation, and revelation.

v. 4: John begins and ends with light (cf. v. 42; 20:31); those who come alive in Christ come out of sin's darkness.

v. 5: Darkness can neither understand, overcome, nor extinguish light.

v. 9: This verse is known as "The Quaker's Text." They used it as the basic text for their doctrine of the inner light. Later Jesus proclaimed Himself the "light of the world" (Jn. 9:5).

v. 11: This verse has been called "one of the saddest verses in the Bible."

v. 12: To "believe in" His name implies a turning from sin, and thus it associates with repentance. How gratifying that some welcomed the Word in faith!

v. 13: While the Jews stressed physical heritage, John wanted to make very clear that becoming God's child is a divine spiri-tual work.

v. 14: This verse is the pivotal statement of the prologue. That the divine *Logos* took on humanity is truly "the most astounding fact of all history." This verse is a key source for the doctrine of Christ's person, and His relationship to the Father. For the incarnate Christ to have "made his dwelling" or "dwelt or lived for a time" among humans could be rendered, He "pitched His tent" or "camped." That Jesus was "full of grace and truth" establishes His equivalence with the gracious God of the Old Testament "abounding in love [*hesed*] and faithful-ness [*emeth*]" (Exod. 34:6). (*hesed* [HEH-sed]: loving,

---

1   Variant textual readings in the original result in the differences we find in our versions.

merciful, showing grace; *emeth* [EH-meth]: faithful, firmness, truth). The glory that Moses saw when the LORD passed before him was now manifested in a human life on earth.

vv. 16-18: these verses are generally thought to be reflections of the author of the Gospel.

v. 18: the incarnation revealed God to humans. Though God is mysterious and invisible, He who shared in kinship and in knowledge "has made him known [Gk. *exegeomai* (ex-egg-EH-o-my)]." This Greek term is defined: explain, interpret, report, describe, cf. to exegete.) The expression "God the One and Only" (or Only Begotten Son) is a unique reference to the divine *Logos*.

I. JESUS' ADVENT AND EARLY YEARS

1. The Lineage of the Promised Messiah (Mt. 1:2-17; Lk. 3:23b-38)

Genealogies were essential in Judaism in order to establish tribal and family origins and determine eligibility for the priesthood. In the first century the Sanhedrin continued to maintain these records, and to make them available in public archives.

The genealogies of the Gospels set forth Jesus' descent through the promised line, and they demonstrate that He qualified as the Messiah and that He was an authentic king. Significantly, the Jews accepted Jesus' genealogy, and they never challenged His claim to be the son of David. Matthew begins his genealogy with Abraham, but Luke takes it back to Adam. Luke implies that Jesus is the second Adam who will renew human life to what it was originally created to be. Paul took up the message when he wrote, "'The first man Adam became a living being'; the last Adam, a life-giving spirit" (1 Cor. 15:46).

Matthew's genealogy is selective with deliberate omissions and three divisions of fourteen each[2], presumably for convenience in memorizing. Each person listed is the ancestor of the one who follows, though not necessarily the immediate ancestor. The order in which each of the two genealogies is given relates to Matthew's view of Jesus as the Jewish Messiah, and Luke's view of Him simply as the Son of Man. Matthew concludes, ". . . Mary, of whom was born Jesus, who is called Christ" (Mt. 1:16). The wording in this verse clearly supports the Virgin Birth and the fact that Mary's husband was not Jesus' father.

God's sovereignty in the Messiah's birth is plainly evident, for Matthew's list includes immoral persons (Judah, David, Tamar, Bathsheba, and perhaps Rahab) and Gentiles. Jesus identified with humans in spite of their faults. The inclusion of

---

2   Actually, there are only thirteen generations listed in the third group, but Mary is named as the fourteenth person.

women in an ancient genealogy is unusual, but three are named and a fourth—Bathsheba—is identified. Of these four women, only Ruth lived an exemplary life. All four women were from alien nations: Tamar and Rahab were Canaanites, Ruth was a Moabite, and Bathsheba was a Hittite. In listing "Jehoram the father of Uzziah" (1:8c), Matthew omits three generations. Jehoram actually was the great great-grandfather of Uzziah. Probably the three kings (Ahaziah, Joash, Amaziah) were omitted because of their connection with the idolatrous house of Ahab.

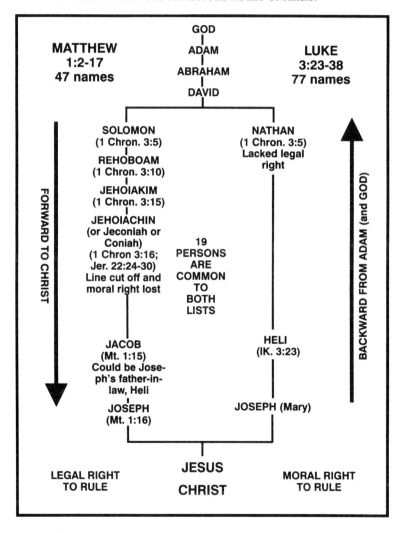

Figure 4: Genealogical relationships of Jesus Christ

Apparently, the Shealtiel in Matthew 1:12 and the Shealtiel in Luke 3:27 are different persons. Matthew states that Shealtiel was the son of Jeconiah (though 1 Chron. 3:17 gives the father his better-known name Jehoiachin); the father of Luke's Shealtiel is Neri. Thus, although each Shealtiel fathered a son named Zerubbabel, these Zerubbabels are two different men.

A widely held proposal to resolve the many differences between the two genealogies holds that Matthew gives Jesus' genealogy through Joseph, while Luke gives it through Mary. In this latter case, Joseph would have been the son-in-law rather than the son of Heli (cf. Lk. 3:23)[3], and this is possible since the Jews did not always distinguish the two relationships. Joseph's line, through sin, had lost the moral right to Israel's throne, though they still possessed the legal right. Mary's line possessed the moral right only. Since Jesus was virgin born, but Joseph was Mary's husband, Jesus inherited both the legal and moral right to the throne without also inheriting the disqualifying moral failure of Joseph's line.

An alternate proposal to reconcile the two genealogies is accepted by some. This view holds that both Matthew and Luke give Joseph's genealogy, but Matthew gives the line of succession-heirs to the throne while Luke gives Joseph's personal family line. Matthew's report is the legal line of royal succession, while Luke's is Joseph's line of natural descent. Two lists are necessary because the line of royal succession did not always run directly from father to son.

Each of the foregoing proposals holds that the two genealogies comprise two different lines, and this assumption, if not the detailed explanations, seems valid. Otherwise, based on agreed upon current insights, the genealogies remain unharmonized. Bible believers definitely hold that both lists are authentic, and the fact that names cannot be verified by modern scholars does not invalidate them.

2. The Annunciation to Zechariah (Lk. 1:5-25)

The lengthy first chapter of Luke consists mostly of the so-called "Infancy Narratives" (cf. Lk. 1:5-80). In verse five, Luke introduces us to Herod (the Great), the Idumean (i.e., from

---

3   Eusebius in *EH* gives an explanation of Joseph's parentage that he credits to Julius Africanus (c. 160-c. 240). According to this report, Matthan of the line of Solomon fathered Jacob and then died prematurely. Melchi of the line of Nathan married Matthan's widow, and their child was Heli. Thus, Jacob and Heli had the same mother. When Heli died without children, since Jacob was his step brother, in the pattern of levirate marriage, he married Heli's widow and Joseph was born of this union. Joseph was therefore the biological son of Jacob, but he was the legal son of Heli. This view is said to have "satisfied the church for many centuries." Though complex, it is possible.

Edom) who had been appointed by the Roman Senate to be king of Judea. Also, we meet the elderly husband-wife team, Zechariah (or Zacharias) and Elizabeth who each had been born into a priestly family. Luke describes the couple who were to be John's parents: "Both of them were upright in the sight of God" (v. 6).

By grounding the message of Christianity in the temple and Jewish history and worship, Luke writes in the style of the Old Testament. To link the two Testaments, he uses the history of John the Baptist and Zechariah and Elizabeth. The announcement of John's impending birth in fulfillment of God's plan was the first authentic word from heaven for nearly four centuries. By this event, and those that followed, God was now breaking into current human affairs on earth. Significantly, He came to one who was found in His house.

Zechariah "belonged to the priestly division of Abijah" (v. 5), which was one of twenty-four divisions. Each division served twice a year for one week. Priests were chosen by lot to offer incense, and the duty was considered such an honor that it was allowed only once in a lifetime. When the incense was actually offered, the priest was left alone in the holy place. Gabriel appeared on the right side of the altar of incense between the altar and the golden lampstand. Since, traditionally, the right side was God's side, Gabriel's appearance there may have multiplied Zechariah's fear.

The angel declared that Zechariah's prayer—clearly prayer for a child—had been heard. The child who was to be born was to be named John. He: 1) would be great in God's sight (v. 15), 2) would be filled with the Holy Spirit from birth (v. 15), 3) would bring many Israelites back to God (v. 16), and 4) would reconcile families to spiritual harmony (v. 17). The name John means: "Jehovah's (or Yahweh's) gift" or "the Lord is gracious" or "the Lord has shown favor." John was to abstain from all alcoholic beverages, and this may have marked him as a Nazirite—the Jewish sect emphasizing holiness—but the matter is debated. Since the Nazirite requirement of uncut hair is not mentioned, John's abstaining from wine may be simply meant to highlight, by contrast, his status of being "filled with the Holy Spirit" (Eph. 5:18).

Because "Elizabeth was barren; and they were both well along in years" (v. 7), Zechariah asked the angel, "How can I be sure of this?" (v. 18). In responding, Gabriel gave his name and position to reassure him, and then announced a confirming sign. Zechariah would be mute until these events were fulfilled, and verse sixty-two implies that he also became deaf. This dialogue delayed Zechariah beyond the scheduled time, but when he emerged, he attempted by means of signs to describe to those waiting what had occurred.

Why Elizabeth, upon becoming pregnant, went into seclusion for five months (v. 24) is not explained. Perhaps it was a custom in that day. Perhaps she wished to complement her husband's mute condition and remain in communication only with God. Basically, however, her pregnancy was a joyous time when she could testify: "[God has] taken away my disgrace among the people" (v. 25). In that culture, for a couple to be childless was considered God's judgment for sin.

3. The Annunciation to Mary (Lk. 1:26-38)

Six months after the appearance to Zechariah, Gabriel appeared to Mary at Nazareth. At that time, Mary was pledged under a covenant to marry, and according to tradition was eighteen years of age. In the original, Scripture three times identifies Mary by the term "virgin" (Gk. *parthenos* [par-THEN-os] cf. Mt. 1:23; Lk. 1:27a, 27b), and four further times pointedly declares that she was with child through the Holy Spirit and not by human agency (cf. Mt. 1:18, 21, 25; Lk. 1:34).

The Biblical doctrine of the Virgin Birth is a vital aspect of the story of the nativity. God entered human life by a supernatural procedure.[4] Because Jesus was born of Mary He was truly human; because He was conceived by the Holy Spirit (cf. Lk. 1:35) He was truly divine and free from the taint of human depravity. The miracle of the Virgin Birth is necessary to explain the miracle of Jesus' divine-human nature.

Gabriel's salutation: "Greetings" (Lk. 1:28) is the Greek counterpart of the Hebrew *Shalom*. The original of the phrase, "blessed are you among women" (v. 28c KJV) is found only in some later manuscripts, and thus these words are omitted in most modern versions. The phrase still occurs, however, in verse forty-two. Though Mary was greatly honored as God's choice to bear His Son, Gabriel made clear that Mary was to *receive* special grace. She was not appointed to be the fountain of grace to others.

Gabriel announced that Mary's Son should be called Jesus (cf. v. 31) which was a form of the Hebrew name Joshua (or Jehoshua) used by Greek speaking Jews. It means "the Lord saves." The angel's promise for her Son paralleled the covenant to David and included: a throne, a house, and a kingdom (cf. Lk. 1:33, 2 Sam. 7:16). By this amazing turn of events, a teenage peasant girl was informed that she was to become the mother of the Messiah for whom all Israel had waited for many centuries.

Mary was not unbelieving, but she asked for an explanation. (cf. 1:34). It has been noted that the first one to question the possibility of a virgin birth was not a modern critic, but Mary herself. She did not request a sign, but she received it anyway in the

---

4   Early in the history of the church, the fact of the Virgin Birth was made a fundamental article of faith and incorporated into the earliest creeds. To reject the Virgin Birth is to reject the firm evidence of Scripture and impugn the validity of Christ's substitutionary death for sinners.

announcement of her relative Elizabeth's impending mother-hood. Mary revealed her submissive faith by identifying herself as the Lord's servant (maidservant) or literally, His "slave girl." (cf. v. 38a). Her words, "May it be to me as you have said" (v. 38b) have been described as "one of the most courageous statements ever recorded."

4. Mary's Visit to Elizabeth. The Magnificat (Lk. 1:39-56)

The phrase "hill country of Judea" (v. 39) identifies the area south of Jerusalem, but the town is not named. Tradition identi-fies it as *Ain Karim* (a village about 8 km. [5 mi.] south of Jerusa-lem), but scholars choose Hebron as the more likely place for Elizabeth's home. Either site would have required Mary's journey to be about 160 kilometers (100 miles) and thus to require four or five days. Though both women were to give birth miraculously, the focus of attention in the meeting was more upon Mary than upon Elizabeth. Elizabeth's experience, however, in being filled with the Holy Spirit, and her utterance of what is called **The Song of Elizabeth** (vv. 42-45), ranks her as a prophetess. This song (which actually was a shouted benediction, cf. v. 42) is the first hymn in the New Testament.

Elizabeth spoke of Mary as "the mother of my Lord" (v. 43), and she thus clearly showed that she understood that Mary's child would be the Messiah. Significantly, however, Elizabeth did not identify Mary as the "mother of God." Elizabeth's usage par-alleled that of David who called the Messiah "my Lord." (cf. Psa. 110:1). The pronouncements of blessing upon Mary (cf. vv. 42, 45) accord with the belief among the Jews that a woman's greatness depends upon the children she bears. Mary's child would make her very special.

Mary's **Magnificat** (vv. 46-56) is a meditation upon God's goodness rather than a reply to Elizabeth. The Savior was not yet born, but God's plan was now in motion and therefore Mary could respond joyfully. Her Magnificat consists almost entirely of Old Testament quotations—one scholar counted twelve different pas-sages—which magnify the Lord by tracing His miracle-hand upon Israel throughout history. The song compares to Hannah's prayer in dedicating Samuel (cf. 1 Sam. 2:1-10).

The Magnificat does not refer to the fact that Mary was to bear a child, nor to the identity of her future Son. Evans com-ments, "The Magnificat reads more like a warrior's song of vic-tory than that of a young woman praising God for the gift of a child."[5] Another writer cites references he considers "revolution-ary" including: scattering the proud (v. 51), bringing down rulers (v. 52), lifting up the humble (v. 52), filling the hungry (v. 53), and sending the rich away empty (v. 53).

---

5   Craig A. Evans, *Luke*. Peabody: Hendrickson Publishers, 1990, p. 26.

After "about three months" with Elizabeth, Mary returned to Nazareth. Apparently, she left Elizabeth just before the birth of John (cf. Lk. 1:56-57). Scripture reports the fact of these events without giving any explanation of the reason for them.

5. The Birth of John; Zechariah's Song (Lk. 1:57-80)

The birth of the baby John, since it was recognized as a miracle, led to great rejoicing. Eight days later, at the infant's circumcision, Zechariah's ability to speak returned when his written memo confirmed Elizabeth's instructions to name the child John. Gabriel had already named him (cf. Lk. 1:13), but the family questioned the name John because none of the relatives had that name. Also, the name had no previous associations, for it does not occur in the Old Testament.

With the return of his speech, Zechariah's first response was to praise God. The result was his prophetic song, known as the **Benedictus** (vv. 68-79). It celebrates God's provision of salvation with a series of Old Testament quotations. He speaks in the past tense, for though Jesus had not yet been born, God's promises were at last being fulfilled. This statement by Zechariah has been called "the last prophecy of the old dispensation." Though he refers to his new son only once, it is the amazing declaration that this child "will be called a prophet of the Most High ... to prepare the way for him" (v. 76, cf. Isa. 40:3). (Note that the yet-to-be-born Jesus is spoken of as "the Most High"—deity is already ascribed to Him.) In adult life, John made this prophecy the basis of his ministry (cf. Lk. 3:4-6).

The expression "horn of salvation" (v. 69) is a Hebrew idiom thought to be Zechariah's poetic reference to a "powerful savior." Metaphorically, a horn speaks of strength or power. The Psalmist wrote, "You have exalted my horn like that of a wild ox. . . . My eyes have seen the defeat of my adversaries" (Ps. 92:10-11; cf. also 2 Sam. 22:2-3; Ps. 18:2). The mention of the sun dispelling the darkness (vv. 78-79) is seen by some to be a theme taken from Isaiah 60:1-3.

The report of John's growth in verse eighty spans a full quarter of a century. Although John was eligible to be trained as a priest like his father, he chose to follow God's call to serve as a prophet. Growing up in the desert, he remained set apart to God's service just as Samson or Samuel. In these years it is possible that he had periodic contact with members of the religiously devout sect of the Essenes.

6. The Annunciation to Joseph (Mt. 1:18-25)

This event took place some time after Mary's third month of pregnancy since immediately following the angel's announcement Mary had "hurried to . . . Judea" (Lk. 1:39) to visit Elizabeth. At this time, an unnamed angel spoke to "Joseph her husband" (Mt. 1:19) in a dream. This instruction was necessary, for on religious grounds Joseph would have expected to divorce Mary. In the custom of the day, a pledged or betrothed couple were considered legally married, but they were in a waiting period before their union as husband and wife. A pledged couple could be separated only by divorce, and a death left the other a widow or widower. One purpose of this waiting period was to confirm the virginity of the bride.

The angel addressed "Joseph son of David" (v. 20) and by that he confirmed Joseph's royal lineage. In his message, the angel announced the fact of Mary's pregnancy and he gave what to Joseph was likely a puzzling explanation, "what is conceived in her is from the Holy Spirit" (Mt. 1:20). He instructed Joseph not to fear (lit. "Stop fearing") to take Mary as his wife. He repeated the instructions he had given Mary concerning the naming of the child (cf. Lk. 1:31): "you are to give him the name Jesus" (Mt. 1:21).

Matthew interpreted these events as a fulfillment of Isaiah 7:14 which scholars understand primarily to concern God's time schedule to achieve Israel's deliverance from her enemies. It is notable, however, that Matthew applies Isaiah's words to depict the miraculous conception of Jesus. The citation identifies Jesus as Immanuel, meaning "God with us," and it implies that God is providing a deliverer just as He did in Isaiah's time.

Joseph obeyed the instructions of his dream and he took Mary as his legal wife. As "a righteous man" (v. 19) he chose not to cast stigma upon Mary, and perhaps as the only man in Mary's life, he shared whatever shame she suffered. Joseph's behavior illustrates New Testament righteousness in sharp contrast with the harsh self-righteousness of religious leaders. Scripture notes that Joseph had no union with Mary until she had given birth to her divine Son. Since Joseph was Mary's husband when Jesus was born, however, Jesus inherited his title that He might be "Son of David" (cf. Mt. 9:27; Jn. 7:42).

7. The Wondrous Virgin Birth (Lk. 2:1-7)

In many non-Christian lands, the people's only knowledge of Christianity is what Luke tells about the birth of Christ. This account in Luke has been called "a little jewel of economical story telling," for he tells the story in only seven verses. He then proceeds to take twice as much space to tell about the shepherds.

Caesar Augustus' decree, which at this point called for registration rather than the paying of a tax, came into effect in the final days of Mary's pregnancy. Joseph's ancestry in David's line, plus the possibility suggested by some that he qualified to possess property there, required that he register in Bethlehem. Everett Harrison comments:

> The enrollment under Augustus looms as one of the clearest indications in all history of the providential control of human affairs by an almighty hand. It is impressive to see how

the administrative machinery of a vast empire was set in motion to fulfill the purpose of God in the advent of his Son.[6]

It is generally held that women were not required to register, but Mary, probably because of her condition and to escape stress and ridicule, accompanied her husband. Though Micah 5:2 had prophesied that Bethlehem would be Messiah's birthplace, it is doubtful that Mary and Joseph truly understood the vital role that they were fulfilling in God's plan.

In about A.D. 150 Justin Martyr wrote that the stable in which Jesus was born was actually a cave, and in A.D. 303 Emperor Constantine built a church over the site. By means of successive restorations, Constantine's Church of the Nativity remains to this day.

In A.D. 525, the monk Dionysus, under a commission from Pope John I, declared that Jesus' birth was on December 25, in the year 1 B.C, just one week before A.D. 1 began. Dionysus based his dating, in part, upon the known dates of the reigns of Caesar Augustus, Herod the Great, and Quirinius (Cyrenius). Many modern scholars have departed from Dionysus, and the consensus suggests that Jesus was born late fall or early winter, 5 B.C. Shepherds and sheep in Palestine spend the night in the open air from April to November, but in the winter season they are brought indoors at night.

Secular dating places the decree of Augustus in 8 B.C, but it is understood that the implementation of the census would take some years. King Herod the Great's death, during whose reign Jesus was born (Mt. 2:1), is dated in 4 B.C. Secular dating holds that Quirinius (Cyrenius) did not become governor of Syria until A.D. 6 and this poses a problem for Biblical identification (cf. Lk. 2:2). One possibility, with some archaeological support, is that in an earlier era Quirinius was involved in Syria as a co-governor with a specific commission from Augustus for a particular project.

8. The Praise of Angels and the Homage of Shepherds (Lk. 2:8-20)

Except for those in the stable, the shepherds were the first people on earth to hear of Messiah's birth. The angel announced: "a Savior has been born to you; he is Christ the Lord" (Lk. 2:11). Thus he added three further designations beyond the name Jesus that had been given: Savior—one rescuing lost mankind; Christ—the Messiah, the one anointed and chosen; Lord—a title denoting deity. These terms, given at the time of Jesus' birth, clearly state the gospel by setting forth a full definition of Jesus' identity and His mission. The shepherds responded to this amazing news by becoming the first worshipers of the baby Jesus.

---

6   Everett F. Harrison, *A Short Life of Christ.* Grand Rapids: Wm. B. Eerdmans Publishing Co., 1968, p. 40.

In many ways the shepherds were unlikely candidates for the high honor that they were granted. In the culture of that day, shepherds were often held in contempt, and they were excluded from mainstream society. The work that they did tended to keep them unclean, and to disqualify them from ceremonial purification. Obviously, God's choice reveals the universality of His provision for mankind. It has sometimes been suggested that Bethlehem shepherds were probably raising sheep for temple sacrifices in nearby Jerusalem. But even if that were the case, they were still simply shepherds.

The glory of the Lord that shone around the shepherds equates with the Shekinah (i.e. glory) that long had been absent from Israel (cf. Ezek. 10:18, 19). The angelic chorus that joined the original angelic messenger sang of "glory to God" and of "peace to men on whom [God's] favor rests" (Lk. 2:14). The traditional rendering of this latter clause: "good will [*eudokia*] toward men" (KJV) is based upon a variant Greek text and an alternate translation of *eudokia*. (*eudokia* [eu-dok-EE-ah): good will, favor, good pleasure, desire or wish). Jesus would bring peace to human hearts by providing reconciliation between God and man.

Significantly, the shepherds did not come to Jerusalem *to see if* the event had occurred, but *to see the event*. They received a very remarkable sign: the Redeemer cradled in a manger. To have to cradle her newborn Son in a manger may have been very distressing to Mary, but it was the uniqueness of the baby in the manger that proved His deity. The shepherds' response was to become "the world's first evangelists" as they "spread the word . . . about this child" (v. 17). For her part, "Mary treasured up all these things and pondered them in her heart" (v. 19).

9. Jesus' Circumcision and Presentation in the Temple (Lk. 2:21-38)

In accordance with the Old Testament standards, Jesus was circumcised when He was eight days old and at that time His name was officially conferred (cf. Mt. 1:25b). Circumcision was a symbol of commitment to the obligations of God's covenant with Israel, and thus totally appropriate for Israel's Messiah (cf. Gen. 17:9-14). The single Scripture verse reporting the circumcision (Lk. 2:21) stands apart from any other Scriptures describing events in Jesus' life. Whether Jesus' circumcision was a formal event in the temple, a ceremony in a synagogue, or a simple home procedure is not reported.

Forty days after Jesus' birth, Mary and Joseph journeyed to the temple in Jerusalem to perform the rites required in the case of the birth of a firstborn male child. These included: 1) the ceremonial redemption of a month-old son, 2) Mary's purification after childbirth. Luke describes the event as the presentation of the child to the Lord, although it appears that in Jewish practice the presentation aspect was overshadowed by the legal procedures.

The redemption of a firstborn male child replaced the earlier Old Testament requirement that every male firstborn should be dedicated to God's service. Since the tribe of Levi now filled this role, other firstborn males were redeemed by a payment of five shekels (cf. Num. 18:15, 16). Thus Joseph and Mary "took [Jesus] to Jerusalem to present him to the Lord" (v. 22) and "to do for him what the custom of the Law required" (v. 27). Luke does not explain that the Law required the payment of five shekels of redemption money.

To provide for her purification, Mary offered a sacrifice of "a pair of doves or two young pigeons" (v. 24). Though this was the minimum offering that was permitted, Luke suggests no alternative. Actually, Scripture prescribed "a year-old lamb for a burnt offering," but it allowed an exception: "If she [a new mother] cannot afford a lamb, she is to bring two doves or two young pigeons" (Lev. 12:8). Apparently, Mary found it necessary to be limited by her poverty.

The holy family's presence in the temple's outer court provided an occasion for the events involving Simeon. This godly, and apparently elderly, man was "waiting for the consolation of Israel" (v. 25). As a devout believer, he counted that God would restore the kingdom to Israel, and it was to him a living expectation. Simeon's song or canticle (vv. 29-32) is known as the **Nunc Dimittis** ("Now dismiss") from its first two words in Latin. As it were, after a lifetime of burdensome waiting, Simeon suddenly found himself gloriously released. Though God's salvation[7] was not completed, Simeon had seen God's instrument of salvation born into the world. His song consists of poetic prophecy praising God for His provision.

Simeon's further prophecy to Mary revealed aspects of the future destiny of the Child. Because of Him she was to suffer bitter personal anguish. The "falling and rising of many in Israel" (2:34) may be paraphrased: "In response to Him many Israelites will undergo a decision crisis, some will stumble over His claims and fall into condemnation; some will receive Him and rise to walk with Him in a new life."

Although Anna was identified by the honored title, prophetess, no specific prophecy by her is recorded. The Old Testament designates only five prophetesses: Miriam (Exod. 15:20), Deborah (Judg. 4:4), Huldah (2 Kings 22:14), Noadiah (Neh. 6:14), and Isaiah's wife (Isa. 8:3) who is otherwise unnamed. Therefore Anna's status is very special. The data concerning her age is ambiguous, but a popular view is that she was at that time about eighty-four years of age and that she had become a widow after only seven years of marriage.

---

7   Luke's emphasis upon the theme of salvation is notable (cf. Lk. 1:69, 77; 2:30, 3:6; Acts 4:12, 13:26, 13:47, 28:28).

10. The Magi Visit the Child King (Mt. 2:1-12)

The pilgrimage of the Magi from one or more countries of the Middle East (e.g., Iran [Persia], Iraq [Babylonia], Arabia) established the worldwide significance of the birth of Jesus. These Gentile men, who were committed to monitoring the heavens, apparently gleaned enough information from the unusual star to launch their journey to Jerusalem. It is commonly held that their journey may have required many months, and that Jesus was no longer an infant when they arrived. Herod's action in selecting as his victims all male children two years and younger is thus explained. Tradition, but not Scripture, declares that there were three Magi, that they were kings, and that their names were Melchior, Caspar (also given as Gaspar), and Balthasar.

The term "Magi" (singular "magus") transliterates the Greek *magos* (MA-gos), and this untranslated form is seen as less misleading than the traditional "wise men." *Magos* is defined: a wise man and priest who is expert in astrology, the interpretation of dreams, and other secret arts. In the Book of Daniel, various types of Magi are designated: magicians, enchanters (or astrologers), sorcerers, Chaldeans, and diviners (or soothsayers) (cf. Dan. 2:2; 2:27). The expression identifying all of these types is "wise men" (Heb. *chakkim* [kak-KEEM]) (cf. Dan. 2:12), and we may conclude that the Greek *magos* is roughly equivalent to the Hebrew *chakkim*. Ordinarily, Magi were pagans, and they were as much committed to astrology as they were to astronomy. Their studies combined both science and superstition.

Scripture does not explain the star (Gk. *aster* [as-TARE]). It appears to have been a special divine creation without natural explanation. Since there are multiplied millions (astronomers speak of quadrillions) of stars in God's creation, He could easily have created a special star. Efforts to establish the star as a conjunction of planets, or similar natural celestial phenomena, are usually not convincing. Some have noted that the Greek term could also be rendered "comet," and they have sought to show that Halley's Comet would have appeared at this time. The fact, however, that the star that they had seen in the East led them from Jerusalem to where Jesus was in Bethlehem complicates any natural explanation.

Though the priests and teachers of the law (or scribes) could correctly inform Herod that the Christ was to be born in Bethlehem, they appear to have had neither faith, nor even curiosity, to pursue the matter further. These Jewish scholars quoted Micah 5:2, apparently from the *LXX*, but rather freely. Micah had stressed Bethlehem's small size—"you are small among the clans of Judah," but in the scholars' version these words became "you . . . are by no means least among the rulers of Judah." They appear to have added a clause from 2 Samuel 5:2.

Though the Magi were Gentiles out of pagan cultures, when they found the "child with his mother Mary . . . they bowed down and worshiped him" (Mt. 1:11). Significantly, they worshiped only the child and not Mary. Neither gold, incense, nor myrrh were local products. They were the type of costly imports that typically would be presented to a prince. Gold suggests a gift to royalty, incense, at least to the people of God, speaks of prayer, myrrh speaks of suffering. It is commonly suggested that these gifts provided funds for the unexpected sudden trip to Egypt.

God used a dream to instruct the Magi not to report to Herod, but to use an alternate route to return to their own country.

11. The Flight to Egypt. Herod Slays the Children (Mt. 2:13-18)

Egypt was a Roman province, but it was beyond the jurisdiction of Herod. The land was about 100 kilometers (60 miles) or three days' journey from Bethlehem. At this time a colony of perhaps one million Jews lived there, and Joseph and Mary may have had friends or relatives among them. The land of Israel's former oppression now became a safe haven for the child Jesus.

In keeping with his depraved outlooks, Herod responded to the exciting news of Messiah's birth with a campaign of murder. His vicious "slaughter of the innocents" stands as one of mankind's blackest deeds. The designated age span would have meant the death of all male children from newborn to those about to have their third birthday.

The quotation "out of Egypt" (v. 15) is from Hosea 11:1, and the reference to mothers crying (v. 18) is from Jeremiah 31:15. In each instance, modern scholars would consider the events to be prophetic types rather than the fulfillment of a direct prophecy. Hosea was concerned with God's deliverance of the nation of Israel from Egypt's bondage; Jeremiah spoke of the weeping of the mothers of Ramah as they lost their children to Nebuchadnezzar's exile.

In his use of the Old Testament, Matthew is described as having "heightened" the words of the prophets. Israel's deliverance from Egypt was given new significance through the return of Jesus from that land, and the sorrows of the mothers of Ramah were intensified in the tears of Bethlehem's mothers. "Rachel" becomes a generic name for all grieving mothers in Israel.

Fortunately for the Jews, Herod the Great, the ruthless tyrant, died shortly after these events, and the rulership of the land was divided. He had ruled Palestine for thirty-seven years. His infamous slaughter of Bethlehem's children was only one minor event in his overall rule of gross injustice and much bloodshed.

II. THE SILENT YEARS IN NAZARETH

1. The Childhood and Youth of Jesus (Mt. 2:19-23; Lk. 2:39-40)

Probably about three years had elapsed when the angel appeared in Joseph's dream and instructed the family to return to Palestine. Since Herod Archelaus, the most dissolute of the sons of Herod the Great, was now ruling in Judea, Joseph, again guided by a dream (his fourth), avoided Bethlehem, and instead returned to his former home in Nazareth which was in Galilee. History records that Archelaus began his reign by murdering 3,000 political opponents.

Matthew saw Jesus' residence in Nazareth as the fulfillment of the message of the prophets (note plural), "He will be called a Nazarene." No specific Old Testament prophecy contains this phrase, but a Hebrew word for "branch" (Heb. *netser* [NAY-tser]) consists of the same basic consonants as "Nazarene." Thus, any Old Testament passage that depicts the Messiah as a branch may be in view. (cf. Isa. 11:1; Jer. 23:5, 33:15; Zech. 6:12). Alternately, Matthew may have had in mind any Old Testament passage that portrayed Messiah's lowliness and obscurity.

Scholars debate the significance of Jesus' being "called a Nazarene" (v. 23), though most agree that it was not a compliment. John quotes Nathanael: "Nazareth! Can anything good come from there?" (Jn. 1:46). The town's location placed it beyond the mainstream of Jewish life, and thus nationalistic Jews tended to make it a target of ridicule. Also, since the town was host to a Roman garrison, Jews who lived there and served the Romans, were thought by some to be national traitors. It is suggested that the unstable nature of the people of Nazareth was exhibited when they responded to Jesus' preaching by attempting to kill Him (cf. Lk. 4:6-30).

The Bible does not mention the neighboring city of Sepphoris that was approximately five kilometers (3 miles) north of Nazareth. Sepphoris was Herod Antipas' capital, and it was second only to Jerusalem in size and importance in Palestine. Beginning in 3 B.C, Herod launched a massive rebuilding of the city (it had been destroyed by military action), and there is evidence that he secured laborers and tradesmen from Nazareth to accomplish these projects. Archeologists report that the rebuilt city, which flourished in Jesus' adult years, included such features as: a forum, a royal residence with an imposing tower, a theater seating 4,000, a gymnasium, a courthouse, public baths, army barracks, and a waterworks system. Since they were carpenters, it is possible that Joseph, and later Jesus Himself, may have been employed in some of these projects.

A probable seven or eight-year span of Jesus' childhood up to age twelve is reported in entirety in Luke 2:40. It is assumed that

Jesus attended synagogue school from age six to fifteen, since the culture of that time expected it. Apparently, He was then apprenticed to the carpentry trade, rather than proceeding to advanced studies to qualify Him as a recognized scholar. Thus, His critics could say, "How did this man get such learning without having studied?" (Jn. 7:15).

Obviously, Jesus pursued His own self study in a disciplined manner. He thus acquired His remarkable familiarity with the Old Testament Scriptures that so impressed His peers. From His formal schooling, plus His ongoing contact with people, Jesus appears to have known three languages: Aramaic—the Hebrew dialect that was the everyday language of the people, Hebrew—the traditional national religious language, and Greek—the language of commerce and of Israel's neighbors. Various clues in the Gospels identify Him with each of these languages.

2. Jesus' First Passover. Life in Nazareth (Lk. 2:41-52)

The three annual pilgrimage feasts, Passover, Pentecost (or Weeks) and Tabernacles, called for the devout to present themselves before the Lord in the temple. Since Passover was combined with the Feast of Unleavened Bread, the ceremonies continued for a total of seven or eight days. Some suggest that Jesus' attendance and participation in the Passover at age twelve, seemingly in His own right, would have been somewhat unusual, but the *Talmud* mentions that a father should prepare his son for manhood at age thirteen by taking him at a younger age to Jerusalem to witness the Passover events. A Jewish boy who was at least thirteen, and had participated in his *Bar Mitzvah*[8] *(bar* MITZ-vah), would be expected to participate as an adult.

Jesus not only attended the Passover, but while there He spent considerable time in the temple academy graduate school where candidates for the priesthood were trained. His leading questions to the teacher-priests no doubt led them into new personal Scriptural insights. On this occasion, Jesus' response to His mother, Mary, becomes His first recorded words in Scripture (cf. Lk. 2:49). The expression "Father's house" (or "Father's business") is the first Scriptural reference to the fatherhood of God. Though Mary had spoken of "Your father and I" (v. 48), (and Joseph was, indeed, Jesus' legal earthly father), Jesus promptly directed the focus to His true Father (v. 49). At this time Jesus evidently was conscious of His divine nature and His vital mission, and He wished to be found at the place where activity was directed on behalf of his Father.

The eighteen years between the Passover and the launching of Jesus' ministry (cf. Lk. 3:23) comprise "the silent years." As a

---

8   The synagogue ceremony by which a Jewish boy, at age thirteen, enters into synagogue membership. In the solemnization of this event the boy is called upon to demonstrate his ability to read from the Hebrew Scriptures.

young adult during these years, though He was the Son of God, Jesus was subject to Joseph and Mary (v. 51), and He underwent a normal balanced human development (v. 52). It appears that God deliberately withheld from Joseph and Mary the full understanding of Jesus' deity, for had they really understood, a normal family relationship would have been impossible.

It is generally held that Joseph had died by the end of this period (tradition says he died when Jesus was sixteen), for the Bible makes no further mention of him. We note that although Scripture reports Joseph's actions (and reactions) there are no recorded words of Joseph anywhere in the Bible. If it is the case that Joseph's death occurred in Jesus' youth, it would have been necessary for Jesus to assume the family support. Presumably, it was not until He was thirty that His stepbrothers took over. William Barclay comments:

> Because [Jesus] spent these . . . years in Nazareth, he knew the problems of making a living, the haunting insecurity of the life of the working man, the ill-natured customer, the man who would not pay his debts. It is the glory of the incarnation that we face no problem of life and living which Jesus did not also face.[9]

III. JOHN THE BAPTIST, JESUS' FORERUNNER

1. John Preaches and Baptizes (Mt. 3:1-6; Mk. 1:2-6; Lk. 3:1-6; Jn. 1:6-8)

The six personalities and events named in Luke 3:1-2 provide the most precise dating in all the New Testament. An enumeration of this sort used to designate a particular historical date is called a "synchronism." Most historians consider that the indicated date would be A.D. 26 or 27, though some place it as late as A.D. 30. Since John the Baptist's ministry was the immediate historical setting for Jesus' ministry, to date John is to date Jesus. The expression "the word of God came to John" (Lk. 3:2) parallels the language that reports God's call to the Old Testament prophets (cf. Jer. 1:11). John was the first divinely-called messenger of God's truth in 400 years.

At this time both Annas and Caiaphas are named as the (high) priests (cf. v. 2). In fact, Annas had been deposed by the Romans in A.D. 15 and replaced by Caiaphas. Many Jews, however, still considered him the rightful high priest. Also, because Caiaphas was Annas' son-in-law, Annas continued to exert a powerful influence over high priestly issues, and, in effect, he continued to rule. When Jesus was arrested and brought to trial, His first hearing was in the court of Annas (cf. Jn. 18:12-13).

---

9 William Barclay, *The Gospel of Luke*. Burlington: Welch Publishing Co., 1975, p. 40.

To introduce and explain John's ministry as a voice calling in the desert with an exhortation to "Prepare the way for the Lord," each synoptic quotes from Isaiah 40:3-5. (Mark appears to add a thought from Malachi 3:1 that in turn was a quotation from Exodus 23:20. In the fourth Gospel, the Baptist later used this same source to identify himself [cf. John 1:23].) John's role was to call upon people to prepare the way for Christ's rule by a life-changing personal repentance. A great King is coming, and the road must be smoothed and straightened. Thus John declared that the Messianic age was at hand.

John's Gospel, written decades after the actual events, introduces the Baptist as the man sent from God who came to testify concerning the Light. The evangelist pointedly notes concerning the Baptist, however, "He himself was not the light; he came only as a witness to the light" (Jn. 1:8). Again it was a message challenging to preparation for Someone very special who was yet to come. The one valid gesture of preparation was repentance.

Scripture reports that in the pattern of Elijah, John dressed and ate as a rugged outdoorsman. He came as a common man, and his lifestyle effectively complemented the message that he preached. Newer versions indicate that the camel's hair (Mk. 1:6) was the material from which the fabric of his garments had been woven. Locusts and wild honey were common food staples in desert regions, since Israel's food laws approved of locusts—which were usually dried—as human food (cf. Lev. 11:22).

John "went into all the country around the Jordan" (Lk. 3:3). Matthew speaks of this area as "the Desert of Judea" (Mt. 3:1), but in modern terms it was more a sparsely-settled barren land than a desert. Though John's ministry was in this rural setting, it attracted widespread attention: "The whole Judean countryside and all the people of Jerusalem went out to him" (Jn. 1:5).

It is evident that John the Baptist served not so much as a prophet, but as an evangelist-baptizer. He called for people to demonstrate their response to his message by submitting to "a baptism of repentance for [Gk. *eis*][10] the forgiveness of sins" (Mk. 1:4)—i.e., a baptism in reference to, or leading to, repentance as a result of the forgiveness of sins. Baptism was the result, not the means of the forgiveness of sins. Candidates are described as "confessing their sins" (Mt. 3:6). For Jews to obey John's call was to admit that they had departed far from God's requirements, and to place themselves in the same category as Gentiles. John's Jewish converts were required to demonstrate humility and contrition. Thus, the success of his ministry is most remarkable.

The Jews appear to have accepted the rite of baptism, perhaps because they knew the ceremonial washings of the law. Although the Jews are known to have baptized proselytes to

---

10 *eis* (ice): for, unto, into, as a result of, on the basis of, with respect to.

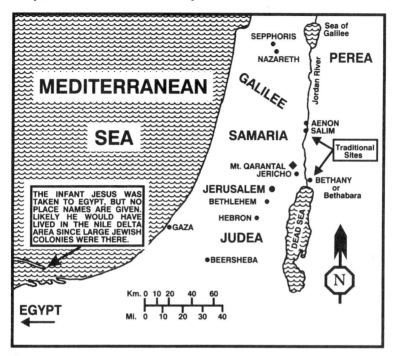

Figure 5: Sites of Jesus' earlier years.

Judaism, most scholars hold that the practice did not begin until after the time of John. Among the Essenes, a religious community within Judaism, repeated washings in the pattern of baptisms were emphasized, but their significance is uncertain. These washing-baptisms appear to have been self-administered.

John's baptism was not a mere cleansing, but a life-changing commitment to a holy life with the confession and repudiation of sin. Jesus implied that John's baptism was "from heaven" (Mt. 21:24)—as it were, it was God's appointed initiation ceremony. Though John's baptism involved an external experience, its value depended upon an inner attitude of responsive obedience to God's moral laws. Scripture indicates that John's rite was not a Christian baptism, so that on occasion, his disciples were rebaptized by Paul (cf. Acts 19:4-5).

2. A Specimen of John's Preaching (Mt. 3:7-10; Lk. 3:7-14)

Both in where he lived and in what he believed, John the Baptist was apart from the mainline religious systems of his day. His call was for people to become separate from such empty religionists. Nevertheless, "many" Pharisees and Sadducees came to observe his ministry. Though they came as curious critics, their presence may have been a subtle confession that in their hearts they had doubts about what they so dogmatically taught. John discerned that they had not come because they wanted to change, but that they might escape judgment in case he was right.

John's denunciation of the Pharisees and Sadducees[11] was powerfully forthright. Though his words were stern and shocking, he was simply being responsibly honest in informing them that they were totally without spiritual hope. By their lives they denied what they taught by their lips. John saw them as vipers—poisonous serpents subject to the judgmental wrath of the coming Messiah. In a second figure, they were trees targeted for total destruction. It is suggested that because the people accepted John as a prophet, they did not actively object to his colorful analogies. As harsh as they appeared, they were necessary, and therefore they were "good news" (cf. Lk. 3:18). Scripture, as well as history (i.e., Josephus), make clear that John was very popular with the people and he won large crowds of followers.

Luke records John's teachings regarding: generosity (sharing) (Lk. 3:11), honesty (vv. 12-13), and truthfulness, gratitude, and thrift (v. 14). John taught the principle that humans should be what they profess to be, and they should "bloom where planted." Though he instructed tax collectors and soldiers to maintain an upright walk, he did not advise either of them to change their vocation.

3. John Promises the Messiah (Mt. 3:11-12; Mk. 1:7-8; Lk. 3:15-18; Jn. 1:15)

In proclaiming the coming Messiah, John declared that though the greater one usually comes first, it was the One coming after who would be greater (cf. Jn. 1:15). For his part, John was not even worthy to carry Messiah's sandals (cf. Mt. 3:11), nor to stoop down and untie their thongs (cf. Mk. 1:7). Such tasks were assigned to the most menial slave, and the rabbis had ruled that these were the only tasks that it was not proper for a disciple to do for his master.

---

11 The Pharisees may be thought of as a denomination in Judaism. They emerged out of Ezra's revival, and their original goal was to teach separation (Pharisees means "separated ones") to perpetuate the revival. In Jesus' time the Pharisees had adopted the tactic of infiltrating Israel's leadership to extend their influence. They taught that the proper service of the Lord was through rigorous and detailed conformity to the Law. Though they were the conservatives of their day, they were mainly the ones responsible for crucifying Jesus. The Sadducees were chiefly prosperous Israelites who had become the equivalent of a political lobby group. They held that human reason and opinion were superior to Scriptural authority, but they accepted the laws of the Pentateuch as the standard for life on earth. They denied any doctrine of an after life with future rewards and punishments.

Whereas John was a "water baptizer," the coming Messiah would baptize "with the Holy Spirit and with fire" (Mt. 3:11). This event would be a divine process, not subject to duplication by humans. Commentators differ on the meaning of the fire aspect of Messiah's baptism, but many see the fire ministry of the Spirit as convicting of sin and expunging it from the believer's life. Mark recorded simply, "He will baptize you with the Holy Spirit" (Mk. 1:8). Jesus fulfilled this promise, and following His resurrection He instructed His disciples: "John baptized with water, but in a few days you will be baptized with the Holy Spirit" (Acts 1:5).

The role of the Messiah in judgment was a necessary part of John's message. A winnowing fork (Mt. 3:12; Lk. 3:17) is defined: "a forklike shovel, with which the threshed grain was thrown into the wind; thus the chaff was separated from the grain."[11] In older versions, this word was rendered "fan." In this figure, the Holy Spirit's fire ministry is seen to be His role in judgment as He consumes the chaff and straw.

4. John's Testimony Before the Leaders (Jn. 1:19-28)

The delegation from "the Jews of Jerusalem" included: priests, Levites and Pharisees (cf. 1:19, 24), and they likely would have come as emissaries of the Sanhedrin. One of the functions of this body was the check the validity of the claims of prophets. John freely confessed that he was not: 1) the Messiah nor 2) Elijah nor 3) the Prophet (cf. Deut. 18:15, 18). He again quoted from Isaiah 40:3 to identify himself as simply a "voice," to stress that it was his message and not his office that mattered. As he repeated his unworthiness to untie Messiah's sandals, he portrayed himself as merely a "water-baptizer." Even as John spoke, it is implied (1:26) that Jesus was standing, unrecognized, among the onlookers.

John specifically denied that he was Elijah (cf. 1:21). It is indeed evident that in the flesh, as the son of Zachariah, John was not a resurrected incarnation of the prophet Elijah of the Old Testament. Nevertheless, as Messiah's forerunner, he was specifically fulfilling Elijah's prophesied role. Thus Jesus would later say, "Elijah has already come" (Mt. 17:12).

The place of John's ministry is given in newer versions as "Bethany on the other side of Jordan," or traditionally as "Bethabara beyond the Jordan" (cf. Jn. 1:28). (According to some scholars Bethany translates as "boat house" and Bethabara as "ferry house.") Since John needed the river to baptize, this Bethany was not the village near Jerusalem. Traditionally, Bethabara is identified with a ford of the Jordan east of Jericho—Hajlah near *Wadi el-Kharrar*—though this site lacks scholarly support.

---

11 William F. Arndt and F. Wilbur Gingrich, defining *ptuon* (PTOO-on) in *Greek-English Lexicon*. Chicago: University of Chicago Press, 1957, p. 735.

IV. JESUS PREPARES FOR HIS MINISTRY

1. The Baptism of Jesus (Mt. 3:13-17; Mk. 1:9-11; Lk. 3:21-23a; Jn. 1:29-34)

Jesus walked the necessary distance and submitted himself to John's baptism so that He might "fulfill all righteousness" (Mt. 3:15). His baptism compares with His circumcision, temple pilgrimages, and payment of the temple tax—Jesus participated in all of these events in order to identify fully with the humans He came to save. In addition, however, Jesus' baptism became the occasion of: 1) His anointing for ministry, 2) the authentication of His Messiahship, 3) God's approval of His person, and 4) God's confirmation of John's ministry. Harrison comments about this event in Jesus' life:

> If John had perceived the depth of meaning in Jesus' submission to baptism he would not have faltered in his faith later on . . . . For Jesus the baptism was not so much the event that launched him upon his ministry, although it was that; even more it was a consecration to the death that awaited him.[13]

All four Gospels mention the dove (or dove-like vision) as an emblem of the Holy Spirit coming upon Jesus as He came up out of the water. Apparently, both Jesus and John the Baptist saw the dove, and in connection with its dispatch Jesus "saw heaven being torn open" (Mk. 1:10; cf. Jn. 1:32). Scholars suggest that the tearing open of heaven depicted the arrival of a new era. The Spirit's anointing was necessary to qualify Jesus for His Messianic role. John the Baptist testified that he identified Jesus by the dove that rested upon Him (cf. Jn. 1:32-33).

Each synoptic records the message of the voice from heaven: "This is my Son, whom I love: with him I am well pleased." (Mt. 3:17; cf. Mk. 1:11, Lk. 3:22)[14] The last clause of this statement may be paraphrased: "in whom my pleasure [i.e., my plan of salvation] rests." God repeated this message at the Mount of Transfiguration (cf. Mt. 17:5). These words are seen as an affirmation of Christ's Messianic status and role. God thus declared His relationship and His approval. The individual simultaneous activities of each Person of the triune Godhead in John 1:33 are a notable revelation of the Trinity.

---

13 Harrison, op. cit., p. 75.

14 Actually, Mark and Luke quote God as saying, "You are my Son." It may be concluded that God indeed spoke directly to Jesus, and Mark and Luke quoted the message verbatim. Matthew assumed an author's prerogative to structure a message for the sake of his readers, and thus he framed the message in the third person.

The account in John's Gospel indicates that Jesus' baptism was on the day after John's testimony before the leaders from Jerusalem. It appears that as Jesus approached to be baptized[15], John the Baptist proclaimed: "Look, the Lamb of God, who takes away the sin of the world!" (Jn. 1:29). To depict the Messiah as the Lamb of God was radically different from the conquering political liberator that the Jews expected. This Lamb would take away the world's sin—Jesus' ministry would achieve the conquest of the principle of sin.

In the Jewish worship system, for community members (common people -KJV) a lamb was an alternate choice for a sin offering (cf. Lev. 4:27-35; 5:1-5). Also, Jews were familiar with the role of the Passover lamb in providing a covering for sin. Thus, even though bulls and goats were the usual first choice in sin offerings, the concept of a lamb who would take away sins would be quite acceptable to John's audience. Many would have known Isaiah's words, "He was led like a lamb to the slaughter, and . . . though the LORD makes his life a guilt offering, he will see his offspring" (Isa. 53:7, 10). Later, Paul would write, "Christ our Passover lamb, has been sacrificed" (1 Cor. 5:7; cf. Rev. 5:6-12; 6:1-17).

John's proclamation at this point was the word of an anointed prophet who did not fully understand the import of what he was saying. He explained, "I myself did not know him" (v. 31), presumably to make the point that he did not recognize Jesus as the Messiah. When the Holy Spirit (as a dove) descended upon Jesus, however, John recognized Jesus' true identity. His concluding testimony at this time was unequivocal: "I testify that this is the Son of God" (Jn. 1:34).

Luke's mention that Jesus "was about thirty years old when he began his ministry" (2:23) is a reminder of Jesus' true humanity, and a useful landmark in calculating chronologies. Just as other humans typically do, Jesus embarked on His vocation when He had acquired sufficient maturity and experience.

2. The Temptation of Jesus (Mt. 4:1-11; Mk. 1:12-13; Lk. 4:1-13)

Mark uses a strong verb to describe Jesus' dispatch into the desert: "the Spirit sent him out [Gk. *ekballo*] into the desert" (Mk. 1:12). (*ekballo* [ek-BAL-oh]: drive out, expel, throw out; but the connotation does not have to include force.) The verb "tempt" (Gk. *peiradzo* [pire-ADZE-so]) denotes: 1) to make trial of, to put to the test, or 2) to entice to sin. The temptation did not really threaten to lead Jesus into sin, but rather to prove that He would

---

15 Another approach to the chronology of events holds that John had baptized Jesus prior to this time, so that here John is publicly testifying to the Messiahship of Jesus.

not sin. As a man, Jesus was not immune to temptation to sin, for Scripture identifies Him as our high priest and says of Him: "We have [a high priest] . . . who has been tempted in every way, just as we are—yet was without sin" (Heb. 4:15).

In rejecting Satan's tempting offers without hesitation, Jesus demonstrated true godliness. The activities to which the devil tempted Jesus were specifically those popularly thought of as feats that would identify the Messiah to the Jews. Because Jesus was truly God, and truly the Messiah, the temptations were powerfully real to Him. By extending such temptations, Satan categorically confirmed his recognition of the divine status of the incarnate Jesus.

Jesus' adversary in His ordeal is called the devil (Gk. *diabolos* [dee-AB-oh-los] —slanderer) by Matthew, and Satan (Heb. *satan* [sat-AN] —adversary, hater) by Mark. The traditional site of Jesus' temptation is Mount Qarantal (*Jebel Quaruntul*), a barren mountain that rises 450 meters (1,500 ft.) above the valley near Jericho. Mark mentions the threat of wild animals, and their presence underscores the loneliness of the place. The forty-day fast stripped Jesus of all advantages, for after that long without food most humans are barely surviving. Matthew's order of the temptations, rather than Luke's, is generally accepted as the actual order in which they occurred. The words "Away from me, Satan!" (Mt. 4:10) following the offer of the world's kingdoms is seen as implying a finality of events.

a. Jesus' First Temptation (Mt. 4:3-4; Lk. 4:3-4)

After a forty day fast, the miraculous production of bread was a very real temptation. Many hold that the devil's words, "If you are the Son of God" (Lk. 4:3) are more accurately translated, "Since you are the Son of God." The devil was not doubting Jesus' deity, but calling on Him to prove it. He hoped that Jesus would satisfy His physical needs in a way that for Him would be sin.

For Jesus to have turned stones into bread would have: 1) declared His distrust of the Father, 2) been a selfish rejection of His Father's will, and 3) separated Him from identifying with ordinary humans. For Him to be a true human it was necessary that He live on terms appropriate to human beings. By quoting Deuteronomy 8:3, "Man shall not live by bread alone," Jesus was saying that the will of God takes precedence over the satisfaction of physical appetites. Because He succeeded in rejecting this temptation, Jesus could validly request self-denial of His followers.

b. Jesus' Second Temptation (Mt. 4:5-7; Lk. 4:9-12)

One leaping from the highest point of the temple could possibly have fallen and slid as much as one hundred and forty meters (450 feet) before coming to rest in the bottom of the Kidron Valley.

For Jesus to have leaped from the temple would have been a public show involving: 1) a presumptuous forcing of God to provide care, 2) evidence of personal ego and bravado independent of the Father, 3) skepticism in regard to God's promises and the requirement that He prove Himself.

Though Satan had used part of Psalm 91:11-12 to justify his appeal, Jesus used Deuteronomy 6:16 "Do not test the Lord your God" to answer Satan and affirm that He was not willing to put His will above the Father's will. Someone paraphrases this Scripture, "You must not make senseless experiments with the power of God." To require God to prove Himself by putting Him to a test is not to trust Him, and it attempts to make Him a servant (cf. Exod. 17:7). We trust God, but we must not dare Him.

c. Jesus' Third Temptation (Mt. 4:8-10; Lk. 4:5-8)

When Satan found he could not divert Jesus from His goal, he proposed a change of the route. Though he gave no Biblical support, he offered Jesus the splendor of "all the kingdoms of the world" (Mt. 4:8). Jesus neither affirmed nor denied the devil's claim, but apparently he could have fulfilled his offer (cf. Jn. 12:31, 2 Cor. 4:4, Eph. 2:2). If Jesus had accepted He would have escaped the cross, but for Him to worship Satan would have been a tragically unwarranted shortcut to the kingdom.

Had Jesus failed this test: 1) there would have been victory without a cross and no refuge for lost sinners, 2) Jesus' victory would have been by satanic means through ruthless conquest instead of self-suffering and sacrifice, 3) Jesus would have become Satan's servant and God's enemy, and 4) supreme authority would be extended to Satan in the total realm of created beings. Jesus responded by quoting Deuteronomy 6:13 and in our versions this became, "Worship the Lord your God, and serve him only" (Mt. 4:10; Lk. 4:8).

Though most evangelicals hold that Jesus could not have sinned because He is God, it is agreed that the tests and conflicts were real. Jesus was human, and humanity is always vulnerable and susceptible to temptation. But Jesus was also divine, and as William Barclay pointed out, "the temptations are such as could only come to a person who had very special powers and who knew that he had them."[16] The outcome of His testing, however, was never in doubt. Because He had successfully met the tempter's testings, Jesus could order, "Away from me, Satan!" (Mt. 4:10). Jesus' human strength was restored as the attending angels served Him (cf. Mt. 4:11).

---

16 William Barclay, *The Gospel of Matthew (Vol. 1)*. Burlington: Welch Publishing Co. 1975, p. 65.

Some notable facts and applications relating to Jesus' temptations include: **1)** The temptations were at God's initiative, not Satan's; **2)** For Jesus, just as for all humans, the temptations were real and they had to be overcome; **3)** The temptations settled and affirmed Jesus' conquest of possible vulnerabilities and "cleared the deck" for His forthcoming ministry; **4)** The weapon that Jesus used in rejecting Satan was the sword of the Spirit—the Holy Scriptures; **5)** Though Satan found needs and appetites (e.g. hunger), these were not sinful in themselves; the possibility of sin lay only in how these needs were gratified; **6)** At this time Satan did not cease to tempt and attack Jesus, but later he used Jesus' enemies and even His disciples.

THREE:

JESUS' EARLY MINISTRY

For perhaps a year and a half Jesus ministered in comparative obscurity. During approximately the first year of this period He ministered in Judea. He then returned to Galilee, and proceeded to lay the foundation for the great Galilean ministry.

I. JESUS' MINISTRY IN JUDEA IN HIS FIRST YEAR

The report of Jesus' first year of ministry is almost entirely limited to John's Gospel. Most events during this period were in Judea, but the wedding at Cana involved a journey to Galilee.

1. Jesus Wins His First Five Disciples (Jn. 1:35-51)

Though in recorded Scripture John the Baptist never identified Jesus as the Messiah, he repeatedly acclaimed Him as the Lamb of God (Jn. 1:29, 36). On these grounds, two of his disciples left him to follow Jesus. One was Andrew, and it is assumed that the other was John, the author of the Gospel. Jesus received them cordially, and invited them to an "open house." Interestingly, the hour is given—John is thought to have used Roman time so that the "tenth hour" would be 10:00 a.m., though by Jewish time it would be 4:00 in the afternoon. William Barclay comments, "When a man really meets Christ he will no more forget that day and hour than he will forget the day of his birth."[1]

Jesus' third disciple, Simon Peter, resulted because Andrew brought his brother. Jesus' first convert had promptly become a soul winner! In view of Peter's later role, it has been said of Andrew's action, "perhaps it is as great a service to the Church as ever any man did." Andrew announced, "We have found the Messiah" (1:41). He had much to learn, however, about the significance of that designation, and the real identity of the One he had found. In Philip's case, it was Jesus who did the finding, but then in turn, Philip found Nathanael.

Upon seeing Nathanael, Jesus declared him to be one in whom there was nothing false, and He revealed that He had already been observing him. Traditionally, one sat under his leafy fig tree as a place of meditation, and perhaps it was there that

---

1 William Barclay, *The Gospel of John* (Vol. 1). Edinburgh: Saint Andrew Press, 1955, p. 71.

Nathanael dedicated his life to God's service. Nathanael rightly identified Jesus: "Rabbi, you are the Son of God; you are the King of Israel" (1:49)—his way of saying that he recognized Jesus as the Messiah. Perhaps Nathanael was familiar with Psalm 2:7-9 that depicted the LORD's Son as king.

The name Peter means "rock" in Greek; *Cephas* is the equivalent Aramaic word. This name was assigned by Jesus after He "looked [*emblepo*] at [Peter]" (v. 42). (*emblepo* [em-BLEP-oh]: to fix one's gaze upon, to discern spiritually, to perceive the heart). Obviously, Jesus named Peter in the light of his potential, even though, while Jesus was on earth, Peter was an unsteady rock. In addressing His disciple, Jesus used Cephas only on this occasion; He used Peter twice (Mt. 16:18; Lk. 22:34), and He used Simon four times (Mt. 17:25; Jn. 21:15, 16, 17).

Philip probably identified Jesus as "the son of Joseph" (Jn. 1:45) because at this time the Virgin Birth was not publicly recognized. Nathanael, mentioned only in John, is thought to be the Bartholomew of the synoptics. Scripture reveals the home towns of four of the new disciples: Andrew, Peter, and Philip were from Bethsaida[2] (v. 44); Nathanael was from Cana (cf. Jn. 21:2). If the fifth disciple, who is unnamed, was John, he probably was from either Capernaum or Bethsaida (cf. Lk. 5:10).

The expression "I tell you the truth" (1:51) translates "*amen, amen*" (ah-MAIN, ah-MAIN) that in older versions is rendered "Verily, verily." This doublet combination is used only in John and this occurrence is the first of twenty-five. The expression "Son of Man" (1:51) was Jesus' favorite to identify Himself and it occurs eighty-two times in the Gospels. In the chronological account of Jesus' life it is used here for the first time. Many scholars suggest that "Son of man" has Messianic implications (cf. Dan. 7:13-14), and it seems uniquely to characterize Jesus' ministry.

The vision of angels ascending and descending (v. 51) conveys the idea of active communication between earth and heaven. The angelic traffic between the two realms symbolizes the flow of earth's appeals and the counterflow of heaven's responses. The presence of the Son of Man on earth uniquely brings God into association with humans and their human needs.

2. The Wedding at Cana (Jn. 2:1-11)

John dates these events on the third day. Likely three days would have been needed to travel from Judea to Galilee—the journey that Jesus had decided to make (cf. Jn. 1:43). Mary's presence at the wedding suggests that this event involved relatives of Jesus. The literal text: "Jesus [he] was invited and his disciples"

---

2   The name Bethsaida is said to mean "fisher town."

(v. 2) led one commentator to remark of the verb *invited*: "singu-lar, as if the including of the disciples were an afterthought." The presence of Jesus' five new disciples may possibly explain the shortage of beverage, and the reason that Mary brought the prob-lem to Jesus.

Since by this miracle, Jesus was "going public" in His minis-try, it was right that He question Mary's involvement. His reply to her was according to the culture at that time, and in effect He ex-plained that her role as His mother did not entitle her to direct His Messianic ministry. For Him to begin to perform miracles was to proclaim that the Messiah had come. He must proceed with this vital milestone at His own pace, and in consultation with the Father and according to His schedule. He chose, however, to honor Mary's implied request.

John records: "This, the first of his miraculous signs [Gk. *se-meion*], Jesus performed in Cana of Galilee" (Jn. 2:11). An imme-diate outcome was that "his disciples put their faith in him" (11:b). Mary's instructions to the servants become a formula for every Christian who seeks a productive ministry in God's service: "Do whatever he tells you" (Jn. 2:5). Of course Jesus could have produced wine without the involvement of the servants, but He chose to use them.

John's presentation of Jesus' "miraculous signs" (Gk. *se-meion* [say-MY-on]) has already been discussed.[3] Two other words are relevant in this regard. "Jesus of Nazareth was a man accred-ited by God to you by miracles [*dunamis*], wonders [*teras*] and signs [*semeion*], which God did among you through him" (Acts 2:22)[4] (cf. Jn. 4:48). According to the usual count, the gospels rec-ord thirty-six miracles performed by the incarnate Jesus.

The passion of that culture for lavish hospitality made the shortage of wine an embarrassing disgrace. The wine produced has been calculated to equal 2,400 servings. Such a large amount may have been necessary because wedding feasts typically contin-ued for up to seven days. For Jesus to transform water to wine set a pattern for His ministry that still continues. Some of His great-est miracles of our day are miracles of transformation.

Most scholars hold that the wine at Cana would be fermented and it could have caused intoxication, because "the ancients knew

---

3 See pp. 18 and 19.

4 *dunamis* (DUNE-a-miss): power, might, strength, force, deed of power, miracle; *teras* (TER--as): portent, omen, wonder, an event so strange as to cause it to be watched. In the New Testament *teras* is found only in the plural (i.e., *terata* [TER-at-ah]) and in conjunction with *semeia* (say-MY-ah): signs.

of no other process to preserve fruit juices." Minority voices argue that "new wine" was fruit juice, and only "old wine" was fermented. In the culture of Jesus' day, wine, whether fermented or not, was normally diluted with water before being served. A common proportion was one part wine to three of water, but on occasion as many as ten parts of water were used.

3. The First Cleansing of the Temple (Jn. 2:12-25)

After the miracle at Cana, Jesus and His party resided briefly in Capernaum before He proceeded to Jerusalem for the Passover. This occasion was just three years before His last Passover when He again cleansed (cleared) the temple (cf. Mt. 21:12-14). Only John tells of this first cleansing—probably he was an eye witness.

Jesus was grievously offended because the sacred Court of the Gentiles had been turned into a merchandise market—popularly it was known as "the bazaar of Annas." Gentile converts to Judaism—"proselytes of the gate"—would be totally discouraged from attempting to worship. On this occasion, Jesus prepared a whip of cords that He could use to drive the animals out of the temple and into the streets. Scripture does not say that He used the whip on humans, and apparently His action was not violent enough to attract the Roman garrison. The force that He used was chiefly moral; conscience made cowards of His enemies.

The animals were, of course, sold for the sacrifices that the devout offered. The moneychangers provided the approved coins required to pay the temple tax. If, as some sources hold, a Jewish one-half shekel was required, these coins had not been minted for at least a century. They were collectors' items with artificially inflated prices. Scholars are unsure how the priests profited from this temple business, but it is certain that they did. The disciples saw these events as fulfilling Psalm 69:9, "Zeal for your house will consume me" (Jn. 2:17). To Jesus, insults against His Father's house were insults against His own person. Though His contemporaries appear not to have recognized it, His actions were not those of a mere reformer; they were the actions of a Messiah.

The Jews responded, not by questioning the validity of what Jesus had done, but by demanding the authority for His actions. In their spiritual blindness, Jesus' reply was a riddle that they misunderstood and misinterpreted. He spoke of His forthcoming death and resurrection, but His hearers heard only literal words concerning the destruction and restoration of the temple. These words were later remembered by the Jews, and for this reason they sealed the tomb (cf. Mt. 27:63-64). After the resurrection, the disciples saw these words as a confirmation of Jesus' deity.

One indication of the spiritual application of Jesus' prediction was His use of the word *naos* (na-OS) for "temple" (cf. 2:19). In strict usage *naos* denoted the inner shrine—the Most Holy Place

	Matt.	Mark	Luke	John
● **PREPARATION FOR MINISTRY**				
Baptism of Jesus	3:13-17	1:9-11	3:21-23	1:29-34
New Year—modern Western calendar				
Temptation of Jesus	4:1-11	1:12-13	4:1-13	
● **MINISTRY IN JUDAH BEGUN**				
First disciples won				1:36-51
Wedding at Cana				2:1-11
First Passover during Jesus' ministry				2:13
Temple cleansed				2:14-25
Nicodemus visits				3:1-11
Samaritan woman				4:1-42
John imprisoned	14:3-5	6:17-20	3:19-20	
● **GALILEAN MINISTRY BEGUN**				

Figure 6: Time line of the estimated dates of the first year of Jesus' ministry. The scale indicates months, and it suggests that Jesus' baptism was in early December. His temptation is shown in the new year in January. The bottom of the chart extends to December of that year, with the Galilean ministry beginning in November. Because of the uncertainties in determining dates, the time line purposely does not label the months.

of the temple, the dwelling place of God's glory. An alternate word *hieron* (he-er-ON) denoted the overall temple structure or its precincts. Popular usage often interchanged these terms, but Jesus' choice of words is always significant.

The Jews' comment concerning the temple building project provides a clue to determine the date: "It has taken forty-six years to build this temple" (v. 20). Secular history dates the beginning of Herod's project to replace Zerubbabel's temple "in about 20 B.C." Thus, forty-six years from that time would locate the current date at about A.D. 27 or 28, and this figure conforms to the usual chronology of the life of Christ. Herod's temple was not completed until A.D. 63 or 64, and in A.D. 70 it was destroyed.

Though "many people saw the miraculous signs . . . and believed" (2:23), their faith in most cases was shallow. They believed what they saw, but they were not willing to commit in an act of life surrender. Because Jesus "knew what was in a man" (2:25), He could know human thought processes directly. In dialog He could ignore what was said and respond to what was thought.

4. Jesus' Conversation With Nicodemus (Jn. 3:1-21)[5]

Nicodemus was a member of the Jewish ruling council—i.e., the Sanhedrin. The nighttime visit was probably to assure secrecy, or at least avoid publicity. By addressing Jesus respectfully as "Rabbi," Nicodemus humbly positioned himself as a learner. Clearly, he was a sincere inquirer, and he came because he wished to know more about Jesus' prophesied Kingdom. Nicodemus appears twice more in Scripture, and each time as Jesus' supporter (cf. 7:50-51; 19:38-42).

The reference to miraculous signs (cf. Jn. 3:2) implies events not otherwise reported in Scripture. Only one sign is known at this time: the changing of the water into wine, and that miracle occurred in Galilee. Jesus chose to pass over Nicodemus' compliments and prior insights, and to proceed directly to speak of the Kingdom. His somewhat cryptic remarks no doubt caused Nicodemus to see the vital difference between the flesh and the spirit—the earthly and the spiritual.

At this point, Jesus introduced the concept of being "born again" (3:3). The Greek phrase combines *gennao* and *anothen* and it may be rendered either: born again, or born from above (cf. *gennao* [genn-AH-oh]: to bear, bring forth, produce, beget; *anothen* [AN-oh-then]: from above, from a higher place, again, anew, over again.) The words denote an experience by which one enters immediately into the life of the world to come, and it stands in radical contrast with natural birth. Jesus taught that this new

---

5   An interesting Bible fact is that John 3 is the 1,000th chapter of the Bible.

birth is an indisputable, non-optional experience, though in its achievement and administration it must remain a mystery.

What Jesus meant by, "No one can enter the kingdom of God unless he is born of water and the spirit" (3:5) is debated. Since verses three and five are each a formula for entering the kingdom, however, it appears that they are simply two different ways of describing the same experience. In verse five, Jesus used a double metaphor to teach that the Spirit has a twofold role in regenerating the penitent sinner: As water He cleanses away the past commitment to sin, and as Spirit He creates a new spiritually motivated being.

In discussing John 3:5 Leon Morris points out that in the context of John's baptism, the water aspect of entrance into the kingdom involves purification. He continues:

> **The meaning then will be that Nicodemus should enter into all that "water" symbolizes, namely repentance and the like, and that he should also enter into the experience which is summed up as "born of . . . the Spirit," namely the totally new divine life that Jesus would impart. Both demands were radical.[6]**

At a later time Paul would teach that the one born into the kingdom enjoys a new divine life—the new creation in Jesus Christ (cf. 2 Cor. 5:17).

Though Nicodemus asked for a clarification of Jesus' teaching, his real need was faith rather than knowledge. Actually, Nicodemus ought to have understood the concept of a second birth. The Old Testament specifically taught the provision of a new heart (cf. 1 Sam. 10:6, Jer. 31:33), so it should not have been a new concept to a Jewish scholar. God's pattern for the restoration of millennial Israel is described: "I will sprinkle clean water on you, and you will be clean; I will cleanse you . . . I will give you a new heart and put a new spirit in you" (Ezek. 36:25,26).

In Greek, wind and Spirit are the same word (*pneuma* [NEWma]), and thus in verse eight the idea of the sovereign ministry of the Spirit is conveyed through a play on words. Older versions expand verse thirteen by adding the words "who is in heaven." If these words do belong in the text, they may be understood as a comment by John describing matters as they stood in his day.

Jesus' future destiny with the cross is hinted in verse fourteen, though the verb "lifted up" denotes not only being lifted above the earth, but also being exalted in glory. In this reference, Jesus was referring to the Old Testament Torah, a book that

---

6 Leon Morris, *The Gospel According to John.* Grand Rapids: Wm. B. Eerdmans Publishing Co., 1971, p. 216.

Nicodemus should have known well. Verse fifteen makes very clear that all who look upon Jesus in faith will have eternal life.

As Christians have long recognized, verse sixteen summarizes the message of the gospel and thus it remains the golden text of the Bible. Someone has commented, "If all the Bible were lost except this one verse it contains enough gospel to save the entire human race."

Some scholars hold that this passage (in vv. 16-21) advances from Jesus' dialogue to John's reflection. But whoever the actual spokesman, the content comprises some great texts of Scripture. Tenney wrote, "The words may be the author's condensation of Jesus' utterance, but [they] were doubtless based on what He said on this occasion."[7] Jesus offers light: those who accept it enjoy God's truth, those who reject it choose judgment. The passage ends with no report of Nicodemus' response, though he had heard a life changing message from the world's greatest Teacher.

5. John the Baptist's Confession of Christ (Jn. 3:22-36)

At this time, John was performing baptisms "in Aenon near Salim, because there was much water there" (v. 23). The name "Aenon" [EE-nuhn] means springs, and it indicates the source of the water. Since Jesus' ministry paralleled that of John, Jesus was also recruiting disciples by baptism. Many of John's followers were transferring to Jesus. These events distressed John's remaining disciples, and they came to him with a questioning protest. "The one you testified about . . . is baptizing, and everyone is going to him" (v. 26).

John's response to his disciples' concerns was a ringing testimony of the greatness of Jesus. He used the figure of a wedding party, and portrayed himself in the role of the friend of Jesus the Bridegroom. He predicted, in what are his last words recorded in John's gospel: "He must become greater; I must become less" (v. 30). By the time that these words were recorded in the Gospel, it was indeed the case that Jesus' life and ministry had far eclipsed that of John the Baptist. No doubt John's attitude toward Jesus served as a model for his disciples.

Scholars suggest that verses thirty-one through thirty-six are another soliloquy by John the evangelist (cf. vv. 16-21). The passage reflects on the superiority of the message of the heavenly Messenger, and it is a major Christological statement of faith. The writer notes that Jesus distinctively was given the Spirit "without limit" (v. 34), (or not sparingly or grudgingly), in contrast with Old Testament prophets whose anointing was measured, and thus limited. The believer is declared to possess eternal life now, and the unbeliever to be the subject of God's wrath now.

---

7   Merrill Tenney, *John: The Gospel of Belief.* Grand Rapids: Wm. B. Eerdmans Publishing Co., 1948, p. 89.

6. Jesus Departs From Judea (Jn. 4:1-3)

In this brief section, John explains how Jesus, who had been ministering in Judea, came to travel northward and thus meet the woman at the well. Apparently the Pharisees saw the rapid increase of Jesus' followers as a threat to their entrenched leadership status. If Jesus had remained in Judea He might have precipitated a premature conflict with the Pharisees. Thus, He judged that at this time, at least from a human perspective, it was better to leave the province.

We have noted that both John the Baptist and Jesus taught the baptism of new converts. Scripture explains that in the case of the apostolic party, the disciples rather than Jesus now officiated at baptismal events. We can assume, however, that Jesus personally baptized His first disciples. They then, in turn, would have baptized others who became His followers.

7. The Samaritan Woman at the Well (Jn. 4:4-42)

Jesus' response to the Pharisees' comparison of His ministry with that of John the Baptist was to return to Galilee. He wished to avoid the impression that He was in competition with John. For Jesus to have gained more disciples than John indicates great popularity. Scripture had previously reported concerning John's ministry: "The whole Judean countryside and all the people of Jerusalem went out to him" (Mk. 1:5).

Presumably Jesus "had to go through Samaria" (Jn. 4:5) to avoid Herod's territory, but more importantly to fulfill an opportunity to witness. The language implies a moral or spiritual necessity. Jacob's gift of the plot of land to Joseph is mentioned in Genesis 48:22. There is no Biblical background for Jacob's well, but what may be the authentic well still exists in Palestine. The well, which now is very deep (38 meters [125 feet]), is fed by an underground spring. Joseph's traditional tomb is nearby. The site of the former village of Sychar continues to be disputed.

The sixth hour of the day, when the apostolic party arrived at Jacob's well, would likely be equivalent to 12:00 noon. If John used Roman time notation, however, it would have been 6:00 p.m. Either hour would be an unusual time for a woman to come to draw water, but probably the woman chose the least popular time because she was uncomfortable in the presence of her neighbors due to her immoral personal life.

As far as is known, no distinctive dress distinguished Jews from Samaritans. Thus it was likely Jesus' speech that indicated that He was a Jew. In a notable example of establishing a point of contact, Jesus spoke of the material world before He moved to the spiritual. The woman was startled by Jesus' request for water, for most Jewish men considered Samaritan women to be ritually unclean. To accept drink or food from them would cause one to become defiled. Jesus pointedly ignored these prejudices.

Jesus' offer of living water (v. 10) had Old Testament precedents, for the LORD through Jeremiah identified Himself as "the spring of living water" (Jer. 2:13, cf. 17:13). Within a few months, at the Feast of Tabernacles Jesus would publicly proclaim Himself the source of "streams of living water" (Jn. 7:38). To describe the permanency of the supply—"will never thirst" (v. 14)—Jesus in the Greek idiom used the double negative. His literal "not never thirst forever" is equivalent to "never never thirst," though, of course, such redundancies are ordinarily not considered to be good English.

As the conversation proceeded, the woman preferred to discuss the merits of Mt. Gerizim[8] over Jerusalem rather than deal with her personal shortcomings. This Samaritan woman would have been taught to accept only the Pentateuch as God's Word. Thus, she looked for a Messiah in the pattern of Moses, based on Deuteronomy 18:15-28, and she had no concept of one who would come of David's royal line. In spite of His tactful approach to her as a person, Jesus firmly rejected Samaritanism as a religion. He declared, "Salvation is from the Jews" (v. 22).

Jesus' statement, "God is spirit, and his worshipers must worship in spirit and in truth" (v. 24), is a fundamental principle of Christian worship. It affirms that worship no longer depends on a specific site, and that material things can never be its essence. One who worships in spirit worships at the level of God's nature. These words effectively elevated Jesus' discussion with the woman above petty issues of time and place.

It has been said, "The woman left her waterpot and went off with the well." Actually, however, the fact that she left the waterpot was evidence that she intended to return. She had first seen herself and then had seen Him, and she had claimed the well of water springing up within. The woman's perception of Jesus advanced throughout the conversation. Either directly or indirectly, she identified Him as: a Jew (v. 9), one greater than Jacob (v. 12), a prophet (v. 19), and at least tentatively as the Christ (v. 29).

Though Jesus appears to have concealed His Messiahship to many, to this outcast woman He plainly revealed Himself as the Messiah (cf. v. 26). By now the disciples had discovered that there was much about Jesus that they could not explain, and thus they were content not to ask about the woman (cf. v. 27). Perhaps Jesus' point about the ripened harvest was that this was one harvest that had not taken four months to ripen (cf. v. 35).

---

8   In Deuteronomy 27:3-7, the Samaritan Pentateuch differs from the usual text (i.e., the Massoretic Text [abbr *MT*]) by replacing "Ebal" with "Gerizim" as the site of the altar in the land.

Jesus declared that there are always rewards for the spiritual reaper (v. 36). Both those who sow and those who reap are entitled to rejoice. Reapers will often enjoy the advantages of another person's labor (v. 38). In teaching these truths Jesus seems to have transcended the present occasion and to have provided insights that would apply throughout the era of the Church, and to all future workers in Christian service.

In the Bible record, the people of Sychar were the first sinners who found Jesus. They were not evangelized by the disciples, but they responded to the woman's testimony (cf. v. 39). Many more became believers as they heard Jesus' words (cf. v. 41). Perhaps these inquirers were already visible when Jesus urged the disciples to lift up their eyes to see the ripened harvest fields (cf. v. 35). That Jesus, a Jew, could remain for two days (v. 40) teaching in Samaria is a remarkable testimony to the degree to which Jesus had won the respect and confidence of these people. The closing words of the townspeople indicate a commendable grasp of truth: "This man really is the Savior of the world" (v. 42b).

II. THE BEGINNING OF THE SECOND YEAR OF MINISTRY

Scripture reports only selected events out of the life of Jesus. The foregoing six events were apparently the only ones selected by the Spirit to represent Jesus' activities during His first year. This phase of Jesus' ministry was recorded only by John; the synoptics omit the entire Judean ministry of Jesus.

1. John the Baptist Imprisoned (Mt. 14:3-5; Mk. 6:17-20; Lk. 3:19-20)

This event was not part of Jesus' ministry, and thus it is inserted later in the Gospel account as an explanation of what had previously happened. In point of time, it is believed to have occurred at about this juncture in the life of Jesus.

John was imprisoned because he rightly denounced Herod Antipas' adulterous relationship with Herodias the wife of his brother Philip (also known as Herod Philip). Matthew reports that Herod "wanted to kill John" (Mt. 14:5). Mark, however, uniquely explains the underlying motivations: "Herodias nursed a grudge against John and wanted to kill him" (6:19), but "Herod feared John and protected him" (v. 20). It is usually suggested that John was imprisoned in the palace at Machaerus, but that his disciples were allowed visitation privileges. When John later was executed, that event interacted with Jesus' ministry[9].

---

9 See pp. 92, 110, 119.

2. The Great Galilean Ministry Begun (Mt. 4:12; Mk. 1:14-15; Lk. 4:14-15; Jn. 4:43-45)

Matthew notes that upon hearing of John's imprisonment, Jesus "departed from there" (Mt. 14:13, NKJV), and Mark reports, "Jesus went into Galilee, proclaiming the good news of God" (Mk. 1:14). Luke adds the spiritual dimension, "Jesus returned to Galilee in the power of the Spirit" (Lk. 4:14). Thus, by transferring His ministry to Herod's jurisdiction, Jesus stepped into the gap that John the Baptist had necessarily vacated. Though Jesus' acceptance in parts of Galilee was to be short-lived, at the outset "the Galileans welcomed him" (Jn. 4:45). In anticipation of future events, John at this point quoted Jesus' saying, "a prophet has no honor in his own country" (Jn. 4:43; cf. Mt. 13:57; Mk. 6:4; Lk. 4:24). The initial popularity assured that Jesus had an immediate audience. Based on data in Josephus, it is estimated that in Jesus' time the population of Galilee was about three million.

In announcing "The time [*kairos*] has come" (Mk. 1:15), Jesus was declaring that the moment of opportunity for the launching of the kingdom of God had arrived. The word *kairos* (ky-ROS) denotes the occasion, moment, or era for action and it contrasts with *chronos* (CHRON-os) which denotes clock or calendar time. Though Jesus announced "The kingdom of God is near" (Mk. 1:15), the Jews chose not to recognize its presence in His person. As a nation, the Jews were ready neither to repent, nor to believe the good news.

The Galilean ministry extended fully a year and one-half or more. The order of events tends to follow Mark and Luke who apparently recorded more or less chronologically. In sections, at least, Matthew appears to have compiled his report topically.

3. The Healing of the Royal Official's Son (Jn. 4:46-54)

Cana was Nathanael's home (cf. Jn. 21:2), and a place where Jesus had friends and followers (cf. Jn. 2:1-11). Thus, as Jesus arrived back in Galilee after having been in Judea, He proceeded to Cana. It was there that He was contacted by the royal official (or nobleman) who persistently begged Him to come and heal his son. By living in Capernaum, which was a port on the Sea of Galilee, the official would have access to Herod's court at Tiberias, which was also a seaport. Capernaum was about twenty-five kilometers (fifteen miles) from Cana.

Jesus' reference to the pursuit of "miraculous signs and wonders" (v. 48) led the official into a firm declaration of faith. He was not seeking a spectacular miracle, but he was seeking the healing of his son, and he saw Jesus as his sole hope (cf. v. 49). Thus, in response to Jesus' word, "Your son will live," the official "took Jesus

at his word" (v. 50). To believe for a healing bestowed on a seemingly casual basis would have required unusually firm faith. The
healing was accomplished at that exact hour, and the fact of the
separating distance was not an issue.

In response to the miracle healing, this Gentile official "and
all his household believed" (v. 53)—i.e., they became converts to
Christ's mission and person. This healing was one of four

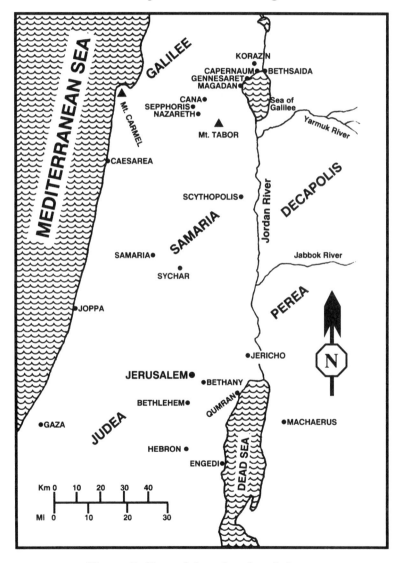

Figure 7: Sites of Jesus' early ministry

performed at a distance, and it was Jesus' second recorded miraculous sign in Galilee. It took place at Cana just as His first miracle. Both miracles were performed before a limited audience so that only insiders knew that they had occurred. In the interim, however, Jesus had ministered in Jerusalem, and there "many people saw the miraculous signs he was doing" (Jn. 2:23).

4. Jesus' First Rejection at Nazareth (Lk. 4:16-30)

Though much that was taught there must have grieved Him, Jesus had attended the Nazareth synagogue since His boyhood. Probably most of those in the audience were long time friends and acquaintances. It was the custom in synagogue worship for the synagogue's ruler to assign volunteers to read the Scripture. Typically, in each service there were two readings, one in the law, the other in the prophets. Jesus read from Isaiah 61:1-2, in what appears to be the Septuagint Version (*LXX*), but since God's age of judgment was yet future, He stopped midway through a sentence and omitted the last clause.

According to custom, Jesus sat down to bring a teaching interpretation of the passage that He had read. The reading had summarized the spiritual effects of His ministry: 1) preach good news to the (economically and spiritually) poor, 2) provide release for (spiritual) prisoners and sight for the (spiritually) sightless, 3) provide release for the oppressed (by sin), and 4) announce the arrival of the kingdom age. For Jesus to say, "Today this scripture is fulfilled in your hearing" (v. 21) was for Him to assume the role of a prophet and to imply that He was the Messiah.

The people were amazed (or astonished) (v. 22), but not necessarily admiring or accepting of Jesus' words. They asked, "Isn't this Joseph's son?" They saw Him only as one of themselves. In the popular view, the Messiah was to come as a mighty conqueror, and they could not reconcile this expectation with the fact that Jesus was a local person. They were unaware that the voice at His baptism had declared that He was God's Son (cf. Lk. 3:22).

The proverb "Physician, heal yourself" (v. 23) implies that a ministry making supernatural claims should exhibit supernatural fruit—they wanted to see miracles. Jesus anticipated this desire, and at least indirectly, He explained why they would not be accommodated. By speaking of Elijah and Elisha He was pointing out that only those who receive the prophet's message can expect to receive the prophet's blessing.

Jesus used these historical accounts to demonstrate that when the prophets found no believers in Israel, they took their ministry to Gentiles. He thus made clear that His ministry would bless the Gentiles, while they, the people of Nazareth, because of their unbelief would miss the blessing. Obviously, hometown nationalistic pride was deeply offended.

The people's response was anger, and a struggle followed as the mob forced Him from the building and attempted to throw Him down a cliff. It is assumed that they hoped that as He lay stunned by the fall they could bury Him with a cascade of stones. Without angry words or actions, however, the majestic Son of God simply walked unhindered through the mob. The traditional Mount of Precipitation is more than three kilometers from Nazareth, and few scholars consider it to be authentic. There is no record that Jesus ever returned to Nazareth.

5. Jesus' New Home in Capernaum (Mt. 4:13-17; Lk. 4:31-32)

At this point Jesus transferred His residence and ministry base from Nazareth to Capernaum (*Kefer-nahum* = village of Nahum) where it appears His headquarters remained for the next two years. This community, in the mainstream of national life, was a manufacturing and merchandising center. Five of Jesus' disciples came from Capernaum: Peter, Andrew, James, John, and Philip. Bethsaida was a residential suburb. Jesus later declared that He had no home (cf. Mt. 8:20), so this move perhaps involved setting up a home for His mother. Matthew saw this event as the fulfillment of Isaiah 9:1-2, for in the person of the Light of the World, light had dawned upon the region (cf. Mt. 4:16).

With the move to Capernaum, "Jesus began to preach, 'Repent, for the kingdom of heaven is near'" (Mt. 4:17). Thus, He was continuing John the Baptist's message. Also, He ministered by teaching in the synagogue. "He went down to Capernaum . . . and on the Sabbath began to teach the people" (Lk. 4:31). Since professional synagogue ministries were scarce, it was customary for an available teacher to be asked to speak.

Jesus' teaching style was uniquely different from that which was usual. In His day, teaching was often stereotyped, concerned with trivia, and limited to what could be supported by quoting from some previous teacher. Jesus' approach was to expound and apply Scriptural truth out of His own insights and without appealing to past human pronouncements. Also, His authoritative teaching spoke to relevant issues that concerned human needs. Thus, until opposition solidified, Jesus enjoyed ample open doors and eager audiences.

6. The Four Called to Become Fishers of Men (Mt. 4:18-22; Mk. 1:16-20; Lk. 5:1-11)

Luke's report of this incident somewhat expands that of Matthew and Mark, but most evangelical scholars hold that the same episode is being described. Events in common include: the same place (Galilee or Gennesaret), two boats, Simon, Simon's partner, James, John, the appeal to be catchers or fishers of men, and the conclusion that they left what they had and followed Him.

Only Luke tells that Jesus first taught out of Peter's boat, from which at Jesus' instruction they later caught a miracle load of fish, and that Peter was thus brought to his knees in worship before Jesus. It has been noted that though Peter was a veteran fisherman, it took the Carpenter to tell him how to catch fish! Peter had been experiencing Jesus' teaching and seeing His miracles for some time, but nothing seems to have had more influence upon him that the miracle of the fish.

The title "Master" (*epistates* [ep-is-TA-tays] v. 5) that Peter used in addressing Jesus (Lk. 5:5) was the usual term a disciple would use to address the one he followed. This term is found only in Luke, the parallel Gospel accounts use "Rabbi" (i.e., Teacher). In addressing Jesus as "Lord" (Lk. 5:8), Peter used the word *kurios* (KUR-ee-os) which in this context appears as a recognition of Christ's Messiahship. Peter had seen deity at work, and his own natural humanity suddenly appeared frail and limited.

About a year earlier Jesus had won Andrew, Peter, and probably John (who at that time was not named) as His followers (see pp. 49, 50). James is named here for the first time. The previous call had been to be disciples (i.e., learners) (cf. Jn. 1:35-51); this call is actually a commissioning to be soul-winning apostles (i.e., sent ones). Those who had previously committed their faith to Jesus are now asked to commit to active ministry.

In leaving their boat and their father, the four fishermen-apostles were giving full allegiance to Jesus. Significantly, Jesus' call to service came not to the idle, but to those who were already busy. He declared, "From now on you will catch (Gk. *zogreo*) men" (Lk. 5:10). (*zogreo* [zoh-GREH-oh]: capture alive, win or recruit). It has been suggested that the proceeds from the sale of the supernatural catch of fish would have provided for the fishermen and their families during the time of vocational transition.

7. Jesus Casts Out an Evil Spirit (Mk. 1:21-28; Lk. 4:33-37)

At the outset, Jesus "went into the synagogue and began to teach" (Mk. 1:21), and again He amazed the people by the authority of His teaching, a fact that Mark reports twice (cf. Mk. 1:22; 1:27). In this setting, however, He was challenged by a man possessed by an evil spirit. Cole comments, "It is a strange commentary on the spiritual situation in Capernaum that a demoniac could worship in the synagogue with no sense of incongruity, until confronted by Jesus."[10]

The evil spirit (or spirits) in the man knew Jesus and sought to oppose Him. The cry of the composite spirits revealed that they wanted to be left alone, and that they feared that Jesus would

---

10 Alan R. Cole, *The Gospel According to St. Mark*. Grand Rapids: Wm. B. Eerdmans Pub. Co., 1988, p. 61.

destroy them. They identified Jesus as "the Holy One of God" (Lk. 4:34). Jesus desired neither the opposition nor the acclamation of an unclean spirit, and He commanded, "Be quiet, and come out of him" (Lk. 4:35). The expression "Be quiet" is literally "be muzzled." After a struggle the unclean spirit departed, and Jesus thus achieved the first of at least five exorcisms recorded in the synoptics. None of these exorcisms are recorded in John's Gospel. This event is the first miracle recorded in Mark.

The exorcism in the synagogue at Capernaum may be realistically visualized because one can visit a partial restoration of an actual ancient synagogue in Capernaum. Based on a hoard of 10,000 coins found under the floor, this synagogue is dated in the fourth or fifth century after Christ. A new synagogue was usually built on the site of the old one, but the Capernaum synagogue appears to have been built over the remains of private homes. Thus, it may or may not mark the site of the synagogue where Jesus ministered. Scripture notes that the synagogue of Jesus' time was built for the Jews by a centurion proselyte (cf. Lk. 7:5).

As an itinerant teacher with a following of disciples, Jesus more or less appeared as the conventional teacher-rabbi who was highly revered in Judaism. The fact that Jesus had cast out an unclean spirit and performed other miracles earned for Him the very special esteem of many. Also, the remarkable freshness and authority of His teaching set Him apart from all others. It was thus understandable that, "News about him spread quickly over the whole region of Galilee" (Mk. 1:28). What the reports missed however, was the fact that he was the Messiah.

8. Jesus Heals Peter's Mother-in-Law and Many Others (Mt. 8:14-17; Mk. 1:29-34; Lk. 4:38-41)

The healing of Peter's mother-in-law was during the Sabbath afternoon, when, presumably, Jesus and His disciples had been invited as dinner guests. In the composite account: she was sick with a high fever, they appealed to Jesus on her behalf, Jesus bent over her and rebuked the fever, He took her by the hand and lifted her up, immediately the fever left her, and she arose and served them. She used her restored health as an instrument to invest in service. Not only did Jesus cure the fever, but He took away the usual aftereffects of a debilitating illness.

To this account of the healing of his mother-in-law, Scripture adds one other glimpse of Peter's domestic life. Paul wrote, "Don't we have the right to take a believing wife along with us, as do the other apostles . . . and Cephas? (1 Cor. 9:5). In later years, apparently, Peter's wife accompanied him in his traveling ministries.

After sundown, when the end of the Sabbath had been signaled by the visibility of at least three stars, the law allowed the sick to be carried and people to travel beyond the Sabbath limitation. At that time, many were brought to Jesus, and in Matthew's words, "He cast out the spirits with a word, and healed all who were sick" (8:16). Such miracles stirred great interest, and Mark reports, "The whole town gathered at the door" (Mk. 1:33). Matthew saw in this group-healing event the fulfillment of Isaiah 53:4 that describes Messiah's passion (cf. Mt. 8:17).

One aspect of Jesus' healing ministry on this occasion is described: "Laying his hands on each one, he healed them" (Lk. 4:40). Jesus' actions on this and similar occasions became a precedent to establish the practices of the early church (cf. Mk. 16:18; Acts 28:8). Although it has roots in the Old Testament (cf. Num. 8:10; 27:18,19; Deut. 34:9), the practice of laying on hands—i.e. imposition—emerges in the New Testament as basically a new procedure. The practice by Jesus showed that He was the source of healing power and that He was concerned for the afflicted one.

Many healings that Jesus performed at this time involved exorcisms. The demons regularly recognized Him as the Son of God, but Jesus took authority over them and He "rebuked them and would not allow them to speak" (Lk. 4:41). Jesus needed no demonic testimonies, and the announcement of His Messiahship was to be solely in the hands of the sovereign God.

Extensive archeological investigations of the site of ancient Capernaum have revealed the remains of stone houses thought to date to Jesus' day. There is some evidence that an ancient Christian church (fifth century), the remains of which have been excavated, was a memorial church built over a venerated room in a private home. Scholars speculate seriously that this venerated room may have been part of Peter's home where the first Christian services in the village were held.

FOUR:

THE GREAT GALILEAN MINISTRY (PART 1)

A t this point Jesus entered into the major ministry activities that were to comprise the backbone of His public outreach. Matthew describes His threefold approach: "Jesus went throughout Galilee, teaching in their synagogues, preaching the good news of the kingdom, and healing every disease and sickness among the people" (Mt. 4:23).

I. THE FIRST PREACHING TOUR IN GALILEE

Jesus' ministry in Galilee had thus far been almost entirely limited to Cana, Nazareth, or Capernaum. He now undertook a planned campaign to reach other towns and villages throughout the Province.

1. Jesus Preaches in Other Galilean Cities (Mt. 4:23-25; Mk. 1:35-39; Lk. 4:42-44)

Before beginning His Galilean campaign, Jesus spent a lengthy time in private prayer that began long before daybreak. In the Gospels' account this is the first of eleven instances in which it is reported that Jesus prayed. Though Peter and his companions sought Him out to tell Him that the local people were looking for Him, Jesus responded: "Let us go into the next towns that I may preach there also" (Mk. 1:38, NKJV). His compulsion to share His message with others overruled the appeal of the crowd from Capernaum who "tried to keep Him from leaving them" (Lk. 4:42). This withdrawal from activity (Mk. 1:38-39) is the first of a total of ten such occasions in the life of Jesus recorded by Mark. (cf. 1:38,39; 3:7-13; 6:6; 6:30-32; 7:24; 8:27; 9:2; 11:11; 11:19).

According to Josephus, at this time there were over 200 villages in Galilee. Jesus apparently shared His preaching and healing ministry with many of them, and He met the needs of multitudes of suffering humans, including those possessed by demons. In 4:25 and elsewhere, for a total of forty-nine references, Matthew speaks of large crowds following Jesus. Unfortunately, the majority of these people were attracted by the miracles, and they did not choose to enter the kingdom in penitent humility. Matthew enumerated the types of infirmities that Jesus healed:

severe pain (those racked with pain—NEB), demon-possession[1], seizures (the epileptic—ASV), and paralysis (cf. Mt. 4:24).

In modern Greek texts for Luke 4:44, the place of Jesus' ministry is given as Judea, though in the parallel passages (Mt. 4:23, Mk. 1:39) it is Galilee. Scholars explain this apparent discrepancy by suggesting that Luke uses the name Judea in its generic sense. Rather than identifying the southern province, here it means simply "the land of the Jews."

2. The Cleansing of the Leper and Subsequent Events (Mt. 8:1-4; Mk. 1:40-45; Lk. 5:12-16)

Usually in Scripture, as on this occasion, the restoration of a leper is called a cleansing rather than a healing. This account is the first cleansing of a leper in Jesus' ministry; in Matthew it comes later, but Mark and Luke place it at this time. Luke reports that this man "was covered with leprosy" (5:12) or "full of leprosy" (KJV). Today's scholars suggest that the term leprosy in Scripture may have identified a variety of skin diseases other than Hansen's disease (today's term for leprosy), but there was a single prescription for all who were diagnosed with leprosy.

It is said that an actual case of leprosy in Bible times would likely run its course in approximately nine years. If other skin diseases were diagnosed as leprosy, however, they probably would not be fatal, and the victim would live indefinitely. Nevertheless, from the moment that one was diagnosed with leprosy, that one was considered to be dead. Levitical law imposed a rigorous quarantine; the leper "must live alone; he must live outside the camp" (Lev. 13:45-46). A leper not only lost his health, he also lost his family, his social circle, and his livelihood. As one of their few concessions, the Jews allowed lepers to attend synagogue services, but they required them to sit in a separate section.

The leper questioned Jesus' will in the matter of healing, but Jesus immediately corrected him: "I am willing; be cleansed" (Lk. 5:13). In order to minister healing, "Jesus reached out his hand and touched the man" (Mt. 8:3). Scholars debate whether Jesus' touch disregarded the rigorous quarantine laws, or if in the synchronization of the healing gift, Jesus actually touched a cleansed man. At least it is clear that by the time Jesus withdrew His touch the leper was cleansed, for it was a cleansing touch and the healing was immediate. For the exiled leper to be touched by a living human hand would itself be a powerful therapy.

Our usual versions describe Jesus as "filled with compassion" (Mk. 1:41). However, since a few source manuscripts read "filled with anger," some versions (e.g. NRSV) show this alternate

---

1   The single word *daimonidzomai* (die-moan-IDZE-o-my] that is rendered demon-possession could also be translated by the word "demonized" and its variants.

reading as a footnote. Jesus could have been angry with the disease even though He was compassionate toward its victim.

Jesus admonished the cleansed leper, "with a strong warning: 'See that you don't tell this to anyone'" (Mk. 1:44). The superficial fickleness of human public acclaim over mighty works made Jesus' request for secrecy necessary. Barclay comments, "The great danger was that men should proclaim Jesus as Messiah without knowing who and what the Messiah was."[2] The Jews desperately wanted a militant political leader to deliver them from Roman rule. They failed to understand a leader whose kingdom was beyond this world and who battled in the Spirit.

In spite of Jesus' instruction, the former leper "went out and began to talk freely . . . . As a result, Jesus could no longer enter a town openly, but stayed outside in lonely places" (Mk. 1:45). For the leper to find his health restored was an event so exciting that he could not be silent about it. Nevertheless, to disobey the Lord's command was to cause needless damage to Jesus' ministry opportunities. The leper had been healed, but he did not respond by conscientiously submitting to Jesus' authority.

Jesus instructed the cleansed leper to show himself to the priest in order to fulfill the requirements of the law. If the leper's quarantine was to be officially lifted, the approval of the priest was necessary. The spiritual restoration of a healed leper involved the elaborate ceremony given in Leviticus 14:1-32 and likely its implementation would have required a three-day journey to the temple in Jerusalem. Since the leper disobeyed Jesus by publicizing his healing, he may have been similarly careless in regard to the law's requirements. If he did show himself to the priest, the priest's confirmation of the healing would have been a notable endorsement of Jesus' ministry.

Luke concludes this pericope by noting that in spite of the uninvited public acclaim, "Jesus often withdrew to lonely places and prayed" (Lk. 5:16). As a man, Jesus desired to know and understand the mind and ways of God through constant communion with Him. He thus is a model to all believers.

3. The Healing of the Man Let Down Through the Roof (Mt. 9:1-8; Mk. 2:1-12; Lk. 5:17-26)

This event took place in Capernaum after Jesus had returned from His tour of the province. It is possible that the house was Jesus' place of residence, or perhaps Peter's house. The roof is described differently between two evangelists. Luke speaks of lowering the "mat through the tiles" (Lk. 5:19). Mark tells of making an opening in the roof and "digging through it" (Mk. 2:4) which implies a roof of mud thatch or clay supported by wooden

---

2   William Barclay, *The Gospel of Matthew* (Vol. 2). Burlington: Welch
      Publishing Co., 1975, p. 164.

beams. Perhaps the house had been remodeled, and the roof combined two different building styles.

Luke reports that "the power of the Lord was present for him [Jesus] to heal the sick" (Lk. 5:17). These words suggest that God maintained sovereign control over the healing ministry of the incarnate Christ. Only Mark notes that there were four carriers, but all three synoptics refer to their faith. Scripture reports no words spoken by either the carriers or the paralyzed man.

The word "son" by which Jesus addressed the man (Mt. 9:2; Mk. 2:5) is an affectionate term meaning literally "lad" or "child." Jesus' exhortation to "Take heart" (or "Cheer up") (Mt. 9:2) is one among six such entreaties by Jesus in the Gospels. Jesus' pronouncement, "your sins are forgiven" (Mt. 9:2) greatly offended the religious leaders who were present. They saw His words as highly controversial, for to forgive sin was to assume the role of deity. Since, however, sin is the root cause of all human ills and the barrier to God's blessing, forgiveness of sin was indeed appropriate. It is possible that the paralytic knew that his condition was the direct result of a dissolute life.

Jesus' critics did not speak their minds in the public setting, but He knew that in their thoughts they were charging Him with blaspheming. Someone translates verse eight: "His spirit read their minds like a book!" In Leviticus 24:10-16 blasphemy involved abusing the name of deity, but the Jews had broadened the term to include making oneself equal to God. In His rebuke, Jesus described His critics' attitudes as "evil thoughts" (Mt. 9:4).

Jesus instructed the paralytic: "Get up, take your mat and go home" (Mt. 9:6). His instructions were instantly obeyed. To pronounce sins forgiven required no visible miracle, but to command a paralytic to walk certainly did. By the visible healing, Jesus validated His pronouncement of forgiveness. Though, as we have noted, Jesus frequently referred to Himself as the Son of Man, this is the only instance in the Gospels that this title is linked with the forgiveness of sins (cf. Mt. 9:6; Lk. 5:24).

This incident, because it involved the forgiveness of sins, marked the beginning in Galilee of opposition against Jesus by the religious leaders. Luke describes the hostile movement's scope: "Pharisees and teachers of the law who had come from every village of Galilee and from Judea and Jerusalem, were sitting there" (Lk. 5:17). The expression "remarkable things" (strange or incredible things) (Lk. 5:26) translates *paradoxa* (par-AH-dox-ah) which becomes the English "paradoxes."

In the original, the "teachers of the law" who were among Jesus' opponents are designated as *nomodidaskalos* [no-mo-di-DASK-al-os] in Luke 5:17, and as *grammateus* [gramma-TOOSE] in Luke 5:21. The first term is a compound of the words "law" and "teacher" and it occurs in the Gospels only in this verse; the second term denotes one who is a scholar of written materials, and in Jewish usage, the rabbinical scholar who is well informed in regard to the law of Moses.

4. The Call of Matthew and His Reception (Mt. 9:9-13; Mk. 2:13-17; Lk. 5:27-32)

Though this account follows in Scripture, many scholars feel that at this juncture there is a gap in the time sequence.

As a tax collector, Matthew (called Levi in Mark and Luke) would have represented Herod Antipas. The Latin word for "treasury" was *publicum*, and thus such collectors were known as "publicans." In Capernaum Matthew would have been involved in: road tolls, customs duties on caravans passing through or entering Galilee, and a harbor tax. He would have been responsible to raise a fixed sum for the provincial treasury. Because he had sold himself to an oppressive ruler, he probably was despised by his fellow citizens; Jews routinely excommunicated tax collectors from the synagogue. Jewish writers described them in terms such as "beasts in human shape" or "licensed robbers."

At this time, Matthew responded without hesitation to Jesus' call to permanent discipleship. Possibly he had previously met Jesus and had been pondering a full commitment. Matthew's "great banquet" (Lk. 5:29) would have required advance planning, and thus some harmonies place it a few weeks later. Guests for the feast included: Jesus, the disciples, tax collectors from Matthew's circle, and "others." Presumably, Matthew's motive in inviting the various guests was to give them opportunity to meet Jesus; as it were, it was an evangelistic outreach. Teachers of the law and Pharisees appear to have been present as uninvited guests.

The Pharisees criticized Jesus because He was eating "with tax collectors and 'sinners' [i.e., outcasts]" (Mt. 9:11). To the Pharisees, anyone who did not observe their intricately detailed laws was a sinner. In His reply on this occasion, Jesus set forth a basic principle of His ministry: "It is not the healthy who need a doctor, but the sick. I have not come to call the righteous, but sinners" (Mk. 2:17). These words, because they represent the refreshingly unique emphasis of Christianity, have been called, "one of the greatest landmarks in the history of morality and religion." Someone has paraphrased Jesus' words as saying, "I mix with sinners because they have a need and I have a cure."

In making this point, Jesus quoted a portion of Hosea 6:6, "I desire mercy, not sacrifice" (Mt. 9:13). This passage teaches that it is God's nature to be merciful, and that He cares first of all about a spiritual attitude of heart, rather than the mechanical performance of religious rituals. By extending His call at this time, Jesus transformed one who had been a greedy tax collector into: an apostle, an evangelist, and a saint. It has been said of Matthew, "He lost a comfortable job, but found a destiny." Far from being contaminated by His associates, the divine Christ worked in them to renew them, and to make them whole in godliness and personal virtue.

5. The Healing at the Pool of Bethesda (Jn. 5:1-16)

This event was during an interlude in the Galilean ministry while Jesus was attending an unnamed feast in Jerusalem. The feast was likely a Passover and if so, it occurred at about this point in Jesus' activities. If it was a Passover, it was the second in the four that Jesus marked during the years of His ministry.

A site that some identify as the Pool of Bethesda (actually there are twin pools) has been excavated in modern times and found, among other things, to have been reached only by two steep stairways. This site seems incompatible, however, with the common belief that the Pool of Bethesda was used to wash animals being taken to the temple as sacrifices.

The man Jesus confronted had suffered from his infirmity, presumably a crippling paralysis, for thirty-eight years. He avoided a direct answer when Jesus asked, "Do you want to get well?" (5:6). Scripture does not mention the man's faith, but the question appears to have brought his faith into focus. Thus Jesus could instruct, "Get up! Pick up your mat and walk" (5:8). The fact that the man could instantly walk and carry his mat after thirty-eight years of infirmity was a vital part of the miracle.

The mention of the angel who stirred the water (cf. v. 4 KJV) is not found in texts prior to A.D. 400. Most modern versions omit it or place it in a footnote. Scripture, otherwise, does not teach that angels minister healing. Though the man's statement concerning action "when the water is stirred" (Jn. 5:7) seems to require an explanation of some sort, the modern text provides none.

The fact that Jesus later found the man in the temple definitely spoke well of him. Nevertheless, Jesus linked the man's infirmity with sin (cf. v. 14), but with no explanation of its nature or the circumstances. This event was unusual in Jesus' ministry, since on other occasions Jesus taught that there is no direct one-to-one correlation between sin and sickness (cf. Jn. 9:1-3).

This healing in Jerusalem on a Sabbath and a feast day would have been a high profile event. In this setting, Jesus chose for the first time to violate the Pharisaic Sabbath laws. He thus fueled the Sabbath controversy that was later to become a major issue with His critics. The "Jews" (v. 10) who objected no doubt were representing the religious leaders in Jerusalem.

6. Jesus' Claims of Divine Prerogatives (Jn. 5:17-29)

In the synoptics, Jesus' usual defense of Sabbath healings was the need of the sufferer. He defended the Bethesda healing, however, by pointing to His status as God's Son and God's example in continuously performing works. Though God's Sabbath rest began when He completed creation, He continues to work in maintaining and governing the universe. Jesus was simply following the Father's example.

At this time Jesus claimed: 1) He worked equally with the Father (v. 17), 2) His power was equal to that of the Father (v. 19), 3) His authority was equal to that of the Father (vv. 22, 27), 4) He offers eternal life (v. 24), and 5) He offers resurrection life (vv. 5, 28). His message included a very notable salvation text: "I tell you the truth, whoever hears my word and believes him who sent me has eternal life and will not be condemned; he has crossed over from death to life" (Jn. 5:24).

Jesus' critics ignored the logic of His defense, but they became even more antagonistic because He referred to God as "My Father" (v. 17). As they "tried all the harder to kill him" (v. 18), Jesus continued to affirm that He was the divine Son of God. He declared that He would share with the Father in the end time judgment. He depicted Himself as an honored participant in the events, including the future resurrection of the dead. To His hearers, these claims were blasphemous.

7. The Witnesses to Jesus (Jn. 5:30-47)

To establish His claim to future authority, Jesus cited supporting witnesses. These included:

(1) **HIMSELF (vv. 30-31).** Because of His personal integrity, His witness is true (cf. Jn. 8:14) even though legally one cannot bear witness to himself.

(2) **JOHN THE BAPTIST (vv. 32-35).** In replying to the official delegation, John had endorsed Jesus (cf. Jn. 1:29-34; 3:25-36).

(3) **HIS WORKS (v. 36).** By this time, Jesus had performed various miracles or sign-works. He presented these now as part of His credentials. Also, He was now bringing people into reconciliation with God.

(4) **GOD THE FATHER (vv. 37-38)** He is "another who testifies in [Jesus'] favor" (v. 32). He had indeed spoken at Jesus' baptism (cf. Mt. 3:17). He was continuing to support and validate Jesus' ministry by performing in human lives that which Jesus preached. Jesus noted that His critics were deaf to the voice of God. They should have known God's voice through the prophets, but they had not heeded it.

(5) **THE SCRIPTURES (vv. 39-47).** Jesus declared that His enemies searched the Old Testament, but were blind to the fact that "The Scriptures . . . testify about me" (v. 39). Actually, to accept that which Moses taught was to be instructed concerning the Messiah, and therefore to know Jesus. (vv. 39-40). Almost all of the 300 or so Old Testament quotations, citations or allusions found in the Gospels specifically pertain to Jesus or were used by Him during His earthly ministry.

Jesus noted, in concluding, that His audience was clearly hostile, and since these people lacked God's love in their hearts, they were prepared to accept anyone except Jesus. If they had really believed Moses, they would have believed Him.

For our harmony, following this insertion of John chapter five, we return to Matthew's order of events.

8. Jesus Defends His Disciples for Not Fasting (Mt. 9:14-17; Mk. 2:18-22; Lk. 5:33-39)

The Pharisees capitalized upon the differences between the disciples of John and those of Jesus in the practice of fasting. These critics hoped to discredit Jesus in the eyes of John's disciples. Jesus' practices ran counter to Judaism's view that fasting indicated one's sorrow for sin and was necessary to prepare for the promised kingdom. Jesus was proclaiming the imminence of the kingdom, but He was not preparing for it by fasting.

John the Baptist had identified Jesus as a bridegroom (cf. Jn. 3:29), but in this passage, Jesus, for the first time, depicted Himself under this figure. In His statement, Jesus implied that the kingdom compares to a wedding feast. Since a wedding is a happy occasion, sacrificial and mournful observances, such as fasting, do not belong. The day would come when the bridegroom would be taken away, and then they could fast. It is suggested that since Messianic traditions said nothing of a bridegroom, His hearers would have totally missed the significance of His reasons for not teaching fasting.

The only required fasting in Biblical Judaism was one day a year on the Day of Atonement (cf. Lev. 16:29). Tradition had added three other mandatory days each year, but the Pharisees of Jesus' time practiced fasting two days a week—usually Mondays and Thursdays. Thus, although the spirit of sacrificial fasting was genuinely Biblical, commonly its application was excessive, and in some cases it was only a vain mechanical formula. The good news of the Christian proclamation was concerned primarily with motives rather than external rules. Though fasting was the old way of responding to God, Jesus was proclaiming a new response based on the model of a joyful marriage celebration.

At this time, in Mark 2:20, Jesus predicted that following the taking away of the bridegroom (i.e., His crucifixion), His followers would practice fasting. This veiled prophecy is Mark's first recorded hint of the cross.

In this section, Jesus gave three parables: the patched garment, wine skins, and the old wine and the new. Old fabric is too flimsy to join to a strong new patch; old wineskins are brittle and would be ruptured by the inevitable fermenting of new wine. The first two of these parables taught that Christianity entailed a total replacement and not a mere repair or enlargement of Judaism. Jesus' new kingdom was His alone, and it was neither traditional

Judaism, nor John the Baptist's modifications. McCumber comments, "It's no longer Jesus or John; it's Jesus or nothing!"[3]

The third parable, which occurs only in Luke, concerned mixing old fabrics and new, or expecting old wineskins still to be flexible. The illustrations depicted Judaism as fixed, complacent and entirely satisfied with existing conditions. Jesus thus explained why the Jews were finding it so difficult to accept His teachings.

9. Jesus Defends His Disciples for Sabbath Breaking (Mt. 12:1-8; Mk. 2:23-28; Lk. 6:1-5)

Traditional versions date this event on "the second Sabbath after the first" (Lk. 6:1 KJV). It is understood as either a reference to the second Sabbath of the New Year, or to the Sabbath that followed Passover. Newer versions speak simply of "One Sabbath." The place is not named, but southern Galilee is probable.

Though they did not violate the fourth commandment, the disciples' actions in the grainfields (cf. Lk. 6:1) on the Sabbath violated man-made Rabbinical law. It has been suggested that to the Pharisees, picking grain was reaping, rubbing it in their hands was threshing, casting aside the husks was winnowing, and eating indicated that they had prepared food. Thus, in their opinion, the disciples committed "four distinct breaches of the Sabbath in one mouthful." Notably, Jesus did not personally participate in this grainfield snacking.

In the practices of Judaism, Sabbath observance had become the fundamental test of a Jew's obedience to God. The rigor and detail that the law was thought to demand were excessive, and at times virtually impossible to obey. Thus, some rabbis publicly declared that if all Israel kept the Sabbath twice, the Messiah would immediately come. Though Jesus was committed to scrupulous observance of God's laws, He objected to these burdensome man-made interpretative applications.

Jesus might have defended His disciples by challenging the Pharisees' arbitrary definition of what constituted Sabbath work. His approach, however, was to show that in this instance the application of the law of the Sabbath was invalid. Thus, He referred to David and the consecrated bread (shewbread) of the temple (cf. 1 Sam. 21:1-6) to teach that there are times when the higher moral law of basic human good takes precedence over conformity to arbitrary religious ritual. If David's circumstances justified him in overruling God's law and eating the sacred bread, how much more is it valid to overrule man-made laws.

Interestingly, on this occasion Jesus used historical precedent to counter the Pharisees' theological claims. He asked, "Have you never read what David did?" (Lk. 6:3). Though most surely they

---

3   William E. McCumber, *Matthew*. Kansas City: Beacon Hill Press, 1975, p. 64.

had read the account, they had never really thought through what it meant in practical living.

Jesus quoted Hosea 6:6 as an Old Testament statement of the principle of the priority of moral law: "I desire mercy, not sacrifice (Mt. 12:7). His words, "The Son of Man is Lord of the Sabbath" (Mt. 12:8) are equivalent to a claim to be deity, for He is affirming His right to reevaluate the Sabbath. Mark uniquely adds Jesus' words: "The Sabbath was made for man, not man for the Sabbath" (Mk. 2:27). The Sabbath is meant to serve human needs, not to add burdens to humans.

In Mark's report, Jesus identified David and the consecrated bread with "the days of Abiathar the high priest" (Mk. 2:26). The Old Testament, however, depicts Ahimelech to be in office at that time (cf. 1 Sam. 21:1). Since the book of Samuel was a large scroll without chapter and verse divisions, Jesus identified the section by its most prominent character. In the aftermath of David's visit, Abiathar was the only priest who escaped Doeg's massacre. Thus, he became high priest during David's reign. For modern readers, Mark's report might be rendered, "In the passage that tells of Abiathar (who was to become high priest), David entered . . ."

10. The Healing of a Man's Shriveled Hand. United Opposition (Mt. 12:9-14; Mk. 3:1-6; Lk. 6:6-11)

This event took place in a synagogue (Mt. 12:9) on "another Sabbath" and it was the man's right hand that was shriveled (withered) (Lk.6:6). Tradition expands the account by claiming that the man had been a plasterer or stone mason, and that his infirmity had cost him his livelihood. Jesus' ministry at this time was primarily to teach, and perhaps His critics had deliberately "planted" the man needing healing since, "Some of them were looking for a reason to accuse Jesus" (Mk. 3:2).

Jesus had the man stand forth so as to be seen by all. He then took the initiative against His critics by asking them what deeds were lawful on the Sabbath. They were silent because they knew that to answer would incriminate them. Mark reports Jesus' response: "He looked around [periblepo] at them in anger [orge]" (Mk. 3:5)[4]. Jesus healed by command, rather than by touch or the application of some symbolic anointing. All that was asked of the man was that he demonstrate public obedience. This event marked Jesus' third involvement in the Sabbath controversy.

Matthew tells of Jesus' argument that since traditional law allowed the rescue of a sheep on the Sabbath, then surely the spirit of the law was not violated when an infirm human was healed. The Pharisees "were furious" (lit. "flew into a mindless rage") over His defense of what they saw as a violation of the law.

---

4   *periblepo* [per-ee-BLEP-oh]: to look round about in a slow penetrating gaze; *orge* [or-GAY]: wrath, indignation, agitation of soul.

As we have noted, Sabbath observance had become a basic emphasis of Judaism, and particularly of the Pharisees. To these Jewish religious leaders, it was equivalent to a cultural trait distinguishing them from the Gentiles. Notably, in their concern over Sabbath events they seem to have totally ignored the healing miracle itself. They chose to take Jesus' power for granted.

The Pharisees' affiliation with the Herodians indicates that opposition to Jesus was now intensifying and organizing. Apart from plotting how they might kill Jesus (cf. Mt. 12:14), in their beliefs and values the Pharisees and Herodians had virtually nothing in common. The real issue was not so much the Sabbath healing but Jesus' assumption of authority over their values and traditions. Later in the Christian era, James set forth a principle that would endorse Jesus' action: "Anyone . . . who knows the good he ought to do, and doesn't do it, sins" (James 4:17).

11. Jesus Teaches and Heals Multitudes by Galilee (Mt. 12:15-21; Mk. 3:7-12)

Though Jesus with His disciples withdrew to what evidently was a remote place on the sea of Galilee, great multitudes followed Him. Mark's list indicates that representatives of all regions of the nation were present. We note that with the exception of Idumea, Jesus later ministered personally in each of these regions. Mark uniquely tells that Jesus found it necessary to request a small boat to be ready to carry Him far enough from the beach to escape the press of the crowds.

At this time Jesus taught and performed healings and exorcisms so that Scripture reports, "he healed all their sick" (Mt. 12:15). Jesus chose to speak to the people both through His words and His deeds. Though evil spirits recognized, "You are the Son of God" (Mk. 3:11), He sought to silence their premature disclosure of His person by His formal Christological title.

Matthew, in 12:18-21, saw this ministry as fulfilling Isaiah 42:1-4. This passage primarily describes the Persian King Cyrus (sixth century B.C.) in his historical deeds on behalf of Israel, but in secondary fulfillment it is certainly a Messianic prophecy applying to Jesus. It depicts Him as a gentle and considerate Savior who would leave His hearers neither depressed nor discouraged. Some see the trinity in verse eighteen: Jesus is the servant, and the Father is speaking to tell of His delight in Him, and to promise to put His Spirit upon Him.

12. Jesus Appoints His Twelve Apostles (Mk. 3:13-19; Lk. 6:12-16; cf. Mt. 10:1-4; Acts 1:13)

At this time Jesus selected from His disciples (learners) a group of twelve that He designated apostles (sent ones, delegates, envoys, messengers). This appointment of the twelve apostles came at the approximate midpoint of Jesus' public ministry.

Mark gives three reasons for Jesus' choice of the twelve: 1) that they might be with Him—and thus be trained, 2) that He might send them out to preach, 3) that they might be authorized to perform exorcisms. These twelve men were to be assigned the vital task of representing Him when He was no longer on earth. The KJV clause in Mark speaks of "power to heal sicknesses" (3:15), but these words are omitted in newer versions because they are not found in the oldest Greek texts.

Just as there had been twelve tribes of Israel, so Jesus chose twelve apostles, and this action suggests the establishment of a second people of God. Thereafter in the gospels era, the designation "the Twelve" became a title to denote this chosen circle:

SIMON (Cephas, Peter): His father was Jonah (Jonas), he was from Bethsaida, and his name means "rock." At first he was impetuous and vacillating, but he became a dependable leader among the apostles and he usually was their spokesman. He is named first in all four lists of the twelve apostles.

ANDREW: He was Peter's brother and thus also from Bethsaida. His specialty was introducing people to Jesus. Tradition tells of his crucifixion on an "X" shaped cross which for this reason is known as a St. Andrew's cross.

JAMES: He was the son of Zebedee and the brother of John. Mark notes that Jesus gave James and John, the name "Boanerges," and He interpreted it as meaning "Sons of Thunder" (cf. Mk. 3:17). James was beheaded by Herod Antipas about A.D. 44, and thus was the first apostle to be martyred.

JOHN: According to tradition, in contrast to his brother, James, he was the only apostle to die a natural death. He outlived all the other apostles, and he became the tender apostle of love.

PHILIP: Little is known of him except that he was from Bethsaida, and his name is Greek.

BARTHOLOMEW (Nathanael): He came from Cana, and Philip introduced him to Jesus. Bartholomew means "son of Talmai" and such a designation is not actually a proper name but a patronymic (i.e., a name derived from that of a father).

THOMAS (Didymus): He is widely remembered because of his doubts concerning the proof of the resurrection of Jesus.

MATTHEW (Levi): His father was Alphaeus, and he was formerly a tax collector.

JAMES (James the Younger): The son of a different Alphaeus from Matthew's father. His mother was Mary (cf. Mk. 15:40).

JUDAS (Thaddaeus, Lebbaeus): He was the brother of James the Younger. (Some texts say "son of James.") Thaddaeus means "big hearted," and this name was preferred in the early church to avoid confusion with Judas Iscariot.

SIMON: As a Zealot (cf. Lk. 6:15) he may have simply been zealous in God's service, or alternately one who belonged to the political party of fiercely nationalistic Jews seeking the overthrow of the Roman government in Palestine.

JUDAS ISCARIOT: His name means "man of Kerioth (a town in Judah)," and thus he was the only apostle who was not a Galilean. He died prematurely at his own hand. When the apostles are listed in the synoptics, Judas is always listed last, but he is not listed in Acts since he was already dead.

Though the order of the names varies, each synoptic and also the Book of Acts (cf. 1:13f) includes a list of the twelve, but there is no list in John. The composite harmony lists a total of sixteen different names, which are taken as variant designations of the same twelve. It is widely agreed that these were ordinary men —in modern terms, laymen. Today's followers of Jesus should be willing to commit themselves to a similar discipleship.

II. THE SERMON ON THE MOUNT

This sermon, following the appointment of the twelve apostles, has been called, "The Disciples' Ordination Address," "The Inaugural Address of the Kingdom," and "The Manifesto of the King" (Otto Dykes). The sermon provides fundamental principles of conduct for all peoples and cultures. McCumber comments: "No piece of ethical literature has been more influential in the course of history."[5]

The sermon is associated with the mountain (actually a foothill) known as the Horns of Hattin (*Kurun Hattin*). This site is close enough to the shores of Galilee for the people to have come from there. The identification, which first appeared in the thirteenth century, is plausible, but it lacks historical validation.

The expanded statement of the Sermon on the Mount is in Matthew's 107 verses. Luke's version has only thirty verses. Matthew includes extensive material pertaining to Jewish law. Luke, writing for a Gentile audience, omits this material. Almost all that is recorded in Luke is also in Matthew.

For the born again Christian, the Sermon on the Mount provides important instruction in lifestyle. It is not a statement of what to do to be saved, but it sets forth important behavioral goals and principles for those who are saved. Though the Sermon's primary concern is kingdom lifestyles rather than church lifestyles, God's ultimate standards are unchanging. His ideal for all who are His children is moral and spiritual perfection (cf. Mt. 5:48 "Be perfect, therefore, as your heavenly Father is perfect."

Most Christians see themselves in process of growth in the development of godliness. Paul spoke of Christlikeness, and then he commented, "Not that I have already obtained all this, or have already been made perfect, but I press on to take hold . . . ." (Phil.

---

5 McCumber, op. cit., p. 33.

3:12). Insofar as the Christian is a citizen of a heavenly kingdom (cf. Phil. 3:20), he or she is challenged to implement the teachings of the Sermon on the Mount. In this life, however, one is also a citizen of a state on earth and there may be a time to stand up for one's constitutional rights. Cultivating maturity in Jesus Christ is the only sure method of achieving a truly Christian lifestyle.

1. The Audience Gathered (Mt. 5:1-2; Lk. 6:17-19)

Jesus, with His newly appointed apostles accompanying Him, apparently moved to a level place on the mountain side. There a "great number of people" gathered. What He had to say, however, was particularly for His apostles, but in a broader sense it was for all His followers. The large company that gathered was no doubt drawn by His healing miracles, but also they were willing to hear His message. Luke comments, "Power was coming from him and healing them all" (Lk. 6:19). This spectacular ministry provided a backdrop to the major sermon that He was about to deliver. Because Luke speaks of a "level place" (6:17), his version is sometimes called "The Sermon on the Plain."

2. The Beatitudes (Mt. 5:3-12; Lk. 6:20-26)

The beatitudes are a series of eight statements describing behavior and attitudes that will result in joyfulness. The word "blessed" is equivalent to happy or fortunate, and it denotes that attitude whereby one contains within oneself all that is necessary for a full and complete life. The word "beatitude" which identifies these statements is derived from the Latin and it simply denotes a statement that pronounces a blessing.

With its religious overtones, a beatitude speaks of a relationship with God. The blessing is not in the state itself (i.e., poor in spirit, meek), but in what that state leads to. Fortunes are reversed because of an immediate direct divine transaction. Thus, much that Jesus taught was opposite from worldly patterns. Also, He emphasized that humans play a large part in determining their own happiness. He pronounced blessing upon:

(1) The poor in spirit: those humble in their own eyes, who feel they deserve nothing, and that they need all that God offers. Such people are likely to respond to conviction of sin and be readily moved to repentance.

(2) Those who mourn: those who are sorrowful for their own sins and failings, and for all the evil in the world. Their destiny is to know ultimate joy.

(3) The meek: those who frankly recognize their dependence upon God and thus they deal gently with their fellows. To those who have been offended, they respond with tender sensitivity.

(4) Those who hunger and thirst for righteousness: those who desire God's kingdom standards to be personally theirs and to

characterize their lives. Those who want more of God discover that He readily responds.

(5) The merciful: those aware of God's mercy to them so that in turn they are merciful to others. Such people participate in what has been called "a self-acting law of the moral world."

(6) The pure in heart: those whose inner life has been cleansed so that they serve God only, and do not at the same time attempt to serve the world.

(7) The peacemakers: those who reject battle and warfare and rightly understand God's will in conflict situations. They not only enjoy inner peace in their own lives, but also they communicate it to others.

(8) The persecuted (or those who are hated [Lk. 6:22-23]): those who uphold God's standards at the cost of their own well being. They join the distinguished company of the prophets and Jesus. Matthew notes that they inherit the kingdom; Luke encourages rejoicing now in anticipation of future reward.

Luke gives only four of the beatitudes, but in different order (1,4,2,8), and with variations of content. He directs the beatitudes (and also the "woes" that follow) to the second person (you) in contrast to Matthew's third person (they, those). Luke does not spiritualize the beatitudes; when he speaks of the poor and those who hunger, he adds no further qualification.

Luke follows the beatitudes with four woes that repeat the previous material in reverse form. It has been suggested that Jews would have known that woes (or cursings) were the obverse side of blessings (cf. Lev. 26). Since Luke wrote for Gentiles, he needed to tell of this relationship.

3. Salt and Light (Mt. 5:13-16)

Just as salt resists decay and spoilage, so the believer is to extend his influence on earth. The salt that is used to preserve is, however, ordinarily itself sacrificed in the process. The idea of "unsalty" salt is seen as a deliberate paradox, though impurities in unrefined salt may sometimes cause it to become insipid and useless. In the spiritual realm, Christians who so adapt to the world that no difference can be seen, become "unsalty salt."

The Kingdom person, as the light of the world, and as one individual lamp, must make his or her influence felt and not attempt concealment. The one thing that a light must do to be a light is shine. The believer is to have a useful effect upon earth, and not exist merely for the sake of personal advantage.

The expression "your Father" (Mt. 5:16) is the Sermon's first of fifteen references that personalize and individualize the Father (e.g. your Father, our Father, my Father).

In speaking of the salt and light Jesus used objects from daily life to portray an aspect of the believer's life. How salt behaves and how people use light are self-evident truths that He could apply to the lives of His hearers. Some speak of illustrations of this type as *true parables*.

4. The Kingdom's Moral Standards (Mt. 5:17-48; Lk. 6:27-30, 32-36)

Jesus taught the responsibility of fulfilling the spirit and principle of Old Testament law in order to give it the meaning that God intended. He moved from the standard set by the letter to the higher standard of spirit. More was expected of the Christian than was expected of the believer under Judaism. Topics that He dealt with included:

(1) Fulfilling the law (Mt. 5:17-20): Jesus was committed to fulfilling rather than breaking the Old Testament law. He represented the preservation of every letter of the law, and its total fulfillment. In commenting on Matthew 5:17 Tasker writes:

> **The moral law of the Old Testament is recognized by Jesus as possessing divine authority, but . . . as Messiah He claims authority to supplement it, to draw out principles that lie latent within it, and to disclaim the false deductions that have been made from it. This is what He seems to have meant when He said I am not come to destroy [or abolish], but to fulfill.**[6]

Such fulfillment came from inner righteousness, not the legalism of the Pharisees and teachers of the law. To violate the Old Testament law, or to teach others to do so, was seriously to reduce one's status in the Kingdom.

In the KJV, Matthew 5:18 reads: "Till heaven and earth pass, one jot or one tittle shall in no wise pass from the law." The word "jot" identifies *yod* which is the smallest letter of the Hebrew alphabet—it appears similar to a superscript. The "tittle" is a small point similar to a serif in Roman letters. Certain Hebrew letters are very similar in form, and it is the presence or absence of a tittle that distinguishes one from the other.

(2) The higher righteousness: Beginning with Matthew 5:21 Jesus taught, not a new law, but a new way of life involving a higher righteousness. Jesus set forth this righteousness in six antitheses relating to: anger, lust, divorce, deception, retaliation, and hate. He emphasized purity of thought as the basis of virtue. Since sin begins in the heart and mind, and only later extends to the act, that which is not thought will not be done.

The seed of murder is anger (5:21-26). One is not to harbor anger against a fellow human, nor to dishonor him with an insulting epithet—someone translates the Aramaic *Raca* as "nitwit." It

---

6 R.V.G. Tasker, *Matthew*. Grand Rapids: Wm. B. Eerdmans Publishing Co., 1961, p. 67.

is suggested that to call one's fellow a fool (v. 22) (Gk. *moros* [moh-ROS], cf. moron) in this context denotes "outcast" or "lost soul," and it therefore is an illegitimate human judgmental pronouncement.

Jesus taught here (5:23-24) that relationships are even more important than worship. If need be, the believer should postpone worship until relationships are reestablished. God's children only enjoy unhindered fellowship with Him if they enjoy fellowship with one another.

The advice concerning legal suits (5:25-26) is wise and practical. If an out of court settlement is possible, it spares all the burdens of slow and costly legal procedures. This principle in spiritual application teaches that the time to be reconciled to God is during life's journey, and not when the day of judgment has already begun.

The seed of adultery is lust (5:27-30). One must deal with the inward cause of sin. An incomplete life is better than an impure life. A capricious divorce (5:31-32), that in Jewish culture often left a woman in desperate economic straits, could result in adultery. Oaths (5:33-37) should not be abused, the word of a believer should be all that is needed. Jesus did not, however, intend a definitive prohibition upon all oaths. Paul called forth God as His witness (cf. 2 Cor. 1:23), and Jesus at His trial broke His silence to identify Himself under oath (cf. Mt. 26:63-64).

Submission to the wishes or needs of another (cf. Lk. 6:28-30) should replace retaliation based on ill will or selfishness (Mt. 5:38-42). Being struck on the cheek (Mt. 5:39) probably indicated insulting disrespect rather than a physical attack. Love should replace hate towards one's enemies (5:43-47). In a radical reversal of values, a forgiving attitude should return blessing for cursing. Love should be unconditional (cf. Lk. 6:32-36), reaching to the undeserving. Those who act out of this unselfish generous love are "sons of the Most High" (Lk. 6:35). Their actions confirm their royal status.

Jesus asked for behavior that totally outstripped that of either Jews or pagans. "Be perfect [*teleios*], therefore, as your heavenly Father is perfect" (Mt. 5:48). (teleios [TEL-eye-os]: fully developed in a moral sense, undivided in obedience to God, unblemished, mature, complete).

5. True Practical Righteousness (Mt. 6:1-18)

Jesus emphasized spirituality in contrast with formalism, and personal integrity in contrast with the hypocrisy of the teachers of the law and Pharisees.

(1) Benevolent deeds (6:1-4): In Judaism at this time, almsgiving was virtually a synonym for righteousness. The Pharisees wanted to be rewarded twice: by acclaim from humans, and by

God. They performed generous acts "before men, to be seen [*theaomai*] by them" (v.1). (*theaomai* [they-AH-oh-my]: be noticed, attract attention, cf. theater). Jesus' message was that motive is what matters. The expression rendered "reward in full" (v. 2, also 5 and 16) in that day was used in receipting paid bills. History has no record of gifts being announced with trumpets (Mt. 6:2), and the words may have been a figure of speech.

(2) Prayer and fasting (6:5-18; Lk 11:2-4): True prayer shuts the disciple in with God. What counts much more than a recitation of needs is the establishment of a relationship with God. A fact that humans often forget is that "your Father knows what you need before you ask him" (Mt. 6:8).

It has been said of the model **"Lord's Prayer"** (Mt. 6:9-13; Lk. 11:2-4) that "Jesus is preaching more than He is praying." The first concern of the prayer is God's glory—His name hallowed (sanctified, honored, respected). The appeal for the kingdom to come looks to the future earthly reign, although the kingdom is now spiritually present on earth. In that future day God's will will be done perfectly on earth. Our daily bread is God's gift to us and not to be taken for granted.

The one place in the prayer which asks something of the believer is in the forgiveness of one's debtors (v. 12, cf. 14-15), (or in Luke's version forgiveness of "everyone who sins against us" [11:4]). The forgiveness of our sins may not depend upon our forgiving others (or any other work), but fellowship with God does.

The petition "lead us not into temptation" (6:13a) is interpreted in two different ways. 1) The words are seen to be equivalent to "Let us not succumb to temptation." It is a prayer for God's provision of sustaining perseverance in trials involving moral decisions. Or, 2) The words are saying "Spare us circumstances that are tempting to us." In this view, the clause "deliver us from the evil one" is an alternate way of expressing the same idea. Elsewhere Scripture teaches: "God cannot be tempted by evil, nor does he tempt anyone" (James 1:13).

Older versions included a doxology: "For yours is the kingdom and the power and the glory forever. Amen." Since these words are missing from manuscripts earlier than the ninth century, they are not found in most modern versions.

In speaking of fasting at this time (cf. Mt. 6:16-18), Jesus makes the point that it must be unobtrusive and inconspicuous.

6. Separation from Earthly Things (Mt. 6:19-34)

Jesus taught single-hearted devotion to God so that all things are valued in relation to Him, and He is seen to be the provider of all elements of life on earth.

(1) Treasure in heaven (6:19-24): The Pharisees held that material blessings were evidences of God's favor. Jesus had a much

better formula for true wealth. He taught that in perceiving those values that really count, some humans are blinded by a fascination with earthly treasures, and in their blindness they are totally overlooking heavenly treasures. In personifying money, Jesus used the Aramaic word *mamonas* (ma-mone-AS) which in older versions was transliterated mammon.

(2) The uselessness of worry (6:25-34): Since there is so much more to life than earthly possessions, to worry about them is not only useless, but it shows a lack of faith in God. By observing nature we can learn of God's providential care. Birds and flowers simply fulfill the purpose for which God created them. The child of God should live simply, trusting in the loving concern of the benevolent heavenly Father. Jesus' words in 6:33 have been called "the key verse to the entire passage."

"Lilies of the field" are thought to be the common purple anemone which grows freely in Palestine.

7. Judgment, Prayer and the Golden Rule (Mt. 7:1-12; Lk. 6:31, 37-42)

The golden rule has its background both in how we evaluate others in judgment, and how we find that God responds in His relationships with us.

(1) Judgment of others (Mt. 7:1-6; Lk. 6:37-42): Humans should work at correcting their own faults before they try either to correct others, or to impose their standards upon them. We should demand more of ourselves and less of others, and should abstain from faultfinding. Unselfishness and generosity, however, provide their own abundant rewards (cf. Lk. 6:38).

Luke recorded Jesus' parables of the blind leading the blind, and the sawdust (mote, speck, splinter) and plank (beam, log, girder). This latter is a hyperbole—a figure of speech in the form of an exaggerated statement. Someone summarizes the principle: "Blinded men make poor oculists." A moral leader must possess suitable moral sensitivities; one who is blind to his own faults cannot rightly criticize others. In this context Jesus affirmed an interesting principle: "A student is not above his teacher, but everyone who is fully trained will be like his teacher" (Lk. 6:40).

In the Jewish culture both dogs and hogs (cf. Mt. 7:6) were allowed to exist as lowly unclean creatures. Jesus seems to have implied that to present the gospel in circumstances that virtually assure rejection only exposes the witness to ridicule or insult. The gospel can be invalidated by lack of common sense. In Jewish usage, just as in English, a clever concise statement or an item of vital information was sometimes called a pearl.

(2) Persisting in prayer (Mt. 7:7-11, Lk. 11:9-13): The imperative verbs, ask, seek, knock are all in the present tense and they imply continuing action. We are to keep on praying and not grow weary. Just as we are not to judge our brother, so we are not to misjudge our Heavenly Father. He wants to bestow answers to prayer, and all His children have equal access to His bounties. He welcomes our prayers and requests, and He can be counted on to do the generous "fatherly thing." God cares, and He never plays cruel tricks upon His children, although we sometimes may not see his "good gifts" (Mt. 7:11) as good.

(3) The Golden Rule (Mt. 7:12, Lk. 6:31): These eleven words sum up all of one's duties to his or her fellows. Although many of the world's religions possess a similar statement, almost all are phrased negatively. According to Jewish tradition, when Rabbi Hillel (c. 70 B.C.-A.D. 10) was asked by a prospective convert to teach him the Law while he stood on one foot, Hillel replied, "What is hateful to you, do not to your fellow." Confucianism's so-called "Silver Rule" is similarly negative: "Do not unto others what you would not have them do unto you." Though the text has become somewhat distorted, God has written the truth of the Golden Rule upon the hearts of all humans.

8. Practical Behavior (Mt. 7:13-23; Lk. 6:43-45; cf. Lk. 13:24)

Jesus taught that humans have only two choices, and what we are inwardly will be expressed in how we behave.

(1) The narrow and wide gates (Mt. 7:13-14): The kingdom way is narrow and restrictive in contrast with the apparent tolerant ease of worldliness. The two ways compare with Moses' blessings and curses (cf. Deut. 11:26-32). Jesus seeks for those willing to make the decision to enter the narrow gate and continue along the narrow road. The synonym for narrow in older versions is "strait," and this term should be distinguished from the word "straight" which has a different meaning.

(2) Trees and their fruit (Mt. 7:15-23, Lk. 6:43-45): Jesus was concerned with the quality of His converts, and that their speech and actions prove the reality of their inner experience. One's lifestyle is a clear indication of the state of one's heart. Where there are false prophets who teach false doctrine, sooner or later the outcome will be aberrant morality. Someone has said, "Their lives will become as crooked as their doctrine." There are humans whose commitment to the Lord is only empty profession, and for them Jesus is Lord in name only. They are so much in error that they are unable to admit it, even to themselves.

9. Conclusion: the Two Foundations (Mt. 7:24-29; Lk. 6:46-49)

A life built upon insincere profession, shallow eternality, and human self-righteousness compares to building a house on a foundation of sand. A life built upon the principles of Christ's teachings is founded upon a rock—the original denotes bedrock.

A prudent human would not build a house on a river sandbar, and even more importantly, each life ought to be firmly founded on the standards and teachings of the Lord Jesus Christ.

Jesus' account of the two foundations is an example of a story parable. This type of parable refers to an event that happened in the past. By analogy, the wisdom learned by those who participated in the experience is applied to the present hearers.

Matthew reports: "When Jesus had finished saying these things, the crowds were amazed [Gk. *ekplesso*][7] at his teaching" (Mt. 7:28). The Gospels report twelve occasions when Jesus' teachings produced this reaction in His hearers. An aspect of the remarkable quality of Jesus' teaching was that it possessed a divinely confirmed authority (cf. Mt. 7:29).

III. THE SECOND PREACHING TOUR OF GALILEE

With the organization of the apostolic company completed, and the basic principles of the Kingdom proclaimed, Jesus was again free to tour Galilee.

1. The Healing of the Centurion's Servant (Mt. 8:5-13; Lk. 7:1-10)

This event in Capernaum was another case of healing at a distance (cf. the nobleman's son, Jn. 4:43-54). According to Luke, the centurion did not appeal in person, but he sent elders to intercede for him. Perhaps the centurion felt it would offend the Jews if Jesus entered a Gentile home. The servant (Matthew's word usage suggests a youth) would actually have been a slave, and such personal concern by the master was unusual. A centurion was a mid-level officer in the Roman army, and in the usual outpost garrison, he commanded from seventy to one hundred men.

At the outset the elders reported, "He loves our nation, and has built our synagogue" (Lk. 7:5). Jesus responded by beginning the journey to the centurion's home. The dialogue between Jesus and the centurion, as Jesus was stopped on the roadway, appears to have been communicated through the centurion's friends. The words are the centurion's, the elders were his mouthpiece. In this indirect manner, he reverently addressed Jesus as "Lord" (Mt. 8:6). The elders had pleaded the centurion's cause on the basis of his good works, but as Jesus in person drew close, such merits became irrelevant. Thus, the centurion hastily declared himself to be unworthy to host Jesus in his home.

Jesus was amazed (or marveled) at the centurion's message so clearly crediting Him with power to command sickness at a distance. The centurion understood the process of a chain of command, with authority residing in the supreme commander. The

---

7 *ekplesso* (ek-PLAY-so): amaze, astound, overwhelm, strike out of one's senses.

only other occasion reported in the Gospels when Jesus was amazed was in response to the lack of faith of the people of His home town (cf. Mk. 6:6).

Two different verbs are used to depict the healing. Jesus used a weaker verb that could be rendered, "I will go and tend him medically" (Mt. 8:7). The centurion used a stronger verb that implied, "Just say the word, and my servant will be healed miraculously" (Mt. 8:8b). Jesus praised the centurion's faith, just as He would later praise the faith of the Canaanite woman (cf. Mt. 15:28). Matthew records Jesus' use of this incident to teach that the exercise of faith qualifies one for the kingdom regardless of geographical or national origins.

2. The Raising of the Widow of Nain's Son (Lk. 7:11-17)

The journey from Capernaum to Nain was about thirty-five kilometers (twenty-two miles), and apparently Jesus and His party traveled during parts of two days. It is of interest to note that Nain was close to Shunem where, centuries before, Elijah had raised the Shunammite's son (cf. 2 Kings 4:18-37). According to the customs of that time, the funeral procession that they met at the gate would have been led by the sorrowful mother. Jesus' words, "Don't cry" (Lk. 7:13) were obviously much more than a human's usual empty cheer.

Since coffins were Egyptian, and not used by Jews, the son's body would have been wrapped in a cloth and carried either on a board or in a shallow open box that would assure that the body would not fall off. Because the soil did not lend itself to the burial of bodies, the Jews ordinarily placed cloth-wrapped bodies in a cave hewn into a hillside rock.

Though he invited personal defilement by touching the bier, Jesus' compassion compelled Him to become involved. He acted without being asked to do so, but no doubt He had great concern for the needs of the widow. In that culture a woman's security depended upon having a male in the home, and a woman whose husband and only son had both died faced a bleak future. This first demonstration of a miracle involving the raising of the dead established Jesus as a great prophet throughout the land.

At this point, some harmonies continue with Luke's account, and thus John the Baptist's messengers now arrive. We choose to insert Matthew 9:35 through 11:30 because these events seem to fit here rather than later.

3. Jesus' Ministry in Summary (Mt. 9:35-38)

These four poignantly descriptive verses provide an impressive picture of the scope of Jesus' Galilean ministry. Since He had access to the synagogues, they provided a ready-made audience. His ministry of "healing every disease and sickness" (Mt. 9:35), no doubt greatly enhanced the appeal of His teaching and preaching. It is not surprising that great crowds followed Him, and that their needs stirred His compassion.

To Jesus the people in the crowds "were harassed and helpless, like sheep without a shepherd" (Mt. 9:36). The word "harassed" denotes "plundered and lying wounded." Jesus had begun the ministry that God had promised, "I will save my flock, and they will no longer be plundered. . . . I will place over them one shepherd, my servant David, and he will tend them; he will tend

	Matt.	Mark	Luke	John
Royal official's son healed				4:46-54
Rejection at Nazareth			4:16-30	
New home in Capernaum	4:13-17			
Commission of 4 fishermen	4:18-22	1:16-20	5:1-11	
● FIRST TOUR OF GALILEE				
Leper healed	8:1-4	1:40-45	5:12-16	
Call of Matthew	9:9-13	2:13-17	5:27-32	
Multitues taught by the sea	12:15-21	3:7-12		
Twelve apostles appointed	10:1-4	3:13-19	6:12-16	
Sermon on the Mount	5:1-7:29		6:17-49	
●SECOND TOUR OF GALILEE				
Centurion's servant healed	8:5-13		7:1-10	
Widow's son raised			7:11-17	
Twelve sent forth to witness	9:35-11:1	6:7-13	9:1-6	
Woman anoints Jesus' feet			7:36-50	
●THIRD TOUR OF GALILEE				
Jesus' Kingdom parables	13:1-52	4:1-34	8:4-18	

Figure 8: Time line of highlights of the second year (January to December) of Jesus' ministry. The scale indicates months.

them and be their shepherd" (Ezek. 34:22-23). Jesus' ministry contrasts with that of false shepherds who destroy and scatter the flock (cf. Jer. 23:1-5).

In His appeal to His disciples Jesus spoke of harvesting rather than shepherding. The shortage of workers to reap the harvest has continued to persist throughout the centuries and to this present day. To ask the Lord of the harvest to send out workers is a vital prayer responsibility, for harvesters must be prayed into service, Significantly, many believers have discovered that "people who pray are likely to become people who go."

4.The Twelve Sent Forth to Witness (Mt. 10:1-16; Mk. 6:7-13; Lk. 9:1-6)

The time of these events is not identified, and some harmonies place them two or three months later. Obviously, the commission to witness had to follow the choice of the twelve (Mk. 3:13-19; Lk. 6:12-16). In turn, it had to be sufficiently prior to their returning report that they had time to fulfill their ministry (cf. Lk. 9:10). Thus, the twelve were likely sent forth in the fall of the second year, and the seventy-two (or seventy) in the fall of the third year. Each group returned in about six months or less.

The witnessing tour of the twelve was directed only to "the lost sheep of Israel," for it was not yet God's time for world evangelization. The Jews were to be given the first opportunity. Jesus instructed these apostle-evangelists: "As you go, preach this message: 'The kingdom of heaven is near. Heal the sick, raise the dead, cleanse those who have leprosy, drive out demons'" (Mt. 10:8). In turn, He equipped them supernaturally to fulfill the healing aspects of this commission. "[Jesus] gave them power and authority to drive out all demons and to cure diseases" (Lk. 9:1). Mark notes that Jesus "sent them out two by two" (Mk. 6:7), and he also uniquely mentions that the disciples "anointed many sick people with oil" (Mk. 6:12).

Jesus instructed that they travel without money, and without extra equipment—the prohibitions against staff, bag, bread and money (Lk. 9:3) are understood to apply to extra supplies beyond the usual clothing and equipment that they possessed. They were to be dependent upon those to whom they would minister, and to expect food and housing to be provided for them by a "worthy person" (Mt. 10:11) in each town and village. They were not to accept an offer which would provide greater luxury, but remain where they were first accommodated.

The act of shaking dust off their feet as their response to a town that rejected them formally proclaimed disassociation. This public act declared that the townspeople were assuming responsibility for their own destiny. Jews practiced shaking off the dust as a gesture to free themselves of Gentile contamination. As it were, the gesture declared that the townspeople were in the same category as unbelieving Gentiles. Their judgment would be more severe than that of Sodom and Gomorrah because their greater light resulted in greater responsibility.

In general, the disciples were to minister according to a comprehensive principle that applies to all of God's witnesses, "Be as shrewd as snakes and as innocent as doves" (Mt. 10:16). Elsewhere in Scripture a snake symbolizes Satan, and a dove symbolizes the Holy Spirit. It is possible that these representations are relevant in applying Jesus' instructions.

5. Responses the Twelve Could Expect (Mt. 10:17-39)

Jesus warned the twelve that they could expect persecution, not only from society's leaders, but from their own family as well. He instructed them concerning their behavior and attitudes in such circumstances. He promised them the ministry of the Holy Spirit to give them the words to say when they were confronted by authorities. Also, He gave some wise advice: "When you are persecuted in one place, flee to another." (Mt. 10:23a).

Jesus' words, "You will not finish going through the cities of Israel before the Son of Man comes" (Mt. 10:23b) convey motivating urgency. Possibly these words indicate that He was promising personally to follow up their evangelistic efforts, and this may have happened at that time. Most scholars, however, see the coming as the Second Coming. Thus, the sending forth of the twelve becomes the model that furnishes the essential patterns for all of Jesus' commissioned witnesses throughout the church age.

We recognize that though the twelve had been sent forth to Israel, the greater mission of Jesus' witnesses through the centuries is the expanded ministry of the Church. Thus, most agree that Scripture at this point is not just recording a historical event. These warnings and instructions apply, not only to the twelve, but also, at least indirectly, to the Church's missionaries throughout the centuries.

The Christian witness should not forget that his Teacher was ridiculed and rejected by unbelieving humans, and thus a similar fate should be no surprise. Nevertheless, Christ's witness has divine resources on his or her side. Ultimately, total truth and absolute justice will prevail. Satan is not to be feared. God rules, and every detail affecting the life of His servants is known and monitored by Him. Where God's witnesses remain faithful, Jesus, in turn, will faithfully acknowledge them before the Father.

Jesus did not attempt to conceal the fact that there is a great cost to discipleship. His words about the possible conflict between the disciple and his family (Mt. 10:34-39) appear, unfortunately, to have been true of His own life. It is said that alienation from one's family can be more traumatic than imprisonment or capital punishment. Nevertheless, the commitment to serve Him must take precedence over all affections, including family ties.

Jesus here (Mt. 10:38), for the first time, speaks of the cross as a symbol of a surrendered life and of death to self will. To "take up one's cross" portrays the action of a condemned victim under Roman law submitting to the events leading to his execution. The paradox of finding and losing one's life (Mt. 10:39) occurs, with minor variations, four times in the Gospels.

6. Rewards of the Workers (Mt. 10:40-11:1; cf. Mk. 9:41)

Though Jesus had spoken of rejection and persecution of those who would go forth as His witnesses, fortunately there is another side. There will be responsive people who receive the message and its messengers. Thus, Jesus has a closing word to these receptive ones. Since in the harvest, His workers represent Him, to receive His workers compares with receiving Christ personally. Loyalty to His people and assistance to them will not go unrewarded, and the rewards will be appropriate to the kindnesses that have been performed. It is suggested that the "little ones" (Mt. 10:42) are those "ordinary" Christians who otherwise are unheralded and unknown.

7. John the Baptist's Question (Mt. 11:2-6; Lk. 7:18-23)

At this time, John would have been in prison approximately seven months. As was previously noted, he had been placed there by Herod Antipas, supposedly to prevent a popular uprising, but actually because he publicly denounced Antipas' immorality.[8] Imprisonment meant that John had undergone a drastic change from a useful and active life to dreary inactivity. He continued to communicate with the outside world, however, by using his disciples to carry messages. The two disciples that John sent would likely have traveled 130 km (80 miles), and this effort indicates the seriousness of their errand.

John's question through his disciples was, in effect, whether Jesus really was the Messiah. John felt there were ambiguities to be cleared up. Though Jesus was performing miraculous works, He had made no move to free John from prison. Jesus proclaimed freedom, but He had shown no signs of destroying the oppressor. How could He continue to minister grace if He was the one who was to exercise judgment? It was John's hope that his disciples would return with totally clear insights into Jesus' identity.

In His response to John, Jesus demonstrated His healing ministry, "At that very time Jesus cured many" (Lk. 7:21). He then dispatched John's disciples to report what they had seen. As it were, Jesus confirmed His Messiahship to John in the same way that He had confirmed it to the nation. Those who knew the Old Testament would recognize Jesus' identification with the Messiah through His healing miracles (cf. Isa. 35:5-6) and the spiritual deliverances that He accomplished (cf. Isa. 61:1).

---

8 See page 59.

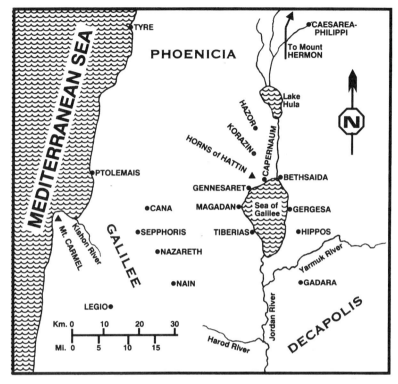

Figure 9: Sites of the great Galilean ministry

8. Jesus' Approval of John (Mt. 11:7-19; Lk. 7:24-35)

Jesus waited until John's disciples had left before He proceeded with a ringing declaration of commendation for John. He saw him as God's prophesied messenger, a second Elijah, and the final voice of the old order (cf. Mal. 3:1; Mt. 11:10; Lk. 7:27). John had served his Lord with courage and self-effacing commitment. Above all, he was great in having fulfilled his role of introducing Jesus. If John's followers had followed through in their commitment to John, they would have clearly recognized that John was the forerunner, and therefore Jesus was the Messiah.

In spite of John's spiritual and personal greatness, however, Jesus pointed out that the most humble Christian qualifies for much greater advantages. John knew only the limited blessings of the old order; he had experienced only natural birth. In contrast, Jesus had come to provide a miraculous new birth for all who would believe in Him. Though John was the greatest man of his age, his age came to an end with the coming of Jesus and the launching of His glorious spiritual kingdom.

Matthew 11:12 is variously translated and interpreted. Some versions see it as a statement of the militant advance of the Church. e.g. "the kingdom of heaven has been forcefully advancing, and forceful men lay hold of it" (NIV). In other versions, the Church is the victim of the violence. e.g. "the kingdom of heaven suffers violence, and the violent take it by force" (NKJV). Barclay suggests a paraphrase that he feels combines the interpretations: "Always my Kingdom will suffer violence; always savage men will try to break it up, and snatch it away and destroy it; and therefore only the man who is desperately in earnest, only the man in whom the violence of devotion matches and defeats the violence of persecution will in the end enter into it."[9]

In view of the model of John's life, Jesus challenged the people to put away their immaturity and childish intolerance. By their constant rivalries and pettiness, and their frequently changing preferences, they behaved like little children playing games. They were content to play neither "wedding" nor "funeral," but with their petty bickering, they succeeded in breaking up every "game." John, who had fasted and talked about sin was too gloomy for them; Jesus, who had attended social events and talked about salvation and liberty was too indulgently lenient (cf. Mt. 11:19). Such critical attitudes were now complicating Jesus' ministry just as they had John's.

The critics who saw Jesus as "a glutton and a drunkard" (Mt. 11:19a) were glaringly prejudiced and inaccurate in their observations. They were ignoring the proverb: "Wisdom is proved right by her actions" (19b). Jesus' actions, and also those of John, proved the validity of the teaching of each of their ministries.

9. Unrepentant Cities Scolded. Rest Promised (Mt. 11:20-30)

The majority of Jesus' mighty works had been performed in the cities that He named: Korazin (Chorazim), Bethsaida, and Capernaum. The mostly Jewish citizens of these cities, however, remained largely untouched and resisted the call to repentance. Elsewhere, Scripture notes that "Israel has experienced a hardening in part" (Rom. 11:25). Jesus pointed out that had similar miracles been performed in the Gentile cities of Tyre and Sidon, their people would have repented. In His message at this time, Jesus compares to an Old Testament prophet pronouncing an oracle of woe. The events of history vindicated Jesus' words, and for many centuries the three cities have been mere ruins.

The truths and understandings that Jesus Christ conveys can be grasped by those of simple and humble heart and mind. The barriers that deprive humans of spiritual understanding are pride and a critical spirit. Intellect that is rightly applied, is a

---

9 Barclay, op. cit. p. 8.

useful tool for spiritual understanding, however, and in itself it is by no means a hindrance. Jesus endorsed little children because they are willing to be taught and are simple hearted, not because they are simple minded! In verses twenty-five through twenty-seven, in which Jesus described God's relationship to human believers, He used the word Father five times.

Jesus' words in Matthew 11:28-30 have been called "The Great Invitation." The bearing of a yoke speaks of submission, and commitment to an occupation. Jesus' yoke, however, imposed no crushing Pharisaic legalistic burden. Instead, His yoke results in liberty. Those who take their place in fulfilling His tasks become His partners, and He freely assumes responsibility for them. People become weary in labor for Him because they attempt to bear the total burden and responsibility themselves.

Jesus depicted Himself as a true friend of the oppressed, and those who are heavily burdened. Rather than imposing the burden of works, He came with His gift of empowering; what He commands, He enables. In being "gentle and humble in heart" (v. 29), He stood forth uniquely in a day in which secular Greek society held that humility detracted from manhood.

In the original, the literary structure of the section extending from verse twenty-five through thirty is rhythmical prose. The style is very similar to that of hymns of thanksgiving in the Dead Sea scrolls.

10. The Sinful Woman Anoints Jesus' Feet (Lk. 7:36-50)

Apparently, out of His wide-ranging human concern Jesus accepted the dinner invitation of a Pharisee. The name Simon was a common Jewish name, and the man is not otherwise identified. The place of his residence is not named, but tradition suggests it was the town of Magadan (Magdala) and that the woman was Mary of Magdala (Mary Magdalene). Simon entertained Jesus, but he ignored the usual host's amenities involving the washing of a guest's feet. Someone speaks of Simon as "a collector of celebrities." His gesture in entertaining Jesus was probably only a patronizing recognition of Jesus' great popularity.

This woman is said to be a sinner, and according to Simon, her reputation for sinfulness was widely known. Whatever her past, however, it appears that prior to this occasion she had responded to Jesus' message and repented of her sin. It is generally assumed that a woman with such a reputation would have been a prostitute, but that assumption goes beyond the Biblical account. Luke identifies her sinful state three times (vv. 37, 39, 47), and he reports that Jesus pronounced her sins forgiven and then assured her, "Your faith has saved you; go in peace" (7:50). What Simon the host seems to have failed to realize was that though the woman was a sinner, she was forgiven; he, too, was a sinner, but he appears not to have been forgiven.

In chapter eight, Luke identifies Mary Magdalene as the one "from whom seven demons had come out" (8:2). If the same woman is in view, her sinful life must have related to the indwelling demons. Jesus' words to the woman in chapter seven, however, do not seem to constitute an exorcism, though the outcome was a total victory. Thus, it would seem that the traditional identification of Mary Magdalene as the woman in Simon's house is not well substantiated.

Most commentators hold that the woman's behavior at least lacked decorum, and probably for that culture was quite improper. To have wiped Jesus' feet with her hair meant that it was loose, and thus it offended the usual standards. Nevertheless, the woman shed genuine tears of penitence, and out of a heart of true devotion she sacrificially administered the anointing perfume. She sought by this means to show her gratitude for the forgiveness of her sins.

The alabaster jar would be a perfume container, likely more or less globular in shape, with a neck that could be broken off to release the contents. Alabaster was a decorative semiprecious stone that was mined in Egypt. Small perfume boxes of this sort were often threaded on a chain and made into a pendant to be worn around a lady's neck. Though the value of the perfume is not given, the fact that it was in an alabaster jar would imply that it was considered valuable.

Since on this occasion Jesus would likely have been reclining rather than sitting at the table (see p. 205), His feet would have been behind Him and away from the table. Thus, they would have been readily accessible to the woman.

The parable of the moneylender and the two debtors established that the measure that one has been forgiven can be expected to relate to the measure of one's love for his or her Savior. Simon correctly understood the point of the parable (cf. v. 43). Concerning Jesus' question, "Do you see this woman?" (v. 44), someone comments, "Simon could not see that woman as she then was, for looking at her as she had been."

In his responses and attitudes, Simon revealed much more about himself than about the woman. Though as a Pharisee, Simon knew a great deal about religion and the law, he had missed the reality that Jesus offered, and which the woman received. Jesus' words clearly applied to Simon: "he who has been forgiven little loves little" (v. 47).

This anointing of Jesus by a woman is held to be a different occasion from the anointing by Mary of Bethany. This latter event took place some two years later in the final days before the cross. Though the host was also named Simon, he is identified as a leper, not as a Pharisee (cf. Mk. 14:3-9; Jn. 12:3-8).

FIVE:

THE GREAT GALILEAN MINISTRY (PART 2)

C hronologies date the beginning of Jesus' Galilean ministry a month or two into His second year. Jesus apparently served in Galilee for at least a year and eight months. More than half of Mark, about half of Matthew, one-third of Luke, and one-fourth of John are devoted to Jesus' Galilean ministry.

I. ANOTHER TOUR OF GALILEE

Scripture does not provide Jesus' precise itinerary and schedule during this phase of His Galilean ministry. Thus, we group the next series of events as simply "another tour."

1. The Ministering Women (Lk. 8:1-3)

Jesus and His party "traveled about from one town and village to another, proclaiming the good news of the kingdom of God" (v. 1). Luke reports: 1) the Twelve accompanied Him (v. 1); 2) some women were in the party (v. 2); 3) these women had experienced healings and exorcisms (v. 2); 4) out of their own means the women helped to support the evangelistic team; 5) the women included: "Mary (called Magdalene) . . . Joanna the wife of Cuza . . . Susanna; and many others" (vv. 2-3). We have noted that the fact that Mary Magdalene was delivered from seven demons does not justify the tradition that she had been a prostitute.

For women to have been in the traveling apostolic party has been described as "an astonishing feature of Jesus' ministry." In that time and culture it is said to have been "unheard of" for women to be included among a traveling rabbi's disciples. Their presence testified to Jesus' high regard for noble womanhood. This group of supporting women has been called, "The first Christian Women's Missionary Society."

2. Jesus and Beelzebub (Mt. 12:22-37; Mk. 3:22-30)

Those who brought the demon-possessed (or "demonized") blind and mute man to Jesus are unnamed. The healing that Jesus performed was an exorcism—one or many demons were cast out—but the result was the man's physical healing. This spectacular healing led the people to begin to ask, "Could this be the Son of David?" (Mt. 12:22), i.e., the Messiah.

The envoys of the Jerusalem establishment, the Pharisees (Mt. 12:24) and teachers of the law (Mk. 3:22), could not object to Jesus' procedure, for exorcisms were a recognized rite in Judaism. The reality of Jesus' miracle was incontestably evident, but they refused to accept His divine status in performing it. Thus they slandered the miracle by claiming that it was accomplished through Beelzebub the ruler of demons. By this tactic they hoped to invalidate miracles as a proof of His divine power.

The name Beelzebub (or Beelzebul, Beelezeboul, Baal-Zebub) appears to be an insulting variant of the name Satan. It derives from 2 Kings 1:2 where it identifies the god of Ekron, a Philistine deity after which Israel's King Ahaziah, the spiritual rebel, sought. It is thought that the original form of the name denoted "princely lord," but by deliberate corruption to the form Beelzebub, it became "god of flies."

These critics at this time blasphemed by saying that Jesus was empowered by evil. Actually, Jesus performed exorcisms by the power of the Holy Spirit. He declared that His ministry of exorcism was an important milestone in God's developing plan. "If I drive out demons by the Spirit of God, then the kingdom of God has come upon you" (Mt. 12:28). Because Jesus ministered in this fashion, we know that the kingdom of God has been launched on earth. God was proceeding with the drama of salvation.

Jesus' response to His critics, as He pointed out the illogical nature of their claims, was one of the few times that He defended Himself. He noted that division always leads to destruction. Yet to cast out demons is to attack forcefully the lordship of Satan. In effect, they were saying that through Jesus, Satan was destroying his own realm. Someone comments, "For all their learning, the Pharisees' criticism of Him is astonishingly naive."

In His parable discussing the achievement of exorcisms, Jesus declared, "No one can enter a strong man's house and carry off his possessions unless he first ties up the strong man" (Mk. 3:27). He implied that an exorcism can be accomplished only if the resident demon is appropriately bound and disposed of. It is not a mere matter of teaching the victim some new behavior.

The principle of Matthew 12:30 provides an evaluative measure to identify Jesus' true followers: "He who is not with me is against me." In these words, Jesus ruled out neutrality as an acceptable relationship to Him. He implied that He seeks those willing to make a decision to commit themselves to Him. Ultimately, there are just two classes of humans: those who choose Jesus, and those who choose the enemy.

Jesus proceeded to discuss the outcome of blasphemy (slander, insult) in relation to forgiveness. He taught that declared opposition to the Holy Spirit will not be forgiven. Where there is deliberate blasphemous speech that is the expression of a hardened heart, that human has chosen to be beyond the reach of repentance and forgiveness. This passage is the basis of the doctrine of the unpardonable sin, or as some prefer, "the unpardoned sin." Probably it is sin of this sort that John had in mind when he wrote, "There is a sin that leads to death" (1 Jn. 5:16b).

The unpardonable sin is the outcome of a chosen act. As it were, it is the deliberate choice of evil as one's good. When a human makes the choice to exclude himself from the convicting and regenerating ministry of the Holy Spirit, he or she becomes "guilty of an eternal sin" (Mk. 3:29). The unpardonable sin cannot be committed accidentally or in ignorance. It cannot be committed by a Christian except he or she makes the choice totally to reject all Christian faith and values (cf. Heb. 6:4-6; 10:26-30). If one fears he has committed the unpardonable sin he obviously has not, for he is still being convicted by the Holy Spirit.

In the Sermon on the Mount Jesus had taught that a tree is known by its fruit (cf. Mt. 7:16-20). Once again, He taught that the principle of knowing a tree by its fruit transfers to the spiritual realm. A genuine believer, in whom the Holy Spirit has imparted a new life, can be expected to display the fruit of godly living. What one is in his or her heart determines not only how one talks, but what one does.

3. A Sign Demanded of Jesus (Mt. 12:38-45)

In asking Jesus to produce a sign, the Pharisees and teachers of the law implied that they were sincere seekers attempting to form an impartial evaluation of His claims. Jesus perceived their hypocritical insincerity, and thus His response was to identify them as evil and adulterous since they were unfaithful to their spiritual vows to God. They had chosen to slander His many healings and exorcisms as the work of Satan, and to discount and reject them as signs. Jesus thus declared that the only sign remaining was the sign of His death and resurrection that was depicted under the figure of Jonah.

Jesus' reference to Jonah was His way of saying that the one truly convincing evidence of His divine Messiahship would be His conquest of death by resurrection. He no doubt avoided a more direct answer because His hearers held false expectations of the Messiah, and Jesus was not prepared to commit Himself to them. He proceeded to point out that in Old Testament times the Ninevites and the Queen of the South made great use of small opportunities. In contrast, His critical hearers were making almost no use of great opportunities.

The parable of the cast-out-demon and the unoccupied house is usually thought to speak of human reformation in contrast with the true new birth by God's Holy Spirit. The demon's former host once again becomes his victim because he responded to God with incomplete dedication, or outright skepticism, in spite of his religious claims otherwise. Some see the parable to apply to Jesus' critics who had blasphemously rejected the Holy Spirit, and who now out of a false spirit were attempting to discern truth.

4. Jesus' Family Seeks Him (Mt. 12:46-50; Mk. 3:20-21; 3:31-35; Lk. 8:19-21)

Mark reported the family visit in two installments—a literary device called intercalation (or bracketing or sandwiching). In Mark 3:21 the family heard that Jesus' ministry left Him so pressured that He could not even take time to eat. They determined "to take charge of him" (lit. "to arrest him") because they felt it was abnormal for Him not to take care of Himself. The story later continues, "Then Jesus' mother and brothers arrived" (Mk. 3:31). Jesus did not respond to their invitation to come with them, but rather He set forth the principle, "Whoever does God's will is my brother and sister and mother" (Mk. 3:35). Months later, John noted, "For even his own brothers did not believe in him" (Jn. 7:5). Obviously, His family's attitude on this occasion was less than sympathetic.

It was not that Jesus rejected His earthly family, but a new relationship now prevailed. He now identified with His larger family that consisted of all who followed Him. He temporarily forsook His mother that He might be every mother's son; and He forsook His brothers that He might be everyone's elder brother. The price of being Jesus' kinsman, however, is a life committed to fulfilling God's will. "Whoever does the will of my Father in heaven is my brother and sister and mother" (Mt. 12:50).

The usual Protestant view, which is attributed to Helvidius of the fourth century, is that these brothers were later children of Joseph and Mary. Luke's words "she gave birth to her firstborn, a son" (Lk. 2:7), strongly suggest that Mary gave birth to other children. Alternate views hold that these "brothers" actually were Jesus' cousins, or that they were children of Joseph by a previous marriage. In a later incident, Matthew records the comments of the citizens of Nazareth: "Isn't his mother's name Mary, and aren't his brothers James, Joseph, Simon and Judas? Aren't all his sisters with us?" (Mt. 13:55-56).

5. Jesus Brings His Parables to Capernaum (Mt. 13:1-52; Mk. 4:1-34; Lk. 8:4-18)

The "Kingdom parables of Matthew 13," and their synoptic parallels, speak of both the present and the end time. This collection provides a unique view of the outcomes of the proclamation of the gospel. Matthew commented, "[Jesus] did not say anything to [the crowds] without using a parable" (Mt. 13:34), and in verse thirty-five he quoted Psalm 78:2 as a statement of God's approval upon the use of parables. About one-third of Jesus' teaching recorded in Scripture consists of parables. The total count of Jesus' parables, including short figurative sayings, is about sixty.

The word "parable" (lit. to place or throw beside) denotes a teaching device that places two realms side-by-side to enable comparison. Parables attract interest, win a hearing, provoke thought and invite commitment, and thus enhance a spoken message. Some rules for interpreting parables include: 1) a parable primarily illustrates one central truth, 2) it is not warranted to seek interpretations of all details in a parable for these may be simply the story's local color, 3) a parable is not necessarily an actual true story, but it is true to life, and 4) parables illustrate, and they are not intended to be the sole support of a doctrine.

Jesus first responded to the disciples' question: "Why do you speak to the people in parables?" (Mt. 13:10). Then, according to the harmonized account, He proceeded with at least ten parables. Most of these began "The kingdom of heaven is like . . ." Their primary insight into the kingdom concerned the present responsibilities of kingdom citizens, and thus possibilities in interpreting the parables are numerous. The discussions that follow give only some plausible identifications or interpretations.

(1) His reason for using parables (Mt. 13:10-17; Mk. 4:10-12; Lk. 8:9-10). Jesus used parables to make the abstract, concrete—to make the moral and spiritual real and practical. By simple stories about objects, events, and people, He made humans discern truth for themselves and apply it to their own lives. He thus revealed truth to those willing to respond.

Jesus also used parables to conceal truth from the unworthy. His quotation of Isaiah 6:9-10 (cf. Mt. 13:13-15; Lk. 8:10) implied that closed minds which chose not to hear His parables were fulfilling that prophecy. Though they heard what was said, their rejection of the truth resulted in their failure to understand. In his day, Isaiah is said to have used "the sarcasm of despair" to react to the failure of his peers to respond to God. As it were, he declared, "Just stay ignorant then." Jesus said to the disciples, "The knowledge of the secrets of the kingdom of heaven has been given to you, but not to [the spiritually indifferent]" (Mt. 13:11).

Parables thus enabled Jesus to reveal truth to those who were responsive, but conceal it from the unworthy. (cf. Mt. 13:1,12). Parables make the pursuit of truth a spiritual challenge that excludes the superficial and uncommitted hearer. The adage rightly declares, "Truth received brings more light; truth refused brings the night."[1]

(2) The Seed (or The Sower and the Seed, or The Parable of the Soils) (Mt. 13:1-8, 18-23; Mk. 4:1-9,13-20; Lk. 8:4-8, 11-15). Identifications include: sower = ministering believer; seed = gospel; field = world of mankind; wayside = careless hearer; stony ground = shallow convert; thorny ground = backslider; good

---

1   Quoted by C. Marvin Pate, *Luke*. Chicago: Moody Press, 1995, p. 188

ground = responsive convert. Plot: The seed is sown and some does well and some does not. Message: The gospel message that is ministered achieves varying responses among different hearers. The difference is not in the seed, but in the soil.

Jesus provided an interpretation for this parable. (cf. Mt. 13:18-23; Mk. 4:13-20; Lk. 8:11-15). His disciples needed to understand the parable of the seed, for it was the springboard to understanding the others. Because of its special role, this parable is sometimes called "The Parable of Parables." Also, in portraying four different soils, it becomes four parables in one.

It has been pointed out that the figures for the harvest increase: one hundred, sixty, thirty (cf. Mt. 13:8) are much larger than normal. A tenfold increase would be considered an excellent harvest. The figures that Jesus uses introduce the added element of divine intervention in achieving the harvest. Jesus' words, "The seed on good soil stands for those . . . who hear the word, retain it, and by persevering produce a crop" (Lk. 8:15) are one of the bases of the doctrine of "the perseverance of the saints."

(3) The Lamp (Mk. 4:21-25; Lk. 8:16-18). Identifications: lamp owner = God; cover = parable; light = truth. Plot: A light is ordinarily intended to be seen. Message: When truth is hidden in a parable, it is only so that it may be more strikingly revealed. In God's kingdom there are no secrets (Lk. 8:17), but neither are there shortcuts (Lk. 8:18). Spiritual insights are achieved by persistent hard work.

(4) The Growing Seed (or Unconscious Growth) (Mk. 4:26-29—note that this is the only parable unique to Mark). Identifications: sower = ministering believer; seed = Word. Plot: After the sower plants, he must wait patiently for the harvest. Message: A seed's rate of growth and ripening to harvest is inexorably determined by its divinely programmed timing.

(5) The Weeds (or the Wheat and the Weeds [Tares]) (Mt. 13:24-30, 36-43). Identifications: sower = Son of Man (or His agent); good seed = believers; weeds = unbelievers; enemy = devil (or his agent); harvest = end time events; reapers = angels. Plot: The Sower sowed good seed, but an enemy added weeds. Message: The church of the gospel age will include true believers and also those who falsely and insincerely profess to believe. At the end time harvest the deceivers will be separated out. Anyone in the kingdom who "causes sin and all who do evil" (Mt. 13:41) will be removed and cast "into the fiery furnace, where there will be weeping and gnashing of teeth" (v. 42). This sad group will apparently include insincere and hypocritical leaders. Comment: The weeds were darnel, a nonproductive plant that during the growing stages is scarcely distinguishable from rye.

(6) The Mustard Seed (Mt. 13:31, 32; Mk. 4:30-32). Identifications: sower = gospel worker; seed = gospel. Plot: A tiny seed becomes a large shrub. Message: From a very small beginning, a great church has grown. Comment: The mustard seed is not literally "the least of all seeds" (Mt. 13:32 KJV), but a popular proverb spoke of it thus. The NIV rendering avoids the problem. In Palestine, a typical mustard plant grows about one meter high, but some may reach twice that height (i.e., about seven feet).

(7) The Yeast in the Dough (Leaven in the Meal) (Mt. 13:33; Lk. 13:20-21). Identifications: dough = the beliefs and practices of the church; woman = heretic; yeast = false doctrine. Plot: By hiding the yeast in the dough, the woman caused the whole lump to be leavened. Message: The church has persistently been infiltrated by paganism and secularism.

An alternate view, typically taught by early twentieth century liberalism, sees the yeast as the gospel permeating human society. It optimistically looked for the total Christianization of society and the church's ultimate triumph. Some evangelicals also see the yeast standing for the gospel, but they look for genuine conversions and not mere Christianization through social service.

(8) The Treasure Hidden in the Field (Mt. 13:44). Identifications (ONE): man = sinner; treasure = Christ. Plot: A man finds a treasure hidden in a field and he sells all that he has to buy that field. Message: A sinner (seemingly accidentally) discovers the priceless Christ and gives up everything to receive Him.

Identifications (TWO): man = Christ; treasure = Church. Message: Christ gave His life to purchase the Church.

(9) The Pearl of Great Value (Price) (Mt. 13:45-46). Identifications (ONE): merchant = seeking sinner; pearl = Christ. Plot: A merchant gives all that he has for a lovely pearl that his search has discovered. Message: The sincerely seeking sinner finds the priceless Christ and gives up everything to receive Him.

Identifications (TWO): merchant = Christ; pearl = Church. Message: Christ gave His life to purchase the Church.

Those who adopt identification ONE hold that the parables distinguish between those who find Christ incidentally (the "man" v. 44) from those who find Him after a search (the "merchant" v. 45). In either case the parables are seen to teach that whether one finds Christ while at his daily tasks, or only after a long search, it is always worth every sacrifice to possess Him.

Traditionally, identification TWO has been popular, but many doubt that the two parables are intended to have duplicate messages. Thus, an alternate older view suggests that the treasure in the field is Israel, and the pearl is the Church. Jesus gave His life for each of these.

(10) The Net (Dragnet) (Mt. 13:47-50). Identifications: fishermen = God's end time angelic reapers; fish = both real and nominal Christians. Plot: The net in the sea encloses both good and bad fish that afterward are sorted. Message: In the end time those who are mere nominal Christians will be sorted out from the true Church.

(11) The House Owner's Treasure (Mt. 13:51-52). Identifications: house owner (or householder) = disciple; treasures = truths of Scripture. Plot: A prosperous house owner may possess a variety of treasures in his storeroom. Message: One who already knows the Old Testament (teacher of the law v. 52), and also embraces the Gospel has a twofold collection of treasures, some old and some new.

In applying the parable of the lamp Jesus had instructed, "Consider carefully how you listen" (Lk. 8:18). He concluded the series by asking, "Have you understood all these things?" (Mt. 13:51), the disciples answered, "Yes." Their later questions, however, confirmed that they really had not.

6. The Stilling of the Tempest (Mt. 8:18, 23-27; Mk. 4:35-41; Lk. 8:22-25)

Matthew records, "When Jesus saw the crowd around him, he gave orders to cross to the other side of the lake" (Mt. 8:18). Perhaps He chose to leave the crowds behind to escape a popular demonstration. Only Mark mentions that He rode in the stern, that there were other boats with them, and that He slept on a cushion. Jesus was able to sleep, not because He was careless or indifferent, but because He was master of the situation and therefore He rested in faith.

Matthew's language: "Without warning, a furious storm [Gk. *seismos megas*][2] came up on the lake" (Mt. 8:24) suggests to some that an earthquake struck. Scripture mentions winds as a factor (cf. Mt. 8:26), however, and both Mark and Luke use the word *lailaps* (LAH-ee-laps) denoting a squall, hurricane, or whirlwind. Sudden windstorms on Galilee are made perilously forceful by the hills that ring the lake. The effect of the violent waves upon a boat parallels what happens to a building in an earthquake.

The cry for help came from the sailor-disciples. Their life had been on the sea, but they could not cope with the storm, and with the waves breaking over the boat. In the Biblical record, this event was the first emergency that they disciples had faced since they began following Jesus. Their response fell short of their potential. Jesus asked, "Why are you so afraid [*deilos*]" (Mt. 8:26). The word *deilos* (die-LOS) is translated cowardly or timid. Though the storm was threatening, as disciples of the divine Christ, their panic did not reconcile with their supposed faith.

Jesus' words to the sea, that are rendered, "Peace, be still" or "Quiet! Be still" (Mk. 4:39), are literally, "Silence, be muzzled!"

---

2 *seismos* (size-MOS): a shaking, an earthquake, a storm on the ocean; *megas* (MEG-as): intense, great, strong.

Jesus used the same verb (Gk. *phimoo* [fim-OH-oh]: to tie shut, or to muzzle) in silencing the evil spirit in the man in the synagogue at Capernaum. (cf. Mk. 1:25, Lk. 4:35). The sudden calming of the waves was an important part of the miracle.

Jesus revealed His human nature as he slept in the stern of the boat, His divine nature as He commanded the waves to be still. He validly scolded the disciples for their little faith (Mt. 8:26), because they ought to have been aware of the provisions assured by His presence. For Jesus to be in the boat did not prevent the storm, but it did assure that they all reached the shore. In evaluating events, the disciples were "terrified" in the presence of divine power. They only partially identified Him, however, for they continued to ask, "Who is this?" (cf. Mk. 4:41).

7. The Demon Possessed Men of Gadara (Mt. 8:28-34; Mk. 5:1-20; Lk. 8:26-39)

In traditional versions, the site of this event is identified as the country of the Gergesenes in Matthew, but the country of the Gadarenes in Mark and Luke. Newer versions speak of the country of the Gadarenes in Matthew, and country of the Gerasenes in Mark and Luke. These differences between the versions result from revisions of the Greek text. It is thought that the variant readings resulted because scribes adjusted place names according to their understanding of geography. The reputed site of the town of Gerasa is some forty-eight kilometers (thirty miles) from Galilee, and Gadara is "a few kilometers." Scripture places Jesus "in the *region* of the Gerasenes (Gadarenes)," however, and the episode began "when Jesus stepped ashore" (Lk. 8:27). We conclude that the location of the town that gave its name to the region remains indeterminate, but it is not an important issue.

Whatever may be correct about the specific place names, at least it is known that this was Gentile territory. Otherwise it was known as Decapolis (meaning ten cities) (cf. Mk. 7:31). Apparently, Jesus had crossed the Sea of Galilee and had come to this place explicitly to minister to the men in the tombs. From a human standpoint, it is possible that the violent storm had blown the boat off the course that had been planned.

Though Matthew speaks of two men, Mark and Luke mention only one—presumably one of the two. One of the men was the spokesman, and perhaps he was the one most seriously afflicted so that he was particularly conspicuous in the events that occurred. McCumber comments over the count of the men: "One, two, or a yardful, Jesus is adequate for their deliverance."[3] The men are said to be "demon-possessed" (Mt. 8:28, cf. Lk. 8:27), or as some would prefer, "demonized."

---

3 William E. McCumber, *Matthew.* Kansas City: Beacon Hill Press, 1975, p. 58.

In Jesus' time, demon possession was not distinguished from mental illness. In either case, there was little or no provision for the care of such patients. Marks tells that the man "had often been chained hand and foot" (Mk. 5:4), but the treatment was ineffective because the man simply broke his restraints. These victims were so totally possessed that they could not distinguish between themselves and the demons. The man ran to Jesus and knelt before Him, not in worship, but in acknowledgment of a greater power.

The demons' message was literally, "What to us and to you?" (Mt. 8:29)—an expression that occurs in Hebrew, Greek, and Latin literature. It was their way of conveying total disassociation from Jesus. The nation's theologians were uncertain of Jesus' identity, but these demons correctly identified Him as "Son of the Most High God." (Mk. 5:7). Ironically, in their terror of Jesus the demons invoked God's protection against Him! Jesus asked for their name (cf. Mk. 5:9), but in reply the demons gave their number. A Roman legion at full strength comprised from 4,000 to 6,000 troops, and for Jesus to confront a legion of demons underscored His divine power.

These demons were fully aware that judgment awaited them, for there will be a day when all demonic powers are disposed of (cf. Mt. 8:29). In the meantime, they strongly desired to be embodied, and they were willing to settle even for embodiment in a herd of pigs. Jesus did not command the demons to enter the pigs, but He gave them permission. Though it seemed contrary to the demons' purposes to allow the destruction of the 2,000 host pigs, it was their nature to cause distress in those that they possessed. The pigs, in frantic disorientation, lost all natural sense of self preservation. Demonization, whether in humans or animals, is a very real victimization and no mere hallucination.

The people of the community were totally without thanks for the healing (curing or literally saving [Lk. 8: 36]) of the demoniacs. They reacted with fear when they saw the former demoniac sitting at Jesus' feet, dressed and in his right mind, and they pleaded with Jesus to leave the area. In their fear of the supernatural, they preferred pigs and demons rather than Jesus. Their attitude has been described as "human selfishness at its worst." Perhaps the destruction of the herd was seen as a major economic blow to local industry.

Before departing across Galilee, Jesus commissioned the leader of the two to a witnessing ministry to tell of his healing, particularly to his family. It is suggested that since this was Gentile territory, Jesus was not afraid of an impetuous crowd that might attempt to make Him Messiah. These instructions, therefore, contrast with His usual warning to tell no one of a healing. Though there is no record that Jesus ever returned to this region, at least He left a witness.

8. Jairus' Daughter Raised and the Hemorrhaging Woman Healed (Mt. 9:18-26; Mk. 5:21-43; Lk. 8:40-56)

When Jesus returned once more to His ministry in Capernaum, He was promptly approached by Jairus who came with an urgent appeal. Jairus was a ruler of the synagogue and he would have been elected to that post by the synagogue elders. He was thus a man who was respected and appreciated by his peers. As a ruler he had oversight of the synagogue building, and he planned and directed the services. His choices decided who would preach, teach, or pray.

Jairus appealed to Jesus because his twelve-year old only daughter was desperately ill. Matthew says she was dead, Mark and Luke say she was dying. Apparently Matthew reported a later turn of events. In response to Jairus' plea, Jesus began the journey to his home and as He went, the crowds thronged around Him. At this point the story is interrupted, and in what is called a "sandwich" or framing construction, the story of the hemorrhaging woman divides the beginning from the conclusion.

Each synoptic tells that the woman's condition had persisted for twelve years, but Mark adds that under the care of many doctors she had grown worse. Her problem likely was a uterine fibroid tumor. Jesus sensed her touch on the edge of His cloak, (or possibly an attached tassel) for "Others thronged Him, [but] she alone touched Him." The healing was not really a matter of the touch of her hand, however, but the grasp of her faith. Her desire to touch Him may have revealed an uninformed and imperfect faith, but it was effective in providing for her need.

Jesus' search for the one who had touched Him was His strategy to lead the woman to declare her faith publicly. The power was not in His garment; the healing resulted by His own active choice. The woman's faith was strengthened by a public witness, and the procedure was necessary to restore her to society. In ministering this healing, Jesus called the woman "Daughter" (cf. Mt. 9:22; Mk. 5:34; Lk. 8:48). She was the only woman thus addressed by Jesus. His declaration "Go in peace" was not merely a friendly farewell, but a notable promise.

While Jesus was dealing with the woman, messengers came with the news that Jairus' daughter had died. Jesus' response to Jairus stands as a classic exhortation to all believers: "Don't be afraid; just believe" (Mk. 5:36).

When Jesus arrived at Jairus' house, the professional mourners were performing. A minimum group would be two flute players and a wailing woman. Jesus expelled (Gk. *ekballo* [ek-BAL-oh]: drive out, throw out, forcibly expel) the mourners just as He would the money changers from the temple—the same verb is used in each account (cf. Mt. 21:12) It is an irony that these "mourners" so quickly forgot their role in order to laugh at Jesus (Lk. 8:53). They were the only people in the New Testament who specifically were said to have laughed.

Jesus' Aramaic[4] command *Talitha koum* (TAL-uh-thuh KOOM) (Mk. 5:41), translated by Mark, "Little girl, get up" is literally, "Little lamb, arise." Perhaps these were the very words that her mother regularly used to awaken her in the morning. The resuscitation of the girl involved the presence of Peter, James, and John, as well as Jesus and her parents, and this was the first of three occasions when Jesus brought these three disciples into an inner circle.

Jesus' instructions for the girl's further care were simply to give her something to eat (cf. Mk. 5:43). Though He had used divine power to raise the dead, He counted on natural means to sustain the living.

9. The Blind and Mute Healed (Mt. 9:27-34)

The two blind men persisted in pursuing Jesus, and for the first time in Scripture they applied to Him the Messianic title, "Son of David" (cf. v. 27). In responding to them, Jesus pronounced a fundamental principle in human relationships with God: "According to your faith will it be done to you" (v. 29). He thus made them responsible for qualifying for their own healing, though of course it was to be faith in Him and not faith in the mere efficacy of faith. Though the blind men received the gift of their sight, they disobeyed Jesus in proceeding to spread news of the miracle.

The man's mute condition was due to demon possession, so that when the demon was exorcised, his powers of speech returned. The spectators were divided in their response, but as usual, the Pharisees were critical and they associated Jesus' power with Satan.

According to the conventional chronologies, approximately at this point Jesus began His third year of ministry. For part of the year He remained in the province of Galilee. He then left Galilee and proceeded with His disciples to the northern area that is often known as Syrophoenicia.

II. THE BEGINNING OF THE THIRD YEAR OF MINISTRY

By this time, Jesus was a recognized itinerant rabbi with a following of disciples, and He qualified to be allowed to speak in

---

4   Aramaic was the usual language of the common people following the return of the Jews from the Babylonian captivity. It is likely that Jesus mostly spoke Aramaic when He taught the people.

Jewish synagogues. Not surprisingly, however, He found His most critical audience in His own hometown.

1. Jesus' Last Public Visit to Nazareth (Mt. 13:53-58; Mk. 6:1-6)

Nazareth is not named, but this place is called His "hometown." Its people knew Jesus' family well enough to name four half-brothers and to recognize His half-sisters. They identified Him as "the carpenter's son" (Mt. 13:55), and also, for the only time in Scripture, as "the carpenter" (Mk. 6:3), but they failed to recognize Him as the Messiah. Their familiarity with Him hindered them from actually knowing Him. The profound wisdom of His teachings puzzled these fellow citizens who likely were farmers and tradesmen. Thus, they asked, "Where did this man get these things?" (Mk. 6:2). They thought they knew all about Jesus, and on that basis they "took offense at him" (lit. were scandalized) (Mt. 13:57; Mk. 6:3).

Jesus' chosen pattern was to perform miracles in response to faith, and therefore He was limited in ministry by the lack of faith of the people of Nazareth. The result was, "he did not do many miracles there" (Mt. 13:58), and "[Jesus] was amazed at their lack of faith" (Mk. 6:6). This mention of Jesus' amazement has been described as "a realistic human touch." By depriving themselves of Jesus' miracles, the people of Nazareth hurt themselves far more than they hurt Him.

2. Herod Antipas Learns of Jesus. (Mt. 14:1-2; Mk. 6:14-16; Lk. 9:7-9; cf. Mal. 4:5)

There were various popular theories concerning the identification of Jesus. He was: 1) John the Baptist resurrected, 2) Elijah, or 3) some other prophet. In response to Jesus' miracle-working exploits, Herod adopted the first theory, and in the process he revealed his personal guilt in John's death. Thus, he spoke of "John, the man I beheaded" (Mk. 6:16; cf. Lk. 9:9). The Gospels expand upon Herod's confusion and they provide a flashback to explain how John had died. Though Herod would have liked to meet Jesus at this time, in fact the two did not meet until a few hours before Calvary.

The popular idea that Jesus was a new Elijah supported the Old Testament prophecy (and Jewish tradition) that a great prophet would come to prepare the way as the forerunner for the Messiah. "I will send you the prophet Elijah before that great and dreadful day of the Lord comes" (Mal. 4:5). Jesus' own view specifically identified John the Baptist as Elijah. Later He declared, "I tell you, Elijah has come, and they have done to him everything they wished" (Mk. 9:13).

3. The Death of John the Baptist (Mt. 14:6-12; Mk. 6: 21-29)

Some harmonies place John's death a month of two earlier. It is reported in Scripture as a flashback, and thus the exact time that it correlates with Jesus' ministry is uncertain.

Herod Antipas had kept John a prisoner for about a year. As previously noted (p. 59), at first Herod wished to kill John. Upon coming to know him, however, Herod found him to be a just and holy man, and he did what he could to protect his prisoner (cf. Mk. 6:20). Nevertheless, in executing John, Herod showed that his word to a dancer meant more to him than justice or the law of God. In that day, female dance entertainers were often prostitutes, and their dances would likely be explicitly licentious.

History notes that Herodias was the granddaughter of Herod the Great. Her first husband had been Herod Philip I, and by him she had her daughter whom Josephus noted was named Salome. Herodias had left Philip to elope with Herod Antipas who was her uncle. He in turn proceeded to divorce his wife to marry her.

Herod's promise of "up to half my kingdom" (Mk. 6:23) was mere rhetoric. Although Herod was given the honorary title of king (cf. Mk. 6:14), in fact he was a tetrarch not a king (cf. Mt. 14:1), and he did not possess a kingdom. Apparently, his pride kept him from backing down on his foolish promise.

4. The Apostles Report. Five Thousand Fed (Mt. 14:13-21; Mk. 6:30-44; Lk. 9:10-17; Jn. 6:1-13)

Mark and Luke tell of the apostles at this time reporting on their witnessing tour of Galilee.[5] John notes that "The Jewish Passover Feast was near" (Jn. 6:4), and thus it was just one year before the cross. Since it was one year since the events of chapter five of John, Jesus was now about to mark the third Passover in His ministry.

At this time, Jesus invited the disciples, "Come with me by yourselves to a quiet place and get some rest" (Mk. 6:31). This occasion was one of many in the Gospels when Jesus attempted to come apart from the crowd (cf. p. 67). By embarking in a boat, Jesus and the disciples would have enjoyed a few hours of rest. Apparently the boat sailed more or less parallel to the shore, so the crowd followed on the shore and when the apostolic party disembarked a large crowd awaited them. The fact that they were now in a remote place led to the need to provide food.

The feeding of the 5,000 is the only miracle recorded in all four Gospels. When Jesus saw such a large group assembled, He "had compassion on them . . . . So he began teaching them many

---

5   cf. p. 90, The Twelve Sent Forth to Witness (Mt. 19:5-15; Mk. 6:7-13; Lk. 9:1-6).

things" (Mk. 6:34). The statement that Jesus "had compassion" (Mk. 6:14) is one of five similar statements in the Gospels. In His ministry at this time, Jesus "spoke to them about the kingdom of God, and healed those who needed healing" (Lk. 9:11).

As the hours went by, the disciples became concerned for the people's need for food. They advised Jesus, in what has been spoken of as "unintended impertinence," to "Send the crowds away" (Mt. 14:15). Instead, Jesus instructed, "You give them something to eat" (Mt. 14:16). The disciples had seen the need, and now Jesus sought to impress them that they shared the responsibility to meet that need. Since there were 5,000 men (cf. Mt. 14:21), the total count of the crowd is projected at three times that number.

Jesus asked Philip concerning the source of supply "to test him" (Jn. 6:6). Most commentators feel that Philip failed the test! Philip's estimate of the cost of a minimum supply of bread was 200 denarii[6], and some versions render this figure as equivalent to eight months' wages for a working man. Because his estimate was discouragingly high, someone speaks of Philip as a "statistical pessimist." Mark notes that besides questioning the disciples, Jesus sent them on a search of the crowd to check on what food was available (cf. Mk. 6:38).

The boy's lunch consisted of five small barley loaves (or buns or rolls), and two small fish (cf. Jn. 6:9) L. Holcomb commented facetiously, "The greatest miracle that day was not that Jesus multiplied [the boy's lunch] into a feast, but that this growing boy still had his lunch uneaten by the middle of the afternoon!" In that day, barley bread was the food of the poor. John's term for the fish denotes those intended more as appetizers than as entrées. It was Andrew who found the boy and brought him to Jesus. Before performing the miracle, Jesus prepared the people by organizing them into ranks of hundreds and fifties.

Though the place was remote, it was not a desert, for there was grass for the people to sit upon (cf. Mt. 14:18). All four Gospels report that before passing out the food, Jesus "gave thanks," and the synoptics add that He first looked up to heaven. In view of this incident, in traditional Catholicism the priest officiating at the mass was instructed to raise his eyes before the act of consecrating the bread.

All four Gospels report the adequacy of the supply of food. In the synoptics "all ate and were satisfied," and in John "all had enough to eat" (Jn. 6:12). John, however, uses a strong compound verb that could be rendered, "All were completely filled up." Someone comments, "When heaven becomes involved in earth's resources, there are enough."

---

6   A denarius was a silver coin that typically was a day's wages for an ordinary laborer.

The miracle appears to have taken place at Jesus' hands in the distribution process: "Then he gave [the loaves and fish] to the disciples, and the disciples gave them to the people" (Mt. 14:19); "Then he gave them to the disciples to set before the people" (Lk. 9:16). At the end of the meal there was more bread than at the beginning, and the remaining fragments were gathered into twelve baskets. Thus there was a basket for each disciple, and each would be privileged to share with Jesus. In this instance, the word basket is *kophinos* (COF-in-os) which usually denotes a large heavy basket—transliterated into English it becomes our word "coffin."

5. Jesus Refuses a Premature Kingship (Mt. 14:22-23; Mk. 6:45-46; Jn. 6:14-15)

The feeding of the 5,000 marked the height of Jesus' popularity. To many, Jesus appeared as the fulfillment of their Old Testament Messianic expectations. Both the Old Testament (cf. Deut. 18:15-18; 33:8-11; Num. 24:15-17), and the intertestamental writings, portrayed a future Messiah combining: kingship, the priesthood, and the gift of prophecy. Jesus clearly demonstrated all of these traits.

At this time, however, Jesus was not prepared to assume Messiah's role on the earthly basis that the people desired. They were willing to acknowledge Him as King, but they were not willing to submit to Him as Lord. He had fed 5,000 men, but He had no desire to recruit them into an earthly army. Thus, "Jesus, knowing that they intended to come and make him king by force, withdrew again into the hills by himself" (Jn. 6:15). Matthew and Luke tell us that He withdrew in order to spend the evening in prayer. No doubt He once more affirmed His obedience to the Father.

6. Jesus Walks on the Water (Mt. 14:24-36; Mk. 6:47-56; Jn. 6:16-21).

It is suggested that "Jesus made his disciples get into the boat and go on ahead of him to Bethsaida" (Mk. 6:45) in order to keep them from becoming involved in a Messianic movement. Their departure gave Him the solitude that He needed for His late night prayer. Apparently, the storm the disciples encountered on the lake blew them off course, and in a change of plan, they were actually to land at Gennesaret (cf. Mk. 6:53).

While Jesus prayed, the disciples were experiencing a continuous powerful head wind. By the fourth watch (3:00 to 6:00 a.m.) they were in the "middle of the lake" (Mk. 6:47), they were "straining at the oars" (Mk. 6:48), and they had rowed "about twenty-five or thirty stadia" (Jn. 6:19, lit. trans.). Thirty stadia equals about five and one-half kilometers or three and one-half miles. The procedure in a storm was to lower the sail, and by the use of oars, attempt to keep the boat heading into the waves.

At this point Jesus appeared walking on the water. Apparently He was traveling parallel to the boat since "He was about to pass by them" (Mk. 6:48). The event was literal and not someone's hallucination, for the disciples "all saw him and were terrified" (Mk. 6:50). In that crisis time they thought their best friend was their enemy. Jesus reassured them: "It is I [lit. I am]; Don't be

	Matt.	Mark	Luke	John
Last known visit to Nazareth	13:54-56	6:1-6		
John the Baptist's death	14:1-12	6:16-29	9:7-9	
Third Passover				6:4
Feeding the 5,000	14:15-21	6:30-44	9:10-17	
Semon on the Bread of Life				6:26-66
● MINISTRY BEYOND GALILEE				
Canaanite's child healed	15:21-28	7:24-30		
Feeding of the 4,000	15:29-38	8:1-10		
Peter's great confession	16:13-20	8:27-30	9:18-21	
The Transfiguration	17:1-8	9:2-8	9:28-36	
● LATER JUDEAN AND PEREAN MINISTRY				
Feast of Tabernacles				7:14-52
Man born blind healed				9:1-41
Good shepherd sermon				10:1-18
Seventy-two sent forth			10:1-24	
Good Samaritan			10:25-37	
Feast of Dedication				10:19-42

Figure 10: Time line of highlights of the third year of Jesus' ministry. The scale indicates months. The Feast of Dedication would be at the end of December.

afraid" (Jn. 6:20). The declaration "I am" is used from time to time in Scripture as a formula of divine self-disclosure. (cf. Exod. 3:14; Isa. 43:25; 48:12; 51:12; Mk. 14:62; Jn. 18:5-6).

Peter marred his experience of walking on the water by focusing on the effects of the wind, and thus weakening his faith. As it were, Jesus assigned Peter a name: "You of little faith" (Mt. 14:31). At least Peter did possess (a) "little" faith rather than no faith at all, and even a little faith is true faith. When the two men entered the boat, the wind ceased and "those who were in the boat worshiped him, saying, 'Truly you are the Son of God'" (Mt. 14:33). It has often been pointed out that though Mark is a record of Peter's memoirs, the account of Peter's walking on the water is found only in Matthew.

Mark connects two different events: "He climbed into the boat with them, and the wind died down. They were completely amazed, for they had not understood about the loaves; their hearts were hardened" (Mk. 6:51-52). The point appears to be that the disciples were still living wholly in the realm of natural human experience. They had no rapport with the things of the Spirit and the life of faith. They continued to measure all things according to earthly causes and values, and were unable to incorporate miracles into their understandings. Their attitude that denied good events compares with some modern humans who practice the denial of painful events.

John reports a further detail, "immediately the boat reached the shore where they were heading" (Jn. 6:21). These words seem to indicate the instant transport of the boat several kilometers across the lake. If such an event did occur, it may correctly be called "the forgotten miracle." It is not ordinarily included in lists of Jesus' miracles because the significance of John's words is debated. Also, the parallel accounts in the synoptics give no hint of such a miracle (cf. Mt. 14:34; Mk. 6:53).

Following the crossing, the party landed at Gennesaret. Jesus exercised a remarkable healing ministry there, so that "all who touched him were healed" (Mt. 14:36). The merit would not have been in the touch itself, but in the faith of which the touch was the expression. These people recognized Him as their healer, but apparently they missed recognizing Him as their Messiah.

7. Jesus' Sermon on the Bread of Life (Jn. 6:22-71)

By walking on the water to join His disciples, Jesus eluded that portion of the crowd that awaited Him at the launch area. When these people realized that fact, they "got into the boats and went to Capernaum in search of Jesus" (Jn. 6:24). By the time they arrived, it appears that Jesus had concluded His healing ministry at Gennesaret (cf. Mt. 14:35; Mk. 6:54-56), and He was now teaching in the synagogue in Capernaum (cf. Jn. 6:59). It is possible that it was the Sabbath, and thus it was the customary time for the Jews to gather in the synagogue.

At this time, Jesus perceived that the crowds were seeking Him for the wrong reasons. Thus, because their attitudes made it necessary, He responded to them with a severity that was almost a hardness. At this stage Jesus wanted only followers with active faith. Those He addressed needed to be brought out of their commitment to the earthly and physical, and brought to terms with the spiritual realities with which Jesus identified.

At the outset, Jesus gave no answer to their question, "When did you get here?" (v. 25), perhaps because the more significant question would have been, "How did you get here?" When the people asked, "What must we do to do the works God requires?" (v. 28) Jesus gave the answer that set the theme for His address: "Believe in the one he has sent" (v. 29). In their response, the people revealed the superficial nature of their interest in Jesus: they asked for a miraculous sign that would justify their belief in Him (cf. vv. 30-31). Apparently, in their unbelief or ignorance, the feeding of the 5,000 did not count.

Jesus spoke of "the true bread from heaven" (v. 32), and explained how they might partake of this heavenly bread. He stated that this bread "gives life to the world" (v. 33) and that "If anyone eats of this bread, he will live forever" (v. 51). Jesus declared: "I am the bread of life."[7] (v. 35, cf. v. 48). As it were, Jesus was saying that: 1) He is the only true source of life that humans seek, 2) He provides this life only through His death. Without at this time explaining the symbolism, Jesus declared, "He who comes to me will never go hungry, and he who believes in me will never be thirsty" (v. 35b).

Since the key to what He was teaching was a commitment of faith, Jesus explained how one becomes a believer. He spoke of the divine process of recruitment: "All that the Father gives me will come to me . . . . this is the will of him who sent me, that I shall lose none of all that he has given me" (vv. 37, 39). The significance of Jesus' teaching on this subject is debated, but those who stress God's sovereignty and the believer's security find support in this passage. Those who stress human responsibility may answer that God's choices depend upon His foreknowledge. Both schools likely agree that all the resources of heaven are committed to providing a salvation that will endure.

---

7 In these words Jesus gave the first of His seven "I am's" in John. The other six include: "I am the Light of the world" (8:12); "I am the Gate for the sheep" (10:7); "I am the Good Shepherd" (10:11); "I am the Resurrection and the Life" (11:25); "I am the Way and the Truth and the Life" (14:6); and "I am the true Vine" (15:1).

Jesus' message concerning God's sovereignty in enabling humans to believe was missed by those who grumbled (cf. v. 41). They continued to apply natural human logical processes to evaluate Jesus and His teachings. Again, Jesus could only tell them that they were deficient in their relationship to God (cf. vv. 44-46). The sole means to everlasting life was a faith relationship to Him who was the bread of life (vv. 47-48). In verse fifty-one He took the metaphor even further by declaring, "I am the living bread," and He added, "This bread is my flesh." (v. 51c).

Those who heard only the literal eating of flesh and drinking blood were repulsed by Jesus' message. They failed to realize what He was really saying: one partakes by believing. To eat and drink Jesus' flesh and blood is to exercise faith in His atoning propitiating power. Christians know that later, Jesus was to prescribe the Lord's Supper as a practice of the Church. In that enacted symbolism, the believer partakes of food and drink that portray an underlying relationship with Jesus Christ in His broken body and shed blood.

Jesus' hearers in Capernaum could not comprehend a relationship that involved the spiritual assimilation of the provisions and character of the Savior, nor could they accept the idea of another human becoming their sacrificial lamb. They responded, "This is a hard teaching. Who can accept it?" (Jn. 6:60). The difficulty was primarily in their hearts rather than in their minds. Centuries later, Augustine summed up the true reality: "Believe and you will have eaten."

The "disciples" who murmured (v. 61) and turned back (v. 66) in the "great defection" were not the Twelve, but the general followers in the pursuing crowds. Jesus asked the Twelve: "You do not want to leave too, do you?" (v. 67). His question was so framed that it indicated that He hoped for a "No" answer. Peter's response, declaring the disciples' faithfulness and identifying Jesus as "the Holy One of God" (i.e., the Messiah) (v. 69), has been described as "well intentioned but not well informed."

In correcting Peter's extravagant claim, Jesus commented "one of you is a devil" (v. 70). These words appear either not to have been heard, or not to have been understood. To speak of someone (identified by John to be Judas) as a devil (Gk. *diabolos* [dee-AB-o-los]) was much stronger than saying that he was demon possessed. Apparently, because Judas would become Satan's channel, he personally identified with Satan.

The events of this chapter, particularly involving His enigmatic teaching regarding the bread of life, marked a turning point in Jesus' ministry. His popular following, that had included the superficial and the merely curious, now began to decline.

8. Increasing Opposition to Jesus (Mt. 15:1-20; Mk. 7:1-23)

By this time, delegations of opponents constantly watched Jesus, seeking for an occasion against Him. A committee of Pharisees and teachers of the law from Jerusalem made an issue of neglect of ceremonial washing by Jesus' disciples—though the complaint cited the failure of the disciples, in reality it was against Jesus. In that era, the Pharisees had adopted a slogan, "To neglect hand washing is as bad as murder." It was not a matter of hygiene, but of ritual purity. Their authority for these demands was "the tradition of the elders" (Mt. 15:2), for Biblical Mosaic law imposed no such extreme demands.

Textual differences in Mark 7:3-4 result in alternate footnote renderings in some versions. Also, an idiom may be involved. The meaning seems clear enough however.

Jesus responded by pointing out the glaring shortcomings of these Pharisees and teachers in negating the true sense of the Word of God by their traditions. He addressed them as "hypocrites" and proceeded to quote a passage from Isaiah 29:13 (*LXX* version) which spoke of those whose "teachings are but rules taught by men." (Mk. 7:7). Their reverence for tradition was a false piety that Jesus rejected, for it meant that they practiced legalism at the expense of morality.

An issue that Jesus targeted was the Pharisees' failure to provide for aged needy parents on the ground that their resources were dedicated to God. They were flagrantly disobeying the fifth commandment. In the name of piety, they lived in affluence while they left their aged parents in abject poverty. Oral tradition defended such practices by teaching that if something was declared to be set apart to God, its owner thereby discharged all earthly responsibilities relating to that possession.

As the system operated, an actual gift to God was not required, but only a declaration of the intention to give. The designated objects remained in the possession of the "donor," and he enjoyed their use. Resources that were so designated were known by the Hebrew loan-word "Corban" (cf. Mk. 7:11) which means "that which is offered." (The pronunciation cor-BAN is Anglicized as COR-ban.) Jesus validly denounced such a system and those who practiced it. They had charged Him with disobeying traditions that were of human origin; He charged them with disobeying commandments of divine origin.

Jesus emphasized that what really mattered was not external washing, but inner purity. No amount of ritual washing could cleanse the heart filled with sensual defilement. The Pharisees were totally in error in their approach. Not surprisingly, as the disciples pointed out, "the Pharisees were offended when they heard this" (Mt. 15:12). The disciples were concerned about this resentment against Jesus. Jesus advised, "Leave them; they are blind guides" (Mt. 15:14). Since they were not God's planting, one day they would be rooted up.

When Jesus was alone with the disciples, they asked for an explanation of His parable about external defilement. Mark reports Jesus' words and then comments, "Jesus declared all foods 'clean'" (Mk. 7:19). Obviously, Peter did not really hear Him at this time! (cf. Acts 10:14). Jesus further replied by enumerating some elements of inner defilement; Matthew lists seven, but Mark lists thirteen. In the NRSV this catalog is translated: "It is from within, from the human heart, that evil intentions [evil thoughts][8] come: fornication [sexual immorality], theft, murder, adultery, avarice [greed], wickedness [malice], deceit [fraud], licentiousness [lewdness, sensuality, indecency], envy [jealousy], slander, pride [arrogance], folly [recklessness, foolishness]" (Mk. 7:20-22). Clearly, in Jesus' view, uncleanness (defilement) is a moral issue rather than a ritual one.

---

8   The words in brackets are used in the NIV or other newer versions.

SIX:

THE MINISTRY BEYOND GALILEE

A pparently at this time Jesus' concern for His disciples' lack of spiritual understanding led Him to withdraw from the crowds. He wanted a less public setting to instruct His select group of followers. Also, with the mounting opposition of the teachers of the law and Pharisees, and the recent fate of John the Baptist, it seemed wiser to retreat to more remote regions. Matthew reports, "Jesus withdrew to the region of Tyre and Sidon" (Mt. 15:21). Later, He would proceed to Decapolis.

1. The Healing of the Canaanite Woman's Daughter (Mt. 15:21-28; Mk. 7:24-30)

The woman from this coastal region is variously identified as: Greek, Syrophoenician, Syrian Phoenician, or Canaanite. Tradition names her Justa, and her daughter Berenice (perhaps a variant of Bernice). Jesus did not intend a public ministry in this area (cf. Mk. 7:24), but when the woman became aware of Him she followed Him and sought His help. Repeatedly, she begged Him to cast out the demon that possessed her daughter, and she reinforced her appeal by dramatically kneeling in front of Him.

Since the Canaanites were known for their corrupt idolatrous practices, it is considered remarkable that this woman should address Jesus as "Son of David" (Mt. 15:22). In doing so, however, she may not have recognized the Messianic significance of that name. Jesus' response to the woman appears out of character: silence (Mt. 15:23), rejection (v. 24), and apparent insult (v. 26). Nevertheless, the woman passed these tests and she was not deterred in her efforts.

Jesus' seemingly harsh comment concerning the crumbs to dogs perhaps related to an actual event at that moment. In the Greek text He used the diminutive (which suggests doggy or puppy), but modern commentators hold that this would not really have softened the insulting term "dog." If He spoke to her in Aramaic—which is likely—it provides no known diminutive. Jesus may have modified the message, however, by the tone of His voice. In that culture dogs were usually repulsive scavengers, and the term ordinarily identified with a very unflattering image.

This woman unflinchingly endured the disciples' objections (Mt. 15:23), as well as Jesus' negative comments. By her agreeable response "Yes Lord" (Mk. 7:28), she became the only person in Mark's Gospel who called Him Lord. Her comment about the dogs eating crumbs primarily displayed faith rather than cleverness. Martin Luther commented, however, "She snares Christ in His own words!" Jesus declared, "Woman, you have great faith! Your request is granted" (Mt. 15:28). The healing was by proxy and at a distance. It demonstrated that Jesus' caring love extends to humans of all national origins.

2. Miracles of Healing in Decapolis (Mt. 15:29-31; Mk. 7:31-37)

Scripture reports, "Then Jesus left the vicinity of Tyre and went through Sidon, down to the Sea of Galilee and into the region of the Decapolis" (Mk. 7:31). Decapolis, meaning "ten cities," identifies the primarily Gentile region of Galilee east of the Jordan River. There "[Jesus] went up on a mountainside and [ministered]" (Mt. 15: 29). Mark uniquely tells of the healing of the deaf man with the speech impediment. Matthew tells of great crowds and "the dumb speaking, the crippled made well, the lame walking, and the blind seeing" (Mt. 15:31). Many Gentiles were reached and "They praised the God of Israel" (Mt. 15:31).

As Jesus pronounced the healing of the deaf man, He uttered a "deep sigh" (Mk. 7:34). The same verb (Gk. *stenazo* [sten-ADZE-oh]) is rendered "groan" in Romans 8:23 (cf. 2. Cor. 5:2). Jesus wholeheartedly identified with those to whom He ministered healing. Mark translates the Aramaic word *Ephphatha* (EF-uh-thuh) as "be opened" (Mk. 7:34). The physical actions by which Jesus conveyed healing to the deaf man served as sign language to communicate encouragement. Though Jesus asked that the healing remain secret, the people disobeyed (cf. Mk. 7:36).

3. The Feeding of the 4,000 in Decapolis (Mt. 15:32-39; Mk. 8:1-10)

Even in the remote regions of Decapolis, healings attracted large crowds who came and stayed—"They have already been with me three days" (Mk. 8:2). Though the feeding of the 5,000 emphasized Jesus' role as the bread of life, this event simply provided for the people's physical needs. Jesus said, "I have compassion for these people" (Mt. 15:32). When the disciples asked, "Where could we get enough bread in this remote place to feed such a crowd?" (Mt. 15:33) they either had not learned through their previous experience, or they did not want to appear presumptuous. Matthew records, "The number of those who ate was four thousand, besides women and children" (Mt. 15:38).

In this case, the original provision consisted of seven loaves and a few small fish. The source of these supplies is not given. Some have suggested that they were the remnants from the twelve baskets after the 5,000 were fed, but this possibility is highly unlikely since that event was several months earlier. The gathered remnants after feeding the 4,000 filled seven baskets.

The word for basket (Gk. *spuris* [spoor-IS]) used here denotes a large rope basket equivalent to a hamper, and the same word is used to identify the basket in which Paul was lowered from the Damascan wall (cf. Acts 9:25).

The majority of people fed at this time were Gentiles, whereas the 5,000 were mostly Jews. Since there was no strong Jewish voice in Decapolis, there was no move to proclaim Jesus' Messiahship. The feeding of the 4,000 affirms that Christ's gospel provides for all nations, and this of course is a fundamental Christian emphasis. Jesus' words, "I do not want to send them away hungry" (Mt. 15:32) has been proposed as an excellent motto for all Christian teachers and preachers. Jesus concluded events in this place by boarding the boat that awaited Him.

4. At Magadan. Conflict with the Pharisees and Sadducees (Mt. 16:1-4; Mk. 8:11-13)

At this time, Jesus apparently was paying a brief return visit to Galilee. The site of these events is given as the "vicinity of Magadan" (or Magdala) by Matthew (cf. 15:39), or "the region of Dalmanutha" by Mark. Neither designation is positively identified, but a location on the western shore of Galilee seems valid. It is possible that the two names: 1) were alternate names for the same place, 2) identified adjacent towns, or 3) in the first case denoted a town and in the second, a district.

Matthew tells that opposition to Jesus now involved the Pharisees united with the Sadducees, again a totally incompatible combination. Commentators suggest that it was only because these two groups joined forces that Jesus was crucified. The Pharisees emphasized debate and talk but alone they might not have acted. The Sadducees were committed to resolute action. Jesus was crucified because the convictions of the Pharisees combined with the actions of the Sadducees.

These critics requested of Jesus a sign from heaven that would validate His claims. The qualification "from heaven" suggests that they discounted physical miracles, such as healings, on the ground that demons could heal. Previously, a committee of Pharisees united with teachers of the law had requested simply that He demonstrate a "miraculous sign" (cf. Mt. 12:38-45). In replying at this time, Jesus basically repeated the points He had made previously: 1) His miracles were qualifying signs but they chose to reject them, 2) the final indisputable sign He would provide would be His resurrection that was symbolized by Jonah's emergence from the fish.

Jesus pointed out that by their success in predicting the weather, they often showed notable skill in interpreting heavenly signs. Nevertheless, they were totally blind to the obvious spiritual signs of their generation. Since they held that Jesus' miracles could be from Satan (cf. Mt. 12:22-37), they concluded that there was nothing in His ministry that would authenticate Him to be from God. In their opinion, He had not produced a "public definitive proof" that He had God's message.

Once again Jesus branded these critics as "a wicked and adulterous generation" (cf. Mt. 12:39; 16:4). They were guilty of spiritual adultery because they professed total devotion to God, but their lifestyle and values were those of the world.

At this point, Jesus boarded the boat and sailed for Gentile territory on the eastern shore of Galilee. This incident marked the virtual close of His ministry in His own territory in the province of Galilee.

5. Jesus Warns Against the Yeast of the Pharisees (Mt. 16:5-12; Mk. 8:14-21)

As Jesus voyaged to the eastern shore, He spoke a warning to His disciples to avoid the yeast (or leaven) of the Pharisees, the Sadducees, and Herod (cf. Mt. 16:5; Mk. 8:15). It is assumed that the three sources provided the same type of infiltrating destructive yeast that is defined as "the teaching of the Pharisees and Sadducees" (Mt. 16:12), and as "hypocrisy" (Lk. 12:1). These views constituted corrupting heresies that hindered belief in Jesus and demanded that He prove Himself by miraculous signs. They represented bad theology and a burdensome legal system that sadly overlooked the real elements of godly living.

Jesus' symbolism at this time quite confused the disciples, for they took His metaphor literally and their response was a discussion of their failure to bring bread. Since they had carelessly embarked on an extended trip without adequate provisions (they had only one loaf, Mk. 8:14), it is understandable that this matter was uppermost in their minds. Their guilty consciences saw a rebuke where none was given.

Jesus expressed disappointment over their lack of spiritual insight, for as someone has described them: "They had blind eyes, deaf ears and short memories" (cf. Mk. 8:18). Jesus proceeded to discuss the matter of the bread, and hopefully it helped them to understand. His questions about the amount of bread left over in the two miracle feeding events seem to have emphasized the fact that with Him the amount of bread was not an issue; He could more than take care of shortages.

6. The Blind Man Healed at Bethsaida (Mk. 8:22-26)

Some scholars hold that this was a different Bethsaida from Capernaum's neighboring town, and thus this event was part of Jesus' trip to the east shore of Galilee. This miracle is one of two found uniquely in Mark (cf. Mk. 7:32-35), and one of three in Mark that were performed privately (cf. Mk. 5:37; 7:33).

In healing the blind man, Jesus involved the sense of touch, for He both spit on the man's eyes, and He formally put (or laid)

His hands on him. The healing is the only one in the Gospels that was achieved in two stages, for at first the man's vision was blurred and unfocused. After Jesus again placed His hands on his eyes, the man saw perfectly. This event has been referred to as, "the miracle that Jesus did twice." It is the only Biblical instance of a so-called "partial healing."

Jesus led the blind man out of the village before He healed him, and afterwards He instructed him "Don't go into the village" (Mk. 8:26). Apparently, at this time Jesus desired to protect His privacy. Some suggest that this secrecy was imposed as a judgment to deprive Bethsaida of the blind man's testimony.

7. Peter's Great Confession of Faith (Mt. 16:13-20; Mk. 8:27-30; Lk. 9:18-21)

At this point Luke resumes his account after having omitted all events since the feeding of the 5,000—the so-called "Great Omission." The cross was now just six months away.

Jesus and the disciples apparently proceeded to the region of Caesarea Philippi[1] in order to find the privacy and solitude that they needed. Jesus now desired extended periods of prayer and undisturbed teaching sessions with the disciples. In this Gentile setting He asked, "Who do people say I am?" (Mk. 8:27). The question was an important one, for Jesus had proved to be so different from the kind of Messiah that was popularly expected.

The disciples cited the current conjectures about Jesus' identity: 1) John the Baptist, 2) Elijah, 3) one of the prophets. Although each of these suggestions could have been considered flattering, each was wrong. Jesus proceeded with His second question: "Who do you say I am?" (Mk. 8:29).

Peter's response to Jesus' question was a ringing confession of His Messiahship, and a confident declaration of His deity: "You are the Christ, the Son of the living God" (Mt. 16:16). Since Jesus received this confession as truth, indirectly He thus declared Himself Messiah. Jesus explained how Peter had arrived at this advanced insight: "this was not revealed to you by man, but by my Father in heaven" (Mt. 16:17).

This event constituted an important milestone in Jesus' earthly ministry, for it marked a formal advance of understanding regarding His true identity. It is essential that the followers of Jesus confess Him rightly, for He must be seen as God's divine Son whom He has given to meet the needs of mankind. Jesus' procedure in addressing a question and receiving Peter's answer has been called, "Peter's midterm exam."

The meaning of Jesus' words, "You are Peter [*petros*], and on this rock [*petra*] I will build my church, and the gates of Hades

---

1 This Caesarea, which was at the foot of Mt. Hermon, was so named in order to distinguish it from Caesarea on the Mediterranean.

will not overcome it" (Mt. 16:18) continues to be debated. Views concerning the rock include: 1) the rock was Peter in the sense that he was a founding member of the Church, 2) the rock was Peter's confession that Jesus is the Christ, 3) the rock was Peter's faith, 4) the rock was Christ—this was Augustine's view.

Many modern Protestants feel that view four best accommodates Scripture as a whole. Scripture elsewhere uses the analogy of a rock to depict Christ. "They all . . . drank from the spiritual rock that accompanied them, and that rock was Christ" (1 Cor. 10:4). It is suggested that Jesus was using a play on words to make His point. Lexicons indicate that Peter's name in Greek (*petros* [PET-ros]) denotes a rock in the sense of a surface stone; the foundation rock of the Church (*petra* [PET-rah]) denotes an outcropping of bedrock. Thus, Jesus was saying that rather than build His Church on a surface rock, He was to build it upon Himself as the foundation stone (cf. 1 Cor. 3:11; Eph. 2:20).

Since Hades is the abode of the dead and is thought of as Satan's kingdom, Jesus seems to have implied: 1) that even death will not thwart the Church, 2) Satan's kingdom will never prevail over Christ's, 3) Jesus will emerge from the tomb, 4) at Christ's order, all believers will be resurrected. In ancient cities, the city gate was the meeting place for the deliberation of the ruling elders. Thus "the gates of Hades" may be equivalent to the "council chambers of Hades."

Peter, on behalf of the Church, was to receive the keys of the Kingdom in the sense that it was his privilege and responsibility through the gospel to proclaim to mankind the conditions of entrance into the Kingdom. Though Peter is addressed here (Mt. 16:19), in John 20:23 Jesus affirmed a similar status for all the assembled company of disciples.

The terms binding and loosing (Mt. 16:19) were used by the rabbis to describe the authority of their declarations when they were acting in their role as judges. To bind was to forbid, to loose was to permit. These expressions relate to humanly administered discipline and leadership rather than ultimate spiritual or moral authority. When Christian leaders impose a set of rules or code for the members of their group, those members who violate that code offend not only their leaders, but also they offend the Lord.

As a conclusion to this confession, "Jesus warned [the disciples] not to tell anyone about him" (Mk. 8:30; cf. Mt. 16:20; Lk. 9:21). Perhaps the reason for this warning was that none of the disciples, including Peter, really understood the true nature of His Messiahship. Further, the nation had rejected Him, for they thought only of a militant leader to deliver them from Roman rule. Thus, it was not warranted that the disciples attempt to convince a prejudiced people who would only misunderstand.

8. Jesus' Prediction of His Death and Resurrection (Mt. 16:21-28; Mk. 8:31-9:1; Lk. 9:22-27)

With Calvary fast approaching, Jesus chose to speak plainly of what awaited Him. He declared that "he must ... suffer many things at the hands of the elders, chief priests and teachers of the law, and ... he must be killed and on the third day be raised to life" (Mt. 16:21). There was no alternative to the cross, it was God's plan that Jesus *"must* be killed" (v. 21; cf. Mk. 8:31; Lk. 9:23 —the same strong wording occurs in the original in all three synoptics). Peter, in objecting to such a fate for his Master, probably was the spokesman for the others also. Apparently Peter was so shocked at the prospect of Jesus' being killed, he didn't hear the promise of resurrection.

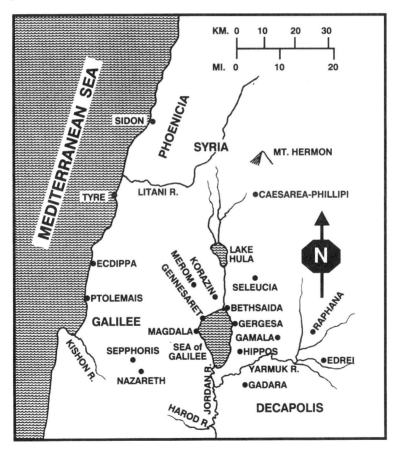

Figure 11: Sites of Jesus' later ministry in Galilee and beyond. During this period of Jesus' life and ministry Scripture provides very few specific geographic identifications.

The disciples' difficulties in grasping Jesus' destiny involved their will more than their mind and understanding. Peter had received Jesus' blessing for his great confession only a few hours before; he now heard the rebuke, "Get behind me, Satan!" (Mt. 16:23). Since Jesus had come to earth to die a redemptive death, any effort to hinder God's plan was satanic. In the third wilderness temptation (Mt. 4:8-10), Satan had tempted Jesus to forsake the cross and take a shortcut to kingship.

Jesus sought to communicate plainly His role as a suffering Savior rather than a conquering Messiah. Only as His followers grasped the conditions of His Messiahship could they know the conditions of discipleship. Jesus "called the crowd to him . . . and said: 'If anyone would come after me, he must deny himself and take up his cross and follow me'" (Mk. 8:34). This denial of self is not a controlling abnormal self-denial, but a positive and willing ongoing affirmation of one's status as God's obedient child.

Cross bearing implies a lifestyle that involves renouncing self advantage and comfort as the dominant elements in one's life. Instead, one purposes to serve God and one's fellows to the limit of one's energies. The guidelines for this behavior are discovered through complete submission to the will of God. To submit to His will repeatedly, as the verb indicates, may not entail martyrdom, but it does entail a constantly renewed spiritual commitment.

Followers of Jesus in the crucified life must repeatedly experience their own personal Calvary. Those who live selfishly and reject Christ will suffer a lost eternity. Those who deny Christ to save their physical life will lose their spiritual life. Jesus taught this truth in a paradox, "Whoever wants to save his life will lose it, but whoever loses his life for me will find it." (Mt.16:25). The obvious answer to Jesus' rhetorical question concerning trading one's soul (some versions use the word life) for the whole world (Mt. 16:26) is that it would be a disastrous loss.

Jesus declared that some who were in His audience would live to see Christ coming in His Kingdom. (cf. Mt. 16:28; Mk. 9:1; Lk. 9:27). There were, indeed, those present that day who later witnessed: the transfiguration, the triumphal entry, the resurrection, the Day of Pentecost, and various remarkable personal experiences. Each of these events were aspects of Christ's kingdom revelation, and also there was the soon-to-occur transfiguration. The fulfillment of Jesus' words, however, may have been intended to be primarily spiritual.

9. The Transfiguration of Jesus (Mt. 17:1-8; Mk. 9:2-8; Lk. 9:28-35)

The transfiguration appears to have been God's way of establishing a connection between Jesus' soon-to-occur suffering, and His future glory. After setting the stage, Scripture reports: "There [Jesus] was transfigured [Gk. *metamorphoo*] before them" (Mk. 9:2). The verb *metamorphoo* (met-ah-morph-AH-oh) is defined: to transform, change in form, transmute, metamorphose. It speaks of a transmutation or transformation that reveals the inner nature in a new form. Luke did not use the term, but he described the process. Perhaps because of his Gentile audience, Luke avoided in any way identifying Christianity with pagan myths of humans being metamorphosed into gods.

In undergoing this process, Jesus' "clothes became as bright as a flash of lightning" (Lk. 9:29). On this occasion Jesus may have, to some measure, changed back into His preincarnate heavenly glory. To the three disciples who witnessed it, the transfiguration was a reassuring proclamation that in spite of Jesus' predicted death, the glory of the Kingdom was still assured. Years later, Peter saw this event as a convincing basis of his faith: "We were eyewitnesses of his majesty" (2 Pet. 1:16).

Matthew and Mark date the transfiguration "after six days" following Jesus' prophecy of the coming Kingdom, and this would be the seventh day. Luke specifies, "About eight days after" (Lk. 9:28). Apparently, Luke counted part of a day as the whole. The transfiguration may have taken place at night, for that would explain the drowsiness of the disciples. Proposed sites are either Mt. Tabor or Mt. Hermon, but the latter is the preference of scholars. At 2,800 meters (9,200 feet) Mt. Hermon is the only "high mountain" (Mt. 17:1) in the region.

The three "inner circle" disciples (Peter, James, John), became "very sleepy" (Lk. 9:32) during the preliminary prayer. They were jolted wide awake upon seeing Jesus in His unveiled glory talking with Moses and Elijah also in glorified bodies. These Old Testament leaders, who were separated by some six centuries in their earthly lifetimes, now appeared together in association with the Messiah. As representatives of the Law and the Prophets, Moses and Elijah effectively endorsed God's divine Son. Their discussion of Jesus' "departure" (Gk. *exodos* [EX-o-dos]) which Jesus "was about to bring to fulfillment at Jerusalem" (Lk. 9:31) confirms Calvary's importance in God's eternal plan. Though *exodos* means departure, it is also a euphemism for death.

Peter's proposal for the construction of three shelter booths was a typical human reaction. Mark saw the suggestion as Peter's effort to cover his own confusion, for "He did not know what to say" (Mk. 9:6). Luke explains parenthetically, "He did not know what he was saying" (Lk. 9:33). Presumably, Peter hoped that physical facilities would assure the perpetuation of spiritual realities—clearly, a false premise. Someone has said of this occasion, "The Mount of Transfiguration is always more enjoyable than the daily ministry or the way of the cross."

The transfiguration concluded with the bright covering cloud and God's heavenly testimony, "This is my Son, whom I love. Listen to him" (Mk. 9:7). Upon the cloud's departure, only Jesus remained. Later, He instructed the three disciples, "Don't tell anyone what you have seen, Comments one writer, "The transfiguration was no miracle at all, the miracle was the veiling of His glory during all the rest of His earthly life."

10. The Descent from the Mount (Mt. 17:9-13; Mk. 9:9-13; Lk. 9:36)

Both Matthew and Mark note that as Jesus and the disciples descended the mountain He requested secrecy regarding what had occurred (cf. Mt. 17:9, Mk. 9:9). The disciples struggled with what Jesus meant in speaking of "rising from the dead." The concept of the resurrection of the Son of man baffled them. Their question about Elijah probably emerged because they had seen him confirm Jesus' earthly role at the transfiguration, but to their knowledge he had not fulfilled his predicted mission by coming as the forerunner of the Messiah. At this time, Jesus plainly declared that Elijah had come in the person of the now martyred John the Baptist (cf. Mt. 17:12-13).

The disciples failed to discern God's plan because they looked only for the physical return of Elijah. They overlooked the fact that John's coming, in the spirit and power of Elijah, could fulfill the prophecy spiritually (cf. Lk. 1:17). Jesus appears to have taught, however, that there would be a later physical fulfillment. He said, "To be sure, Elijah comes and will restore all things" (Mt. 17:11). This verse suggests that a resurrected Elijah will return to earth in a restorative ministry prior to Jesus' earthly kingdom. This interpretation would permit Elijah to be one of the two witnesses during the tribulation (cf. Rev. 11:3-12). Such events would comprise a twofold fulfillment of the return of Elijah. He came in spirit in John the Baptist, and he will come again literally in the end time to fulfill his own unique mission.

11. The Healing of the Boy Possessed by an Evil Spirit (Mt. 17:14-21; Mk. 9:14-29; Lk. 9:37-43a)

The disciples who were unable to minister healing to the boy possessed by an evil spirit are identified by Mark as "the other disciples" (Mk. 9:14). Presumably they were the nine who had not been present at the transfiguration. The critical teachers of the law, who apparently were dogging Jesus' footsteps, took advantage of the disciples' plight to "argue with them" and no doubt to belittle their ministry. The power to "drive out all demons" had been among those that Jesus had conferred when He sent out the Twelve some six months previously (cf. Lk. 9:1-2). For whatever reason, these disciples were unable to exercise this power.

To plead the cause of his son's healing, the father knelt humbly before Jesus and prayed, "Lord, have mercy" (Mt. 17:15). These words became a model for early Christian prayers. The father proceeded to name the affliction: "He has seizures [*seleniadzomai*] (sel-ane-ee-ADZE-o-my): (lit.) be moonstruck, thus be mentally unbalanced, suffer seizures, suffer epilepsy. (*selene* [sel-AYE-nay] = moon, cf. selenium)" (Mt. 17:15). Actually, of course, the boy was possessed by a demon. Jesus' response, "O unbelieving generation" is usually seen to have been directed either to the nation overall as represented by those present, or possibly to the disciples, rather than at the father. The failure to cope with evil spirits was ultimately a spiritual failure, and its primary cause was lack of faith.

Even as the boy was brought to Jesus, he suffered another convulsive attack. Literally, the demon "dashed him down" (Lk. 9:42) as a boxer might knock down an opponent. (cf. Gk. *rhesso* [RHAY-so]: throw down, dash to the ground). The father had said, "If you can do anything . . . " (Mk. 9:22), and thus he seems to have doubted Jesus' power. Jesus responded by challenging the man's faith, and reassuring him of the scope of divine power. He declared the principle, "Everything is possible for him who believes" (Mk. 9:23). The only limitation upon the power of God is human faith. In performing the exorcism Jesus gave two commands: 1) come out of him, 2) never enter him again.

Jesus explained the disciples' failure: "Because you have so little faith" (Mt. 17:20), and He instructed: "This kind can come out only by prayer" (Mk. 9:29). Sincere prayer vitally links with the exercise of faith, particularly in performing exorcisms. Perhaps the disciples were careless at this point, and they counted too much on their status and authority. The father's words, "I do believe; help me overcome my unbelief" (Mk. 9:24) have been paraphrased, "Help me just as I am, a doubter." He had come to Jesus with his need, and he pleaded for—and received—a response on the basis of whatever faith he now had.

In newer texts, the KJV references to prayer and fasting in Matthew 17:21, and to fasting in Mark 9:29 are omitted. Whatever the correctness of the text, it should be noted that externals, such as prayer and fasting, do not constitute spiritual power. Externals may or may not be evidence of a true inner reality. In the crisis of need, Jesus neither prayed nor fasted; He simply commanded the spirit to depart. In His personal lifestyle, however, Jesus always lived at that level of dedicated submission in which prayer and fasting were common events.

12. Jesus Again Predicts His Death and Resurrection (Mt. 17:22-23; Mk. 9:30-32; Lk. 9:43b-45)

At this time, Jesus with His accompanying disciples "left that place and passed through Galilee [on the way to Capernaum]. Jesus did not want anyone to know where they were, because he was teaching his disciples" (Mk. 9:30-31). Although Jesus was passing through Galilee, He had concluded His ministry there and He did not intend to revive it. For the second time, Jesus plainly told the disciples of His forthcoming death and resurrection. The fact that he would "be betrayed into the hands of men" (Mk. 9:31) was a new element, but He did not say that His betrayer would be one of the twelve disciples.

Once again, the disciples totally missed the promise of a resurrection. Mark reports, "they did not understand what he meant and were afraid to ask him about it" (9:32), Luke explains, "it was hidden from them, so that they did not grasp it" (9:45). Probably the disciples deliberately took refuge in their inability to understand, and they chose to reject the evidence of the predicted crucifixion. In their culture, power was revered, and a betrayed and slain Messiah was simply unthinkable.

13. Jesus Pays the Temple Tax (Mt. 17:24-27)

This visit to Capernaum was private, but the collector of temple taxes used the occasion to ask Peter about Jesus' payment of the temple tax. Since the tax, which was commonly called "the didrachma" (dy-DRAK-muh), related to Jewish temple worship, its payment was voluntary. The tax was based on Moses' assessment when the tabernacle was being built, but in Jesus' day the proceeds were used to operate the temple. Each adult male was expected to contribute a two-drachma piece (cf. Mt. 17:24) annually—usually during the Passover season. This amount would equal about two day's wages for a day laborer.

In His discussion with Peter, Jesus pointed out that since the temple was His Father's house, He actually was not required to pay the tax. For the sake of the impression that it would make if He ignored the tax, however, He was willing to pay. Jesus surrendered His privileges, but not His principles.

The four-drachma coin (Gk. *stater* or *tetradrachmon*, cf. Mt. 17:27) that Peter found in the fish's mouth, paid the tax for both Jesus and Peter. Five miraculous aspects of the incident of the coin in the fish's mouth are noted: 1) the fish was caught, 2) it was the first one caught, 3) there was money in it, 4) the money was the exact amount needed, and 5) it was in the fish's mouth.

A Galilean fish, the musht, is popularly called "Peter's fish" because tradition identifies it as the species that Peter caught on this occasion. The musht are attracted to bright objects, and they carry their incubating eggs in their mouths until they hatch. Since musht feed only on plankton, however, and they ignore a baited hook, scholars doubt the popular identification.

14. Jesus and the Children (Mt. 18:1-6; Mk. 9:33-37; Lk. 9:46-48)

When Jesus confronted His disciples about their dispute concerning which was greatest, they were embarrassed to have to admit the topic of their supposedly private argument. Their guilt before Jesus indicates that they were beginning to develop some sensitivities, though they were still thinking in terms of an earthly kingdom.

Jesus proceeded to use the occasion to instruct them concerning true greatness. He stated the fundamental spiritual principle as a paradox: "If anyone wants to be first, he must be the very last, and the servant [Gk. *diakonos*] of all" (Mk. 9:35). (*diakonos* [dee-AH-con-os]: a servant, one who freely attends to the needs of others.) By singling out a little child, Jesus declared that the most childlike person is the one of greatest worth. The evidence of greatness is not ambition to rule, but willingness to serve. Children exemplify teachablenss and obedience.

Tradition says that the child that Jesus chose at this time grew up to be St. Ignatius. Scholars have pointed out, however, that since He was in Capernaum, Jesus likely was in Peter's house (cf. Mk. 1:29), and probably the child was Peter's. By teaching the unique value of little children, both on this occasion and the one that followed, Jesus raised the estate of childhood for all time.

15. John's Mistaken Zeal Rebuked. Children Defended (Mt. 18:7-11; Mk. 9:38-50; Lk. 9:49-50)

In reply to John's report of forbidding one, not of the Twelve, to cast out demons in Jesus' name, Jesus declared that they should not have stopped him. A man who was a follower of Jesus and the enemy of Satan should be free to minister though he was not one of the Twelve and apparently had no commission or authorization from Jesus. Since they had failed to deliver the demon possessed boy (cf. Mt. 17:14-21), the disciples may have been jealous of the man's success.

Jesus affirmed the principle, "whoever is not against you is for you" (Lk. 9:50), or as Mark recorded it, "whoever is not against us is for us" (Mk. 9:40). These words have been called "the great minimal condition" of a relationship to Christ. At this time, Jesus was primarily teaching His followers not to hold a spirit of exclusivity. In Luke 11:23 His focus was to teach that nonbelievers may not hold a spirit of neutrality: "He who is not with me is against me."

Returning to His message concerning children, Jesus emphasized the disastrous results of offending little ones. In speaking of being thrown into the sea with a large millstone about one's neck, He used a startling figure. A large millstone would be one turned by a donkey as opposed to a smaller hand mill. Jesus declared that physical injury is much less serious than the spiritual destruction that will be suffered by those who lead children into sin. In their relationships, His followers must reject from their lives whatever offends. Jesus' rules for relating to children would apply similarly in relating to new converts and "spiritual babes."

Mark's quotation (9:48) concerning hell (Gk. *geenna* [GEH-en--na, cf. Gehenna]) is cited from Isaiah 66:24 (*LXX* version), and scholars suggest that he included it for the sake of his Roman readers. Mark 9:49 has no generally accepted explanation, but it perhaps is a reference to the universal human destiny to undergo judgment—though, of course, the believer's sins were judged on Calvary. In the Scriptural pattern, salt and fire are each symbols of purification. Just as salt purified Old Testament sacrifices, the Spirit's fire will today purge the human who sacrificially submits to God (cf. Mk. 9:50).

Jesus' statement "[Little ones'] angels in heaven always see the face of my Father in heaven" (Mt. 18:10), is one of the major

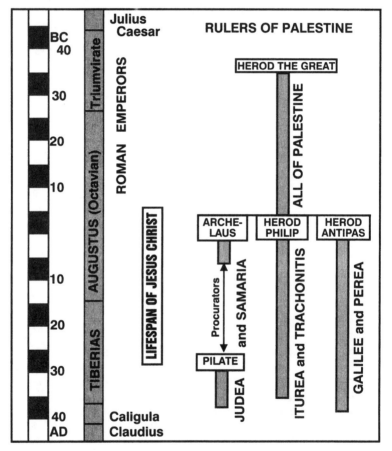

Figure 12: Time line relating rulers of Palestine during the gospel era. Herod the Great ruled all Palestine; at his death (4 B.C.) his kingdom was divided among three of his sons. The left column shows the succession of Roman emperors. The time line is marked in five-year increments, and the duration of a ruler's reign is shown by the shaded bar attached to his name.

texts used to support the doctrine of personal guardian angels (cf. also Ps. 34:7; Heb. 1:14). Modern versions omit Mt. 18:11 as a scribe's annotation, but the same words occur in Luke 19:10.

16. Jesus' Discourse on Forgiving Offenses (Mt. 18:15-22)

In this discourse Jesus set forth basic principles for a discipline process in the church. Notably, Jesus named His church only twice: 1) in this passage, and 2) in the promise of its building (cf. Mt. 16:18). The rules for restoring an offender provide for neither retaliation nor vengeance, but their goal is to gain a brother. 1) In cases of behavior requiring disciplinary action, the initiative rests upon the one who recognizes or suffers the wrong. In a private interview, he should seek to show the offender his fault. 2) If there is no response, there should be a conference between the two before witnesses. 3) If there is still no response, the parties should bring the case for a hearing before the entire church. 4) As a last resort, the rebel should be cut off from Christian society.

In this teaching, Jesus stressed that He was imparting an official mandate. Decisions by believers on earth would be ratified in heaven (cf. Mt. 16:19). United prayer was assured a special effectiveness: "if two of you on earth agree (Gk. *symphoneo* [sumphone-EH-oh]: to be of one mind, to harmonize, cf. symphony) about anything you ask for, it will be done for you by my Father in heaven" (Mt. 18:19). For believers to come together in His name (cf. v. 20) is to be submitted to His lordship.

Though the rabbis taught that three times were enough to forgive an offender, Jesus' response to Peter's question indicated that there should be no limit to forgiveness. Some versions render the count in Matthew 18:22 as seventy-seven (e.g., NIV); others render it seventy times seven (e.g. KJV, NASB). In either case, Jesus clearly taught that "forgiveness is not a matter of mathematics, but of love and character." The parable concerning the unforgiving servant that followed expands this idea. It is suggested that Peter may have raised this issue due to an actual problem between him and another disciple.

17. The Parable of the Unforgiving Servant (Mt. 18:23-35)

This parable sets forth the nature of forgiveness in Christ's Kingdom, and thereby grounds forgiveness in the nature of God. The king forgave a debt equivalent to the entire budget of the Roman Empire for a year. Such a vast figure represents each human's debt to God. The servant refused to forgive or show patience with a debt equivalent to a laborer's wages for a few weeks. The debtor was imprisoned, and also tortured.

The usual reason for torture in a debtor's prison was to force confession of hidden resources that could be applied to the debt. In this case, the torture would be only judgmental and penal. The outstanding generosity that the servant received from the king placed him under obligation to his fellow debtor.

In applying the parable, Jesus said, "This is how my heavenly Father will treat each of you unless you forgive your brother from your heart" (Mt. 18:35). If a believer adopts pagan standards, he will be judged as a pagan. The master: 1) withdrew his cancellation of the servant's debt, and 2) consigned him to a debtor's prison. Jesus appears to be teaching: 1) a believer's unforgiveness of another is a sin, 2) God will withdraw forgiveness from a believer who fails to forgive another.

18. Counting the Cost of Discipleship (Mt. 8:19-22; Lk. 9:57-62)

These incidents are not dated, but they are thought to relate to the Galilean ministry and therefore we insert them here.

The teacher's commitment, "I will follow you wherever you go" (Mt. 8:19), evidently impressed Jesus as shallow and smug. The Lord's response, "the Son of Man has no place to lay his head" (Mt. 8:20), probably was meant to emphasize that His interests were not material and earthly. He chose deliberately to discourage all but the most dedicated. Those who would follow Christ must recognize that this world is not their home. Scripture is silent concerning the teacher's response.

The disciple wished to bury his father first, but Jesus requested that he give first place to the eternal and heavenly. There is no duty above the disciple's duty to Christ, and this man had his priorities wrong. If the father was already dead, then his soul was now beyond the son's reach. If the son was saying that he desired to care for his father until he died, Jesus' point was that those without spiritual life could do that. The basic challenge to the disciple was to pursue those spiritual exercises that would develop his own soul. Scripture does not support the tradition that identifies this disciple as Philip.

The challenge to the one who requested time to bid farewell to those at home was similar. In that culture the farewell would likely be a week-long event with ongoing feasting. Jesus compared the disciple who looked back to prior interests to an incompetent plowman. A lightweight eastern plow would only maintain a correct furrow with constant guidance and attention. Since Jesus has gone ahead, the believer's eyes must be fixed on Him.

SEVEN:

THE LATER JUDEAN AND PEREAN MINISTRY (PART 1)

The story of Jesus in His exploits outside Galilee during His last half year of ministry brings together material from the synoptics, and also from John's Gospel. The first period of this era extends from the Feast of Tabernacles (probably October) to the Feast of Dedication (late December). It should be noted that Perea is not a Biblical name, but it traditionally identifies the land east of Jordan that the Bible describes as "beyond Jordan." Josephus was among the ancients who made reference to Perea.

I. JOHN'S REPORT OF THE FIRST PERIOD OF THIS MINISTRY

This section begins with a four-chapter portion from John's Gospel. Apart from one brief incident from Luke, all of the material that pertains to this period is unique to John. These four chapters are often headed: "The period of conflict," for they tell of the growing opposition to Jesus' ministry.

1. The Unbelief of His Brothers and Others (Jn. 7:1-9)

We have noted that Jesus had concluded His public ministry in Galilee. He seems to have returned there to visit His family, however, and for a time He remained there privately instructing His disciples. Out of this setting, Jesus' unbelieving brothers, in effect, advised, "Leave Galilee and go to Judea, for there you will have a larger audience and a higher profile."

Apparently the brothers saw Jesus with the potential to organize the Jews and mount a revolt against Roman rule. Their advice to Jesus at this time, however, put them on the side of the Jewish authorities who sought to destroy Him. Since Jesus responded that He would proceed to Jerusalem for the feast "at the right time," His brothers departed without Him. When Jesus later made the same journey, He did so in secret.

Although Jesus knew He was safe in God's plan, in order not to assume upon the Father, He acted prudently. "Jesus went around in Galilee, purposely avoiding Judea because the Jews there were waiting to take his life" (Jn. 7:1). Later, when He was in Judea and teaching in the temple His condemnation of the Pharisees led to their violent hatred toward Him. At that time, God's sovereign protection was evident: "No one seized him because his time had not yet come" (Jn. 8:20b).

2. Jesus Goes Privately to Jerusalem (Lk. 9:51-56; Jn. 7:10)

Jesus was committed to attending the Feast of Tabernacles events in Jerusalem, but He chose to travel privately through Samaria and to avoid the usual pilgrim caravans. He sent messengers ahead to arrange for Him and His party to stay in an unnamed Samaritan village. The Samaritans' awareness of His plans led them to deny the reservation, since these people resented anyone who identified with the Jews. Their rejection was the more tragic because had they known it, He was going to Jerusalem to provide salvation for them and for all mankind.

James and John proposed responding by repeating Elijah's miracle in bringing fire down upon his enemies (cf. 2 Kings 1:9-12). Such action was totally out of character for Jesus during His first advent—His fire ministry awaits His end time judgments. His rebuke upon the disciples may have begun the transformation that later led to John's spiritual ministry to these very people (cf. Acts 8:14-25). Probably this incident, or one similar to it, led Jesus to attach the name "Boanerges" (boh-uh-NUHR-jeez) —"sons of thunder"—to James and John (cf. Mk. 3:17).

3. Events at the Feast of Tabernacles (Jn. 7:11-52)

When Jesus appeared in Jerusalem about midway through the eight-day feast, He proved to be a prominent but controversial figure. He was present, not only to keep the Feast, but also to proclaim His message. The Jews watching for "that man" (v. 11) were likely made up of the hostile leaders and Sanhedrinists. They are distinguished from "the crowds" (cf. v. 12).

Jesus proceeded to teach in the temple courts, and though the people were amazed by his teaching, His unconventional background prompted questions. They asked, "How did this man get such learning without having studied?" (v. 15). They saw Him as unlearned because He had no credentials from a recognized rabbinical training school. Thus, He would have received no instruction in the traditional methods of Scripture interpretation. Nevertheless, Jesus brought informative and often exciting expositions and applications that warmed His hearer's hearts.

Jesus declared that God was the source of His teaching. He set forth the principle, "If anyone chooses to do God's will, he will find out whether my teaching comes from God or whether I speak on my own" (Jn. 7:17). He was willing to submit His doctrine to a pragmatic test: when it was applied, it would be found to work.

The teaching dialogue of Jesus (vv. 16-36) proved to be stern and uncompromising. He spoke of His heavenly calling and destiny, and He challenged the people to obey the spirit as well as the letter of the Old Testament law. He won followers, but He also won enemies. Among His listeners there was confusion regarding His status. One group attempted to apprehend Him (v. 30), and the chief priests and the Pharisees sent temple guards to arrest Him (v. 32). The listening crowed, however, apparently had no insight into the intentions of their leaders, and they thought His concerns for His life were illusionary (cf. v. 20).

Jesus answered the crowd's objections to His healing of the man at the pool on the Sabbath (Jn. 5:1-18) by pointing out that infants were routinely circumcised on the Sabbath. Thus, there was inconsistency in their application of the law of Moses. Jesus instructed, "Stop judging by mere appearances, and make a right judgment" (v. 24). The critical crowd was twice in error in identifying their Messiah. Though they declared "when the Christ comes, no one will know where he is from" (v. 27b), in fact Scripture predicted He would come from Bethlehem (cf. Micah 5:2). The crowd claimed to know "where this man is from" (v. 27a), but again they were in error for they associated Jesus only with Nazareth (cf. v. 41, Mt. 21:11).

Jesus declared that He was not on His own, but He was on a mission for the One who had sent Him (vv. 28-29). Since He had previously taught (cf. Jn. 6:44) that He had been sent of the Father, many would have known that He was speaking of being on a mission for His heavenly Father. Jesus' remark that in a short time He would go where they could not find Him (cf. 7:44) puzzled His hearers. They understood only in the natural realm, and matters of the spirit confused them. Ironically, their sarcastic suggestion that He must be intending to go to minister to the Jews of the dispora and to the Greeks was an accurate prophecy of the future course of the Christian outreach.

Out of this atmosphere of hardness and hostility, Jesus extended His invitation to His followers to experience outflowing streams of living water. In Jesus' time, the Feast of Tabernacles emphasized the pouring out of water. According to one version of events at that time, each morning for seven days, the priest, bearing a golden pitcher of water to be poured out on the temple altar, led a procession from the Pool of Siloam. The eighth day he carried no water, but with all the concluding activities otherwise, it was the "greatest day of the Feast" (Jn. 7:37).

Jesus' offer of "streams of living water" (v. 38) on the so-called "waterless day" was His special gesture to fill the lack. He applied the water symbolism of the Feast to speak of His promise of the gift of the Spirit of life. His reference to believing "as the Scripture has said" appears to link with His promise to the woman at the well (cf. Jn. 4:14), and to such Biblical accounts as Numbers 20:11; Zechariah 14:8; Ezekiel 47:1-9; Isaiah 44:3; and Joel 3:18. In extending His offer, Jesus stood up and called out in a loud voice in order to achieve maximum visibility and authority. John explains that He was announcing a new relationship to the Holy Spirit. In the new era, humans could enjoy both an indwelling and an outflowing of the Spirit that would constitute a divine-human partnership providing for new heights of spiritual enrichment.

Jesus' audiences sharply disagreed concerning His identity and credibility. Some among those who accepted Him were prepared to recognize Him as the Prophet (cf. v. 40; Deut. 18:15-19), while others saw Him as the Christ (i.e., Messiah). Part of the problem was incomplete or false information about Him and His place of origin that we have already noted. Some of the ignorance was no doubt deliberate. Listed reactions included: disagreement (vv. 40-44), hostility (vv. 45-49), and cautious faith (vv. 50-52). Just as in our day, when humans are confronted by the divine Christ, they cannot remain neutral but their response is often irrational and misinformed.

The guards sent to arrest Jesus (cf. v. 32) came back empty handed and they reported: "No one ever spoke the way this man does" (v. 46). They inferred that He spoke like God. The response of the Pharisees, and their arguments and denunciations reveal their blind prejudice. They rejected the report of the guards, and they scoffed at the ignorance of the mob who believed.

When Nicodemus spoke of due legal process, rather than respond to his logic, they attacked his person: "Are you from Galilee, too?" (v. 52). At this time, the only real objection they could find against Jesus was the supposed place of His birth. In denouncing Galilee, they apparently forgot that the prophet Jonah was from that province.

4. The Woman Taken in Adultery (Jn. 7:53-8:11)

Though this story is in 900 manuscripts, its right to be in the Bible is questioned because it is not in two of the earliest, nor in eleven later manuscripts. Also, it is rarely cited by church fathers, there are numerous textual differences between many manuscripts, and Eusebius (c 260-340) specifically assigns it to the *Apocrypha*. Those who defend its inclusion suggest that it was indeed a part of John's original manuscript, but that it was temporarily removed by overzealous scribes who felt it condoned immorality. An alternate view, held by some, is that this is an authentic account of an incident in Jesus' ministry, but it is a later addition to John's Gospel.

The setting implies that the teachers and Pharisees, with the woman as their prisoner, arrived as an interruption to Jesus' teaching session in the temple. The incident was arranged as a plot to attempt to trick Jesus into ruling contrary to the Law of Moses and in favor of their traditions. "They were using this question as a trap, in order to have basis for accusing him" (v. 6). How it was that they had apprehended only the woman, and what had become of her partner, is not explained.

Although Moses had said, "both the adulterer and the adulteress must be put to death" (Lev. 20:10), it appears that at this time this law was not being enforced. The Romans did not ordinarily allow the Jews to inflict capital punishment[1], and they had no concern for violations of Jewish law. No doubt Jesus' critics hoped that He would take a stand on the matter. He could either reject the Law as too harsh, or He could demand its enforcement. If He rejected the law they could charge Him with sabotaging Scripture, if He asked for its enforcement He would drastically offend the public. Also, if He called for her death He would be violating Roman law.

Jesus' action in stooping down and writing on the ground would have served to increase the dramatic tension and, in effect, to refer the argument to the consciences of the critics. As each departed, he tacitly confessed his own guilt. An ancient version adds a clause, "He wrote in the dust the sins of each one of them." Although this addition is not confirmed, it suggests a possible reason for the outcome.

Mosaic Law required two or three witnesses to pronounce judgment upon a wrong doer, and for a witness to cast the first stone. The incident involving the woman was shabby and sordid, and it called to question the sinlessness of the witnesses. The accusers were defeated by their own consciences, and when the last two made their exit, the case against the woman collapsed. Jesus, the sinless One, alone had the right to dismiss the woman. In freeing her, Jesus upheld the law's standard of justice, but He pointedly instructed her to leave her life of sin.

5. Jesus' Discourses in Jerusalem. The Hostility of the Pharisees (Jn. 8:12-59)

Jesus' "Light of the world" discourse (8:12) may have been prompted by the lamplight activities at the Feast of Tabernacles. As part of the festivities each year, four very large lamps (or candelabra) were lit in the temple courtyard. The people gathered to sing and worship by their light. According to the *Talmud* these lamps were fifty cubits high (about seven stories). Since the Feast was over at this time, the great candelabra would no longer be lit.

The Pharisees objected to Jesus' self-endorsement in pronouncing Himself the light of the world, for they rightly recognized that by these words He was claiming to be the Messiah. Traditionally, one of the titles of the Messiah was "Light," and David had written, "The LORD is my light and my salvation" (Ps. 27:1). In replying to the Pharisees, Jesus used the first personal pronoun twenty-three times. He claimed the prerogative of bearing witness on His own behalf (v. 14), for light needs no confirmation—if it shines, it shines.

---

1 Apparently there were times, such as at the stoning of Stephen (cf. Acts 7:54-60), when the action of a Jewish mob defied Roman rule.

Jesus' procedure in His dialog with the Pharisees was to enumerate His status and destiny and to contrast His exemplary divine credentials with their confused and invalid human credentials. In contrast with the Pharisees, Jesus knew His origin and destiny, but they did not (v. 14). He passed judgment on no one (though His life was a judgment); they judged by human standards (v. 15). In failing to recognize Him, the Pharisees were ignorant of the Father (v.19). Jesus was from above; the Pharisees were from beneath (v. 23); He was not of this world, they were of this world (v. 23). Jesus' supporting witnesses were: 1) His own word, and 2) His Father (v. 18).

	Matt.	Mark	Luke	John
Jesus ministers in Perea	19:1-2	10:1-2	13:22-30	
Man with dropsy healed			14:1-6	
Teaching on humility			14:7-14	
Parables of Luke 15			15:1-32	
Raising of Lazarus				11:1-44
● THE LAST JOURNEY TO JERUSALEM				
The ten lepers			17:11-19	
Rich young ruler	19:16-30	10:17-31	18:18-30	
Request of James and John	20:20-28	10:35-45		
Conversion of Zacchaeus			19:1-10	
Parable of the minas			19:11-27	
Jesus nears Jerusalem				11:54-57

Figure 13: Time line of highlights during the last three months of Jesus' ministry—probably January through March.

The passage consisting of verses twenty-one to thirty has been compared with Jesus' discourse with Nicodemus. In verse twenty-four His literal words were: "For if you do not believe that I am, you will die in your sins." These words link with Exodus 3:14. (For a further comment see the discussion on verse 58 below). To the question, "Who are you?" Jesus replied, "Just what I have been claiming" (v. 25). He thus avoided a direct confrontation on the issue of His identity as the Son of God. Jesus declared that He would be known through His crucifixion and in response "many put their faith in him" (v. 30). They responded to His testimony of Himself.

Though Jesus addressed "the Jews who had believed him" (v. 31), in the replies that followed, beginning with verse thirty-three, He seems to have been dialoguing with unbelievers. In verse thirty-two, however, He set forth a major spiritual promise: "you will know the truth, and the truth will set you free." The Jewish claim that they had "never been slaves of anyone" (v. 33) was false, for they had a long history of national bondage under a succession of five nations, and they were slaves of sin. They boasted of their heritage in Abraham, but Jesus pointed out that their attitudes and actions denied them a place in the chosen line (v. 40). Someone has commented, "They had Abraham's blood in their veins, but not his faith in their hearts."

Their claim "We are not illegitimate children" (v. 41) is seen by some commentators (beginning with Origen in the third century) as a veiled sneer against Jesus' person, in view of the circumstances of His birth. Since they rejected truth and embraced lies, Jesus declared, "You belong to your father, the devil" (v. 44). Their charge, "you are . . . demon-possessed" (v. 48), was their way of saying that He was insane. Jesus had heard the charge that He was demon-possessed before, and He would hear it again (cf. Jn. 7:20; 8:52; 10:20).

In verses fifty through fifty-nine, Jesus proclaimed Himself as the One who would deliver from death. No doubt by the question "Who do you think you are?" (v. 53), Jesus' opponents hoped to provoke Him into blasphemous claims that would give them the excuse to stone Him. When He declared that He was a contemporary with Abraham (v. 56), they responded, "You are not yet fifty years old" (v. 57), and thus, either carelessly or deliberately, they estimated much too high (cf. Lk. 3:23). It is possible that they used fifty as a marker, for in that culture one was counted a senior at age fifty.

In verse fifty-eight, for the third time in this address, Jesus identified Himself as the absolute "I Am." (cf. vv. 24, 28, 58, cf. Exod. 3:14). The NIV twice adds the words "the one I claim to be" (vv. 24 and 28) and thus somewhat disguises Jesus' claim. (The corners enclosing the clause are NIV's way to indicate added non-textual material.) In declaring Himself to be the "I Am," Jesus affirmed His past and future eternity, and depicted Himself sovereign over time.

Confronted with the absolute timeless Christ, the majority of His Jewish audience remained hostile and unbelieving. They saw His claim as totally blasphemous. From their previous actions in name calling, they now exhibited their total defeat in argument by resorting to physical violence and taking up stones with the intention of stoning Him. Perhaps Jesus' escape was in part through blinding their eyes to cause Him to be unrecognized. Augustine wrote, "Jesus, as a man, fled from the stones; but woe to that one from whose heart of stone, God flees."

6. The Healing of the Man Born Blind (Jn. 9:1-41)

The man blind from birth was probably simply a beggar to his neighbors, he was an object of theological debate to the disciples, and to the Pharisees he was a potential trap for Jesus. But to Jesus, he was a human being in need. The issues involved have much in common with Job's tragedies, and apparently human understanding had progressed very little from the time of Job.

The Pharisees tended to see all sickness as the result of one's personal sin, and the disciples seem to have adopted this view also (cf. v. 2). Someone describes it as "an all-too-cheap pastoral recipe that tastes like the theology of Job's friends." To account for one born physically challenged, the Pharisees suggested such possibilities as: he had sinned in another life, or he had sinned while still in the womb, or he would sin in his future life and God was acting on the basis of His foreknowledge.

In the case of this man, Jesus denied that anyone was guilty of a specific sin that had caused his infirmity. He saw the man's illness as an opportunity for God's glory rather than the basis of a problem. Though it was the Sabbath, out of a heart of compassion, Jesus proceeded to minister healing.

Jesus' use of clay made from spittle was an eccentric, and to some an offensive procedure, that was surely not required to convey a miracle healing. The use of clay would, however, involve the blind man's senses, and require his participation in washing it from his eyes. Kneading clay was specifically forbidden in the Pharisees' Sabbath regulations, and thus Jesus may have chosen this procedure to force a confrontation.

A notable aspect of the blind man's involvement was obedience, for he responded by proceeding as instructed. John notes that Siloam means "Sent" (cf. v. 7), and perhaps the pool was given this name because it stored water conveyed or "sent" from the Gihon Spring by Hezekiah's tunnel. The open air pool was about the size of a small swimming pool, and a landmark in Jerusalem. After the man "came home seeing" he faithfully witnessed to his neighbors (9:8-12), to the Pharisees (9:13-17), and to the hostile Jews (9:24-34).

There was nothing about the healing that the Pharisees could deny, and honest members among them recognized it as a "miraculous sign." (cf. v. 16). When the critical ones said of Jesus, "We don't even know where he comes from" (v. 29), the former blind man responded, "If this man were not from God, he could do nothing" (v. 33). The petty action of the Jewish leaders in "throwing out" (vv. 34,35)[2] the man clearly admitted their defeat. Though the KJV quotes Jesus "Dost thou believe on the Son of God?" (v. 35), most modern versions, reflecting manuscript revisions, read: "Son of Man."

In a later contact, as the man looked upon the face of Jesus for the first time, he affirmed His Messiahship and proceeded to worship Him (cf. vv. 37-38). Jesus concluded the incident by pointing out that His ministry involved both opening the eyes of the blind, and bestowing judicial blindness upon the willfully ignorant. He declared, "For judgment I have come into this world" (v. 39). Though "God did not send his Son into the world to condemn the world" (Jn. 3:17), unfortunately, many reject Christ and come under judgment. For them, the One who came to bring salvation becomes the occasion of condemnation.

Scripture vividly traces the blind man's growth in belief. At the outset, he obediently followed Jesus' instructions (v. 7). He testified openly and enthusiastically, identifying Him as "the man they call Jesus" (v. 11). He recognized Jesus as a prophet (v. 17). He defended Jesus and the reality of his healing in spite of the Pharisees' ridicule (vv. 24-34). He endured persecution for his faith (v. 34). He continued to want to know more about Jesus (v. 36). He confirmed his belief and worshiped Jesus (v. 38). In these seven steps the former blind beggar reached belief's final stage—the sincere worship of Jesus Christ.

7. The Discourse on the Good Shepherd (Jn. 10:1-21)

This passage is notable in being a "figure of speech" (v.6)[3] rather than John's usual direct discourse. Though Jesus was really teaching about human spiritual destiny, He talked about sheep. Scholars count at least eighteen statements that describe the shepherd, and five that provide facts about the sheep. In oriental practice, a shepherd leads his sheep—they are driven only

---

2　The Greek verb is simply *ekballo* (ek-BAWL-oh) which means to drive out, expel, throw out more or less forcibly. However, verse 22 notes that anyone who acknowledged Christ would be "put out of the synagogue." Thus, the NEB renders verse 34 "Then they expelled him from the synagogue." In addition to the spiritual and religious loss, the victim of expulsion would likely be socially ostracized from the local community.

3　Gk. *paroimia* (par-oy-ME-ah): figure of speech, a cryptic saying, similitude, allegory, illustration. In usual references, a *paroimia* is clearly distinct from a parable.

when on their way to slaughter. Thus, the role of following the shepherd is indeed a suitable figure for Christian discipleship.

The implied scenario of the Biblical figure (vv. 1-5) is a sheep-fold at the beginning of a new day. Several flocks have spent the night in an enclosed sheep pen. A shepherd has arrived and he is admitted by the watchman. The shepherd assembles his flock by calling. Only his sheep respond to his voice. In that culture sheep were primarily raised for wool rather than for meat. Thus, individual sheep might remain with the shepherd for years. There was ample opportunity to teach them to respond to the shepherd's call and to their own name.

The interpretations implied include: **sheep pen** (sheep-fold)—the earthly church, particularly as it mirrors the heavenly Church; **the shepherd of the sheep**—Jesus; **the watchman** (doorkeeper)—the Holy Spirit working through His ministers; **the sheep**—the Lord's people within Judaism, and also Gentile believers outside Judaism (cf. other sheep, v. 16); **a stranger** (v. 5)—a false leader; **gate** (vv. 7, 9)—God's way of salvation embodied in Jesus Christ; **the hired hand** (hireling, v. 12)—a "professional" religious leader (as the Pharisees); **thieves and robbers** (v. 8)—false saviors, "sheep stealers," self-appointed teachers and leaders, thieves steal by plan, robbers use violence; **the wolf** (v. 12)—Satan.

In every reference in the original, the word "sheep" is in the plural. The focus is upon the Lord's concern for His people as a corporate body. The words , "I am the gate (door)" (v. 9), depict the oriental shepherd standing in the gate to the sheep pen. There, he inspects and passes the sheep one by one as they come and go. He permits their freedom, but restrains them when danger threatens, and, of course, keeps out predators. The figure of the gate is also used in the Old Testament: "This is the gate of the LORD through which the righteous may enter" (Ps. 118:20).

Although the expression "good shepherd" (v. 11) is the usual translation, the adjective used (Gk. *kalos* (kal-OS): beautiful, precious, noble, blameless) would warrant "beautiful shepherd," or even "brave shepherd." Jesus indeed laid down His life for the sheep (vv. 11, 15, 17, 18), for He died, not because He fell victim to crucifixion, but because He voluntarily plunged into death.

In the figure, verse sixteen is describing the situation when there is a very large flock. In that case, the shepherd would divide them and assign each divided group to an individual fold to spend the night. By day, the entire flock would be rejoined. The unity of the flock continues to be assured because the sheep respond to and obey one shepherd. Jesus is teaching that the unity of the church is not primarily a matter of rigid or clever human organization, but of a loyal response to Him.

Once again some who heard Jesus' words declared Him to be demon-possessed (cf. v. 20). But at this time, also, there were those who accepted and defended His ministry (cf. v. 21).

8. Discourses During the Feast of Dedication (Jn. 10:22-39)

Some harmonies interject Luke chapters ten to thirteen prior to these events. They visualize a two to three-month interval between John 10:21 and 10:22. Since this chronology is uncertain, however, we will complete this portion of John.

In modern times, the Feast of Dedication is usually called the Feast of Lights, or Hanukkah. It involves, among other things, an eight-day candle lighting event, and it is observed by the Jews at a time more or less parallel to the Christian's Christmas. Hanukkah commemorates the victory of the Jewish leader, Judah (Judas) Maccabaeus (or Hasmonean), over the Syrians, making possible the cleansing and rededication of the temple in 164 B.C.

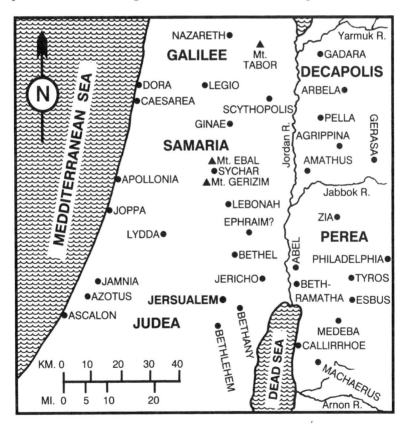

Figure 14: Scripture names few sites of Jesus' later Judean-Perean ministry but He probably knew many of these places.

In the year previous, Judas had led a successful rebellion against the Syrian conquerors who, under the leadership of Antiochus Epiphanes (an-TIE-uh-kuhs eh-PIF-uh-neez), had attempted to impose paganism upon the Jews.

On this occasion, Jesus was confronted by a group of Jews as He walked in Solomon's Colonnade (or porch) in the temple. The spokesman asked, "If you are the Christ, tell us plainly" (v. 24). These critics apparently wanted to provoke Jesus into making a definitive statement of His deity that they could use to charge Him with blasphemy. They then would have grounds to demand His execution.

Jesus replied by pointing out that He had already told them, but they did not believe because there were not His sheep (cf. vv. 25-26). The problem was not that Jesus had not informed them, but because of their prior prejudices and misconceptions, they had not correctly heard what He had said. In responding to these shortcomings and confusions, Jesus proceeded to describe the traits that distinguished believers from unbelievers.

Christendom has long debated the meaning of Jesus' words: "I give [my sheep] eternal life, and they shall never perish; no one can snatch them out of my hand" (v. 28). The Calvinist sees this passage as a definitively strong statement of the believer's security. The Arminian may agree that heaven's resources assure the stability of the provision of salvation, but he typically argues that even those who are soundly saved retain their powers of choice. Though no other person, including Satan, can snatch away the convert, that one himself has the power to choose to give up his faith. Fortunately, however the issue is settled, most agree that teaching on the believer's security should be balanced with teaching on the believer's responsibility.

The Greek text of John 10:29 is disputed, but the NIV chooses a rendering based on the older text. An example of the newer text is NRSV: "What my Father has given me is greater than all else, and no one can snatch it out of the Father's hand." Apparently, the fact that the newer text seems to introduce confusing concepts has encouraged many scholars to reject the change.

In declaring "I and the Father are one" (v. 30), Jesus used the neuter gender for the word "one." The statement, therefore, does not say that they are one person, but that they are a unity. It has been said, "His words are more a matter of relationships than a matter of metaphysics." Jesus thus made a strong public declaration of His divine status, and the Jews clearly understood these words to affirm His deity. Their immediate response was to pick up stones and threaten to stone Him (cf. v. 31).

To defend His right to identify Himself as one with God, Jesus referred to Biblical usage in Psalm 82:6 (cf. vv. 34-38). There, certain flesh and blood humans are called "gods," apparently in recognition of their status as leaders or royalty. Jesus argued that if those men could be called gods, then He was not guilty of blasphemy when He declared, "I am God's Son" (v. 36). In this discourse, Jesus declared incidentally the principle: "the Scripture cannot be broken" (v. 35). These words are a definitive comment affirming the binding authority of Scripture.

In stressing His special relationship with the Father, Jesus declared: "the Father is in me, and I in the Father" (v. 38). Later, in His upper room discourse to His disciples, He repeated these identical words (cf. Jn. 14:11). At this time this statement stirred the Jews to great hostility.

9. Jesus' Retreat to Perea (Jn. 10:40-42)

As His response to such glaring animosity, Jesus chose to withdraw from ministering in the city of Jerusalem. He "went back across the Jordan to the place where John had been baptizing in the early days. Here he stayed (Jn. 10:40; cf. Jn. 1:28; 3:28). Scripture notes simply, "In that place many believed in Jesus" (Jn. 10:42). As far as Scripture records, He did not return to Jerusalem until Palm Sunday.

II. LUKE'S ACCOUNT OF THE SECOND PERIOD OF THIS MINISTRY

An eight-chapter narrative block (Luke ten through seventeen), that is almost entirely unique to Luke, now follows in the gospel harmony. These events are dated in January and February during Jesus' last three months of ministry. Luke chapters ten through thirteen (to verse twenty-one) will be covered in the balance of this chapter.

1. The Mission of the Seventy-Two (Lk. 10:1-24)

The seventy-two, or in traditional manuscripts, the seventy, included the twelve disciples plus other dedicated followers of Jesus. The Twelve had been instructed, "Do not go among the Gentiles. . . . Go rather to the lost sheep of Israel" (Mt. 10:5-6). The thirty-six (or thirty-five) teams of this group were assigned to no particular target, and they may have included some Gentile communities in their ministry. It is assumed, that in contrast to the Twelve who ministered in Galilee, they ministered primarily in Judea. They were to be advance heralds announcing Jesus' planned visit that would follow.

Jesus instructed these missionaries to consider themselves part of the family in which they were staying, rather than visitors or paying guests. Their ministry in healing the sick (v. 9) would open doors for them. They should not seek luxury, but appreciatively accept whatever fare the home provided. They were appointed as official representatives of their Lord: "He who listens to you listens to me; he who rejects you rejects me" (v. 16).

Because they traveled without funds or any extra equipment, their acceptance in a community and a home required a decision. People had to choose to accept them and contribute their accommodation as a gift. Most of these conditions had applied previously when the original Twelve were sent forth (p. 90).

It was likely several weeks later when the seventy-two returned. They joyfully reported, "Lord, even the demons submit to us in your name" (v. 17). Jesus' comment regarding Satan's fall (v. 18) may relate to Satan's past moral failure that resulted in his expulsion from residence in God's holy mount (cf. Ezek. 28:12-15 [Satan is described under the figure of the king of Tyre]; Isa. 14:12-15; 1 Tim. 3:6). Since Satan still has access to the heavenlies (cf. Job 1:6; Eph. 6:12), Jesus' words may also have been prophetic. In the future there is to be a further casting down of Satan (cf. Rev. 12:7-9).

The mention of "authority to trample on snakes and scorpions" (v. 19) can be taken as literal, since in that land these creatures were hidden hazards. A spiritual application is also possible, since Satan is depicted as the "ancient serpent" (Rev. 20:2). Jesus pointed out that a greater work than any the disciples had done had been done for them: "rejoice that your names are written in heaven" (v. 20).

In responding to their achievements and report, Jesus was "full of joy [Gk. *agalliao*] through the Holy Spirit" (Lk. 10:21). This occasion is the only one in Scripture in which Jesus is described as joyful. The verb *agalliao* (a-gal-lee-A-oh) denotes: to exalt, be glad, be overjoyed, or even to jump for joy. As He summarized their experience, Jesus pronounced a special beatitude upon the seventy-two: "Blessed are the eyes that see what you see" (Lk. 10:23). They had enjoyed experiences denied to great leaders such as prophets and kings.

2. The Parable of the Good Samaritan (Lk. 10:25-37)

This parable, which is found only in Luke, is one of the best known and loved of all of Jesus' parables. Since it provides a direct example of behavior that should be imitated, it is classified as an illustrative parable. A parable such as the wheat and the weeds that teaches by analogy is known as a story parable.

The expert in the law, or lawyer, related, of course, to the law of Moses. His question was meant "to test Jesus," or as one version renders the scenario, "[he] tried to trap him [i.e., Jesus]" (TEV). In his first response to Jesus, the lawyer-theologian commendably quoted Deuteronomy 6:5 and Leviticus 19:18. Since the question was not sincere, however, when Jesus gave him a simple but adequate answer, the lawyer sought to complicate it. The parable of the Good Samaritan was Jesus' response to his question, "Who is my neighbor?" (v. 29).

The events that Jesus described were sufficiently common in the experiences of that culture that the Jerusalem-Jericho road was known as "the path of blood." This road was approximately twenty-seven kilometers (seventeen miles) in length, and the journey from Jerusalem to Jericho involved a descent of over a kilometer (one-half mile). In the parable, the priest showed "dainty neglect," and the Levite showed "cold curiosity." All of Christendom speaks of the "good Samaritan," but this combination of words does not occur in the parable.

Jesus' choice of the Samaritan as the hero of the parable would likely have conflicted sharply with the lawyer's prejudices. Thus, he would not bring himself to identify the Samaritan by name, and he spoke only of "the one who had mercy" (v. 37). He did, however, recognize the principle of neighborliness, and show he had gleaned the lesson: Our neighbor is whoever needs our help. Jesus' instructions, "Go and do likewise" could be literally rendered, "Keep doing likewise" (v. 37). Since Jews of that era held that only another Jew could be one's neighbor, these words would be to the lawyer a radical challenge.

3. Jesus the Guest of Mary and Martha at Bethany (Lk. 10:38-42)

During His last few months on earth, Jesus appears to have made His home with Mary, Martha, and Lazarus in the village of Bethany near Jerusalem. Typically, the younger sister, Mary, was found at Jesus' feet as an eager student. Thus, verse thirty-nine reports the first of three such occasions (cf. Jn. 11:32; 12:3). On this occasion, Martha's housekeeping duties became oppressive so that they caused her to be "distracted by all the preparations" (v. 40), (Gk. *perispao* [per-is-PAH-oh]: dragged about in several directions, or pulled all around.)

Though the NIV records simply that Martha "came to [Jesus]" (v. 40b), since the verb often connotes suddenness, the J.B. Phillips version reads, "she burst in." Martha accused Jesus of being uncaring: "Lord, don't you care . . . ?" Jesus responded with a gentle rebuke. He did not disapprove of her dedication to household tasks, but only of her worry and excessive concern.

Jesus' statement, "Mary has chosen what is better" (lit. Mary has chosen the good part) (v. 42), was a defense rather than a comparison. That which was better (the "good part") was fellowship with Him through attending to His eternal Word. To be occupied with Christ is more to be desired than to be occupied for Christ. The "only one thing needed" seems to many scholars to relate to the cultivation of spiritual life in preparation for the life to come. Some suggest, however, that in these words Jesus was telling Martha that a simple one-dish meal was all that was necessary to feed her siblings and Him.

4. Jesus Again Teaches His Disciples to Pray (Lk. 11:1-13)

Jesus' prayer on this occasion (v. 1) is not given. At this time, however, He again shared a prayer model with His disciples. The so-called "Lord's prayer" had been given probably sixteen months previously (Mt. 6:9-13), but this later version is more general in its description and identification of God. Both Catholics and Protestants in worship usually recite Matthew's version, though the Catholic form is based upon an edited manuscript that omitted the traditional Protestant doxology.

The parable of the friend at midnight depicts God as He appears to many humans who come to Him in prayer with a need. The special insight that the parable reveals is that God will do what is consistent with His character by responding to the prayer that persists. The quality that achieves results in the man who asks is his boldness (v. 8)[4]—older versions spoke of importunity. The homeowner complained about the hour and the inconvenience, but not about his friend's boldness.

There is much more to the theology of prayer than this one truth, but because persistence is such a vital principle, in making this point, the parable serves its purpose. In general, Scripture depicts God as a kind heavenly Father who cares and loves. He is not at all reluctant to provide for His people, though He desires that they persist in asking. The pattern of asking, seeking, and knocking[5] assures the perpetuation of a vital Father-child relationship so that the believer's God is warmly personal. The best earthly father-child relationship is a model of that which God is prepared to extend toward His children.

5. Jesus Again Accused of Being in League with Beelzebub (Lk. 11:14-36)

At this time, Jesus was apparently ministering in Judea where demon possession was less common than elsewhere. The demon He exorcised had caused his victim to be mute. A parallel event, perhaps eighteen months earlier in Galilee, involved a victim who was both mute and blind (cf. Mt. 12:22-32). In each of these instances, Jesus was charged with performing an exorcism through the power of Beelzebub (i.e., Satan), the prince of demons. His critics recognized that His works were supernatural, but they questioned the source of His power. The earlier occasion had led to the discourse about the unpardoned sin.

Jesus responded to the charges of Satanic empowering much as He had previously. He again pointed out that if He was working by Satan's power, then Satan was working against himself. Jesus indicated that He drove out demons "by the finger of God" (v. 20,

---

4 Gk. *anaideia* (an-AY-die-ah): persistence, impudence, shamelessness, importunity.

5 These verbs are in the present tense implying continuous action.

cf. Exod. 8:19), and this expression is understood to be a reference to the Holy Spirit. The description of the exorcised evil spirit who returns with seven other spirits (vv. 24-26), is thought to teach the futility of mere human reformation in contrast to a radical new birth. The one who only "turns over a new leaf" and whose heart is undecided concerning Jesus Christ is vulnerable to renewed Satanic attacks.

The exclamation of the woman in the crowd (vv. 27) was clearly intended to confer honor and acclaim upon Mary. Jesus used the occasion to declare His approval of those who would believe in Him. He declared that fleshly ties are secondary to genuine faith and obedience. Without dishonoring His human mother, He pronounced a blessing upon all who heard God's Word. To associate with Him spiritually was more significant than to be His relative in the flesh. One's status in the family of God was the one supremely important relationship.

In yet another effort to impress the message, Jesus again spoke of the "sign of Jonah" (v. 29). The experiences of this Old Testament prophet confirmed the significance and reality of Christ's forthcoming resurrection. The fact that He would conquer death and emerge from its bonds would constitute Jesus' ultimate credential. Jesus declared, however, that He was able to offer very much more than either Solomon (v. 31) or Jonah (v. 32). He was not so much comparing Himself with prior servants of God, but He was saying that a new set of spiritual provisions was being introduced. The NIV attempts to convey this interpretation in footnote renderings: "something [instead of "one"] greater than Solomon . . . something greater than Jonah."

At this point, Jesus apparently repeated part of the teaching He had given in the Sermon on the Mount (cf. Mt. 6:22-23). Though people use a lamp correctly, they do not always show the same wisdom in the use of spiritual light. The problem in those who reject the Lord is not in the light, but in their failure to respond to it. The heart that is truly open to the light will receive light from Christ, the true light. The "good" or "single" eye (v. 34) is one that sees a clear undistorted image; it is not confused by double vision or lack of illumination. People are meant to see clearly by faith. When they deliberately will not to see the truth, they sink into darkness and error.

6. Jesus Dines with a Pharisee but Denounces Pharisees (Lk. 11:37-54)

The meal appears to have been a midmorning snack or brunch, with only light foods or fruit being served. Thus, no elaborate washing preparation was really called for, and the issue was not hygiene but religious belief. It is said that some Pharisees' obsession with washing was based on the superstition that one's hands could be contaminated by demons, and these could be washed off with water.

Jesus responded to criticism by explaining that washing in water did not cleanse one's heart. External behavior was no substitute for genuine inner penitence. In turn, Jesus addressed the shortcomings of the Pharisees (vv. 39-44), and then those of the experts in the law (lawyer-theologians). He pronounced three woes upon each group. Newer versions have deleted references to teachers of the law (scribes) in Jesus' denunciations, but this group is named among Jesus' enemies at the conclusion of the dialogue (v. 53). In view of the severity with which Jesus addressed His hearers, this discourse has been said to be "one of the most solemn passages in the whole of Scripture."

The Pharisees wrongly confused tradition and culture with God's law. They thought that rigorous attention to tradition was all that God required. From this section and elsewhere, five errors of the Pharisees emerge: 1) They stressed symbols and rituals at the expense of morality and true duties, 2) They substituted these externals for true godliness, 3) They lacked a sense of proportion—they stressed trivia (tithing herbs in a garden plot) and ignored justice and the love of God, 4) they served primarily to be seen by others, and 5) they misled their followers by their errors. We note that Jesus did not condemn them for tithing, but for their failure in more serious matters.

An unmarked grave (v. 44) was a ceremonial and spiritual hazard because someone could unwittingly walk over it and be defiled by it. The teaching and behavior of the Pharisees purported to convey God's truth, but in reality they stood for many unrecognized errors that could defile without warning.

Jesus also denounced the "experts in the law [KJV—lawyers]." (cf. vv. 46-51). These were the theologians and theoreticians who compiled and interpreted the traditional laws. It was their teaching that the Pharisees practiced. These experts had codified the Law of Moses into 365 prohibitions and 248 commandments, for a total of 613 precepts. Obviously, such laws were burdensome and complex, but though the experts were responsible for formulating them, they were totally disinterested in helping the people that they burdened.

The stories of the two martyrs, Abel and Zechariah (v. 51, cf. Mt. 23:35) are told in Genesis 4:8 and 2 Chronicles 24:20-21. These books were the first and last in the Hebrew canon, and naming the two, spans the whole of Jewish history.

The Pharisees' reaction to Jesus' scolding was "to oppose him fiercely and to besiege him with questions, waiting to catch him in something he might say" (vv. 53-54). They had no interest in listening to be instructed or challenged to godliness.

7. Jesus' Ministry to the Great Multitude (Lk. 12:1-59)

In spite of the opposition of the Jewish religious leaders, Jesus was still popular with the people. His audience for this major address was "a crowd of many thousands . . . so that they were trampling on one another" (v. 1).

(1) Miscellaneous Warnings and Encouragements (vv. 1-12).

His topics included:

A warning against hypocrisy (vv. 1-3). Hypocrisy is speech and behavior apart from reality—as an actor in a play. In the light of God's detailed knowledge hypocrisy is totally futile. It is impossible to hide from Him what we truly believe.

Fear no one but God (vv. 4-5). Humans should fear only God, and under His power and care they should be free from any fear of their fellows. The power of humans does not reach beyond the grave. This passage (v. 4) was the only occasion in the Gospels when Jesus called His disciples "friends." The word rendered "hell" is *geenna* (GEH-en-nah)—better known in its Latin form as *gehenna*.

Count on God's watchful care (vv. 6-7). God cares about every detail, even the fate of a sparrow and the number of hairs on our head. To Him, individual humans are much more than a detail. God is always aware of what is happening to His children, and He values them supremely.

The challenge to witness (vv. 8-9). The believer's witness on earth on behalf of Christ is echoed by Christ's witness in heaven on behalf of that believer.

A warning against blaspheming the Holy Spirit (v. 10). Since the Spirit has a vital role in administering God's forgiveness, those who blaspheme Him are rejecting divine forgiveness (cf. Mt. 12:32).

A promise to the persecuted (vv. 11-12). A believer on trial before authorities because of his faith has the specific promise of divine help. The Holy Spirit will ensure a wise defense.

(2) Rebuke of greed. The Rich Fool (vv. 13-21). This parable was Jesus' response to the man who requested His help to persuade his brother to divide an inheritance. Jesus rejected the request, for "He came to bring men to God, not to bring property to men." By the parable, Jesus taught that true human worth is not a matter of possessions (cf. v. 15). He thus expressly contradicted the Pharisaic claim, "Whom the Lord loves, He makes rich." The rich fool (shortsighted one, simpleton) thought only in material terms, and only for his own selfish earthly advantage. In the Greek, the few sentences that the man spoke contain twelve personal pronouns. That very night his soul (life) was recalled. The verb is plural—"*they* demand"—perhaps speaking of the multiplicity of divine involvement. The man's problem was not so much having riches, but trusting in riches. The only worthwhile wealth is to be "rich toward God" (v. 21).

(3) Warning against worldly anxiety (vv. 22-34). Jesus taught neither indifference nor improvidence, but He did teach that His people should not worry. Excessive worry is the mark of pagans, but those who place God and His kingdom first can live without worry. Believers should not worry because: 1) a human is more than a body, 2) all God's creatures are under His care, 3) anxious care cannot extend one's life, 4) God will provide better than humans ever can, 5) God's care of growing plants is reassuring, and 6) God the Father knows the needs of His people.

Wise believers submit to God's rule in their hearts and lives, and they find models for their trust by observing birds and flowers. His gifts of material goods should be used, not only to provide for the needs of this life, but as the means to store up treasure in heaven. They fulfill this purpose when they are used to achieve spiritual goals.

(4) Wise and unwise servant-managers (vv. 35-48). The believer serves under his Lord as a servant-manager, and at no time can he allow himself to be careless. Persistent watchfulness is essential (cf. v. 36). Jesus used the customs of His culture to teach the believer's ongoing responsibility. An extended wedding feast was often casually scheduled, even in the matter of the days of its duration.

In summarizing Jesus' teaching in this parable, someone proposes the "Beatitude of persistent watchfulness: When we expect Him least, we must expect Him most." Persistent watchfulness will assure readiness for the master's return, and as well, it will promote a closeness in spirit between the master and his servants.

This parable also teaches the principle of the responsibility of authority: The more that is entrusted to one, the more that will be expected of that person (cf. vv. 47-48). The expression "cut him to pieces" (v. 46) is taken as a hyperbole for severe punishment.

Jesus' hearers would have taken special note of one aspect of this parable. In sharp contrast with that day's customs, Jesus depicted a master who served his servants (cf. v. 37). This unusual twist of events would have highlighted the special relationship that Jesus holds with His followers. Though the term "manager" (v. 42) is now usually used, traditional versions used "steward." This term derives from "sty ward," i.e., warden of a [pig]sty. It reflects humble backgrounds!

(5) Jesus' Messianic ministry (vv. 49-53). Jesus is here depicted in His judgment role, and as a divider of humans. He is Savior, but He also is Judge who one day will send fire upon human rebels. "[God] has given him authority to judge because he is the Son of Man" (Jn. 5:27). He will deal with human shortcomings and limitations realistically, and not gloss over disqualifying defects. He is scheduled to judge: sin, Satan, and all humans who have chosen to be unbelievers. In His scale of values, spiritual and moral issues take precedence over human ties of blood and friendship. He requires that His servants give Him first place above all others.

Jesus said of the future judgmental fire "I wish it were already kindled" (v. 49). He seems to be saying that He was eager to do battle with Satan and destroy his kingdom. The longer Jesus maintains His role as Savior, however, the more humans will be saved, even though Satan will do more damage.

(6) The necessity for spiritual vision (vv. 54--59). The practice of predicting weather again led Jesus to speak of paying heed to prophetic signs. He spoke of the need of interpreting the present time (Gk. *kairos* [kair-OS]: point of time, day), perhaps in distinction from the present hour or period (Gk. *chronos* [CHRON-os). Judgment was imminent, but they chose to be blind to it. About six months previously, He had similarly addressed this topic (cf. Mt. 16:1-4; Mk. 8:11-13), though in the context of a request for a sign from heaven. On this occasion there was no recorded entreaty from the crowd.

The theme of Jesus' conclusion was not perpetuating stubborn quarrels. Not only is it prudent in law to make peace with one's adversary, but wise humans should recognize that they are under a sentence as sinners and they should urgently seek God's forgiveness and to be reconciled to Him.

8. The Cause of Disasters. The Barren Fig Tree (Lk. 13:1-9)

A question to Jesus at this time concerned major disasters that humans suffer. His questioners recalled the tragedies of Pilate's massacres of the Galilean Jews who had gathered to worship. Probably implicit in the question was an effort to provoke Jesus into passing judgment upon the value of Galileans (whom Judeans looked down upon), and the rule of Pilate. History tells of two major massacres, one involving 3,000 victims, the other, 20,000, but scholars remain unsure whether one of these, or some other event, is in view. In Jesus' day it was commonly held that those who suffered great catastrophes deserved their fate because of extraordinary personal sin.

In His response, Jesus made the point that there was no direct connection between earthly tragedy and personal sin. He exempted even the eighteen workers who were killed when the tower of Siloam collapsed during construction. Since these workers were accepting money that Pilate had illegitimately appropriated from the temple, many saw their death as God's deliberate judgment, but Jesus disagreed.

The parable of the barren fig tree illustrates God's patience and longsuffering. A fig tree normally matured in three years, and if it did not it became a liability to the owner. In this case, the unproductive tree was extended a year of grace. God could be expected in a similar way to grant grace to undeserving humans. Nevertheless, they must recognize they were living on borrowed time, and that sooner or later "fruit" would be required. When the time that God has allocated to allow for repentance is fulfilled, He proceeds with judgment.

9. The Crippled Woman Healed (Lk. 13:10-21)

This event marks the last recorded ministry of Jesus in a synagogue, and presumably after that, synagogues were closed to Him. His act of calling the crippled woman to Him was unusual, and He ministered her healing without being asked. Her infirmity was organic—probably an extreme case of curvature of the spine—but Jesus described her as one "whom Satan has kept bound for eighteen years" (v. 16).

The ruler of the synagogue was angry because the healing was performed on the Sabbath. He objected, not for the sake of God's law, but because the tradition of the Pharisees had been violated. Thus, Jesus responded to him with justified severity. He pointed out the hypocrisy of those who denounced a Sabbath healing, but routinely on the Sabbath took care of the physical needs of their domestic animals. God's intention for the Sabbath was so much more than imposing restraining bonds upon humans. The crowds supported Jesus in this response, and "all his opponents were humiliated" (v. 17). Though this humiliation ought to have led to repentance, it appears to have resulted in only a temporary setback to their inflated self-image.

Luke concludes this section with his version of two parables: the mustard seed, and the yeast. (cf. Mt. 13:31-33, see pp. 102-103). We have noted (p. 145) that some harmonies place Jesus' discourses during the Feast of Dedication at the juncture of these events.

EIGHT:

THE LATER JUDEAN AND PEREAN MINISTRY (Part 2)

Jesus had now largely concluded His public ministry in Judea, and in these final weeks He was to be found either in Perea or in more remote communities. This season of His ministry was to conclude when He arrived at Jerusalem for His last week.

I. THE THIRD PERIOD OF JESUS' MINISTRY IN JUDEA AND PEREA

During these weeks, Jesus ministered publicly in Perea and privately in Judea. Except for John's account of the raising of Lazarus (Jn. 11:1-44), only Luke reports these events.

1. Jesus' Teachings in the Cities of Perea (Lk. 13:22-30)

Since Jesus taught as He "made His way to Jerusalem" (v. 22), His route apparently took Him through Perea. There He was asked, "Are only a few people going to be saved?" (v. 22). Even in that era, honest humans recognized their lost estate, and they saw the need to be "saved." Both Jews and Gentiles used the term (cf. Mt. 19:25; Acts 16:30). In reply, Jesus did not give a number, but His discussion implied that there would be only a few.

Jesus encouraged His hearers to "make every effort [*agonidzomai*] to enter through the narrow door" (v. 24). (*agonidzomai* [ag-own-IDZE-o-my]: to struggle, strive, strain every nerve, cf. agonize) To have been so near to Him on earth, and yet not to have received His salvation would be a tragedy. He reviewed their argument: "We ate and drank with you, and you taught in our streets" (v. 26). Nevertheless, if they had not entered while the door was open, they would hear Him say, "I don't know you" (v. 27). There was a basic difference between being a true believer or merely relating to Him socially.

Jesus depicted being saved as entering through a narrow door (cf. Mt. 7:14) into a home where a feast was to be served. After a time the host would close the door and admit no one else. Many of Jesus' Jewish listeners would be excluded and replaced by Gentiles. "People will come from east and west and north and south, and will take their places at the feast in the kingdom of God"

(v. 29). For Gentiles to be saved and Jews to be condemned was a startling reversal of their expectations (cf. v. 30).

2. Jesus' Message to Herod Antipas. He Mourns Over Jerusalem (Lk. 13:31-35)

The Pharisees' report to Jesus that Herod Antipas was seeking to kill Him may have been only a ploy to drive Him from the area. Jesus responded in effect, that despite Herod, He would stay and minister, for He refused to let Herod set His agenda. In addressing His message to "that fox," Jesus used the feminine form—vixen. Perhaps His message was directed to Herod's wife, Herodias. Since a fox is furtive and sly, the term appears to be used here by Jesus as an expression of stern disapproval.

Jesus' statement "on the third day I will reach my goal" (v. 32b) implies that He would follow His own schedule. He was ministering by divine power and was not subject to Herod's whim. By this claim Jesus clearly revealed His knowledge of His destiny and His commitment to fulfill it.

The mention of Jerusalem (v. 33) led to Jesus' lament (vv. 34-35). What He said now, He was to repeat during the last week of His ministry (cf. Mt. 23:37-39). That the city harbored those who would destroy Him was reason for its own destruction. Nevertheless, Jesus would gladly have offered to provide Jerusalem with His delivering care. He conveyed His offer under the figure of a mother hen protecting her chicks under her wings.

3. A Man is Healed of Dropsy (Lk. 14:1-6)

This occasion is the third time that Jesus accepted hospitality from a Pharisee, though this one was "prominent" or a "ruler." Scripture hints that the presence of the man with the dropsy had been deliberately arranged, particularly because it was the Sabbath. Dropsy involves the gathering of fluids in body tissue and cavities, so as to cause severe and sometimes grotesque swelling.

The healing of the man with the dropsy led to yet another confrontation on the issue of Sabbath keeping. Though Jesus twice directed a question on the subject to His critical observers, they "had nothing to say" (v. 6). No doubt they realized that an attempt to respond would expose their inconsistency and hypocrisy. In fact, both the Old Testament and rabbinical law allowed help to a trapped animal on the Sabbath. By His teaching, and actions, Jesus made the point that creature needs and a loving heart take precedence over rigid law.

This event is the sixth and final occasion when Jesus was involved in disputes concerning the Sabbath. There had been four previous public healings that generated objections: the invalid at Bethesda (Jn. 5:9), the man with the withered hand (Lk. 6:6), the man born blind (Jn. 9:14), and the woman with the crooked spine (Lk. 13:10). Also there had been the incident of the disciples in the grain field (Lk. 6:1). Jesus had performed two other healings on the Sabbath: the demon possessed man in the synagogue (Lk. 4:33) and Peter's mother-in-law (Lk. 4:38), but there is no record of resulting criticism. Since there are twenty-six individual healing miracles by Jesus reported in the Gospels, the seven Sabbath healings would constitute twenty-seven percent of the total.

4. Jesus' Discourse on Humility (Lk. 14:7-14)

This discussion about humility, which Luke calls a parable (v. 7), was Jesus' response to dinner guests scrambling for the chief places. His discourse has been called, "The Parable of the Arrogant Guests." To these people the seating was important because the closer one sat to the host, the more he was honored. On at least three other occasions, Jesus dealt with the same problem (cf. Mt. 23:6; Mk. 12:39; Lk. 20:46).

Jesus pointed out that to appoint themselves to the chief place, was a formula for humiliation. His way of modest self constraint was the formula for honor. Verse eleven provides a vital spiritual principle, "For everyone who exalts himself will be humbled, and he who humbles himself will be exalted." These words have been paraphrased, "The way up is the way down."

This portion of the discourse ends with Jesus' lesson on true hospitality. The sharing of what one has is first a spiritual ministry, and it is at its best when extended to those who cannot repay. To those who share generously, Jesus promised, "you will be repaid at the resurrection of the righteous" (v. 14). John identified this future day as the "first resurrection" (cf. Rev. 20:6).

5. The Parable of the Great Supper (Lk. 14:15-24)

The chance remark of a Pharisee who was a fellow dinner guest led to this parable. In referring to the blessing of those who will eat in the kingdom, the Pharisee obviously implied that he would be among them. Through His parable, Jesus showed that the man's presumption was not valid.

In the culture of that time, a dinner often involved two invitations. The first announced the event and placed the guests "on call." The second announced that the food was ready and alerted the guests to gather. If one accepted the first invitation, he was obligated to come when the food was ready. The excuses of the guests who rejected the second invitation indicated: 1) attachment to possessions, 2) preoccupation with business, and 3) priority to other relationships. These concerns may not have been evil in themselves, but they competed with the invitation and deprived the intended guests of their place. These prospective guests revealed that they valued the banquet below their personal interests. The outcome was that beggars replaced them.

The parable applies to the Jews, and to all nominal Christians. All humans are invited as God's kingdom guests, but what counts is not the fact of the invitation but what one does with it. Jews are to be replaced by Gentiles, and arrogant religionists by

humble but obedient penitents. Most of the privileged ones were
ignoring the invitation. The master's instruction, "Make them
come in" (v. 23) is seen as an oriental expression implying insis-
tent hospitality rather than compulsion.

To people who smugly held that earthly health and prosperity
proved divine favor, Jesus' teachings were radical. He replaced
the respected elite of His culture with physical and social out-
casts. He was later to express His theme: "The Son of Man came
to seek and to save what was lost" (Lk. 19:10). Note that He concluded this parable by speaking of "my banquet" (v. 24).

6. The Cost of Discipleship (Lk. 14:25-35)

Even at this late date, for some, to follow Jesus was still the
popular way. Thus, He found it necessary to instruct in the demands of true discipleship. Someone comments, "Jesus had just
told them that the banquet was free, but He wants them to know
it isn't cheap." His use of the term "hate," employed the typical
Semitic language style with its extreme contrasts. Although love
and hate are emotions, they also relate to the choices of will and
they speak of acceptance and rejection. Jesus did not purpose to
destroy family affection, but He taught that all earthly attach-
ments must take second place to one's commitment to Him.

One's cross (v. 27) is whatever burden or responsibility Christ
has chosen to impose. It is a burden that results because of one's
commitment to follow and serve Jesus Christ. As we have noted,
in that culture one who carried a cross was probably a condemned
criminal under a sentence of death. The cross that Jesus imposes
upon the Christian often relates to an aspect of character or attitude that ought not to exist (cf. Rom. 6:6; Col. 3:5). To be a disciple
was to be a learner of the ways of Jesus. In later usage, the words
"disciple" and "Christian" were frequently interchanged.

The parable of the tower builder, and the parable of the war-
ring king, each teach that cost must be counted in advance. Jesus'
hearers were likely aware of Pilate's abandoned aqueduct as an
example of an unfinished tower.

Christian devotion is often tested by what one is willing to do
with his possessions. Serving Jesus requires commitment: "Any
of you who does not give up [apotasso] everything he has cannot
be my disciple" (v. 33). The verb apotasso (a-po-TASS-oh) denotes:
renounce, give up, yield right of ownership, assign, or delegate.
The Christian is to see himself as merely the manager of whatever possessions the Lord has placed in his control. Jesus again
spoke of savorless salt. (cf. Mt. 5:13; Mk. 9:50). He implied that
for salt not to be salty is an anomaly, and grounds for considering
it totally worthless. He thus challenged His followers to manifest
His imparted nature, and truly to represent Him.

7. Jesus' Parables of a Lost Sheep, Coin, and Son (Mt. 18:12-14; Lk. 15:1-32)

These parables, which have been called "The Gospel of the Outcast" were Jesus' response to the objection of the Pharisees and teachers of the law to His association with "tax collectors [publicans] and sinners (*hamartolos*]" (Lk. 15:1). (*hamartolos* [ham-ar-toe-LOS]: sinner, irreligious one, heathen, outcast) People from these groups were increasingly being attracted to Jesus. Since many of these people were sincere seekers after God, Jesus could associate with them without compromising His life or message. The Pharisees' complaint stands as one of the glories of the gospel: "This man welcomes sinners." (v. 2b).

Each of the three parables (some see them as one parable in three parts) portrays aspects of the abounding grace of God: 1) it seeks the lost, 2) it persists in a restoration, and 3) it revels in its success. To depict Jehovah (Yahweh) as a God who seeks people is unique; no other religion views its god in this way. The parables primarily focus on restoration to God's family. They concern the backslider's recovery rather than the sinner's conversion.

1) The lost sheep (Lk. 15:1-7; Mt. 18:12-14). The shepherd searched for the lost sheep until he found it, and when he did so his concern turned to rejoicing. After carrying the sheep home, the shepherd shared his rejoicing with his neighbors. Similarly, heaven rejoices over a penitent sinner far more than it does over the works of the righteous. The Pharisees would have noted that the shepherd carried the sheep home without rebuke or judgment. They held that God hated sinners and rejoiced only in their death. The mention of "righteous persons who do not need to repent" (Lk. 15:7) is considered an instance of Jesus' use of irony. In fact, there are no such persons!

2) The lost coin (Lk. 15:8-10). In the search a lamp was lit, the floor swept, and the effort continued until the coin was found. The coin was probably a major part of the woman's dowry, and its recovery was essential to her future security. The church ought to be equally motivated, and under the Holy Spirit's illumination to search as persistently in seeking to restore the backslider. Paul taught, "Brothers, if someone is caught in sin, you who are spiritual should restore him gently" (Gal. 6:1).

3) The prodigal son (Lk. 15:11-32). Out of forty recorded parables by Jesus, this "crown of parables" is one of the best known. It has been called "The world's greatest short story." Interpretations are: father—God; prodigal—willful sinner or backslider who chooses to waste his life; elder brother—self-righteous believer. The best robe bestowed honor, the ring conveyed authority, and sandals portrayed sonship—slaves went barefoot. The fatted calf would be the most luxurious meat available, and far more delicious than the young goat the elder brother visualized having with his friends.

The prodigal illustrates the essential element of voluntary repentance that was not taught in the first two parables. In this parable, the father waited for the son to follow through on his decision to return home. It was not until the son "came to his senses" (v. 17), however, that he began his journey home. The son was separated from his father's fellowship in the distant country but not from his love. In spite of the son's condition the father received him; he was instantly forgiving and his greeting was without the hint of a reproach. Significantly, the prodigal recognized that his sins were ultimately against God (cf. Lk. 15:21).

Though the elder brother was a son, his perspectives were those of a servant. He harbored resentment and bitterness: "All these years I've been slaving for you and never disobeyed your orders" (Lk. 15:29). He owned resources that he left untapped, and he possessed privileges that he had never enjoyed. He failed to realize that he was his father's heir, and always in his presence. R.C. Foster commented, "The prodigal was lost in the far country; the elder brother was lost in his father's house."[1] Notably, the father took the initiative in going out to greet the elder brother, just as he had greeted the prodigal (cf. Lk. 15:20, 28).

Jesus made no application of this parable; He left His hearers to write their own conclusion. Some suggest that since the father's love is really the emphasis, a more descriptive name for it would be "The Loving Father." Alternately, because the father was so extravagantly generous (i.e., prodigal) to his son, someone suggests the parable should be named "The Prodigal Father!"

8. The Parable of the Shrewd Manager (Lk. 16:1-18)

This parable was addressed to the disciples, but the Pharisees were the ones convicted by it and they responded by "sneering at Jesus" (Lk. 16:14). In this instance, Jesus used what appears to be a bad example to teach a right principle.

The parable concerns a manager (steward) who was given notice of dismissal by his employer because he was guilty of mismanagement. He evaluated matters frankly, and determined a feasible course of action "to cushion his fall." While he still possessed the authority, he obligated his master's debtors toward him personally by arbitrarily arranging a reduction of their debt.

Scripture speaks of "the dishonest manager" (Lk. 16:8), but it is possible that his actions may be partly justified. It has been suggested that the amounts quoted were the value of the commodity owed, plus the interest-commission that was charged for such loans in that culture. Since olive oil was a volatile high risk commodity, the interest rate was one hundred percent. The rate for wheat, that was more stable, was twenty-five percent. Thus, the

---

1   R.C. Foster, *Studies in the Life of Christ*. Joplin: College Press Publishing Co., (1995 reprint), p. 934.

manager simply reduced the outstanding amount by canceling the interest. His master would still receive back his original investment, though without the gain that had been indicated.

In the parable, the rich master and not God commended the manager because he had "acted shrewdly" (v. 8). The parable teaches that God's servants must wisely use their present material resources on earth to achieve credit in the eternal realm. Previously, Jesus had instructed, "Store up for yourselves treasures in heaven" (Mt. 6:20). The traditional expression "unrighteous mammon" (v. 9) (Gk. *mamona tes adikias* [ma-mo-NAH tays a-duh-KEE-as]), typically rendered "worldly wealth" in modern versions, derives from the Hebrew term for earthly property.

This parable offended the Pharisees because they loved money as a means of pleasure. Jesus pointed out that God does not change His standards because humans believe otherwise. He drew examples from His previous teachings to illustrate the authority of God's Word and law. There is one pattern for entering the kingdom (v. 16, cf. Mt. 11:12), there is a permanence to Scripture (v. 17, cf. Mt. 5:18), and to marriage (v. 18, cf. Mt. 5:32; 19:9). The law and Word of God are the only real authorities, and all aspects of human life must be measured by their values.

9. The Rich Man and Lazarus (Lk. 16:19-31)

Most evangelical Bible scholars hold that the story of the rich man and Lazarus is actual history, and they deny that it is a parable (i.e., a fictitious story). Facts support this view: 1) the account is not called a parable, 2) a major participant is actually named, 3) there are no comparisons with something else in a higher realm for "Abraham's side" and "hell" are themselves the higher realm, and 4) the after life is reported in the past tense in contrast with the usual present or future tense of parables.

The individual earthly experiences of the rich man and Lazarus (the Greek form of Eleazar [i.e., God helps]) were totally dissimilar. In their treatment of Lazarus, the dogs who provided his only comfort were kinder than the rich man. In the after life the rich man called Abraham "Father" (v. 24), and Abraham called him "Son" (v. 25), but between the separate realms there was an unbridgeable chasm. The rich man's effort to communicate with heaven, and his missionary concern on behalf of his brothers, were now pathetically too late. The brothers needed the solid instruction of Scripture, not a resuscitated beggar.

Scripture does not teach that the rich are condemned because of their riches. This rich man, however, appears to have used his riches only for self-indulgence. His problem was not so much that he had done evil, but that he had failed to grasp opportunities to do good. In the after life his memories of events on earth (cf. v. 25) may have been more painful than the fire that he was suffering. Lazarus was not pronounced righteous because he was poor, but because his faith and life met God's standards. The fate of these two men in this account disproved the Pharisaic teaching that God loves the rich and rejects the poor.

Older traditions named the rich man Ninive (or Nimeusis or Neues), but the Latin Vulgate rendered the words "rich man" as "Dives," and this term is commonly used as his name. Modern versions speak of Lazarus being carried to Abraham's side (v. 22), but the traditional and literal expression is "Abraham's bosom" (Gk. *kolpon Abraam* [KOL-pon ab-ra-AM]: the bosom, breast, or chest of Abraham). The term was the usual Hebrew idiom for the place where God's presence could be enjoyed.

The story of the rich man and Lazarus is one of the few Bible portions that provide a glimpse into the intermediate state—that realm of human existence immediately following this life on earth and prior to the future end time judgments. Conventional doctrine holds that Hades (v. 23), which misleadingly is often translated "hell," is the immediate realm of all departed souls, both wicked and righteous. In Hades there are two compartments: 1) Paradise (Abraham's bosom), and 2) Hades proper. Since the resurrection of Christ, the Paradise portion has been in the heavenlies in the Lord's presence. At death, the soul of the wicked proceeds downward to Hades, and the soul of the righteous proceeds to the Lord's presence in the heavenlies.

10. The Unworthy Servants (Lk. 17:1-10)

Though His message was addressed to His disciples, Jesus was probably prompted by His critics to speak of "things that cause people to sin" or "offenses" (Gk. *skandalon* [SKAN-dal-on]: temptation to sin, stumbling-block, cf. scandal). A deliberate offense against the gospel can become a death trap to a new convert. God plans the future destruction of those who impose offenses upon spiritual babes.

Believers are to forgive one who is their brother in the faith. Notably, Luke used the term "brother" in this sense for the first time in his book, but the person designated is a sinning brother. The believer should rebuke the sinning brother, but forgive him if he repents, even if the process is repeated seven times in a day. The rebuking of the sinning brother, or the forgiveness of the one repenting, are equal responsibilities for the Christian.

The disciples responded to Jesus' teaching on forgiving a brother by asking for an increase in faith. The expression "small as a mustard seed" was a Jewish idiom for a tiny portion. The important aspect of faith is its quality rather than its quantity. Faith is that which contacts God to achieve the impossible such as uprooting a mulberry (sycamine or fig) tree (which are said to grow up to ten meters [thirty-five feet] tall) and replanting it. Faith does not possess virtue of its own, but its virtue and power are in God, who alone accomplishes the miraculous.

The parable of the unworthy (unprofitable) servants (vv. 7-10) teaches the Christian worker not to think of himself of special value to God. Neither is he to think that he deserves God's reward. In all his efforts, he is simply doing his duty. Fortunately, even though a servant is unprofitable, it does not mean he is worthless. His efforts may still accomplish what is needed. Most servants in Bible times were slaves, and they lived lives of sacrifice and self-denial. God's servant should expect the same.

11. The Raising of Lazarus (Jn. 11:1-44)

This event, reported only by John, interrupts Luke's lengthy exclusive reporting of this era. The raising of Lazarus is John's seventh and last reported miracle apart from Jesus' resurrection. When John wrote, long after the events he describes, Mary, through her identity with Jesus in His passion and resurrection (cf. vv. 1-2)[2], had become the best known of the Bethany family.

In sending word of Lazarus' sickness to Jesus, the sisters no doubt expected His prompt response. Scripture suggests that Jesus' delay was because of His love for the family (cf. vv. 5-6). The Gospels record no other occasion when Jesus delayed in responding to a call for His help. As death's conqueror, however, He knew that He did not need to hurry to Lazarus' side. Also, His delay and subsequent resuscitation of Lazarus gave the sisters vastly greater joy than would have resulted from an earlier healing.

Jesus had been "across the Jordan" (Jn. 10:40) (presumably in Perea), but now He was willing to return to Judea in spite of the disciples' concern for His safety and theirs (cf. vv. 8, 16). Bethany was on the eastern slope of the Mount of Olives about three kilometers (two miles) southeast of Jerusalem. Jesus' itinerary was according to the will of God that to Him was equivalent to walking in the light of day (cf. vv. 9-10). As "God's Son" (v. 4), He could rightly speak of death as only the state of having "fallen asleep" (v. 11). He used this incident, and the fact of His absence, to authenticate Himself to His disciples. "For your sake I am glad I was not there, so that you may believe" (v. 15).

Although we frequently speak of "Doubting Thomas," here he is "Heroic Thomas"—or possibly "Pessimistic Thomas." On this occasion Thomas moved to a place of leadership among the disciples by exhorting his colleagues, "Let us also go, that we may die with him" (v. 16). At this point, Thomas had not understood the promise of resurrection, so that instead of expectant faith, he exhibited only loyal despair. It appears, in fact, that Bethany was sufficiently distant from Jerusalem that Jesus and His party were not in jeopardy there. The disciples may not have agreed with Thomas' pessimism, but they followed his suggestion and accompanied Jesus to Bethany.

---

2   Though John at this point mentions Mary's act of anointing, the account of the event is not given in his Gospel until the next chapter (cf. Jn. 12:1-3).

When Jesus arrived at Bethany Martha was energetic and outspoken. Mary was tearfully worshipful, and she greeted Him by falling at His feet (v. 32). Jesus declared to Martha, "I am the resurrection and the life" (v. 25), and these words become the fifth of John's "I Am" revelations of Christ. Martha responded with a ringing confession of the Messiahship of Jesus: "I believe that you are the Christ [Messiah], the Son of God" (v. 27). Martha's report to Mary, "The Teacher is here" (v. 28) underscores a unique aspect of Jesus' ministry: He pointedly ignored the usual prejudices of a Jewish rabbi against instructing a woman.

Jesus reacted to the weeping of Mary and her friends by being "deeply moved [*embrimaomai*] in spirit and troubled" (v. 33). Since the verb *embrimaomai* (em-brim-AH-o-my) may mean either to be deeply moved or to be angered, versions reflect this ambiguity. It is possible that Jesus became angry as He reflected on all the damage caused by sin (including death), but it is more likely that He was simply deeply moved as He empathized with the sorrowful people around Him. The words that follow: "Jesus wept" (v. 35) comprise the shortest verse of the Bible, and they appear to confirm the empathy and compassion of Jesus.

In speaking of weeping, the original uses different verbs. "When Jesus saw [Mary] weeping [*klaio*] and the Jews . . . also weeping [*klaio*] . . . . Jesus wept [*dakruo*]" (Jn. 11:33, 35). The verb *klaio* (KLY-oh) denotes: to sob or wail aloud, to weep bitterly or vehemently, to bewail or lament. The verb *dakruo* (dak-RU-oh), that is used only here in the New Testament, denotes to shed tears or to weep, and it suggests a restrained quiet weeping.

Although she knew the body would have begun to decay, Martha agreed to open the tomb. Jesus first briefly returned thanks to God, then in a loud voice He commanded Lazarus to come out of the tomb. This event was a resuscitation rather than a resurrection, for Lazarus would die again. Lazarus emerged from his tomb in a natural human body and bound with his grave clothes. Jesus showed His concern for Lazarus' human needs by instructing that he be helped out of his grave clothes.

In the fourth century a church was built over what was said to be Lazarus' tomb that consists of a cave cut into the rock of a hillside. Its arrangement, with a stone to close the mouth, is similar to that of Jesus' traditional tomb.

12. The Sanhedrin Actively Plots to Kill Jesus (Jn. 11:45-54)

The news of the raising of Lazarus attracted new followers, but it also generated new active hostility from the Pharisees and chief priests who were members of the Sanhedrin. In the special meeting that they had called, they argued that if Christ should continue ministering the whole nation would follow Him. They saw Rome interpreting such events as an uprising, and proceeding to crush Israel and destroy its people and their leaders.

In the discussion, Caiaphas the high priest advised, "It is better for you that one man die for the people than that the whole nation perish" (v. 50). John explains that with these words Caiaphas unknowingly spoke a prophecy. Also, he reports the Sanhedrin's policy in regard to Jesus: "From that day on they plotted to take his life" (v. 53). To Caiaphas, Christ's death would solve a political problem; God planned it to solve the sin problem. While the rulers plotted Jesus' death, great numbers of the people were still eagerly seeking to hear His message. The village called Ephraim (v. 54) where Jesus took refuge is not identified today.

II. JESUS' MINISTRY DURING HIS JOURNEY TO JERUSALEM

There are unrecorded travels by Jesus during this period, but in general it was a time when He was journeying southward on His way to Jerusalem. He appears to have followed a roundabout route, and perhaps at times to have retraced His steps.

1. The Healing of the Ten Lepers (Lk. 17:11-19)

This event occurred in a border village between Samaria and Galilee, and the ten lepers included at least one Samaritan. The lepers asked only for pity, but Jesus chose to provide the gift of healing. By telling the lepers to show themselves to the priests (which presumably meant a journey to Jerusalem), Jesus confirmed His respect for the Mosaic law. The priests served as the nation's health inspectors, and for the lepers to appear before them to confirm their healing was an act of faith. Had they not been healed, they would have been ridiculed.

The one healed leper who came back "praising God in a loud voice" was a Samaritan, and apparently the only "foreigner" (v. 18) in the group. He clearly showed that he knew the source of his healing (cf. v. 16), and he appears to have responded to his healing the moment it happened, and before showing himself to the priest. It has been said, "Nine received benefits through Christ; one received Christ through His benefits." Jesus declared, "Your faith has made you well (Gk. *sodzo*)." The verb *sodzo* (SOWED-zoh) is translated: preserve, save, bring to safety, heal, or keep. Jesus' pronouncement appears to have conveyed spiritual salvation as the complement of the physical healing.

2. The Coming of Christ's Kingdom (Lk. 17:20-37)

Jesus' discourse at this time was prompted by the Pharisee's question concerning the coming of the kingdom. Though they asked when, He answered by telling where. He indicated that it was not a matter of looking for future signs, nor of searching among human institutions, for one day it would occur with spectacular visibility. The important issue was to recognize Him. The phrase "within you" (v. 21) is rendered "in your midst" by Moffat and "among you" in Alford[3] and the footnote in the NIV, and many feel these translations are preferred. At that very moment they were looking at the King himself. The Jews' part in attaining the kingdom was not to await God's future, but to recognize the Messiah who had come. There was no point in discussing a future coming when they were blind to His presence in their midst.

In Jesus' day and up to the present time, the kingdom is spiritual. Traditional language describes the kingdom as existing on earth in "mystery form." Jesus had said, "If I drive out demons by the finger of God [and He did], then the kingdom of God has come to you" (Lk. 11:20). Those on earth who commit their allegiance and loyalty to "King Jesus" comprise the present kingdom. It remains the invisible kingdom of the heart.

Jesus proceeded to declare to His disciples (vv. 22-37) the fact of His future return and kingdom. Luke's record is a little preview of the larger Olivet Discourse, and it parallels Matthew 24:15-44. Further discussion will follow there. Luke ends by noting, that in the inauguration of the kingdom, Israel would become a place of death, attracting great numbers of scavenger birds.

3. Two Prayer Parables: the Persistent Widow, and the Pharisee and Tax Collector (Lk. 18:1-14)

Luke explains that Jesus told the parable of the persistent widow and the unjust judge "to show them that they should always pray and not give up" (v. 1). Though the parable depicts God only by way of contrast, it highlights persistence as an important working tool that can be used by all who desire God's intervention. Even an irreverent and oppressive Roman judge would be moved to favorable action by the persistent appeal of an otherwise helpless widow. Since she was unable to influence by bribes or threats, the widow's only power against what appeared to be callous indifference lay in her persistence.

The judge declared that he would "see that she won't eventually wear me out [Gk. *hupopiazo*] with her coming" (v. 5). In making this statement, he used a colorful verb that a prize fighter would use: *hupopiazo* (hoop-oh-pea-AD-zoh): strike under the eye, give a black eye to, fly in the face of, torment, maltreat. The woman surely did not see herself with such powers!

The reason that "chosen ones . . . cry out to [God] night and day" (v. 7) is because they know that sooner or later they will get results. When the believer prays, help is on the way (v. 8). The persistence of a believer's prayer reveals his or her estimate of God's character. A major reason that God delays in administering justice is that sinners might have opportunity to repent. Presumably, the reason that there will be limited faith on the earth

---

3   James Moffat's version of the New Testament first appeared in 1913, that of
      Henry Alford in 1869.

when Jesus comes (cf. v. 8b) is because far too many humans will fail to persist in actively awaiting His coming.

In the parable, the "prayer" of the Pharisee (vv. 11-12) was really a soliloquy of self-congratulation, and his reminder to God of how great he was. He used the pronoun *I* four times. In contrast, the tax collector not only demonstrated self-effacement, but he made prayer an occasion of sincere personal penitence. He offered God neither a statement of his virtues, nor excuses for lack of virtue. Thus Jesus concluded, "this man . . . went home justified before God" (v. 14). The tax collector availed himself of God's gift of grace; the Pharisee counted on his own merits. To Jesus' audience with their perspectives of pious Pharisees and despised tax collectors, this parable would have been startling.

The tax collector's plea, "God, have mercy [*hilaskomai*] on me" (v. 13) has been rendered "O God, be propitiated unto me."[4] The verb *hilaskomai* (hil-ASK-o-my) is translated: propitiate, conciliate, show mercy, expiate. Paul and John used derivatives of this verb to develop the New Testament doctrine of propitiation, though modern versions render the word "atonement" (Rom. 3:25) or "atoning sacrifice" (1 John 2:2). Similarly, the later state of the tax collector who "went home justified before God" (v. 14) introduces the subject of justification that Paul meaningfully developed (cf. Rom. 5:1; 8:30; Titus 3:7).

At this point, the Gospel harmony returns to Matthew's account and the parallel passages in the synoptics. With relatively minimal exceptions, in the remaining chapters of each Gospel, the synoptics agree on the order of events.

4. Jesus' Teachings Concerning Divorce (Mt. 19:1-12; Mk. 10:1-12, cf. also Lk. 16:18)

At this time, Jesus "left Galilee and went . . . to the other side of the Jordan" (Mt. 19:1). Crossing the Jordan meant He was returning to Perea. Herod Antipas ruled both Galilee and Perea, and thus Jesus remained in Herod's territory, but He was probably following the normal route for pilgrims to Jerusalem.

As Jesus taught and ministered healing to large crowds, some Pharisees "to test him" (Mt. 19:3) asked His opinion about divorce. Since the divorce issue was controversial and divisive, their question probably was not sincere, and likely they hoped He would take a stand that would offend His supporters.

Pharisees who followed Hillel allowed divorce on trivial grounds, but followers of Shammai allowed it only for immorality. Both schools quoted Moses in Deuteronomy 24:1 "If a man marries a woman who becomes displeasing to him because he finds something indecent about her [or some uncleanness in her] . . . he writes her a certificate of divorce." Views on what constituted

---

4 *The Emphasized New Testament.* J.B. Rotherham.

"something indecent" varied all the way from adultery, to inability to cook, and it was out of this dispute that the two radically divergent schools emerged.

Jesus responded to the Pharisees' question with a counter question concerning their knowledge of the divine origins of marriage that God instituted at creation. Jesus showed that God had not changed His original intention. The Mosaic provision was a departure from the creation ordinance. Deuteronomy 24:1 tolerated divorce, but it did not establish it as an approved institution of society. Thus, Jesus did not so much debate divorce as state the basic philosophy of marriage. He pointed out that Moses introduced divorce, not to improve upon the divine order, but in response to the hardness of human hearts.

Significantly, in His brief comments, Jesus portrayed the wife as an equal partner with her husband. In Jewish practice at that time, only the man could proclaim a divorce—women were property and they had no power to end a marriage. Jesus defined marriage with mutual responsibilities between husband and wife, and He declared that a divorced man, by remarrying, could commit adultery against his first wife. In Mark's account, the wife is depicted as divorcing her husband (cf. 10:12), though such an event was unthinkable in Judaism in that day—but not in secular Roman society.

Jesus declared that divorce and remarriage ordinarily result in the committing of adultery, but in Matthew's account of His reply to the Pharisees He introduced a further clause: "except for marital unfaithfulness" (Mt. 19:9). Scholars debate how this exception is to be understood, and the matter remains controversial. In Matthew, the discussion closed with Jesus' comments about celibacy. He declared that it was a valid option for those who chose, but He did not depict it as a superior life-style.

Mark continues the discussion when "they were in the house again [and] the disciples asked Jesus about this" (Mk. 10:10). In His reply, Jesus repeated His statement that remarriage constitutes adultery, but this time there was no "exception" clause. Jesus thus appears to have held a strict view regarding divorce, particularly involving His followers. Nevertheless, by His kind treatment of those with marital irregularities, Jesus showed them loving social acceptance (cf. the woman at the well [John 4:6-26]; the woman caught in adultery [John 8:3-11]; or the sinful woman who anointed His feet [Luke 7:36-50]).

5. Jesus Blesses the Children (Mt. 19:13-15; Mk. 10:13-16; Lk. 18:15-17)

At this point, Luke's separate accounts end, and he returns to the gospel harmony in the events that he reports.

In Bible times, parents customarily brought their infants and small children to a distinguished rabbi to be blessed. On this occasion the event was marred because "the disciples rebuked them" (Mk. 10:13). Though the usual scene pictures the mothers with the children, the pronoun "them" is masculine and it refers either to "parents" or "fathers." Thus, Jesus' visitors seem to have been family groups. Mark tells that Jesus reacted with indignation against the disciples, and He firmly instructed them to permit the children to come (cf. Mk. 10:14).

To convey a blessing, Jesus apparently took the smaller children in his arms (cf. Mk. 10:16), or if they were older, He placed His hands upon them (Mt. 19:15). As God, He did not merely pray for a blessing but actually bestowed it. He explained that the spirit of childhood paralleled the spirit of the kingdom. Qualities such as: confident trust, simplicity, obedience, acceptance of others, and meekness belong to children and to citizens of the kingdom. A child accepts parental provision simply because it is given—that should be the believer's attitude toward God.

6. Jesus and the Rich Young Ruler (Mt. 19:16-30; Mk. 10:17-31; Lk. 18:18-30)

Mark reports that the young man ran up to Jesus and knelt before Him, and Luke notes that he was a ruler—he may have been a member of the Sanhedrin (though for a young man that was unlikely), or a ruler of a synagogue. His complimentary address to Jesus, "Good Teacher," may have been mere tact, for he did not answer when Jesus pointed out that such a title implied His deity. It has been suggested that a better question than "What . . . must I do?" would have been, "What must I be?"

By responding to Jesus' instruction to obey the commandments by asking "Which ones?" the young man may have been confessing that he had not kept all of them. Jesus passed over the first four commandments dealing with relationships with God, but He cited the fifth through the ninth commandment dealing with man's relationship to his fellows. Jesus added the summary, concerning loving one's neighbor. The young man claimed he had kept all that Jesus was prescribing, but he still revealed his lack of spiritual assurance by asking, "What do I still lack?"

The young man may have qualified in terms of the laws that Jesus had specified, but many feel he failed the tenth commandment: "You shall not covet" (Ex. 20:17). If he kept the letter of the law, he failed to meet its spirit, and he was possessed by his possessions. Although Jesus "loved him" (Mk. 10:21), He imposed two essential conditions: 1) sell all that he had, and 2) follow Him. The young man had to do the first to do the second, for his possessions stood between him and God. These requirements were necessary for the young man, but no other convert was asked to dispose of his wealth in this manner. Tragically, this young man became the only earnest seeker in the Gospels who "went away sad" (Mt. 19:22) from the presence of Jesus.

It has been pointed out that Jesus specified, "obey [Gk. *tereo* {tay-REH-oh}: keep, guard, preserve, fulfill] the commandments" (Mt. 19:17). The young man replied, "All these have I kept [Gk. phulasso {foo-LASS-oh}: observe, follow]" (Mt. 19:20). Perhaps the young man deliberately used a weaker verb, although the point is debatable. What is evident is that he changed verbs and thus he avoided responding precisely to Jesus.

Jesus enumerated commandments as the route to eternal life, but He knew that the problem was that humans are unable to keep the commandments. Later, Paul explained that "the law was put in charge to lead us to Christ" (Gal. 3:24). As long as the young man trusted in his good behavior, instead of throwing himself on God's mercy, he did not qualify to receive eternal life.

His discussion with the rich young ruler led Jesus to state the principle, "It is easier for a camel to go through the eye of a needle than for a rich man to enter the kingdom of God" (Lk. 18:25; cf. Mt. 19:24; Mk. 10:25). In each synoptic He added words to the effect "but with God all things are possible" (Mt. 19:26). It has been said, "It takes a miracle to save a rich man, but it takes a miracle to save a poor man too." The authority and privileges that money buys make it difficult for one to be a humble penitent sinner. The disciples, who had long been taught that wealth was an evidence of godliness, were "amazed at his words" (Mk. 10:24, cf. v. 26).

Many efforts have been made to explain the terms "eye of a needle" and "camel." Concluding that He meant just what He said seems preferable, so that He was saying that humanly speaking it was impossible. Many suggest that Jesus was quoting a popular Jewish proverb. He chose the largest animal and the smallest opening within the common experience of His hearers to convey the idea of that which is humanly impossible. He thus was stressing the fact that salvation is the work of God.

Peter's remark concerning the disciples' self-sacrifice and the question "What then will there be for us?" have been criticized as mercenary. Jesus acknowledged the disciples' sacrifice, however, and He declared that they would be rewarded both in this life and the life to come. In the afterlife there would be many reversals of position; the status of humans today is not necessarily what will be hereafter. Futurists see the "renewal of all things" ("regeneration"—KJV) (Mt. 19:28) as the millennial kingdom, others may see it as the new creation and the eternal abode of the righteous. The word rendered judging could also mean ruling.

7. The Laborers in the Vineyard (Mt. 20:1-16)

This parable serves to expand Jesus' answer to Peter's question about the reward of the disciples. It depicts a landowner who hires workers for his vineyard at five different times during the day. The last group worked only one hour before quitting time. When the pay was distributed, all workers were paid the amount agreed upon for the first workers—one denarius (cf. v. 13). The workers who had served all day, enduring the oppressive heat of grape harvest time, complained that they were treated unfairly. But in fact the landowner had not cheated them, for they received just what they had been promised. The problem was not injustice, but the worker's jealousy over the master's generosity.

The parable rebukes the hireling spirit among God's workers, and it teaches that God may not reward according to human patterns. Two principles emerge: 1) God assigns work according to the needs of His vineyard, 2) Work is rewarded according to the choices of God's sovereign love, power, and compassion. Actually, every one of God's servants will be overpaid for his or her labor (cf. Lk. 17:10), and God's first concern is for human motives and attitudes rather than accomplishments.

Someone has said, "This parable is in fact the gospel of the penitent thief." If the ultimate reward is heaven, the one who serves as a Christian for a lifetime is no more saved than one who is converted only moments before death. Though the first workers served all day, those hired at the eleventh hour responded to their first invitation.

8. Jesus Again Foretells His Death (Mt. 20:17-19; Mk. 10:32-34; Lk. 18:31-34)

In reacting to Jesus' persistence at this time in His journey to Jerusalem, His disciples were astonished and His followers were afraid (cf. Mk. 10:32). As far as they understood matters it appeared to them that Jesus was deliberately going to His death. He chose, however, to ignore the threat of hostility and violence, but He again made a special point of taking the Twelve into His confidence to tell them what would happen to Him.

In this, His third discussion of His forthcoming crucifixion (cf. Mt. 16:21; 17:22), Jesus added further details. He identified Jerusalem and being handed over to the Gentiles, and He mentioned the mocking, the flogging (scourging), and the insulting, and for the first time He used the word "crucify" (Mt. 20:19). Again He declared that there would be a resurrection on the third day. In spite of His clear statements, Luke reports, "The disciples did not understand any of this. Its meaning was hidden from them, and they did not know what he was talking about" (Lk. 18:34). The disciples appear to have been obsessed by their expectation of a conquering political deliverer.

9. The Request of James and John (Mt. 20:20-28; Mk. 10:35-45)

Matthew identifies "the mother of Zebedee's sons" as the one who approached Jesus, but Mark simply names the two sons, James and John. Apparently it was a family project, and though their mother was involved in the request, in the dialogue that followed, James and John spoke for themselves. In Matthew, where the mother was the spokesperson, the two sons answered Jesus' first question (cf. Mt. 20:22). From a comparison of Scripture (cf. Mt. 27:56; Mk. 15:40), it is inferred that the mother's name was Salome, and she was Jesus' aunt.

In asking if they could drink the cup, Jesus was asking if they could share His fate and undergo the experience that was to be His route to the throne. They thought only of glory, but Jesus thought of agony. His "baptism" in this context would be the overwhelming calamity of His crucifixion that the two disciples clearly could not share. Jesus used the occasion to teach a fundamental principle, "Whoever wants to become great among you must be your servant" (Mt. 20:26). The model servant-leader is, of course, Jesus Himself: "The Son of Man did not come to be served, but to serve, and to give his life as a ransom [Gk. *lutron*] for many" (Mt. 20:28; cf. Mk. 10:45). (*lutron* [LOO-tron]: a ransom, the price of release, the purchase of the deliverance of someone who could not free himself).

The indignation of the ten (Mk. 10:41) has been described as evidence of spiritual immaturity equal to the brothers' ambitious request. It is often suggested that the reason they protested was that they had not thought of making the request first!

10. Jesus Heals Blind Bartimaeus and his Companion (Mt. 20:29-34; Mk. 10:46-52; Lk. 18:35-43)

This event associates with Jericho just before His journey's end at Jerusalem. Apart from the cursing of the fig tree, this miracle was Jesus' last. In Jesus' day the city had spread to both sides of the valley (or wadi). As Jesus left one part (Mt. 20:29), at the same time He was entering another (Lk. 18:35). The blind men wisely were placed where help could be found. Perhaps they knew that in beginning His Messianic ministry Jesus had proclaimed "recovery of sight for the blind" (Lk. 4:18).

Only Matthew speaks of two blind beggars, Mark and Luke speak of one, and Mark supplies the name Bartimaeus. All three synoptics emphasize the blind men's call to the "Son of David"—a deliberate Messianic address. They may have been blind, but they rightly knew who Jesus was. Though He was on the way to Jerusalem, Jesus stopped, for as the poet wrote: "The cry of a beggar can stop God as He marches by."

Mark provides unique details about the call of the crowd to the blind man: "Cheer up! On your feet! He's calling you." (Mk. 10:49). Probably the blind man's cloak was his most precious possession, but since it hindered his response to the Lord, he threw it aside. All three synoptics reveal that Jesus provided healing only after He had been asked to do so. The request became a means by which the blind men expressed their faith.

Matthew reports that Jesus was motivated by compassion and that He healed by touching their eyes. In Mark and Luke

Jesus pronounced, "Your faith has healed you." The three synoptics report that the former blind men proceeded to follow Jesus as disciples. Luke adds, "When the people saw it, they also praised God" (Lk. 18:43).

11. The Conversion of Zacchaeus (Lk. 19:1-10)

Since Jesus had already healed the blind men, His presence in Jericho was an exciting event. Great crowds thronged Him, and Zacchaeus, because he was short of stature, necessarily found an effective observation post in a tree.

The title "chief tax collector," which identifies Zacchaeus, occurs nowhere else in Scripture. Evidently Zacchaeus was the overseer of other tax collectors, and his role made him particularly despised by the people. Jesus, knowing all aspects of the situation, took the unprecedented step of stopping beneath the tree, singling out Zacchaeus by name, and inviting Himself to Zacchaeus' home.

Jesus' words, "I must stay at your house today" (Lk. 19:5) indicate the fulfillment of a divine plan. Apparently, Jesus judged that of all the citizens of Jericho, Zacchaeus was most ready for a new life experience. The crowd reacted unfavorably, and they complained, "He has gone to be the guest of a 'sinner'" (v. 7).

Zacchaeus had apparently enjoyed a conversation and a meal with Jesus before he stood up and announced his new policies. He proved his conversion by announcing: 1) that he would give half his goods to the poor, 2) that he would restore fourfold anything that he had robbed. Obviously, a converted Zacchaeus had a totally new attitude toward his social responsibilities. Mosaic law exhorted, "Do not be hardhearted or tightfisted toward your poor brother . . . give generously to him and do so without a grudging heart" (Deut. 15:7, 10). Exodus 22:1 prescribed that a stolen ox should be restored fivefold, but a stolen sheep fourfold. According to tradition, Zacchaeus went on to be a Christian leader, and he became bishop of Caesarea.

Jesus' concluding observation "the Son of Man came to seek and to save what was lost" (v. 10) would have had Messianic significance to His Jewish audience. Some consider these words to be the key verse of Luke.

12. The Parable of the Minas (or Pounds) (Lk. 19:11-27)

A mina (MEAN-uh) was a large silver coin. Its purchasing power compares with wages for from one day to one week for a modern worker. Ten minas would probably be equal to wages for two to three months. The people who heard this parable would have known the story of Archelaus (ahr-kuh-LAY-uhs). Following his father's death, this son of Herod the Great assumed the rule of Judea (cf. Mt. 2:22) expecting to be crowned king. Throughout his rule of about a decade he remained uncrowned because a delegation of Jews blocked his coronation. Archelaus was thus denied the kingdom, though in the parable the nobleman received it in spite of protests. Interestingly, this parable was the only one known to involve actual historical events.

In the larger context, the parable is about King Jesus and His subjects. To those who expected an earthly kingdom immediately, the parable proclaimed: "Not now, but later." Those to whom He came as Messiah-King would reject Him. Unlike Archelaus, however, Jesus would be crowned in spite of opposition. In heaven Jesus has received the crown and the kingdom and He now awaits His return to earth to assume His rule. Associated with His coming will be the rewarding of His faithful servants, and the judging of His enemies (cf. v. 27).

This parable depicts an equal gift given to each servant, and in this it contrasts with the parable of the talents where the contributions were not equal (cf. Mt. 25:14-30). The parable teaches that in spite of the Master's absence, each believer is responsible for using God's gifts wisely. Here, each believer is considered to have an equal opportunity before God, although the parable reports a reckoning of only three of the ten servants.

The man who laid away his mina in a piece of cloth was scolded and his mina given to the one who had ten. These events led to what has been called the law of forfeited stewardship: "To everyone who has, more will be given, but as for the one who has nothing, even what he has will be taken away" (v. 26). Spiritual gifts flourish from use and die of disuse. Though Christ's servant may not be motivated to win a reward, he must conscientiously seek to fulfill his responsibilities.

NINE:

THE PASSION WEEK (Part 1)

By returning to Jerusalem, Jesus knowingly became vulnerable to His enemies. Though they were determined to destroy Him, He was determined to fulfill the plan of God. The usual dating places these events in the spring of the year, and of course, Christendom commemorates them as the Easter season. At this, the outset of Jesus' final week, we have covered seventy percent of the harmonized gospel account.

I. JESUS' FINAL PUBLIC MINISTRY IN JERUSALEM

Jesus used His last week in Jerusalem to conduct both a public and a private teaching ministry.

1. The Setting For His Last Week's Ministry (Mt. 21:17; Lk. 21:37-38; Jn. 11:55-12:1, 9-11)

John explains: "When it was almost time for the Jewish Passover, many went up from the country to Jerusalem" (Jn. 11:55). He tells that these pilgrims anticipated that Jesus would be present at the Feast. Jesus was, indeed, among the incoming pilgrims: "Six days before the Passover, Jesus arrived at Bethany, where Lazarus lived" (Jn. 12:1). His arrival resulted in great public interest and a rapidly growing following. "A large crowd of Jews found out that Jesus was there . . . [and] many . . . were going over to Jesus and putting their faith in him" (Jn. 12:9-10b).

The foregoing text, along with what is said in the synoptics, indicates that during this final week, Jesus made His home with Mary, Martha, and Lazarus in Bethany. This village on the eastern slope of the Mount of Olives was about three kilometers (a mile and two-thirds) from Jerusalem. (cf. "He left [the crowds after the triumphal entry] and went out of the city to Bethany, where he spent the night" [Mt. 21:17]).

Jesus' strategy in spending His nights in Bethany placed Him beyond the reach of the Jerusalem authorities at those times when He would have been vulnerable. In the daytime, the crowds that thronged Him were His protection. The authorities noted that one of the reasons for Jesus' popularity was the report of the resuscitation of Lazarus. Thus, these enemies began to plot how they might kill Lazarus and, as it were, destroy the evidence of Jesus' miracle power (cf. Jn. 12:10).

2. The Triumphal Entry Into Jerusalem (Mt. 21:1-11; Mk. 11:1-11; Lk. 19:28-44; Jn. 12:12-19)

Up to this time, Jesus had accepted the status of Messiah by implication, but He had avoided any public demonstration or claim to His Messiahship. The time had now come to present Himself to His people and He proceeded to initiate what is traditionally known as the triumphal entry. The crowds that had gathered for the Passover, many of whom were pilgrims from Galilee, were in an expectant mood. John notes, "They kept looking for Jesus, and . . . they asked one another, 'What do you think? Isn't he coming to the Feast?'" (Jn. 11:56).

As the Messiah, Jesus acted to fulfill the prophecy of Zechariah 9:9 "Shout, Daughter of Jerusalem! See, your king comes to you, righteous and having salvation, gentle and riding on a donkey, on a colt, the foal of a donkey." The Gospels record a free quotation of this verse that was apparently the way it was remembered (cf. Mt. 21:4; Jn. 12:15). Though for Jesus to have ridden on a horse may have suggested greater status, princes and kings in Bible times also rode on donkeys (cf. Judg. 5:10, 10:4, 12:14; 2 Sam. 16:1-2). When Jesus comes as the world's conqueror, He will ride a white horse (cf. Rev. 19:11-16).

The quoted prophecy concerning the colt, with the previous line repeated in slightly altered form, illustrates Hebrew poetry's typical synonymous parallelism. Two animals were brought to Jesus, a donkey and her colt (cf. Mt. 21:2,7), but it is usually held that He rode only the colt. The mother donkey, however, accompanied her colt, and the disciples' cloaks served as a saddle (cf. Mk. 11:7). The surrender of their cloaks was a mark of homage, and the overall event, as it were, proclaimed Jesus king.

In the morning, after leaving Bethany, Jesus paused at the village of Bethphage (BETH-fuh-jee) on the Mount of Olives to send two disciples for the colt. That He would ride on a young unbroken animal posed no problem. The colt's owners apparently were believers, for they readily consented for Jesus to use it. The colt and mother donkey likely were returned that afternoon.

As He rode toward Jerusalem, a very large crowd of people joined in the demonstration, some marching before Him, and some after Him. Apparently some had followed from Bethany (cf. Jn. 12:17), and as they reached the summit of the Mount of Olives and viewed Jerusalem before them, they "began joyfully to praise God in loud voices" (Lk. 19:37). As they entered the city, a new group met them (cf. Jn. 12:18).

Even before He arrived at the city, Jesus replied to the Pharisee's request that He silence the crowd, "If they keep quiet, the stones will cry out" (Lk. 19:40). Matthew reports, "the whole city was stirred" (21:10), and John quotes the Pharisees as saying, "Look how the whole world has gone after him" (12:19). It is estimated that the population of Jerusalem at Passover time would be several hundred thousand, and great numbers of these would be pilgrims with spiritually responsive hearts.

The people's cry of "Hosanna" meant literally, "do save now," and it denoted the prayer, "Save us now, we pray." It derived from Psalm 118:25-26. Jews of Jesus' day used "Hosanna" to express joy, much as some modern Christians use the word "Hallelujah." Linking their joy to the acclamation of Jesus had definite Messianic implications. The Roman authorities, however, apparently did not see these events as any threat to their rule of the nation, and they made no objection to what was occurring.

The people who acclaimed Jesus at this time were moved, but most fell short of a transforming spiritual experience. They were a "crowd of disciples" (Lk. 19:37), but they did not really see Him as God's Son. Except He perform miracles or assume power they were not prepared to see Him as the long-awaited divine Messiah. They identified Him superficially: "This is Jesus, the prophet from Nazareth in Galilee" (Mt. 21:11). Since the people of Judah denied that the Messiah could come from Galilee, this appraisal meant the dismissal of Jesus' Messianic status.

For Jesus to participate in the triumphal entry was an act of great boldness. He thus made Himself totally conspicuous, and placed Himself in full view of His enemies. Nevertheless, this occasion was a deliberate proclamation of His kingship. As it were, Jesus was making one last public appeal. Because He rode on a donkey, however, He was declaring that His was a kingdom of peace and love. By this dramatic event He was inviting the people of Jerusalem, and ultimately all people, to recognize Him on His own unique terms as their divine King.

Someone comments, "The parade was permanent in that we live with its effects, but within a week's time, it was as if the parade had never happened." Even for Jesus, the effects of the acclaim were notably short-lived. Luke reports, "As he approached Jerusalem and saw the city, he wept over it" (Lk. 19:41). Jesus wept as He realized that this city, that would reject His rule, would soon lie in desolate ruin. Though the weeping does not seem to have dampened the demonstration, it likely puzzled those close beside Him who became aware of it.

This occasion is known as Palm Sunday because John reports that the people "took palm branches and went out to meet him" (Jn. 12:13). To the Jews, the palm suggested victory, and their nation's triumph. Matthew and Mark each tell that the people spread their cloaks and branches, but they do not name the kind of branches. It has been suggested that since the reference to palms is so minimal, "Parade Sunday," rather than "Palm Sunday," would better identify this occasion. Also, some suggest that "Royal Entry" would be better than "Triumphal Entry," since Jesus' triumph awaits the Second Coming.

After His entry, Jesus "looked around at everything" (Mk. 11:11) in the temple and then He "went out of the city to Bethany, where he spent the night" (Mt. 21:17). The crowds probably had expected Him immediately to confront the Roman rulers.

3. The Barren Fig Tree (Mt. 21:18-22; Mk. 11:12-14, 20-26)

The incident involving the fig tree occurred as Jesus returned to Jerusalem the day after the triumphal entry. The tree was in leaf, but there was no fruit "because it was not the season for figs" (Mk. 11:13). In Palestine, a fig tree usually bears green "early figs [first ripe]" (Mic. 7:1) beginning in March, followed by regular figs (commonly black) which are ripe by midsummer. Most of the early figs soon fall, but the later figs, if not picked, remain on the tree in edible condition for many months. In April, Jesus found neither type of fig on the tree.

When He found only leaves, Jesus spoke to tree, "'May you never bear fruit again!' [and] Immediately the tree withered" (Mt. 21:19). Peter called this pronouncement a curse (cf. Mk. 11:21), but primarily it was a teaching device. Scholars speak of the event as "an enacted parable" or "a parabolic action," and note that it is the sole destructive miracle in the Gospels. Jesus not only showed His disapproval of promise without fulfillment, but His action dramatically portrayed the certainty of His future role as judge. Many see the fig tree as a symbol of national Israel and its tragic destiny. Its destruction was a tangible declaration of the judgment that was about to fall on Jerusalem.

Jesus responded to the disciples' reaction to the withering of the tree by speaking of what faith can do to remove hindrances to His work (cf. Lk. 17:6). His words led to a striking prayer promise: "Whatever you ask for in prayer, believe that you have received it, and it will be yours" (Mk. 11:24). To these words, He added an important instruction, "when you stand praying, if you hold anything against anyone, forgive him" (Mk. 11:25).

Mark 11:26 of the KJV is omitted from versions that use the newer Greek text. The substance of this passage, however, is part of the Sermon on the Mount (cf. Mt. 6:15).

4. The Second Cleansing of the Temple. Jesus Preaches (Mt. 21:12-16; Mk. 11:15-19; Lk. 19:45-48)

Just as at the beginning of His ministry (cf. Jn. 2:12-22), now during His last week, Jesus again acted against those who were desecrating the temple. This event was "the next day" (Mk. 11:12) after the triumphal entry. Once more God's house had become a money making carnival, and as one has said, "The breath of mammon became the atmosphere of the place." By permission of the high priest, merchants had set up stalls in the court of the Gentiles, and they were selling sacrificial animals there. Almost certainly, the priests and temple officials, either directly or indirectly were profiting from this courtyard business.

In achieving this cleansing, Jesus drove out those buying and selling, and overturned the tables of the money changers and the benches of those who sold doves. On this occasion, there is no mention of a whip, nor of driving out sheep and cattle. Previously He had objected to the turning of His Father's house into a market. This time all three synoptics report that He objected to their making it "a den of robbers." To validate these actions, Jesus cited Isaiah 56:7 referring to the "house of prayer" and Jeremiah 7:11 referring to the "den of robbers."

Jesus' popularity with the people protected Him from immediate reprisals. No doubt He was not alone in resenting the commercialism of the Gentile court. Following the cleansing, "The blind and the lame came to him at the temple, and he healed them" (Mt. 21:14). Also, a company of children began repeating the shouts of acclaim that had been heard at the triumphal entry, "Hosanna to the Son of David" (v. 15). The priests and teachers of the law had accepted the cries of the hawkers and their animals, but they became indignant at the cries of the children. Jesus defended the children by quoting Psalm 8:2.

Some harmonies insert the visit of the Greek inquirers at this point. We have placed it just prior to the Olivet Discourse (p. 188).

5. Jesus' Authority Questioned (Mt. 21:23-27; Mk. 11:27-33; Lk. 20:1-8)

The delegation confronting Jesus consisted of: chief priests, elders, and teachers of the law. Probably many were members of the Sanhedrin. Most of the priests were Sadducees, and therefore shallow and critical in their beliefs about God and Scripture. Their challenge at this time no doubt was their response to the cleansing of the temple. They demanded to know what authority entitled Him to perform such a presumptuous act.

Jesus parried His critics' question about His authority by asking their opinion of John the Baptist. Since whatever answer they gave would have discredited them, they chose to relinquish their authority as the nation's religious leaders and refused to answer. Jesus, therefore, was likewise entitled to decline to answer. In his role as Jesus' forerunner, John was Jesus' authentication. The Jewish leaders chose to be undecided about John because to endorse him was to endorse Jesus, and this they refused to do.

6. Parables for Israel's Religious Leaders (Mt. 21:28-22:14; Mk. 12:1-12; Lk. 20:9-19)

Many harmonies of the events of Christ's life hold that His last day of public ministry began with these parables and extended through His Olivet Discourse. Typically, it is suggested that all these events occurred on Tuesday, and that Wednesday was a day of rest. An alternate view sees these final teachings and discourses extending over two days and thus to have included Wednesday as also a day of ministry. In most people's opinion, the evidence that is currently available does not support a definitive conclusion in regard to these matters.

The three parables at this time communicate Jesus' evaluation of the status of Israel's national religious leaders and their followers. In particular, the parables speak to the representatives of the Sanhedrin who were the ones questioning His authority.

1) The two sons (Mt. 21:28-32). This parable indicted the hypocritical Pharisees, elders, and teachers of the law who claimed to be doing the will of God when they were not. In God's sight, it is what a person does that matters, not what he merely talks of doing. Those who actually involve themselves are the only ones who really count. In applying the parable, Jesus dared to declare that tax collectors and prostitutes would enter the kingdom ahead of the nation's religious hierarchy. His words sweepingly condemned the entire body of religious leaders.

2) The wicked tenant-farmers (Mt. 21:33-46; Mk. 12:1-12; Lk. 20:9-19). It has been said that the patience and longsuffering of God are so remarkable that, to portray them, Jesus had to invent the situation and characters of this parable. No actual owner would endure such hostile treatment from his tenants. The parable is, of course, an allegory of God's dealings with Israel. Perhaps some of His perceptive hearers would have recognized that God was the landowner, and Jesus was the son.

In the parable, the owner responded to their rebuffs and cruelty only after great delay. At that future time "He will come and kill those tenants and give the vineyard to others" (Mk. 12:9). The tenants, with the fully equipped vineyard generously at their disposal, represented the Jews with all the religious advantages that God had granted to them. This parable was addressed to the people as well as their leaders (cf. Lk. 20:9).

Jesus quoted the metaphor of the rejected capstone (cornerstone) from Psalm 118:22,23—said to be a reference to an actual incident during the building of Solomon's temple. Though originally it applied to Israel, Jesus now applied it to Himself. In effect, it was declaring that in the future, God would overrule the rejection of His Son. At that time He would bestow doom upon the entrenched religionists of that day. Mark comments, "They knew he had spoken the parable against them" (12:12).

3) The wedding-feast of the king's son (Mt. 22:1-14). This parable depicts mankind's rejection of God's message and His messengers. It applies both to national Israel and to the Gentiles. The groom's father, representing God, invites anyone available to replace the chosen guests who indifferently reject the first invitation. Such an invitation requires one either to: 1) accept it, or 2) reject it. The incident in the parable of the man without wedding clothes is a parable within a parable. Humans are invited to come to God, but they must come on His terms. Everyone needs all He provides. At the wedding of the Lamb, the bride will wear "Fine linen, bright and clean . . . Fine linen stands for the righteous acts of the saints" (Rev. 19:8).

This parable teaches that the acceptance of the gospel is equivalent to partaking of a banquet feast. The invitation is to all who can be reached: goodness does not merit the invitation, nor does "badness" prevent it.

7. Jesus Answers and Asks Questions (Mt. 22:15-46; Mk. 12:13-37; Lk. 20:20-44)

Jesus' enemies carefully planned the extensive questioning during this day. They hoped that together they would succeed in trapping Him. Instead, He won resounding victories.

1) Pharisees and Herodians ask about tribute to Caesar (Mt. 22:15-22; Mk. 12:13-17; Lk. 20:20-26). Jesus responded bluntly to the extravagant flattery of the Pharisees and Herodians, "You hypocrites, why are you trying to trap me?" (Mt. 22:18). At that time the discussion of tribute money generated great emotion and it emphasized differences. The Pharisees saw the payment of tribute as humiliating, the Herodians supported it, the Zealots refused to pay it, and Judas the Galilean taught that it was the beginning of slavery. Most Jews found the tax a galling irritating burden, particularly because it was used chiefly to support the occupying Roman army.

The Roman denarius, that was to be used to pay the tax, likely included an inscription that declared that Caesar was the son of God and the high priest of the nation. The Jews held that a coin with the image of a human violated God's commandment in Exodus 20:4. The claim that this ruler was divine was blasphemy. Thus, pious Jews avoided carrying such a coin, but Jesus' questioners were able to produce one to show to Him.

Jesus' reply to His questioners was amazingly shrewd. It has been said to have "distinguished without dividing the secular and sacred," and to have "united without unifying the two spheres in which His disciples must live." Though secular rulers may be corrupt, Scripture teaches that both the state and the church are ordained by God. Jesus' statement not only silenced His enemies, but it serves as a basic guideline for the believer's relationship to civil government. At a later time Paul wrote, "The authorities that exist have been established by God" (Rom. 13:1). Early in the third century, Tertullian made application of this incident: "Give to Caesar his image stamped upon his coin, and give to God His own image stamped upon you."

2) Sadducees ask about resurrection (Mt. 22:23-33; Mk. 12:18-27; Lk. 20:27-40). The Sadducees generally denied the resurrection and the reality of the spirit world, including the existence of angels (which Jesus mentioned in His reply [cf. Mt. 22:30]). The Sadducees' story of the sevenfold widow was selected from their repertoire of well-worn arguments. The practice of levirate marriage, that required the survivor to marry his brother's widow, was based on Deuteronomy 25:5-10. The Sadducees hoped that Jesus' response would discredit Him in the eyes of His followers. Perhaps they had heard that He promised resurrection, and they wished to make Him look ridiculous.

In replying, Jesus did not try to struggle with their artificial problem, but He focused on the unscriptural and false beliefs upon which the problem was based. His words, "You are in error" (Mt. 22:29) are literally "You deceive yourselves." False doctrine in response to Biblical truth is a voluntary choice. Though the Sadducees professed to accept the Pentateuch, which teaches life after death, they denied this doctrine. Jesus quoted from Exodus 3:6 to refute their denial. His point was that in Moses' time the LORD (Jehovah or Yahweh) would not have been the God of the patriarchs if they had ceased to exist when they died.

Mark and Luke spoke of "the account of the [burning] bush" (Mk. 12:26; Lk. 20:37) to provide a reference to the Exodus passage when God spoke to Moses from the bush. Several centuries would intervene before the provision of our system of chapters and verses that allows us to pinpoint references. Both Mark and Luke expanded on Matthew's account to make the application clearer. Luke adds the comment of the teachers of the law, Jesus' usual critics: "Well said, teacher!" (Lk. 20:39).

3) Pharisees and teachers of the law ask about the great commandment (Mt. 22:34-40; Mk. 12:28-34). The questioner is described as an expert in the law (lawyer) in Matthew and a teacher of the law (scribe) in Mark. It would be easily possible for a man to be a teaching-lawyer. In replying to the question about the greatest or chief commandment in the law, Jesus quoted Deuteronomy 6:5, and He added to it Leviticus 19:18. Truly loving God and effectively loving one's neighbor are closely related. Jesus thus set aside the complex Jewish system of 613 laws, and He proceeded to the true heart of God's revelation.

The questioner, evidently an honest man, approvingly repeated and applied Jesus' answer in the manner of a professor evaluating a student. The comment that to show love was "more important than all burnt offerings and sacrifices" (Mk. 12:33) was a surprising admission in the lawyer's response. It has been suggested that some of the lawyer's associates probably would have resented his approval of Jesus.

The lawyer was silenced when Jesus, in turn, evaluated him with the words, "You are not far from the kingdom of God" (Mk. 12:34). When humans sit in judgment of Jesus, they need to know that He is judging them. Whether the lawyer actually crossed over into the kingdom is not known. Mark added, "From then on no one dared ask [Jesus] any more questions" (v. 34b). Perhaps the Pharisees refrained from further questions because they feared that His wise answers might convert some of their people to become His followers. **4) Jesus asks how Christ is David's son (Mt. 22:41-46; Mk. 12:35-37; Lk. 20:41-44).** Jesus now turned the tables and asked the Pharisees (cf. Mt. 22:41) a question: Whose son is the Messiah? When they answered that he was the son of David, Jesus asked them to explain Psalm 110:1 that indicates that the Messiah is the Son of God. How could the same person be David's son and also be David's LORD? For the Pharisees this question was unanswerable. They expected only a human Messiah, and they were not prepared to see Him as the Son of God. If He was not God they could not explain how He could be David's LORD.

The answer to Jesus' question is provided by the New Testament understanding that Jesus was both God and man. Those who denied Messiah's deity held a defective view of His nature. Matthew reports, "No one could say a word in reply" (22:46). McCumber comments, "The critics are silenced but not converted. They will answer Him next with whips and nails."[1] Nevertheless, the common people cheerfully identified with Jesus and "the large crowd listened to him with delight" (Mk. 12:37).

8. Jesus Warns Against Hypocritical Leaders (Mt. 23:1-39; Mk. 12:38-40; Lk. 20:45-47)

In His final public discourse (the Olivet Discourse was primarily directed to the disciples) Jesus spoke an extended indictment against the teachers of the law and the Pharisees. At this time He repeated and expanded upon some of His previous denunciations (cf. Lk. 11:37-54). He objected to these leaders, not so much because of what they taught (though in His woes He denounced aspects of their teaching), but because of their teaching style and their unworthy lifestyles. They saw themselves as the nation's religious authorities—"[they] sit in Moses' seat"[2] (Mt. 23:2). Tragically, in their own lives they glaringly failed to measure up to that which they taught. Thus, Jesus declared, "They do not practice what they preach" (Mt. 23:3).

Matthew reports seven woes (i.e., inevitable judgments) that Jesus pronounced against the Pharisees: 1) they were hypocrites who hindered people from achieving heaven (vv. 13-14); 2) they perverted their proselytes (v. 15); 3) they confused moral distinctions (vv. 16-22); 4) they served God in petty details and ignored Him in major matters—as someone has said, "They magnified trifles and trifled with magnitudes" (vv. 23-24); 5) they were immoral (vv. 25-26); 6) they were hypocrites who concealed inward corruption (vv. 27-28); and 7) they were inconsistent and

---

1   William E. McCumber, *Matthew*. Kansas City: Beacon Hill Press, 1975, p. 174.

2   A scholar interpreting Moses' teaching would be an authoritative voice. Some synagogues provided a "Moses' seat" for a respected scholar.

deceiving (vv. 29-33). The tragedy is that these denunciations applied to people who thought they were holy. Probably the great majority of the Pharisees did not consciously deceive; they were merely blind to their faults.

The brief reports in Mark and Luke add two further shortcomings of the Pharisees: 1) pride, and 2) greed. Their desire for

		Matt.	Mark	Luke	John
Jesus arrives at Bethany					12:1
Triumphal entry		21:1-11	11:1-11	19:29-44	12:12-19
Cleansing of the temple		21:12-13	11:15-18	19:45-46	
Teaching in temple		22:1-46	12:35-40	20:1-44	
Anointing by Mary		26:6-13	14:3-9		12:2-8
Judas bargains to betray		26:14-16	14:10-11	22:3-6	
Last Supper & Gethsemane		26:17-46	14:12-42	22:7-46	13:1-18:1
Trial and Crucifixion		extended references			
Entombment		27:57-66	15:42-47	23:50-56	19:38-42
Resurrection		28:1-10	16:1-8	24:1-12	20:1-18

Figure 15: The final week of Jesus' ministry. The scale indicates days, with His arrival at Bethany shown to have been on Friday. Since most events in Scripture are not dated, scholars do not agree on the specific assignment of days.

human recognition was excessive, and they engaged in pompous display. Some among them were voraciously grasping in their pursuit of donations. Their fundraising projects targeted the defenseless: "they devour widows' houses" (Mk. 12:40). They did things such as: charge for their help, cheat as trustees, mismanage, and foreclose unfairly. The basic content of these additions in Mark and Luke was formerly given in Matthew 23:14 as an eighth woe. Currently accepted Greek manuscripts no longer include Matthew 23:14.

A phylactery (Mt. 23:5) was a small case, usually of leather or metal, that held slips of paper (or parchment or papyrus) inscribed with Scripture passages. Jewish custom involved suspending this box on a ribbon and displaying it either on the forehead or in the crook of the left arm. The practice emerged from the literal application of Deuteronomy 6:8 and 11:18.

Jesus did not condemn titles, but the love of them (v. 7); He instructed, "Nor are you to be called 'teacher,' for you have one Teacher, the Christ" (Mt. 23:10). The word for "teacher" (*kathegetes* [ka-they-gay-TAYS]) that is used here has been carried over into modern Greek to denote a college professor. However, in Bible times, the word implied a master of Biblical exegesis and interpretation, and this role was reserved for Jesus.

The Pharisees imposed on their converts all the burdens of legalism but provided nothing that mattered spiritually (v. 15). They practiced deceit by invalidating promises and oaths by qualifying them with trivial and arbitrary distinctions (v. 16). The principle of tithing was valid, but Jesus condemned the system of bookkeeping that the Pharisees used (v. 23). In effect, they strained out the smallest creature, the gnat, and they swallowed the largest creature they knew, the camel (v. 24).

In concluding His condemnation of the Pharisees, Jesus used very severe language: "You snakes! You brood of vipers! How will you escape being condemned to hell [*geenna*]?" (Mt. 23:33). (*geenna* [GEH-en-na]: Gehenna). Someone remarks, "As Gehenna was Jerusalem's garbage dump, so God has His cosmic garbage dump." Jesus added that these perverted religionists would further compound their offences by rejecting future Christian messengers that He would send (cf. Mt. 23:34). The Book of Acts reports outcomes of the apostles' efforts to minister the gospel to the Jews (cf. Acts 6:9; 17:5-6; 18:4-6).

We have noted (see Luke 11:51) that the stories of the two martyrs: Abel and Zechariah (cf. Mt. 23:35) occur in Genesis 4:8 and 2 Chronicles 24:20-22. Jesus' examples speak of the first and last and all between, as we might speak of "from Genesis to Malachi." Jesus called Zechariah "son of Berekiah," whereas 2 Chronicles lists him as "son of Jehoiada." The difference is usually explained by the Jewish casual usage of "son of" as equivalent to "descendant of."

Jewish historical scholars have often protested that Matthew Chapter 23 gives a distorted picture of the Pharisees. It is widely agreed that not all Pharisees were corrupt, and that the movement as a whole had good intentions and some worthy objectives. (See footnote, p. 42, discussing the origin and agenda of the Pharisees.) Harrison comments on this matter:

> If one studies the Pharisees in their historical development apart from their contact with Jesus, one gets a rather consistently favorable impression of them; but when one sees them depicted in Matthew 23, the impression is quite different. This leads to the conclusion that ... the worst features of this group were only really drawn out by their contact with Jesus.[3]

Once again, Jesus mourned over the city of Jerusalem. (cf. Mt. 23:37-39). In prophetic vision He saw the blackened ruins that were to be the city's destiny shortly after His death. He pointedly spoke of "your house" (Mt. 23:38) rather than "my Father's house." The larger fulfillment of Matthew 23:39 (which quotes Ps. 118:26 and which was shouted by the crowds at the triumphal entry) is taken to be Jesus' Second Coming when His role of Messiah-deliverer will truly be recognized.

9. The Widow's Donation to the Temple Treasury (Mk. 12:41-44; Lk. 21:1-4)

The temple collection boxes, of which tradition says there were thirteen, were located in the court of the women. This area marked the limit within which women were permitted to enter, and thus it was the most readily accessible and busiest area of the temple courtyard.

In giving two small copper coins (Gk. *leptos* [lep-TOS]: about one-eighth of a cent), the woman made the smallest contribution allowed. She gave all that she had, however, and thus this story is not about giving according to one's means, but giving as an act of total commitment to God. It is likely that the woman would have gone hungry because of her gift.

In spite of the abuses of the leaders, this woman's worship exhibited genuine piety and sacrifice. Not only did Jesus see what the widow gave, He also saw what she had left. It was on the basis of the latter that He commended her. It is significant that Jesus did not suggest that the woman should be exempt from giving because of her poverty, and that He commended her giving though it was to an imperfect organization.

---

3   Everett F. Harrison, *A Short Life of Christ*. Grand Rapids: Wm. B. Eerdmans Pub. Co., 1968, p. 134.

10. The Greeks Seek Jesus. The Unbelief of the Jews (Jn. 12:20-50)

These Greek pilgrims to the Jerusalem Passover are thought to have been God-fearing Gentiles who may have been proselytes to Judaism. It is widely agreed that they were not simply Greek-speaking Jews. Perhaps they chose Philip as their spokesman because his name was Greek. John does not tell us whether they obtained their requested interview with Jesus, and nothing further is reported about them. Nevertheless, their presence was important, for as Leon Morris noted:

> The fact that the Greeks had reached the point of wanting to meet Jesus showed that the time had come for Him to die for the world. He no longer belongs to Judaism, which in any case has rejected Him. But the world whose Saviour He is, awaits Him and seeks for Him.[4]

The presence of the Greeks led Jesus to speak of the present moment's significance in relation to His life on earth (cf. v. 23). Since the cross was to be the means to His glory, Jesus could compare His death with the planting of a grain of wheat. He recognized that His pending death would provide for a new relationship for mankind. On the basis of the cross, both Jews and Gentiles could enjoy a new life. In this discourse (vv. 23-26), Jesus clearly stated the purpose of the incarnation. He was born to die, just as a seed must be sown if it is to germinate and grow. He could offer no earthly throne or glory, but only the privilege of being a servant.

As He realized the nearness of the cross, Jesus became deeply distressed, but He proceeded to reaffirm His commitment to the plan of God. The majority of manuscripts punctuate with a question mark His words, "Father, save me from this hour" (v. 27). Thus, Jesus' soliloquy proceeded as rendered in the NIV. God's confirming voice responded from heaven. John reports, "The crowd . . . said it had thundered; others said an angel had spoken to him" (v.29). This occasion marks the third time during Christ's incarnation that God spoke audibly from heaven. (cf. His baptism [Mt. 3:17]; His transfiguration [Mt. 17:5]).

Jesus' declaration that He would be "lifted up from the earth" (v. 32) clearly predicted His forthcoming crucifixion. The crowd was puzzled, for they were blind to His identity as the Son of Man—i.e., the Messiah (cf. v. 34), because Jesus did not measure up to the popular idea of what the Messiah would be like and the conditions He would fulfill. Jesus declared that their time to achieve understanding was running short. "You are going to have the light just a little while longer" (v. 35).

---

4 Leon Morris, *The Gospel According to John*. Grand Rapids: Wm. B. Eerdmans Pub. Co., 1971, p. 590.

John's comments at this point discuss unbelief. It was illogical (v. 37), nevertheless it fulfilled predictions (vv. 38, 40, cf. Ps. 53:1; Isa. 6:10), and it was bestowed judicially by God (vv. 39-40). For all its irony and tragedy, the rejection of the Messiah was in accord with Old Testament prophecies. John, however, added an important qualification: "At the same time many even among the leaders believed in him" (v. 41). Humanly speaking, had these leaders had the courage of Nicodemus and Joseph of Arimathea, they might have swayed the vote in the Sanhedrin.

Though Isaiah had written of his vision of the "LORD Almighty" (Isa. 6:3), John declares that what Isaiah had seen was "Jesus' glory" (v. 41). He thus identifies Jesus as one with the Almighty LORD. Jesus, in His closing word in this section, declared that to believe in Him is to believe in God (v. 44). Belief in Him brings light (v. 46), and unbelief is the act of a rebel. His message offers everlasting life (v. 50).

II. THE OLIVET DISCOURSE

Except for the book of Revelation, the Olivet Discourse is Scripture's most detailed record of the future. It is sometimes called the "Eschatological Discourse" or the "Little Apocalypse."

1. The Setting for the Discourse (Mt. 24:1-3; Mk. 13:1-4; Lk. 21:5-7)

This discourse was Jesus' response to the disciples' question concerning the future destruction of the temple. In His discussion, Jesus undertook to answer three questions that the disciples had asked: **1) When would this happen?** That is, when would the temple be destroyed? **2) What would be the sign of His coming?** (*parousia* [par-ou-SEE-ah]: coming, advent, presence, arrival). They appear to have meant His coming to assume the rule of His kingdom as Messiah-King. **3) What would be the sign of the end of the age?** The word "age" (Gk. *aion* [ay-OWN]: present age) denotes the current earthly order. According to Mark, these questions were asked by a quartet of disciples: Peter, James, John, and Andrew (cf. Mk. 13:3). Matthew's record provides no answer to the first question, but it is dealt with in Luke's account. The second and third questions are answered both in Matthew and in Mark.

Portions of the Olivet Discourse comprising Jesus' answer to the disciples' questions about the future of the temple are found in all three synoptics. Matthew's account is, however, the most extensive. In Matthew and Mark the discourse was given after Jesus had left the temple and He was sitting in a restful spot on the Mount. In Luke, He appears to have been still teaching in the temple and its adornments and substantial stones were in view (cf. Lk. 21:5). It is possible that Jesus began His discourse in the temple as Luke implies, but when the disciples came to Him privately (cf. Mt. 24:3) on the Mount of Olives, He repeated and expanded upon appropriate portions.

2. The First Stage of the Future (Mt. 24:4-14; Mk. 13:5-13; Lk. 21:8-19)

Many scholars consider that this section describes what the disciples and their successors could expect during the course of the age. Thus, they title the section, "The course of the present age." Others consider this section to be describing the future tribulation. They apply the passage basically to Israel, with only secondary applications to Christians. They minimize the discourse's application to the fate of the Church. The schools likely agree that Jesus primarily was talking to His disciples as Jews, and thus talking about their temple and city and their future.

In Matthew 24 Jesus declared that the future would bring: 1) false Christs and Messiahs (vv. 4-5), 2) wars and rumors of war (vv. 6-7), 3) famines (v. 7), 4) earthquakes (v. 7), 5) persecutions and martyrdoms (v. 9), 6) false prophets (v. 11), 7) increasing evil and apostasy (vv. 10, 12), 8) the gospel of the kingdom preached worldwide (vv. 13-14).

Interpretations that apply this prophecy to Israel usually suggest that the conjunction "then" (v. 9) introduces a new era: the final three and one-half years of the tribulation. The previous general troubles (vv. 5-7) were the beginning of birth pains, and now Antichrist unleashes his fury against Israel. The "gospel of the kingdom" (v. 14) differs from the Christian gospel. It is John the Baptist's message of repentance that will be revived to prepare humans for Messiah's coming kingdom.

For most of Jesus' message, Mark and Luke focus on the immanent persecution that the disciples would suffer. There would be trials and imprisonment, betrayals, and hatred based on prejudice. Jesus promised that when His people were arraigned in public hearings, He (Lk. 21:15) and the Holy Spirit (Mk. 13:11) would give them words to speak. The promise, "But not a hair of your head will perish" (Lk. 21:18) is usually seen in the ultimate sense. Though the disciples did not realize it, all except John and Judas would become martyrs, and they thus perished physically. Mark's promise, "He who stands firm to the end will be saved (Mk. 13:13) is usually understood by pretribulationists to apply primarily to the Jews. The verse that follows (v. 14) appears to speak of events in the great tribulation.

3. Signs of the Great Tribulation (Mt. 24:15-26; Mk. 13:14-23; Lk. 21:20-24; cf. 17:22-23)

The disciples' questions concerned the near future and the distant future. In the near future, that we know as Titus' conquest in A.D. 70, the temple would be thrown down and its stones scattered. In the distant future, the great tribulation would be ended by the return of the conquering Messiah-King.

1) The soon-to-occur conquest of Jerusalem. Jesus' primary counsel concerned their response to a forthcoming conqueror who would invade and conquer Jerusalem and desecrate the temple. Jesus advised: When they hear news of the temple's desecration, they must drop what they are doing and run for their lives. Jesus pointed out that there were particular travel complications for pregnant women or nursing mothers, and in the winter, or during Sabbath travel restrictions. These instructions involve a dual fulfillment: near and far. The near fulfillment was in the siege and conquest under Vespasian and Titus (A.D. 66-70); the far fulfillment will be during the tribulation when Antichrist unleashes his destructive forces.

It is said that Christian Jews who heeded Christ's warning and fled to Petra under Vespasian's siege and before Titus' final conquest were spared destruction. The significance of the shortening of the days (cf. Mt. 24:22) is debated. Some suggest that the count of prophesied days will be reduced, others suggest that the days will be less than twenty-four hours.

2) The appearance of the "abomination that causes desolation." This expression (cf. Mt. 24:15) derives from Daniel 9:27, and it links with a time of tribulation and horror. Futurists understand this occurrence as the launching of Antichrist's idolatrous false religion. It is a particularly devastating event because Antichrist uses the facilities and probably the vocabulary of Judaism, and he brazenly proclaims himself to be deity. The same concept of "great tribulation" is named in Revelation 7:14. In the distant future, the Jews could anticipate a time of horrible tribulation that they would only survive because the Lord would intervene to shorten the days. The "elect" (Mt. 24:22) are the Jews who are destined for Christ's kingdom.

3) The proliferation of deceivers. In the end time tribulation, Antichrist and his associates will specialize in deceit. (cf. Mt. 24:23-26). The Jews, who are eagerly seeking their Messiah, will be especially vulnerable. Jesus warned that rumors of a Messiah, known only locally, would inevitably be false.

4. The Second Coming of Jesus Christ (Mt. 24:27-30; Mk. 13:24-26; Lk. 21:25-28; cf. 17:24-25, 37)

When Jesus chooses to return, He will be revealed on a world wide basis as he appears as a lightning flash across the sky. The only reference to the time of this event given here is that He will return as the finale to the great tribulation. After all the dark tragedies, there will be the shining presence of Jesus Christ, the Son of Man. The expression "Second Coming" refers to Jesus' return as conquering Messiah-King; it does not denote His coming in the rapture.

Jesus declared, "Wherever there is a carcass, there the vultures will gather" (Mt. 24:28). Just as surely as vultures gather to eat decaying flesh, so judgment will strike where there is spiritual corruption. The Second Coming will result in great destruction of rebel humans. The event will trigger a frightening disruption of the heavens (cf. Mt. 24:29-30). The sign of the Son of Man is not described, but on the basis of Isaiah 11:10 some see the sign to be Jesus Himself. Others suggest that since the cross so universally identifies with Jesus, it is possible that in some way the sign relates to the cross.

5. The Gathering of the Jewish Elect (Mt. 24:31-35; Mk. 13:27-31; Lk. 21:29-33)

In conjunction with the Second Coming of Christ, surviving Jewish people who have not migrated to the land of Israel will receive a call to return. In this context and stage of history, the Jewish people are the Messiah's elect. Though the call will be mediated by angels, neither resurrection nor translation will be involved. This return will be of living humans in their natural physical bodies.

In many applications, the fig tree (Mt. 24:32) is considered a symbol of national Israel, but the parallel passage in Luke 21:29 declares, "Look at the fig tree and all the trees." In this passage, Jesus apparently intends no special symbolism that relates Israel to the fig tree. He is simply advising them to be aware of natural signs. Many trees, including the fig tree, lose their leaves each fall and produce new ones in the spring. Students of nature read the seasons through observed seasonal stages of deciduous trees, and similarly, prophetic students should interpret historic events.

Jesus declared in Matthew 24:34 (cf. Lk. 21:32): "This generation [Gk. *genea*] will certainly not pass away until all these things have happened." The term *genea* (gen-eh-AH) is defined: those with a common ancestor as a race or clan, those born in the same era (i.e., contemporaries), the span of time during which a generation lives. Scholars debate which definition applies here. Thus, Jesus may simply be saying that the generation witnessing the end time desecration will be the generation witnessing the Second Coming and the launching of Christ's kingdom.

6. The Time of the Second Coming (Mt. 24:36-44; Mk. 13:32-33; Lk. 21:34-36; cf. 17:26-35 or [36])

When Jesus delivered this discourse, the time of His Second Coming was known neither by man nor angels. Even Jesus, as the human Son, did not know the time of His return. While incarnate, He had voluntarily emptied Himself of His omniscience (cf. Phil. 2:5-8). The exact timing of the prophetic clock is God's secret. To illustrate this point, Jesus talked of Noah's flood, and of coworkers in the field, or at a grinding mill. In these illustrations, the ones who are taken suffer judgment; those who remain are spared to enter the new order of life. In Noah's time "the flood came and took them all away" (Mt. 24:39). Similarly, at Christ's Second

Coming, multitudes will be taken in judgment. The illustrations are the reverse of the rapture, and in spite of the similarities, they do not speak of Christ's coming to rapture the Church.

Jesus appealed to His hearers to watch and be alert for the time of His conquering Second Coming. Again, this appeal is not primarily to the Christian to watch for the rapture, though obviously the situations are parallel, but an appeal to the Jewish survivors on earth during the tribulation time. The great threat to the Jewish survivor is to be deceived by Antichrist so that he is not prepared for the return of his Messiah.

To warn His people, Jesus tells of the homeowner who fails to be watchful and suffers a burglary (cf. Mt. 24:42-43; Lk. 12:39-40). Jesus is not likening Himself to a thief, but He thus illustrates His unexpected future return. When His people think earthly conditions are too good or too bad for His return, that may be the very time of His Second Coming. Paul wrote, "the day of the Lord will come like a thief in the night" (1 Thess. 5:2).

7. The Parable of the Servant (Mt. 24:45-51; Mk. 13:34-37; cf. Lk. 12:41-46)

Not only is there to be watchfulness in anticipation of the return of the Messiah, but also faithful and conscientious service during the period of waiting. God's people on earth are responsible for serving in a faithful and wise manner. They compare with servants left in charge while the master is absent, and they are expected to remain watchful for his return.

This parable illustrates "the law of double reference." In context, it primarily refers to national Israel and their preparation for the Second Coming and the inauguration of the millennial kingdom. Secondarily, and also validly, it refers to the Christian Church, and it is a message to prepare faithfully for the rapture. Mark's account concludes with the admonition: "What I say to you, I say to everyone: 'Watch!' [Gk. *gregoreo*]" (Mk. 13:37). This verb *gregoreo* (gray-gor-EH-oh) (be on the alert, be watchful) is the root for the popular name in Christendom: Gregory.

8. The Parable of the Ten Virgins (Mt. 25:1-13)

The doctrinal point made by the parable of the ten virgins is stated in verse ten: "The virgins who were ready went in with him to the wedding banquet." Those who were ready were admitted to the marriage supper, and those who were not were excluded. One prepares by qualifying in advance for whatever terms are imposed. There is no gospel of the second chance. Advance preparation is necessary because the kingdom will come suddenly after an unexpectedly long delay.

Jesus' listeners would probably have visualized the lamps as torches, since they were to be carried outside. A typical torch consisted of a pole with a bundle of fabric at the top as a wick. The wick maintained a bright flame as long as it was saturated with oil. The system required frequent replenishing of the oil, and one who carried a torch needed an oil supply. Although oil is considered a symbol of the Holy Spirit because both function in anointing (cf. Exod. 29:7; 1 Sam. 16:13; Lk. 4:14; 2 Cor. 1:21-22), most scholars prefer not to interpret the symbolism of the oil in the parable. The issue is preparedness, and in the parable it was conveniently measured by the presence or absence of oil.

Many scholars today deny the traditional futurist view that saw this parable as primarily a picture of Christ coming in the rapture for His Bride the Church (cf. Rev. 19:7-9). There may be parallels, but these are better interpreted as secondary. Rather, the parable is seen as addressed to Israel and concerned with Christ's conquering Second Coming. The bride never appears in the parable, and the main action of the groom was to pronounce judgment against the latecomers. Someone has written, "The bridegroom is swallowed up in the figure of the inexorable Judge." Both the wise and foolish virgins spent their time sleeping, and thus neither group appears to represent the Church.

9. The Parable of the Talents (Mt. 25:14-30)

In context this parable, which is the longest parable in Matthew, speaks of the fate of Israel during the tribulation, but it also has a wider application. It clearly speaks to the Lord's servants in every era. In the parable of the minas (Lk. 19:11-28) ten men received equally, but in this parable three men receive different amounts. A talent was a measuring standard for a substantial sum of money, but over the years it related to different metals with differing values and no precise value is agreed upon. Suggestions of a talent's value in terms of its equivalence to a worker's salary range from about two weeks to four months or more.

The parable of the talents teaches the principles of accountability and industry. It focuses on the believer's use of his Lord's investment in him to count for His glory. One is not expected to do the impossible, but each must attempt at least something. At the end time, the Lord will evaluate the ministries of His servants, and He will reward especially those who conscientiously did their best. His disfavor will rest upon those who failed to use that with which He had entrusted them. He treats His servants as partners, and expects them to perform as such.

The third servant gave a speech before returning his master's talent. His words reveal that he really did not know his master in spite of his claims that he did. At the level where it counted, he totally blundered in attempting to fulfill his master's wishes. The master's action in taking away the talent formally ended the master-servant relationship between them.

10. The Judgment of the Nations (Mt. 25:31-46)

This section describes events that will occur "when the Son of Man comes in his glory" (v. 31) to assume His role as King (v. 34).

The word "nations" (*ethne* [ETH-nay]) denotes Gentiles. Jesus' words here differ from the preceding sections in being a direct prophetic message instead of a parable. Jesus describes the judgmental activities that will be involved in His Second Coming at the close of Armageddon. He will proceed in a military operation against rebel humans in their natural bodies upon earth.

The standard by which the nations are to be judged is their treatment of Christ's brothers (cf. v. 40). Since the whole of the Olivet Discourse is from the standpoint of Jesus' Jewish audience, a consistent interpretation would see His brothers as the people of national Israel. His message at this time is that those who favor the Jews will be spared to enter Christ's millennial kingdom; those who are indifferent or hostile to the Jews will suffer Christ's wrath. These relationships will not be entirely casual, for during the tribulation a Gentile who goes out of his way to favor a Jew may do so at the risk of his life. No doubt many Gentiles who choose to take this risk are motivated by their own commitment to Jesus Christ.

TEN:

THE PASSION WEEK (Part 2)

The Jewish leaders were now resolutely committed to the death of Jesus. They had issued a warrant for His arrest (Jn. 11:57), "and the leaders . . . were trying to kill him. Yet they could not find any way to do it, because all the people hung on his words" (Lk. 19:47-48; cf. Mk. 12:12; Lk. 20:19).

I. EVENTS RELATING TO THE LAST SUPPER

In these final days, Jesus resorted to secrecy in His plans and activities. He thus retained control of His life until His ministry was fulfilled. We have noted that He spent His days in Jerusalem but He outwitted His enemies by returning to Bethany beyond the Mount of Olives to spend His nights (cf. Mt. 21:17; Lk. 21:37).

1. Jesus Reveals His Impending Death (Mt. 26:1-5; Mk. 14:1-2; Lk. 22:1-2)

To His disciples at this time, Jesus declared, "As you know, the Passover is two days away—and the Son of Man will be handed over to be crucified" (Mt. 26:2). Thus, Jesus clearly set forth: the fact, the method, and the time of His death. Over the months the predictions had become increasingly specific, and Jesus now named the actual day. The Passover, which as Mark and Luke indicate (cf. Mk. 14:1; Lk. 22:1), included the Feast of Unleavened Bread, was a week-long sacred holiday. We have noted that during that time, pilgrims swelled the population of Jerusalem from the normal 50,000 to several hundred thousand.

Though Jesus declared the future with certainty, the Sanhedrin continued to plot how they might accomplish their plan. Scripture identifies their membership: chief priests, elders, and teachers of the law. This body gathered for an unofficial meeting at the home of Caiaphas, the high priest. Matthew reports, "They plotted to arrest Jesus in some sly way and kill him. But not during the Feast . . . or there may be a riot among the people" (Mt. 26:4-5). There was no longer a question about executing Christ; the only question was when to do it.

2. Mary of Bethany Anoints Jesus (Mt. 26:6-13; Mk. 14:3-9; Jn. 12:2-8)

This event took place in Bethany when Jesus was being entertained in the home of one called Simon the leper. Scholars suggest that Simon probably had been healed by Jesus and that his story may have been told anonymously (cf. Mk. 1:40-45). Though many aspects of this event were similar, this anointing is clearly distinguished from that by the sinful woman in Galilee about eighteen months previously (cf. Lk. 7:36-50). In addition to Jesus and Mary, among those present were: Lazarus, as a guest, and Martha as a server. The context indicates that this gathering took place on the evening following Jesus' last day of public ministry when He had given His Olivet Discourse.

To anoint Jesus' head and feet, Mary used costly oil of spikenard (Gk. *nardos* [NAR-dos]), a perfume derived from a plant native to the Himalayas, and normally considered a gift for a king. As on the occasion of the previous anointing, the alabaster jar would likely have been a flask with a slender neck that could be broken off to release the contents. Though the anointing of someone's feet was a standard courtesy to a guest, the anointing of the head was at least a gesture to a special guest, or in the right circumstances, could be equivalent to a crowning. For Mary to use her hair to wipe a man's feet (cf. Jn. 12:3) would be as startling and unconventional in that day as it would be in ours.

Mary "acted out of love's impulsive extravagance" and she showed her faith and devotion to her Lord by bestowing a gift worthy of a king. In modern versions the "three hundred denarii" of the original (Mk. 14:5; Jn. 12:5) has been replaced by an interpretative phrase such as: "a year's wages" or "a fortune." John speaks of "about a pint of pure nard" (Jn. 12:3). Perhaps now that she had seen Jesus' power over death in the case of Lazarus, preserving her treasured flask of embalming fragrance was no longer important to her. Perhaps also, she saw her gift as a thank offering for what Jesus had done.

Judas led the disciples in criticizing Mary for her extravagance, and her apparent indifference to the poor (cf. Jn. 12:4). Jesus' reply was a stirring defense and tribute to this devoted woman: "She has done a beautiful thing to me . . . . She did it to prepare me for burial" (Mt. 26:10,12). Jesus certainly was not insensitive to the poor (cf. Mk. 14:7), nor did He set His approval on poverty, but His point was that the poor could always be helped. Nevertheless, He would not always be physically present on earth. The occasion was extraordinary, and an extraordinary expenditure was justified.

3. Judas Bargains to Betray Jesus (Mt. 26:14-16; Mk. 14:10-11; Lk. 22:3-6)

Scripture appears to imply that Judas went to the Sanhedrin authorities directly from the home of Simon the leper. Possibly, he was smarting from Jesus' rebuke in response to his criticism of Mary. Judas' bargain with the Sanhedrin did not change the outcome, but it changed the schedule of their plans. Before Judas' involvement, the Sanhedrin had intended to wait until after the

Passover. The plan called for Judas to betray Jesus into their hands at a time when the public was not present. With Judas on their side, the Sanhedrin were now kept informed. They had only to await the signal to dispatch the arresting party at the right time and to the right place.

Scripture does not state Judas' reason for betraying Jesus, but love of money seems to have played a major role. He had questioned the chief priests: "What are you willing to give me if I hand him over to you?" (Mt. 26:15). The thirty silver coins, which appear to have been paid out immediately, have been said to be the price Judas set on his own soul. Since the coinage is not identified, the money value is unknown. Thirty silver coins, however, were the redemptive value of a slave (Exod. 21:32), and the price paid the rejected shepherd (cf. Zech. 11:12).

Luke reports, "Then Satan entered Judas" (Lk. 22:3). No one else in Scripture is said to have been personally indwelt by Satan. Before Judas sinned in betraying his Lord, he had sinned in his mind and in lesser matters. John reports, "he was a thief; as keeper of the money bag, he used to help himself to what was put into it" (Jn. 12:6). Though Judas had associated with Christ daily, he had achieved no victory over entangling sin.

4. Preparations for the Passover Meal (Mt. 26:17-19; Mk. 14:12-16; Lk. 22:7-13)

The usual chronologies provide a day of rest between the events of this day and those which went before. Mark dates this day as "the first day of the Feast of Unleavened Bread, when it was customary to sacrifice the Passover lamb" (Mk. 14:12). Jewish customs appear to have allowed some variations in the scheduling of Passover events (cf. Lev. 23:5-6). In order that the disciples might participate, Jesus sent Peter and John into Jerusalem to make preparations. It was appropriate that Jesus and His disciples should gather in this fashion, for the Jews considered the Passover meal to be the highlight of their family life. To be able to eat the Passover in Jerusalem was considered an added privilege and blessing.

Secrecy was necessary to conceal the plans from Judas—who would have reported them to the authorities—and thus avoid Jesus' premature arrest. Thus far, Jesus had left Jerusalem each evening so that He might not be found vulnerably isolated there. We have noted that by day, the crowds that surrounded Him were His protection. The Passover meal, however, was to be eaten by night. Jesus was now proceeding to complete God's plan: "My appointed time is near" (Mt. 26:18), but He still must retain control of the schedule. A man carrying a water jar (or pitcher) (cf. Mk. 14:13) would be conspicuous, since normally only women carried water jars and men carried wineskins. According to tradition, the owner of the home with "a large upper room" (Mk. 14:15) to which the disciples were led was the father of John Mark.

In Jerusalem, the two disciples arranged for the room, and obtained the items needed for the Passover supper, including the Passover lamb. Upon completing their errand they returned to Bethany. It is possible that the room chosen for the last supper was the same upper room in which the disciples gathered after the Ascension (cf. Acts 1:13). The restored room (by the Crusaders A.D. 1099) in modern Jerusalem is called the COENACULUM (Latin for "dining room") or CENACLE (English form).

5. The Passover Meal. The Disciples' Rivalry (Mt. 26:20; Mk. 14:17; Lk. 22:14-16, 24-30)

The Jewish leaders were now resolutely committed to the death of Jesus. They had issued a warrant for His arrest (Jn. 11:57), "and the leaders . . . were trying to kill him. Yet they could not find any way to do it, because all the people hung on his words" (Lk. 19:47-48; cf. Mk. 12:12; Lk. 20:19).

The problems of attempting to harmonize the Biblical accounts with the Jewish festival calendar have led some scholars to suggest a two-day Passover option that year. In this schema it is thought that Jesus, in preparation for the cross, chose the earlier day, while most Jews opted for the second day. If this were the case, then the time that Jesus died on the cross was the same time that most Jews were slaying their Passover lambs.

A two-day observance would explain the report concerning the officers on the day of the crucifixion who in delivering Jesus to the Romans: "To avoid ceremonial uncleanness . . . did not enter the palace; they wanted to be able to eat the Passover" (Jn. 18:28). Suggested explanations for two official Passover days include: 1) that year the date of the Passover was disputed and some chose the earlier date, 2) the temple facilities could not cope with the vast number of sacrificial lambs in only one day and two days were provided out of practical necessity.

In Jewish custom, the lamb was slain and dressed during the afternoon, so that it could be eaten that night. The slaying in the temple courtyard began at 3:00 o'clock, and it involved thousands of pilgrim family heads, each with a lamb.[1] The assembly-line-like procedure included: pouring out the blood on the altar, dressing the carcass, giving the fat to the priests, and bringing home the meat wrapped in the fleece. The Passover day began at sundown—approximately 6:00 p.m., and the Passover meal proceeded just as soon as the lamb was roasted. Besides the lamb, the meal included: unleavened cakes, bitter herbs (a salad that included lettuce, chicory, horseradish, and other spices), and

---

1   In the year of his observation Josephus reported a count of 256,500 lambs slain in the brief afternoon period prior to Passover evening.

haroseth (charosheth) (a paste of crushed fruits including dates and raisins moistened with vinegar).

In these solemn moments as the disciples began their Passover last supper, "a dispute arose among them as to which of them was considered to be the greatest" (Lk. 22:24). Seemingly, they still had not heard Jesus' teaching, and they had been deaf to the message of His imminent crucifixion. Once again He instructed them in the nature of true greatness: "The greatest among you should be like the youngest" (Lk. 22:26), and He made clear that in His kingdom the pattern is opposite from that of worldly kingdoms. In His kingdom, one rules by serving. Jesus is the role model: "I am among you as one who serves" (Lk. 22:27).

Despite their misunderstanding, Jesus proceeded to reassure the disciples. He declared, "I confer on you a kingdom . . . so that you may eat and drink at my table in my kingdom and sit on thrones, judging the twelve tribes of Israel" (Lk. 22:29-30). Though Jesus' followers are far from perfect, His grace provides for their lack and equips them for a glorious future.

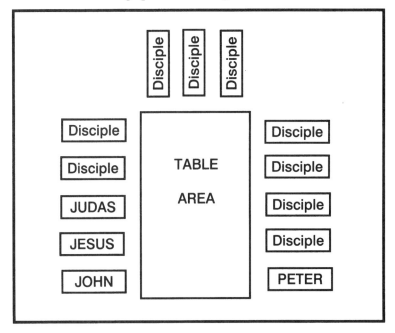

Figure 16: Edersheim's suggestion of the place arrangements at the last supper. In his view, Judas had preempted Peter's usual place of honor, and thus Peter was left to occupy the last place. The result was the argument between the disciples over which one was greater. This arrangement accommodates Scripture, but it is only a possibility, and apart from specific textual data.

6. Jesus Washes the Disciples' Feet (Jn. 13:1-17)

The emphasis in this incident is Jesus' love for His disciples. "Having loved his own who were in the world, he now showed them the full extent of his love [lit. that he loved them to the uttermost]" (v. 1). By relating to them in this loving way He responded to their striving to be great. His love was not discouraged by the treachery of Judas (v. 2), His divine status (v. 3), nor by His knowledge of Peter's forthcoming denial (v. 38). The footwashing was a significant action that foreshadowed the cross, for it was this same spirit of humble service that led Jesus to Calvary.

Textual variations govern the versions in their report of the timing of this event. The words of the KJV "Supper being ended" (Jn. 23:2), are replaced in the NIV with "The evening meal was being served." The latter accords more smoothly with the account that follows, for supper had evidently not ended. Jesus' removal of His outer clothing would leave Him dressed in a tunic that was the usual garb of a servant. Tradition holds that Judas contrived to be the first to have his feet washed.

The washing of a guest's feet was normally provided by the host through his servants. Since at this supper there were neither host nor servants, and none of the disciples volunteered, Jesus took the initiative Himself. He thus performed an enacted parable. Peter, in his usual rash manner, at first emphatically refused to submit to foot washing. His literal words were, "Not never shall you wash my feet ever!" (v. 8). R. Tasker comments,

> In making this protest Peter was in fact displaying the pride of unredeemed men and women who are so confident of their ability to save themselves that they instinctively resist the suggestion that they need divine cleansing. They desire to do everything for themselves.[2]

Jesus replied to Peter: "Unless I wash you, you have no part with me" (Jn. 13:8). Presumably it was not so much the application of water to Peter's feet, but Peter's overall submission to avail himself of Jesus' cleansing blood. In reply to Peter's request that his feet, hands, and head all should be washed, Jesus set forth the spiritual principle that the uncleanness of the whole person could be removed once and for all. Incidental contamination, however, must be removed by a periodic ongoing cleansing experience through daily prayer and confession.

In a further message, Jesus exhorted, "you also should wash one another's feet" (v. 14). The majority in Christendom accept these words as a spiritual directive instructing in attitudes and relationships with fellow believers. The words describe an example rather than prescribe an ordinance. Jesus is seen to be teaching the spirit of humble service to one another as a principle of

---

2   R.V.G. Tasker, *The Gospel According to John.* Grand Rapids: Wm. B. Eerdmans Pub. Co., 1980, p. 155.

everyday living. Christians are challenged to respond in service to the needs of their fellows. In most modern cultures, foot washing is not likely a useful gesture to a guest, instead, one relieves him of his coat and provides refreshments.

Jesus' words, "You are clean, though not every one of you" (Jn. 13:10) are taken as a reference to Judas, and some hold that they indicate that he was never really saved. Jesus said of Himself, "I have set you an example (Gk. *hypodeigma*)" (v. 15). The word *hypodeigma* (hoo-PAH-deig-mah) is defined: example, model, pattern, that which spurs one on to imitate it. Harrison summarizes this event:

> When did such lofty dignity ever combine with such lowly labor? More than feet were washed that night. Hearts as well were held in the Master's hands and were cleansed.[3]

Scripture concludes with a beatitude:"You will be blessed if you do [these things]" (v. 17).

7. Jesus Declares Judas to be the Traitor (Mt. 26:21-25; Mk. 14:18-21; Lk. 22:21-23; Jn. 13:18-30)

In preparing for His disclosure of Judas, Jesus quoted David: "He who shares my bread has lifted up his heel against me" (Jn. 13:18, cf. Ps. 41:9). Only the worst kind of traitor would betray one with whom he had shared food. To lift up one's heel suggests behaving in contempt and animosity, and the expression may link with the idea of a kick by a horse or mule. In being "troubled in spirit" (Jn. 13:21), Jesus revealed the reality of His humanity.

When Jesus declared plainly, "One of you will betray me" (Mt. 26:21) each disciple responded, "Surely not I, Lord" (v. 22). When it was Judas' turn, his words were, "Surely not I, Rabbi [i.e., Teacher]" (Mt. 26:25)[4]. Jesus had explained that it would be "the one to whom I will give this piece of bread when I have dipped it in the dish" (Jn. 13:26). Though giving the bread to Judas seemed to be a clear signal, none of the other disciples understood. They neither wanted to know what *would* happen, nor wanted to believe that the predicted events *could* happen.

Customs of that day probably partly determined events at the last supper. A group sharing a meal would recline on low couches. The couches would be placed on three sides of the low rectangular table—the fourth side was the serving side. Diners would support themselves on their left elbow, and they would more or less face the back of their neighbor. Such an arrangement complicated both conversation and observation. Because Jesus could speak

---

3 Everett F. Harrison, *A Short Life of Christ.* Grand Rapids: Wm. B. Eerdmans Publishing Co., 1968, p. 146.

4 Leonardo Da Vinci's "Last Supper" is intended to depict events at the moment described in this verse.

privately to Judas, it is widely held that he was positioned in the place of honor to the left of Jesus, the host. Jesus could speak to him by turning and speaking over His right shoulder. By raising Himself and turning, Jesus could hand him the bread.

The dish or bowl (cf. Mk. 14:20) into which Jesus dipped the bread is thought to have contained the *haroseth* sauce that, as we have noted, was traditionally used at Passover. Judas understood the significance of Jesus' gesture, but only he appears to have done so. The incident became the moment of his deliberate choice in favor of infamous treachery. John reported, "As soon as Judas took the bread, Satan entered into him" and Jesus instructed "What you are about to do, do quickly" (Jn. 13:27).

By revealing His awareness of Judas' duplicity, Jesus, in effect, dismissed him from their company. John notes, "He went out. And it was night" (13:30). The symbolism is obvious. In their naiveté, the other disciples interpreted Judas' departure as an occasion to buy more food, or to donate to the poor.

Judas' absence gave Jesus one last opportunity to bring a message to those who were genuinely His disciples. Jesus could now proceed to institute the memorial supper. Scripture progressively monitors the progress of evil within Judas. He is called a devil (Jn. 6:70), a thief (Jn. 12:6), a man prompted by the devil (Jn. 13:2), and a man indwelt by the devil (Jn. 13:27). Clearly, Judas would not have belonged in the memorial supper[5].

Luke recorded Jesus' words, "The Son of Man will go as it has been decreed [determined —KJV], but woe to the man who betrays him" (Lk. 22:22). Mark reported this statement, "The Son of Man will go just as it is written about him. But woe to that man who betrays the Son of Man! It would be better for him if he had not been born" (Mk. 14:21). In His foreknowledge, God knew of Judas' treachery, and He allowed it to be an element that fulfilled His sovereign plan. Nevertheless, the choice to betray Jesus was Judas' own and he was totally responsible for what he did.

8. The Memorial Supper Instituted (Mt. 26:26-30; Mk. 14:22-26; Lk. 22:17-20)

These Scriptures are most familiar to those who worship in non-liturgical churches where Bible portions are read at communion services. Matthew and Mark tell of the presentation of the bread first, and then the cup; Luke appears to interweave these events. The bread would be the unleavened bread (*matzo*

---

5 Luke seems to suggest that Judas was still present during the memorial supper. He quotes Jesus when He announced the cup: "The hand of him who is going to betray me is with mine on the table" (Lk. 22:21). Scholars suggest that Jesus was not speaking of Judas' physical presence, but of the fact that he was still officially part of the group. Judas still definitely had a hand in what was occurring and what would occur, and as it were, his hand lay heavily upon Jesus' earthly future.

*Figure 17: A nineteenth century artist's rendering of guests re-clining at a table. This scene is **not** meant to depict the Last Sup-per, but Scripture describes that occasion: "When evening came, Jesus was reclining at the table with the Twelve" (Mt. 26:20). Paintings, descriptions, and archeology confirm such customs.*

[MAT-suh]) used by the Jews at their Passover meal (or Seder [SAY-der]). Scripture does not name the liquid element, but sim-ply speaks of "the cup" or the "fruit of the vine."

Commentators suggest possibilities in understanding Luke 22:17, 18, 20. Either: 1) the cup of verse 17 is part of the Passover celebration (the third or fourth cup in Passover custom) and therefore it links with verses 14 and 15, or 2) Though Jesus filled the memorial cup at this time, He did not distribute it until after the bread that He shared after the supper (cf. v. 20). The expres-sion "blood of the covenant" (Mt. 26:28) refers to the new cove-nant that replaces the law of Sinai. The new covenant is God's commitment to pronouncing forgiveness upon each human who accepts the shed blood of Jesus.

As Jesus distributed the bread and the cup He declared, "This is my body" (Mk. 14:22), and "This is my blood" (Mk. 14:24). Scholars suggest that He probably was speaking Aramaic in which there is no word "is." Thus, He actually would have said, "this—my body" and "this—my blood." Since He was present with them in a healthy human body, and His body had not yet been broken or His blood shed, it would have been obvious to all that He was speaking figuratively rather than literally. The ele-ments at the table could only be emblems or representations of another kind of reality.

The bread and the cup were teaching aids used by Jesus at this time. He wanted them to know that His soon-to-occur broken body and shed blood would become the means by which sinners could be transformed into saints and kingdom citizens. He wanted them to know that they were to enter the kingdom through entering His body, the Church. By speaking of the cup as the emblem of His "blood of the covenant [testament —KJV]" (Mk. 14:24) He indicated that He was extending a grant or a provision in the manner of a will. In Christ's eternal kingdom He will renew with His disciples this ceremony that He began in the upper room (cf. Mk. 14:25). Paul reviewed and reinforced the gospels' account, and to a limited measure he interpreted it theologically (cf. 1 Cor. 11:23-34).

The memorial supper is one of two ordinances that is almost universally practiced by Christians. From the original expression (Mt. 26:27; Mk. 14:23; Lk. 22:17) rendered "he gave thanks" (Gk. *eucharisteo* [eu-car-is-TEH-oh]) the term "eucharist," one of the formal names for the memorial supper, is derived. The term "communion" is provided by 1 Corinthians 10:16 in the KJV. This ordinance serves both to remember Christ's death, and also to look forward to His coming again. There are many parallels between the New Testament report of the memorial supper and the Jewish *Mishnah's* prescription for the Passover.

Significantly, the Passover ritual closed with the singing of the Hallel (Praise) Psalms (113-118), and likely Jesus and the disciples sang all or part of this portion (cf. Mt. 26:30; Mk. 14:26). These Scriptures state, "they went out to the Mount of Olives," but John's expanded account suggests that they lingered in the upper room for Jesus' further farewell discourses. His words in John 14:31 "Come now; let us leave" follow the added teaching of that chapter. Harmonies that see these words as marking the departure from the upper room suggest that the instruction of John fifteen begins at this point.

Three more chapters of teaching and prayer follow (John 15-17), however, before John reports, "When he had finished praying, Jesus left with his disciples and crossed the Kidron Valley" (Jn. 18:1). Perhaps John 14:31 depicts leaving the table, and 18:1 depicts leaving the room. Some hold that Jesus spoke these final messages as the group walked together to Gethsemane.

9. Jesus' First Farewell Discourse. He Foretells Peter's Fall (Mt. 26:31-35; Mk. 14:27-31; Lk. 22:31-38; Jn. 13:31-38)

John reports that Jesus now spoke of His special destiny and of His role in glorifying the Father. He would glorify the Father by His obedience to the Father's plan to provide salvation for sinners. As He had told the Jews (cf. Jn. 7:34; 8:21), Jesus' journey into the life beyond would necessarily be a solitary one. He thus wished to convey necessary final instructions to these that, in this single instance in the Gospels, He called, "My children [little children —KJV]" (Jn. 13:33). The new commandment "Love one another. As I have loved you, so you must love one another" (Jn. 13:34) established "the primacy of love."

Matthew tells that Jesus now declared, "This very night you will all fall away on account of me" (Mt. 26:31). He proceeded to cite Zechariah 13:7 concerning the striking (smiting) of the shepherd and scattering of the flock. He, of course, knew that the effects of the striking would be temporary for He would rise, and all but one of the flock would be restored. Against this backdrop, Peter responded with his self-confident claim: "I will lay down my

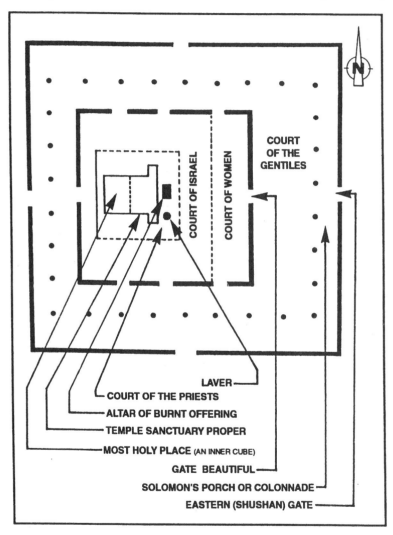

Figure 18: A general plan of the temple in the time of Christ. Many details, including the location of various meeting and utility rooms, are unknown to today's scholars.

life for you" (Jn. 13:37; cf. Mt. 26:33; Mk. 14:29; Lk. 22:33). Jesus replied to him, "tonight—before the rooster crows twice you yourself will disown me three times" (Mk. 14:30; cf. Mt. 26:34; Lk. 22:34; Jn. 13:38). Peter continued to argue emphatically: "Even if I have to die with you, I will never disown you" (Mk. 14:31).

Peter, apparently, neither understood nor appreciated it, but Jesus assured him that He had prayed that Peter's faith would not fail in spite of Satan's efforts (cf. Lk. 22:31-32). Wheat underwent rather violent treatment when it was subjected to a sifting process, but the outcome was that the weeds and chaff were separated from it. The "you" in verse 31 is plural, indicating that Satan desired to sift all the disciples, but the "you" in Jesus' report of prayer for Peter is singular and therefore distinctly personal. Jesus' words to Peter, "when you have turned back" (Lk. 22:32) are taken to be His way of saying: "when you have retraced your steps" or "when you have returned to Me."

Jesus' instruction to sell one's cloak to buy a sword (Lk. 22:36) is a difficult passage, for it seems so contrary to His teaching otherwise. The following explanations are suggested:

1) The context proceeds with quoting from Isaiah 53:12, "he was numbered with the transgressors" (v. 37). In order to fulfill prophecy, and to provide an excuse for His enemies to apprehend Him, it was thus necessary that the apostolic party be armed. Since His enemies were engaging in a ridiculous charade, Jesus was instructing His disciples to play the part and take on the appearance of a rebel group. In responding, "That is enough" (Lk. 22:38), to the report of two swords, Jesus indicated that they indeed constituted legal arms. With only two swords among the twelve, however, they were not really an armed body.

2) Though previously all of their needs had been met (cf. v. 35), Jesus was now instructing His disciples to equip themselves suitably for the challenges of His work whatever these might be in the culture in which they found themselves. In the new order of events, they must be responsible for their own upkeep. The Lord's work was no longer only an evangelistic tour; from now on it involved the ongoing maintenance of organizational and institutional structures, including such aspects as security measures.

3) Jesus' words "That is enough" were spoken in resignation to their mistaken intention to defend Him by physical combat. An alternate translation might be: "Enough of this!" or as Marvin Pate suggests, "I give up!"

The foregoing suggestions may not be compatible, and the student must choose the explanation that is personally satisfying. We note that at least one of the swords may have been on hand because it had been needed to kill the Passover lamb.

10. Jesus' Further Farewell Discourses (Jn. 14:1-16:33)

In this final teaching session, Jesus attempted for the last time to inform His disciples concerning His plans and ways. As we have noted, during at least part if not all these sessions, the group probably remained in the upper room where they had partaken of the Passover meal. Among devout Jewish families, it was customary to linger at length at the Passover table discussing the Scriptures and the evidences of God's hand in the past year and what He might do in the future.

1) Faith, hope, love, and obedience (Jn. 14:1-14). In effect, Jesus' message at this time was a reply to Peter's question of John 13:36: "Lord, where are you going?" Jesus began His response by asking His disciples to maintain personal faith in Him (cf. v. 1), and He thus made Himself one with God. The "rooms" (mansions[6]) (v. 2) were "abiding places" or "rest stops" that would provide for believers in the life to come. Though Jesus declared that the disciples knew the way to the heavenly home, Thomas directly contradicted Him (cf. vv. 4-5). In response, Jesus proclaimed, "I am the way and the truth and the life" (v. 6), and these words constitute a major statement of the Gospel that ranks with John 3:16. Jesus presented Himself as the key to all mysteries, and the bridge to God's heaven.

Philip was not so much unbelieving as baffled by Jesus' words, for he perceived in the material realm so much better than in the spiritual realm. Jesus explained that His person, His words, and His works, all revealed the Father (cf. vv. 8-11). In depicting the complete unity between Jesus and the Father, verse ten has been called "the formula of reciprocal immanence." By his request "Show us the Father" (v. 8), Philip indicated that he had entirely missed the point of what Jesus had just said (cf. v. 7). Every day during the past years Philip had enjoyed the experience that he was now requesting.

The verb "believe" in verse eleven, is plural, and the subject appears to be all the disciples and not Philip only. If they really loved Him, they would be obedient to His commandments. The "even greater things" (v. 12) may include spiritual miracles in transformed lives, or it may mean touching a greater number of lives over a longer lifespan and expanded outreach—which some Christian workers have certainly done. John 14:14 is a remarkable prayer promise: "You may ask me for anything in my name, and I will do it." The fact that all must be in His name guides and refines what is asked. The Father considers what is asked "in Jesus' name" as if He were the one asking it.

2) Promise of the Counselor (Jn. 14:15-31). The Holy Spirit or Counselor (v. 16, Gk. *paracletos* [par-AH-clay-tos]:

---

6   This KJV translation echoed the Latin Vulgate *mansiones* which simply meant dwelling.

helper, intercessor, advocate, counselor, paraclete, one called alongside) was to be Jesus' provision for His disciples for the future. Since Jesus called Him "another Counselor," B.H. Carroll identifies Him as "the other Jesus." The significant designation "Spirit of truth" (v. 17) is unique to John. The Spirit would: indwell God's people, teach them truth, and embody God's presence to ensure that they were not left as orphans (comfortless —KJV). (cf. v. 18, Gk. *orphanos* [or-fan-OS]: deprived of one's parents, comfortless). Though Jesus announced He was sending the Counselor to replace Him in His absence, He also assured His disciples that in the future He would return to them (cf. v. 19).

Judas (Thaddaeus) asked, in effect, how Jesus could return and show Himself to them and not to the world. In reply, Jesus indicated that lack of love, and failure to obey, would deprive humans of knowledge concerning Him. He thus implied that His kingdom was spiritual, and awareness and insight depended upon spiritual sensitivity.

In detail through verse twenty-seven, Jesus described how the Holy Spirit would function in making His revelation real. He would confirm, not replace, efforts to study and learn—one can only be reminded (cf. v. 26) of what he has already learned. As the Prince of Peace, Jesus bequeathed His peace to His disciples (v. 27), and in His case peace came with power to achieve it, and it was no mere empty greeting. His peace has been described as "the inward serenity based upon reconciliation with God."

In the final verses in this chapter Jesus gave His disciples farewell instructions and encouragement. He announced once more His unique love for His father. The words, "Come now; let us leave" (v. 31) suggest two possibilities that we previously noted: 1) At this invitation they rise from the table but they remain in the room while He continues teaching; or 2) After singing the Hallel Psalms together they leave the room but Jesus continues to teach them as they walk towards Gethsemane.

3) The vine and the branches (Jn. 15:1-17). Jesus' words "I am the true vine" (v. 2) are the seventh of His "I am's" in John. He used the allegory of a vine to depict the relationship that His disciples should maintain with Him. The fruit of vines grows only on branches and not on the main vine stock. Jesus stressed the principle of abiding, by which in order to bear fruit, the believer must dwell permanently in Him and in His Word and in His love. He also taught, however, that fruitless branches would be cut off; viticulture consists mainly of pruning. The verb translated "prunes" (v. 2) is literally "cleans," and it is not the normal word for pruning. It is suggested that He used that word because He was really talking about people, not plants.

In discussing Jesus' analogy of the vine and branches, Leon Morris notes:

Left to itself a vine will produce a good deal of unproductive growth. For maximum fruitfulness extensive pruning is essential. This is a suggestive figure for the Christian life. The fruit of Christian service is never the result of allowing the natural energies and inclination to run riot.[7]

Jesus described the characteristics of a fellowship of believers and for them prescribed the eleventh commandment: "Love each other as I have loved you" (v. 12). He declared that if God's people practice love for one another, they will resolve the problems of disunity. Elements of this love include: sacrifice (v. 13), intimacy (vv. 14-15), initiative (v. 16a), and productivity (v. 16b). Christ's workers are His friends (v. 15), and they have been chosen by His sovereign grace and not because of their merit.

4) Further persecution for His witnesses (Jn. 15:18-16:4). Jesus plainly warned His disciples to expect hostility from the world. The lives of virtuous believers are a reproach to the wicked. If they persecuted Him, they would persecute His followers. Humans were hostile because Jesus' coming to teach and instruct had deprived them of all excuse for their sin. Their hostility was only in themselves, and thus Jesus cited Psalm 69:4 "They hated me without reason" (v. 25). Though this citation was from the Psalms, Jesus credited it to the Law—the term "Law" identified the Old Testament Scriptures overall. Jesus suggested two counter measures to reduce the world's hostility: a) the Spirit's ministry (v. 26), and b) their witness (v. 27).

Jesus' reference to the "Spirit of truth who goes out from [proceedeth from —KJV] the Father" (v. 26) was a key verse in the medieval "procession controversies" in the church. The Eastern churches held that this sole verse that speaks of procession relates the Holy Spirit to the Father only. Thus, they rejected the Western claim that the Spirit "proceeds from the Father and the Son." The disagreement was one of the major issues that in 1054 led to the separation of the Eastern (Orthodox) Church from the Western (Roman Catholic) Church.

In 16:1 Jesus stated His basic purpose in the previous discourse: "All this I have told you so that you will not go astray." He then illustrated in greater detail what hatred from the world would mean (cf. 16:2). By putting someone out of the synagogue, the Jews considered that they were cutting him or her off from God. Such hostile persecution would occur because rebel humans know neither the Father nor the Son (cf. 16:3).

5) Parting comfort for His disciples (Jn. 16:5-33). Although Peter had framed the words, "Lord, where are you going?" (Jn. 13:36), Jesus apparently saw Peter's concern to be only for his anticipated loss, and not at all for Jesus' destiny. Thus,

---

7 Leon Morris, *The Gospel According to John.* Grand Rapids: Wm. B. Eerdmans Publishing Co., 1971, p. 669.

Jesus could rightly say, "None of you asks me, 'Where are you going?'" Jesus now addressed the problem of the disciples' depression over what He had said (v. 6). He explained that His coming departure was a necessary step in the unfolding plan of God, that the Holy Spirit might proceed to act. Jesus set forth the classic ministry of the Holy Spirit in convicting (v. 8)—He would subpoena the sinner, convene a trial, and furnish proof of guilt. The primary sin of humans is failure to believe in Jesus Christ.

Jesus now spoke of the Spirit's work in guiding the believer (vv. 12-13). To guide into all truth is taken as a ministry to impart understanding concerning Jesus' provision for humans. By this ministry the Spirit is to bring glory to Christ (vv. 14-15).

The meaning of Jesus' statement concerning not seeing and then seeing Him (v. 16) is debated by commentators just as it was by His disciples (cf. v. 18). Views include: 1) He was referring to His coming entombment and resurrection, 2) He was referring to His departure from earth so that they would be deprived of His physical presence, but granted spiritual insight to behold Him. His use of two different words for "see" in verse sixteen is cited in support of this view, 3) He was referring to His Second Coming, which In God's timing is "after a little while."

Jesus' intimation of His forthcoming death and departure from earth in the ascension left His disciples depressed and with a question (cf. vv. 19-20). Rather than answer their question, Jesus addressed their emotional need. He pointed out that they would sorrow while the world rejoiced. His enemies would rejoice that they were rid of the One who so troubled them. But the disciples were to experience a restorative future joy. They were, of course, to know the joy of witnessing the resurrection, and later they were to discover the reality of resurrection life.

Verse twenty-four is a generous prayer promise, and verse twenty-five is a promise that many associate with the teaching role of the Holy Spirit. Jesus assured the disciples, "The Father himself loves [Gk. *phileo*] you" (v. 27). This Scripture is one of only three in which the verb *phileo* (I love) is used when God (the Father) is the subject (cf. also Jn. 5:20; Rev. 3:19). The usual verb is *agapao* (at least fourteen times in the New Testament) when God is the subject. Most scholars hold that whereas *agapao* (ag-ah-PAH-oh) denotes loving as a choice of will based on understanding, *phileo* (fill-EH-oh) denotes loving as an emotional attitude because of a warm personal affection (cf. p. 246).

Jesus continued the above verse, "You have loved me and have believed that I came from God" (v. 27b). The disciples responded, "This makes us believe that you came from God" (v. 30). The NIV rendering of verse thirty-one: "You believe at last!" thus seems valid, although in other versions (e.g., KJV, NRSV) it is a question: "Do you now believe?" The original at this point is ambiguous. Notably, however, Jesus proceeds to point out that they all would soon forsake Him, for their belief still had some shortcomings. Jesus concluded by renewing His declaration of peace, and declaring His victorious overcoming of the world.

11. Jesus' Last Prayer for His Disciples (Jn. 17:1-26)

Jesus' prayer at this time is known as His high priestly prayer, since in content it parallels that of the traditional liturgy used by the high priest on the Day of Atonement. In the gospel record it is Jesus' longest prayer. By allowing the disciples to listen as He shared His heart in prayer to the Father, Jesus instructed them in their future tasks and status on His behalf. The location of the apostolic party at this time remains unspecified: they may still have been in the upper room; they may have paused in their walk towards Gethsemane; or they may have been in the temple court to which they had paid a quick visit.

In this prayer Jesus began with prayer for Himself by asking that He might be glorified so that He could glorify the Father and bring Him greater glory (cf. vv. 1-5). In the second section (vv. 6-19), Jesus prayed specifically for His disciples. His concern was a committed core of disciple-evangelists who would reach the world with His message. He prayed especially that God would protect the disciples from the evil one in the face of His imminent departure (vv. 11, 15). In verse eleven He used the expression "Holy Father" which occurs nowhere else in Scripture, although of course the concept is taught repeatedly.

Jesus prayed that God would sanctify the disciples (cf. vv. 17, 19). To "sanctify" in this context stresses the idea of being set apart and being entirely dedicated to God's service. The disciples were to take over Christ's mission to the world (cf. v. 18).

In the third section (vv. 20-26), Jesus committed Himself to pray for all believers (v. 20). He prayed for their unity, "that all of them may be one" (v. 21). The root and model of Christian unity is the unity of the divine Father and Son. True unity is divine in its source, and not the outcome of human efforts to harmonize diverse interests. Though ecumenical movements that seek for organizational unity are to be commended, our Lord's concern is for unity of heart, mind, and will. The unity of believers would convince unbelievers of the validity of Christ's mission (v. 23).

In concluding His prayer, Jesus expressed the desire that all that the Father had given Him would believe and be one with Him in glory (v. 24). Christ's glory is an expression of divine love, manifested in His gift of saving grace. Though Jesus had addressed God as "Holy Father" (v. 11), He now addresses him as "Righteous Father" (v. 25). He thus distinguished the heavenly Father from unholy and unrighteous fathers on earth.

II. THE ARREST AND TRIALS OF JESUS

John's Gospel describes the transition to Gethsemane. "When he had finished praying, Jesus left with his disciples and crossed the Kidron Valley. On the other side there was an olive grove, and he and his disciples went into it" (Jn. 18:1). The Kidron Valley, through which a brook flows in the rainy season, separates Jerusalem from the Mount of Olives.

1. Jesus Prays in Gethsemane (Mt. 26:36-46; Mk. 14:32-42; Lk. 22:39-46; Jn. 18:1-2)

Gethsemane (meaning "oil press") was a private garden and olive grove located on the slopes of the Mount of Olives about a kilometer from Jerusalem. Apparently, the owner had given permission for its use, and during His final week Jesus had regularly taken the disciples there. Luke reports, "Jesus went out as usual to the Mount of Olives" (Lk. 22:39). Because Judas knew that Gethsemane was Jesus' favorite retreat, he soon was to arrive with the arresting party. "Judas . . . knew the place, because Jesus had often met there with his disciples" (Jn. 18:2).

The first human pair had failed the test in the garden of Eden, but now another human in another garden was to struggle and prevail in victory for all mankind. Jesus left the main company of eight disciples as sentries at the gate, He took Peter, James, and John a little further, and He then proceeded "about a stone's throw" (Lk. 22:41) beyond them to His place of solitary prayer. Jesus did not ask the disciples to pray for Him, but to pray for themselves: "Pray that you will not fall into temptation" (Lk. 22:40). For His part, Jesus "fell with his face to the ground" (Mt. 26:39), and He prayed with great fervency.

The Gospels use three different verbs to describe Jesus' anguish of soul at this time: 1) "he began to be sorrowful" (Mt. 26:37, Gk. *lupeo* [loop-EH-oh]: to be distressed, to grieve, to be anguished), 2) ". . . and troubled" (Mt. 26:37, Mk. 14:33, Gk. *ademoneo* [ah-dame-on-EH-oh]: to be in anxiety[8], to be full of heaviness, to be depressed), 3) "he began to be deeply distressed" (Mk. 14:33, Gk. *ekthambeo* [ek-tham-BEH-oh]: to be greatly amazed, to be horrified, to be dismayed). Our language lacks the forcefulness to do full justice to each of these powerful verbs, and their lexical definitions tend to overlap. In spite of all the strengths Jesus possessed, His humanity struggled piteously in anticipation of what He must experience. Someone has said, "The agony of Gethsemane was greater than the agony of Calvary."

---

8 Jesus' anxiety was His sinless response to His anticipated ordeal. The Scripture, "Do not be anxious about anything" (Phil. 4:6) uses the verb *merimnao* (mer-im-NAH-oh) to identify morbid anxiety or worry that is wrong for Christians (cf. Lk. 12:11, 25). Even as He faced Calvary, Jesus' anxiety was not of this type.

Jesus divided His prayer into three sessions, but from the beginning He prayed, "Abba, Father, ... Take this cup from me. Yet not what I will, but what you will" (Mk. 14:36).[9] This prayer was obviously not an attempt at rebellion, but it was a response of His overwhelming dread of the terrors that awaited Him. In His humanity He must endure excruciating torture; in His deity He must endure the horror of becoming sin and being separated from God. The strengthening angel (Lk. 22:43) enabled Him to continue though "his sweat was like drops of blood falling to the ground" (Lk. 22:44). His human nature continued to have the usual needs and responses of humans.

Each time that Jesus returned to the disciples He found them asleep. Since by now it must have been well after midnight, the disciples were sleepy. The first time, Jesus wakened them and asked, "Could you not keep watch for one hour?" (Mk. 14:37). After that He let them sleep until the arresting party arrived, for by then He had moved beyond the need of human companionship. Though the disciples meant so well, they proved useless as watchmen for Jesus, or even in praying for themselves. He gave the best possible interpretation to their behavior: "The spirit is willing, but the body is weak" (Mk. 14:38). Also, Luke explains, they were "exhausted from sorrow." (Lk. 22:45).

The successive prayers of Jesus simply confirmed His commitment to the will of the Father. Thus, "once more [He] prayed the third time, saying the same thing" (Mt. 26:44). A.B. Bruce, in the nineteenth century, suggested that the three prayers represent three stages in Jesus' attitude. The first simply unburdened His heart, the second solemnly faced His fate, the third constituted the abandonment to the divine will. When the time for prayer had ended, Jesus instructed, "Rise, let us go! Here comes my betrayer" (Mt. 26:46).

2. Jesus is Betrayed, Arrested, and Forsaken (Mt. 26:47-56; Mk. 14:43-52; Lk. 22:47-53; Jn. 18:3-12a)

Judas led the arresting party to Gethsemane where he was sure he would find Jesus. Since it was during the night, there were no crowds to interfere. The arresting party included: Jewish temple police, Roman soldiers from the occupying garrison quartered in the Tower of Antonia, and officials representing the chief priests, teachers of the law, elders, and Pharisees (cf. Mk. 14:43; Jn. 18:3). These people were the only ones in Scripture that Jesus specifically identified as sinners (cf. Mt. 26:45). Matthew refers to

---

9   In this Scripture, the expression "*Abba*, Father" is used for the first time. *Abba*, which was the Aramaic word for father, was a Hebrew child's way of addressing his father familiarly, and it spoke of intimacy between father and son. The word father that follows translates the usual Greek. This bilingual repetition combines intimacy with universality in addressing the heavenly Father.

"a large crowd" (26:47), and John speaks of "a detachment of soldiers" (Jn. 18:3). A detachment normally consisted of 600 men, but likely only representatives were sent. Estimates place the total arresting party at from 200 to 600. They were armed with swords and clubs, and they carried torches and lanterns (cf. Jn. 18:3). It was the season of the full moon, but apparently they brought lights in case Jesus tried to hide.

By prearrangement, Judas identified Jesus to the officers by greeting and kissing Him. This procedure assured that in the dim light the arresting party would not confuse their quarry. Judas' treachery is first evident in his salutation that was literally: "Rejoice (be merry, glad to see you), Master (teacher)" (Mt. 26:49). Though the expression may have been somewhat conventional (as our use of "Good day" even in adversarial situations), there was irony in Judas' choice.

The kiss was a further evidence of treachery. Judas appears to have ignored the standards of his day that considered the disciple impudent who kissed his master before the master kissed him. All three synoptics mention Judas' act in kissing Jesus, and Matthew and Mark use the compound verb *kataphileo* (cat-ah-fill-EH-oh) which suggests the act of kissing in a vigorous and fervent manner. Luke reports Jesus' challenge: "Judas, are you betraying the Son of Man with a kiss?" (Lk. 22:48). John adds in parentheses what he so vividly remembered: "Judas the traitor was standing there with them" (Jn. 18:5).

Jesus' response "Friend, why have you come? (Mt. 26:50 footnote) has been called "a rebuke by a question." This footnote rendering in NIV (cf. also KJV) reflects the literal original (Friend, why here?), whereas the NIV text, "Friend, do what you came for" is an interpretative paraphrase.

In delivering Himself to His enemies, Jesus who knew "all that was going to happen to him" (Jn. 18:4), remained in complete control. Twice He asked who it was they sought (cf. Jn. 18:4, 7). In the first instance, upon their reply, "Jesus of Nazareth," He answered simply, "I AM." In reaction "they drew back and fell to the ground" (Jn. 18:6), overcome by what someone has described as "numinous awe." Leon Morris comments:

> The soldiers had come out secretly to arrest a fleeing peasant. In the gloom they find themselves confronted by a commanding figure, who so far from running away comes out to meet them and speaks to them in the very language of deity.[10]

Though most versions supply a pronoun and render Jesus' answer as "I am he," to Jesus' enemies with Jewish backgrounds, the words "I am" had very special significance. It was by these words that the God of Israel identified Himself (cf. Exod. 3:14). If

---

10 Morris, op. cit., p. 743.

Jesus' words in the Garden had power to shock, in His future coming His words will be as a sharp two-edged sword.

By restoring Malchus' ear, Jesus undid the damage resulting from Peter's impetuous swing of his sword. Probably, Peter's sword was one of the two that had previously been noted (Lk. 22:38), and it may only have been a large dagger rather than a full sword. Though John's description speaks of the "cutting off" of the ear (18:10), the verb actually denotes "ripping off" or "tearing off" and it suggests that the sword was dull. Jesus commanded Peter, "Put your sword back in its place," and He added, "Do you think I cannot call on my Father, and he will at once put at my disposal more than twelve legions of angels?" (Mt. 26:53). Since up to 6,000 soldiers constituted a legion, the potential complement of twelve legions was 72,000 angels. That number contrasted dramatically with the company of twelve humans consisting of Jesus and His eleven fearful disciples.

Jesus pointed out to the arresting party that He had been teaching daily in the temple courts and they could easily have arrested Him. Now they had come with swords and clubs as if to capture a rebel leader. This occasion marked the only time that Jesus protested an indignity to Himself, and here He simply objected to the manner of His arrest. They, of course, were doing things in the pattern dictated by their fear of the people. Their action in binding Him (cf. Jn. 18:12) was contrary to Jewish law except in cases when the prisoner resisted, which Jesus did not. At this point, Scripture poignantly comments, "Then all the disciples deserted him and fled" (Mt. 26:56; cf. Mk. 14:50). Apparently, the arresting party made no effort to apprehend them.

The concluding incident in Mark's Gospel concerns the young man in a linen garment who was following Jesus. To avoid arrest he fled naked (cf. Mk. 14:51). Many hold that the young man was Mark himself in a cameo appearance in his Gospel. As tradition depicts matters, the last supper had been in Mark's parents' home, and when Jesus was praying in Gethsemane, he was home asleep. Mark had been awakened either because the arresting party first came to the upper room before proceeding to Gethsemane, or by a servant with news of events in the Garden. He had rushed to the scene wearing only his sleeping garment and thus had become vulnerable to the events that occurred.

3. Jesus' Examination Before Annas and Caiaphas (Mt. 26:57, 59-68; Mk. 14:53, 55-65; Lk. 22:54a, 63-65; Jn. 18:12b-14, 19-24)

John reports that Jesus' captors first led Him before Annas, the high priest emeritus. Officially, Annas was without authority in the case since the Romans had deposed him fifteen years previously. Many Jews, however, considered Annas still their legal high priest, for by their law the priest was appointed for life. Whether in or out of office, Annas continued to exert considerable influence. The fact that the present incumbent, Caiphas, was his son-in-law, and that over the years five of Annas' sons occupied the high priest's office assured his continuing involvement.

Annas began what was to be the most infamous trial in all history with incriminating questions. Since the correct legal procedure required the questioning of witnesses, not the accused, at the very outset, Annas violated the law. In replying to the question about His disciples and His doctrine (Jn. 18:19), Jesus declared that He had taught publicly and therefore Annas should "Ask those who heard me. Surely they know what I said" (Jn. 18:21). In response to these words, a nearby officer slapped Jesus, and after a further brief interchange, Jesus was led "still bound, to Caiaphas the high priest" (Jn. 18:24). In the original, the word rendered "slapped" actually denotes "administered a severe blow." Such violence made mockery of legal process.

The examination before Caiaphas, who as high priest presided over the deliberations, was in his home by night. Matthew's mention that the membership of the Sanhedrin "had assembled" (26:57) hints that they had gathered while Jesus was being examined by Annas. The full membership of the Sanhedrin totaled seventy-one, but as few as twenty-three was a quorum, and perhaps many were absent. Those present included: teachers of the law, elders, and the chief priests. The hearing was conducted as an actual trial, with the obvious intention that its decision should stand. Rather than being a gathering pursuing justice, it actually was nothing more than a kangaroo court—the machinery to pronounce the death penalty upon a prejudged man.

In its initial strategy, the "Sanhedrin were looking for evidence against Jesus so that they could put him to death .... Many testified falsely against him, but their statements did not agree" (Mk. 14:55-56). Oddly, the Sanhedrin respected justice to the extent that their witnesses must agree, but they had met to accomplish a totally unjust deed. The two witnesses misquoted Jesus when they claimed that He had said He could destroy and rebuild the temple. He had actually said, "[You] destroy this temple, and I will raise it again in three days" (Jn. 2:19). John explains, "The temple he had spoken of was his body" (v. 21).

Eventually, Caiaphas demanded of Jesus, "I charge you under oath by the living God: Tell us if you are the Christ, the Son of God" (Mt. 26:63). In the NIV, Jesus reply is rendered: "Yes, it is as you say" (Mt. 26:64). More accurately (as in NRSV) Jesus replied: "You have said so" (Mt. 26:63). Mark reports Jesus' answer, "I am" (Mk. 14:62). Matthew apparently cites the Jewish idiom that Jesus would actually have used, whereas Mark paraphrased it into its basic meaning in any language. In either case, Jesus had made His accuser confess His true identity.

Although Jesus did not contradict Caiaphas, He proceeded with a prediction of His future glory. His destiny at God's right hand (cf. Lk. 22:69) links with Psalm 110:1. His coming in the clouds of heaven (cf. Mt. 26:64) links with Daniel 7:13. To be seated at God's right hand suggests a role as the judge of all humans. By applying these Scriptures to Himself, He was affirming that He was the Messiah. In response to these words, Caiaphas tore his clothes according to the formally regulated ritual of the day, and he pronounced Jesus guilty of blasphemy. The Sanhedrin members obsessively chorused, "He is worthy of death" (Mt. 26:66). They took the position that for Jesus to claim to be the Messiah was a capital crime.

It is significant that in Mark's account of the foregoing events, Caiaphas phrased his question, "Are you the Christ, the Son of the Blessed One?" (Mk. 14:61). To identify deity as "the Blessed One" instead of simply saying "God" has been called a "reverential circumlocution." For the high priest to adjust his words to avoid naming God is one more evidence of the low level of piety that prevailed at that time.

The fate of Jesus was decided in this illegal meeting of the Sanhedrin. It has been pointed out that on at least five grounds, the action was a breach of justice and a legal review would certainly have dismissed the case: 1) the Sanhedrin met in a home rather than in the temple, 2) it met at night though only day meetings were legal, 3) witnesses were bribed and the accused was forced to testify against Himself, 4) a prisoner's confession was used judicially, and 5) the trial was not dismissed in spite of disagreement between witnesses. It was to preserve a facade of justice that the early morning daytime meeting of the Sanhedrin was called to rubber stamp this action and make it official.

Although these were the nation's elders and members of its highest judicial body, the events following the pronouncement of the verdict unleashed the savage behavior of a mob. "Then some began to spit at him; they blindfolded him, struck him with their fists, and said, 'Prophesy!' And the guards took him and beat him" (Mk. 14:65). The Jewish mockery at this time ridiculed Jesus' prophetic powers (which He refused to use); the later Roman mockery (cf. Mk. 15:16-20) ridiculed His claims to kingship. Apparently, this first round of atrocities continued while they waited for daybreak and the hour for their official Sanhedrin meeting. Meanwhile, a tragic drama was occurring in the courtyard.

4. Peter Denies Jesus Three Times (Mt. 26:58, 69-75; Mk. 14:54, 66-72; Lk. 22:54b-62; Jn. 18:15-18, 25-27)

The record of Peter's denial is found in all four Gospels. Apparently the Holy Spirit chose to tell and retell the event to remind other humans of their frailty and the vital need to depend on divine strength. John appears to interweave these events with his report of the trial before Annas, but they clearly occurred during the trial under Caiaphas. The crowing rooster marked daybreak, and the speedy conclusion of the Jewish trials.

Though Peter was courageous enough to proceed to the place of the trial rather than flee into hiding, his courage was soon to fail him. He was admitted into the high priest's courtyard because he was introduced to the young lady doorkeeper by "the other disciple who was known to the high priest" (Jn. 18:16). The identity of this so-called "mystery disciple," who apparently was not challenged, has been variously proposed as: John, Nicodemus, or Judas, but John is the most popular choice.

Peter's three denials appear as follows: 1) to the servant girl of the high priest, who was the doorkeeper: "Woman, I don't know him" (Lk. 22:57). Perhaps at this time, "the rooster crowed"[11]. 2) to female (and possibly male) bystanders an hour later: "Man, I am not [one of them]" (Lk. 22:58). 3) to those standing near including a relative of Malchus whose ear had been cut off: "I don't know this man you're talking about" (Mk. 14:71). He preceded this denial by invoking curses, and while he was speaking the rooster crowed for the second time.

Scripture describes events at the third denial: "[Peter] began to call down curses on himself and he swore to them, 'I don't know the man!'" (Mt. 26:74). Many scholars hold that the procedure of calling down curses was a way of affirming innocence—if the curses did not occur he would be assumed innocent. It would not necessarily be the case that Peter used profanity.

Peter had no sooner pronounced his third denial than Jesus was led past and His eyes, in a penetrating gaze, met Peter's (cf. Lk. 22:61). Believers can only feel heartfelt sympathy for this all-too-human disciple who "went outside and wept bitterly" (Mt. 26:75). Though Scripture does not say that Peter repented, it certainly implies that he did. Thus, someone comments of Peter: "He was a great sinner, but he was a great repenter!"

5. Jesus' Formal Condemnation by the Sanhedrin (Mt. 27:1; Mk. 15:1a; Lk. 22:66-71)

At daybreak (cf. Lk. 22:66) the Sanhedrin proceeded with a further official meeting to fulfill the legal requirements for referring Jesus to the Roman authorities. It is usually thought that this meeting would be in the Gazith, the Sanhedrin's official council chamber in the temple. Though some suggest that this morning meeting was simply the final act of the night meeting, the fact that "Jesus was led before them" (Lk. 22:66) appears to indicate that this was a separately convened session. The early hour likely was chosen in order to assure that Jesus' case was included on Pilate's agenda for that day. The meeting simply reenacted the key events of the night's examinations.

---

11 Some manuscripts include these words in Mark 14:68, but modern versions either omit them or show them as a footnote. Even if we are not definitively told when the rooster first crowed, at least we know that after Peter's third denial "the rooster crowed the second time" (Mk. 14:72).

Once again Jesus' declaration of Himself as the Messiah was the issue, and again He simply endorsed what His accusers were saying. "'Are you then the Son of God?' He replied, 'You are right in saying I am.'" (Lk. 22:70). On the basis of these words this daytime Sanhedrin meeting reached its formal trial decision, and again prescribed the death penalty. Since the judicial powers of the Jewish state were limited by Rome, they saw their decision as a recommendation to the Roman authorities. Although they were later to say to Pilate, "We have no right to execute anyone" (Jn. 18:31), they sometimes did execute people, particularly by stoning (e.g., Stephen). Their concern for Roman initiative in this matter appears to have been a response of their conscience to the fact that they were executing an innocent man.

The decision makers are specifically identified as "the chief priests, with the elders, the teachers of the law and the whole Sanhedrin" (Mk. 15:1). This group "came to the decision to put Jesus to death" (Mt. 27:1), but the count of those voting is not given. We have noted that a quorum for the Sanhedrin was twenty-three; a decision would have required a majority of at least two. Thus, Jesus could have been condemned by as few as thirteen votes. It is possible that those members of the Sanhedrin who were known to be favorable to Jesus were not invited to this early morning meeting.

6. The Remorse and Suicide of Judas (Mt. 27:3-10)

When Judas saw that Jesus had been condemned, he was seized with remorse. "I have sinned . . . for I have betrayed innocent blood" (v. 3). It is possible that Judas had expected Jesus to free Himself, and he had thought of his actions only as a scheme to raise money. Thus, Judas brought back the thirty pieces of silver to the chief priests and elders, and when they showed no interest in accepting the money, he "threw it into the temple and . . . went away and hanged himself" (v. 5). Though Judas had shown remorse, there was no evidence of repentance.

The authorities used the money that Judas returned to buy a burial ground for foreign strangers or indigents. The burial ground was named "Akeldama," (ah-KEL-da-ma) which in Aramaic means "field of blood" in recognition that it was purchased with blood money. It formerly had been a field where potters dug for clay. The fulfilled prophecy cited in Matthew 27:9 identifies closely with Zechariah 11:12-13, but Jeremiah refers to the potter (18:2), and he speaks of buying a field (32:6-15).

The parenthetical note in Acts 1:18-19 tells of Judas' undergoing a fatal fall that ruptured his body cavity. The church has long held that the two accounts do not necessarily conflict. In the fifth century, Augustine suggested that in the hanging the rope broke, and the resulting fall caused the body to rupture.

7. Jesus' First Appearance Before Pilate (Mt. 27:2, 11-14; Mk. 15:1b-5; Lk. 23:1-5; Jn. 18:28-38)

Pontius Pilate was the Roman governor (procurator) of Judea, and the man in whom the power to enforce the death penalty by crucifixion was vested. In handing Jesus over to him, the Jews were careful not to pass the entrance of the Praetorium, which was Pilate's official residence and the building from which he administered. They were concerned that in a Gentile building there might be contaminating leaven, or even a burial, and they were particularly eager to avoid defilement at Passover (cf. Jn. 18:28). They were scrupulous about ceremonial defilement, but they were vigorously participating in a judicial murder.

Two possibilities for the conduct of the trial are suggested: 1) Pilate allowed the Jews to remain outside while He proceeded to examine Jesus inside the Praetorium and he commuted between this inner chamber and the street or court outside where he came periodically to consult with the Jewish accusers, or 2) Pilate conducted the hearing outside in the courtyard so that the Jewish accusers could observe and participate. Probably he had his judicial bench brought outdoors. This view is suggested by the fact that after Jesus had been sentenced "The soldiers led Jesus away into the palace (this is, the Praetorium)" (Mk. 15:16), but since the flogging followed the sentencing, that may have been the reason that Jesus was outside.

There had been three Jewish trials (or hearings) and now there were to be three Roman trials. Though the Jewish and Roman authorities thought that Jesus was on trial, in reality, it was they, and the whole human race, which was on trial.

The Jewish officers at first tried to avoid stating their grounds for requesting the execution of Jesus. They responded to Pilate's inquiry concerning the charges: "If he were not a criminal . . . we would not have handed him over to you" (Jn. 18:30). They had hoped that Pilate would simply confirm their sentence, but instead, he opened a new trial. When charges were stated, they were political rather than religious: 1) He subverts (misleads, teaches sedition) our nation, 2) He opposes payment of taxes, and 3) He claims to be a king (cf. Lk. 23:2). They based this latter charge on His claim to be Christ (the Messiah), and they made Christ to be equivalent to king. Thus, they had changed the basic charge from blasphemy to treason.

Pilate appears to have dismissed the first two charges as utterly false, but he made an effort to follow through the claim to be king. If Jesus was claiming to be a king, He was declaring Himself to be a rival of the Roman emperor, and He would be a threat to Roman rule. All four Gospels report that Pilate began his examination by asking Jesus if He was the king of the Jews. In the account in the synoptics, Jesus replied to the effect that it was so (cf. Mt. 27:11; Mk. 15:2; Lk. 23:3), but He did not proceed to defend or justify Himself. Pilate thus determined that this man was harmless, and he therefore announced, "I find no basis for a charge against this man" (Lk. 23:4; cf. Jn. 18:38).

John records that Jesus replied that He had come to this earth to be king, but not in a military or political sense. He concluded, "Everyone on the side of truth listens to me" (Jn. 18:37). To these words, Pilate responded with his classic question: "What is truth?" and thus he may have implied that no one could determine absolute truth in religion. If that was Pilate's conviction, then he would have seen no reason to condemn Jesus on what he considered to be sectarian religious grounds. John, just as Luke, concludes the account of the trial with Pilate's declaration that he found no basis for a charge against Jesus.

8. Jesus' Trial Before Herod Antipas (Lk. 23:6-12)

In the uproar resulting from Pilate's pronouncement, Jesus' identification with Galilee was mentioned. When Pilate "learned that Jesus was under Herod's jurisdiction, he sent him to Herod, who was also in Jerusalem at that time" (Lk. 23:7). The referral was Pilate's opportunity to rid himself of a troublesome case.

Herod was pleased to meet Jesus, for "He hoped to see him perform some miracle" (v. 8)—obviously a wrong reason. However, though Herod asked Him many questions, Jesus maintained total silence. Apparently, Jesus considered Herod to be a shallow insincere profligate, particularly since he had capriciously executed John the Baptist. Not only was Herod unworthy of His reply, but so also were the clamoring chief priests and teachers of the law who were in Herod's court.

Eventually, the baffled Herod seems to have decided that Jesus was an irrational religious fanatic. After he and his soldiers had contemptuously ridiculed and taunted Jesus, they dressed Him in a mocking robe, and sent Him back to Pilate. In effect, by this gesture, Herod pronounced Jesus innocent. Scripture notes "that day Herod and Pilate became friends—before this they had been enemies" (v. 12). Perhaps Pilate's recognition of Herod's jurisdiction over Galilee healed past rivalries, or perhaps their mutual conviction of Jesus' innocence provided a shared concern.

9. Jesus is Sentenced to Death by Pilate (Mt. 27:15-30; Mk. 15:6-20a; Lk. 23:13-25; Jn. 18:39-19:16a)

With Jesus once more before him, Pilate reviewed the accusations. Mark describes Pilate as "knowing it was out of envy that the chief priests had handed Jesus over to him" (Mk. 15:9). Thus, Pilate for the second time declared Jesus' innocence: "I . . . have found no basis for your charges against him. Neither has Herod . . . as you can see, [Jesus] has done nothing to deserve death. Therefore, I will punish him and then release him" (Lk. 23:14-16). The people however, incited by the chief priests and elders (Mt. 27:20), and possibly assembled at their call, reacted to this pronouncement by shrieking their objections. The only prisoner they would accept for release was Barabbas.

The custom of the release of a prisoner at Passover—the so-called "Pascal amnesty"—is known only through the New Testament. Some see a reference to the practice in the Jewish *Mishnah*, but the passage is vague and controversial. Roman law, however, recognized amnesties, and various notable instances are known, though they are not related to a fixed custom. Scripture appears to emphasize the Barabbas episode by reporting it in all four Gospels, and only Luke does not explain that the release of a prisoner was according to custom.

Barabbas, the people's choice for amnesty was guilty of all the crimes of which Jesus had been charged. In addition, he had led a failed rebellion against Rome, and he was a robber and murderer. The choice of Barabbas rather than Jesus is a glaring example of the ugly outcomes of the "mob mind" syndrome.

The sequence of events that followed may be gleaned from the composite harmony as follows:

1) Pilate, presiding from his official judge's seat, continues his efforts to have the crowd accept Jesus as the one to be released (Mt. 27:17; Jn. 18:39). Since serious charges had been laid, and no defense offered, Pilate had no legal option but to condemn Jesus. Nevertheless, an amnesty would have spared him from having to pronounce judgment.

2) A dream affirming Jesus' innocence leads Pilate's wife to send him a message of warning (Mt. 27:19). Some traditions hold that Pilate's wife had become a Jewish proselyte, and that she had concluded that Jesus was the prophesied Messiah.

3) The crowd cries for the release of Barabbas (Lk. 23:18).

4) Pilate proceeds to wash his hands (Mt. 27:24,25)—this was a face-saving action that perhaps avoided a full-scale riot and Pilate's loss of control of the people.

5) Pilate approves Barabbas' release (Mt. 27:26; Jn. 18:39-40).

6) To appease the crowd and incite sympathy, Pilate orders that Jesus be flogged (cf. Jn. 19:1). In that culture, flogging (scourging) was brutally cruel. As the strokes fell on the bared back, bone or metal weights on the ends of the many throngs of the lash tore away chunks of flesh. Some victims did not survive. Following the flogging, the soldiers led Jesus to the Praetorium (the palace) and there they staged a mock coronation. They dressed Jesus in a purple robe (Jn. 19:2-5; Matthew saw it as scarlet [27:28]), and placed a crown of thorns on His head. This is the soldiers' first mocking.

7) Pilate presents the beaten wounded Jesus to the crowd, "Here is the man" (Jn. 19:5). Harrison comments, "Pilate was a poor psychologist," and he quotes Marcus Dods, "Pilate failed to take into account the common principle that when

you have wrongfully injured a man you hate him all the more."[12]

8) The crowd (actually "the chief priests and their officials") continues to cry, "Crucify! Crucify!" (Jn. 19:6).

9) The Jews argue: "According to [our] law he must die because he claimed to be the Son of God" (Jn. 19:7). They called for an execution on the basis of their misguided view of Scripture.

10) Pilate's last private interview with Jesus (Jn. 19:8-11). His contacts with Jesus were making him increasingly uneasy, and now "he was even more afraid" (Jn. 19:8). He chose to cover his uncertainties by a show of authority. Jesus pointed out that Pilate's power was given him from above, and that the one guilty of greater sin was he who had handed Jesus over—presumably a reference to Caiaphas.

11) The crowd threatens to charge Pilate with treason if he releases Jesus (cf. Jn. 19:12). In fact the Jewish leaders and the motley crowd were the ones guilty of treason, for they rejected the authority of Pilate, their legal governor. Pilate was intimidated by their threats, for his political future depended upon his remaining popular and thus staying in Caesar's good graces. The decision which he upheld, was not by a judicial finding, but because he "decided to grant [the mob's] demand" (Lk. 23:24).

12) Pilate sits in the judge's seat (*Gabbatha* in Aramaic) to indicate he is ready to announce his decision (Jn. 19:13). The judge's seat was a raised platform in the paved courtyard where a magistrate could announce a decision to an audience.

13) In defeat, Pilate capitulates: "Here is your king" (Jn. 19:14).

14) The chief priests, speaking for the crowd, declare, "We have no king but Caesar" (Jn. 19:15). These words have been called, "The crowning apostasy of Judaism." They chose a pagan emperor in place of Jesus their Messiah.

15) Pilate hands over Jesus to be crucified (Jn. 19:16). He handed Him over to the will of the Jews and to the custody of the Roman soldiers who were appointed to carry out crucifixions. Pilate chose to approve Jesus' execution in order to minimize trouble for himself. For the record, however, the official Roman charge against Jesus was treason, since He had acknowledged that He was King of the Jews.

16) Once again in the Pretorium the soldiers brutally mock Jesus while they await the hour of crucifixion (cf. Mk. 15:20; Mt. 27:31a).

17) The soldiers return His clothes and prepare to escort Him to the cross (Mt. 27:31b; Mk. 15:20b)

---

12 Everett F. Harrison, op. cit., p. 214.

From the time of His arrest, Jesus had undergone six trial hearings before: Annas, Caiaphas, the Sanhedrin, Pilate, Herod, and Pilate. The Roman authorities, Pilate and Herod, had five times declared Him innocent: Herod (Lk. 23:15), Pilate (Jn. 18:38; Lk. 23:14; Lk. 23:22; Jn. 19:4). Short of actually dismissing the case, Pilate had tried every possible means to free Jesus: 1) declared Him innocent, 2) tried to win sympathy and satisfy the people by flogging Him, and 3) offered to release Him on the basis of the annual custom. The Jews declared their responsibility for Jesus' death (cf. Mt. 27:25), but because Pilate agreed to it, and sentence was under Roman auspices, he too was responsible. In reality, the Son of God was crucified by all mankind.

In spite of all the cruelties and injustices of Christ's trial, God remained in charge, and He never lost control. The vicious ugly schemes of wicked men and of Satan were somehow countered by the wisdom of God and woven into His plan, many details of which had been prophetically declared in Scripture. Jesus willingly chose to enter into the events so that He might provide an unassailable salvation for every penitent sinner.

ELEVEN:

THE CRUCIFIXION AND RESURRECTION

It appears that Jesus' trial hearings were fairly brief, and the entire official process took only a few hours. In addition there were, of course, the illegal night meetings. The Sanhedrin's legal meeting had to await daybreak, or about 6:00 a.m. Their recommendation proceeded to Pilate, to Herod, and back to Pilate. There was no effort to delay sentencing to assure a more fair trial, and in fact the proceedings were deliberately rushed.

I. THE CRUCIFIXION OF JESUS

With Pilate's approval of the death penalty, and the soldier's conclusion of their sadistic mockery of a coronation, the events of the crucifixion proceeded. Jesus' own clothing was returned to Him for the torturous march through the streets.

1. Jesus on the Way to the Cross (Mt. 27:31-34; Mk. 15:20b-22; Lk. 23:26-32; Jn. 19:16b-17)

It was customary for four guards to escort the condemned one to the place of crucifixion. They may also have been accompanied by an officer who would be a centurion. This macabre procession would often include those who wished the death of the victim, but in Jesus' case the followers included a large number of people, particularly women, who mourned and wailed for Him.

Jesus began His death march "carrying his own cross" (Jn. 19:17). Apparently at some point, however, the soldiers took the cross from Jesus and conscripted Simon for the task of carrying it. Jesus was taken to Golgotha—"The Place of the Skull" (Mt. 27:33; Mk. 15:22; Lk. 23:33; Jn. 19:17), that probably was so named because of its shape. The word for "skull," through translation into Latin, became Calvary.

In Roman custom there was no fixed place of execution. They executed criminals in any convenient place where many would see them, and be deterred from similar deeds. Golgotha at that time was simply a roadside site where people regularly passed. Thus, while Jesus hung on the cross, "those who passed by hurled insults at him" (Mk. 15:29). Hebrews reports, "Jesus . . . suffered outside the city gate" (Heb. 13:12), and these words imply that Golgotha was outside the city walls that existed at that time.

Scripture does not explain why Simon, who was a visitor from Cyrene, was given Jesus' cross to carry. It is usually assumed that after suffering the prolonged hours of brutality through the night, Jesus no longer had the strength to carry the cross Himself. Cyrene was a city in Libya in North Africa, and there was a large Jewish colony there, so Simon was likely either a Jew or a Jewish proselyte—his name is Jewish. Presumably he was in Jerusalem as a pilgrim attending the Passover festival.

Simon is said to be the father of Alexander and Rufus (Mk. 15:21), and his identification in this manner implies that his sons were known in the early church. In his letter to the Romans, Paul wrote, "Greet Rufus, chosen in the Lord, and his mother, who has been a mother to me, too" (Rom. 16:13). These references suggest the possibility that Simon was converted through his contact with Jesus. Thus, Simon's wife became a mother to Paul, and his son became a prominent Christian in Rome.

As He marched to the cross, Jesus addressed the women mourners who followed. He advised these "Daughters of Jerusalem" not to weep for Him, but for themselves and their children, in view of the horrors that the people of the city were to suffer (cf. Lk. 23:28-31). Barrenness that now was considered a curse, would then be considered a blessing. His cryptic words (Lk. 23:31) are taken to say, "If men treat your King thus, what will it be like when a dry and apostate nation suffers the judgment stroke?" Future disasters would exceed even this present tragedy.

Tradition identifies the route of Jesus from Pilate's palace to Calvary as the VIA DOLOROSA (Sorrowful Way). Fourteen "stations" or events are designated. These include Biblical events— Simon taking the cross, or Jesus' message to the women of Jerusalem, and non-Biblical events—three occasions when Jesus fell, or when the sweat of His face was wiped by Veronica. Since Jerusalem of His day was destroyed, and most landmarks altered beyond recognition, traditional sites cannot be authenticated.

The Temple Mount, however, is more or less a constant. Also, Emperor Hadrian's reconstruction of Jerusalem, which began in A.D. 135, leads to other identifications. Hadrian, to scorn both Jews and Christians, built a temple to Venus over the ruins considered the site of the crucifixion of Jesus. Two centuries later, when the Roman Empire was being Christianized, the Roman temple was replaced by a Christian church. Thus, the Church of the Holy Sepulcher, which dates to A.D. 336, seems very likely to mark the site of Golgotha and of Jesus' tomb.[1]

When Jesus arrived at Golgotha, as a preliminary to the crucifixion, He was offered "wine to drink, mixed with gall; but after

---

1   The alternate site known as Gordon's Calvary, or the Garden Tomb, is popular
     with Christian visitors to Jerusalem, but it is not supported by the majority
     of scholars.

tasting it, he refused to drink it" (Mt. 27:34). Mark describes the mixture as wine and myrrh (cf. Mk. 15:23). The gall or myrrh is thought to be some type of bitter drug that reduced sensitivity to pain, and the incident may have fulfilled Psalm 69:21: "They put gall in my food."

Tradition says that women of Jerusalem, who comprised the equivalent of a charitable organization, were regularly on hand to provide a narcotic drink to victims of crucifixion. They hoped to modify the pain and fulfill Proverbs 31:6-7, "Give . . . wine to those who are in anguish; let them drink . . . and remember their misery no more." In Jesus' case, it may have been either these women, or the soldiers, or some of His followers who offered the wine. Jesus refused any measures, however, that would have allowed Him to escape the excruciating reality of the cross or to dull His senses and understanding.

2. The Act of Crucifixion (Mt. 27:35; Mk. 15:23-24; Lk. 23:33; Jn. 19:18)

The Gospels simply state: "They crucified him," without describing the process. Clearly, however, Jesus was subjected to the fiendishly cruel procedure of nailing the victim's hands and feet to a wooden support. Following the resurrection, Thomas insisted, "Unless I see the nail marks in his hands and put my finger where the nails were . . . I will not believe" (Jn. 20:25). In prophecy David had described Calvary: "they have pierced my hands and my feet" (Ps. 22:16), and when Jesus comes again "every eye will see him, even those who pierced him" (Rev. 1:7).

Death by crucifixion resulted through thirst, hunger, shock and exhaustion. There would be loss of blood through the wounds, but probably not enough to cause death. Usually, the victim died through asphyxiation, since the shock of being suspended on the cross caused eventual paralysis of the diaphragm. Breathing could only be accomplished by continually thrusting the legs upward. If the victim's legs were broken, they could no longer support his breathing, and death would soon result.

The horrors of crucifixion (the word "excruciating" comes from the same Latin root) were made more vivid by the discovery in a Jerusalem suburb in 1968 of the actual bones of one who had been crucified. The victim was a young Jew of about twenty-five whose name was Yehohanan (a form of John) son of Hagakol. His two heel bones were pinned together by a large nail that had struck a knot in the wood of the cross and had become too firmly anchored to be removed. In disposing of the remains, the feet had been amputated and buried with the nail and the knot still in place. Analysis of the arm bones indicated that nails had been driven above the wrists, but most of the weight of the body had been carried by a small seat attached to the cross. Though the bones were reburied after study, scholars continue to analyze and debate their implications.

Jesus' cross elevated Him above ground level. When the man wished to touch Jesus' lips with a moistened sponge, it was necessary for him to put it on a stick (cf. Mk. 15:36). The vertical post that extended beyond the crossbeam provided a place to attach the sign that proclaimed the charges against Him. Thus the cross must have been in the traditional form as it is commonly pictured. The Romans usually crucified their victims naked, but it is suggested that in respect to Jewish sensitivities they may have allowed a loincloth. The soldier's action in dividing Jesus' garments into four shares and casting lots for His seamless tunic (undergarment) is seen by John as the fulfillment of Psalm 22:18.

3. The First Three Hours on the Cross (Mt. 27:36-44; Mk. 15:25-32; Lk. 23:34-43; Jn. 19:19-27)

Mark records, "It was the third hour when they crucified him" (Mk. 15:25). John, however, says of the time when Pilate rendered his decision, "It was . . . about the sixth hour" (Jn. 19:14). There is no generally accepted reconciliation of these time designations. Though Pilate would have observed Roman time and Mark would have reported in Jewish time, both systems counted the hours of the day beginning at 6:00 a.m. Thus, Mark's third hour was 9:00 a.m., and "about the sixth hour" was "going on noon." Since John says "about," perhaps he intended only to suggest "the forenoon."[2] Traditionally, Mark's statement of the time has been accepted as the hour of the crucifixion.

The sign on the cross above Jesus' head was written in Hebrew (Aramaic), Latin, and Greek (cf. Mt. 27:37; Jn. 19:20)—an unwitting prophecy of Christ's universal kingship. Its full text appears to have read, "THIS IS JESUS OF NAZARETH, THE KING OF THE JEWS." Probably these words were the only identification of Jesus committed to writing while He still lived on earth. Though the chief priests protested the words "King of the Jews," Pilate refused any changes, and he responded, "What I have written, I have written [or What I have written stands]" (Jn. 19:22). Harrison comments concerning the sign: "To the Roman mind this suggested Zealot sympathies; to the Jewish mind it suggested a (false) Messiah; to the Christian mind it suggested the Lord of glory whom sin-blinded men had failed to recognize."[3]

While He was being crucified, Jesus prayed for His tormentors: "Father, forgive them, for they do not know what they are doing" (Lk. 23:34). Ignorance did not excuse the men, but it made

---

2 Out of twenty-three references to time in the New Testament, twenty use designations of three, six, or nine. This usage supports the suggestion that time commonly was identified generally by the period rather than precisely by the hour.

3 Everett A. Harrison, *A Short Life of Christ.* Grand Rapids: Wm. B. Eerdmans Publishing Co., 1968, p. 220.

their act forgivable. This prayer is the **first word** of Jesus' seven words from the cross. He could pray this prayer because He had already forgiven them. For this reason, this word has been called "the most sublime of all the seven words." David Gooding wrote:

> This prayer, uttered in the moment of fearful pain, on behalf of those who were causing the pain, has rightly moved the hearts of millions . . . . [It has] become the ideal which has taught countless sufferers not to yield to blind retaliation, but to seek the good of even their enemies.[4]

All four Gospels speak of the two lawbreakers, one on either side. In the NIV, Matthew and Mark refer to them as robbers, Luke calls them criminals, and John simply refers to "others." Since Roman law did not regard robbery as a capital offence, the two had likely committed an act of insurrection rather than mere robbery. The word rendered "robber" (*leistes* [lays-TAYS]) also means revolutionary or insurrectionist, and the two may have belonged to the same insurrectionist group as Barabbas. Modern versions have dropped Mark 15:28 from the text, but scholars agree that this situation fulfilled Old Testament prophecy: "he . . . was numbered with the transgressors" (Isa. 53:12).

Even in this tragic hour, Jesus' persecutors could not rest. Among those who taunted and sneered were: passersby (Mt. 27:39), rulers (chief priests, teachers of the law, and elders) (Mt. 27:41; Mk. 15:31; Lk. 23:35), soldiers (Lk. 23:36) and at least one of the lawbreakers (Mt. 37:44; Lk. 23:39). The first group of persecutors apparently knew of the false charges raised in Caiphas' palace (cf. Mk. 14:58) concerning the destruction of the temple. The second group, which consisted of the leaders, may have come to savor their victory or perhaps to protest the message of the sign proclaiming Jesus King of the Jews. This group mockingly cried, "He saved others, but he can't save himself" (Mt. 27:42; Mk. 15:31). It was true that Jesus could not save Himself, for that was the condition upon which He could save others.

Only the one lawbreaker spoke in Jesus' defense, and perhaps only after he had reconsidered his earlier attitude (cf. Mt. 27:44). As one who feared God, he rebuked his companion, and he testified of Jesus, "this man has done nothing wrong" (Lk. 23:41). He requested, "Jesus, remember me when you come into your kingdom" (Lk. 23:42). Jesus' response became the **second word** from the cross. "I tell you the truth, today you will be with me in paradise" (Lk. 23:43). In Jewish usage, "paradise" was the usual term for the dwelling place of the righteous dead.

Standing by the cross at this time was a company of several women that included, Mary the mother of Jesus, Mary's sister, Mary the wife of Clopas (or Cleophas), and Mary Magdalene. Also

---

4 David Gooding, *According to Luke*. Grand Rapids: Wm. B. Eerdmans Publishing Co., 1987, p. 342.

at the cross was John, the disciple whom Jesus loved (cf. Jn. 19:25-26). Herschel Hobbs commented:

> Jesus died in an ocean of hate. But in that raging ocean there was a tiny island of love. [5]

In spite of His suffering, Jesus addressed Mary and John and committed each to the other as mother and son. "Dear woman, here is your son . . . Here is your mother" (Jn. 19:26-27). These instructions, constituting a bequest, became Jesus' **third word** from the cross. John accepted this charge, and from that hour he took Mary to his own home. It is possible that because Mary had accepted Jesus' cause, His stepbrothers were so unsympathetic that they were unwilling to receive her into their homes.

4. The Three Hours of Darkness. Jesus' Death (Mt. 27:45-50; Mk. 15:33-37; Lk. 23:44-46; Jn. 19:28-37)

The three hours of darkness were God's response to the awful scene on earth. They were equivalent of an eclipse of the sun, but Luke says simply, "the sun stopped shining" (Lk. 23:45). During this time, Jesus experienced the horror of separation from God. Because "God made him who had no sin to be sin for us" (2 Cor. 5:21), the Father necessarily forsook Him. Toward the close of this period, Jesus cried out in Aramaic, "*Eloi, Eloi, lama sabach-thani?*" which translates to, "My God, my God, why have you forsaken me?" (Mt. 27:46). These words parallel Psalm 22:1, but in a very different context. This cry was Jesus' **fourth word** from the cross, and it is the only recorded occasion when Jesus did not address God as Father. Some bystanders concluded that His fourth word in Aramaic was a call to Elijah, and this impression seems to have motivated a response to His fifth word (cf. Mk. 15:35-36).

Jesus' words, "I am thirsty" (Jn. 19:28), His **fifth word** from the cross, brought Him the assistance of a bystander. By means of a stick (reed stalk), a sponge moistened in sour wine was placed upon Jesus' lips to help to soothe His raging thirst. He had previously refused treated wine, but He accepted this liquid because He needed it to be able to proclaim His final words. Perhaps, also, it was the fulfillment of Psalm 69:21b, and Psalm 22:15.

John reports Jesus' **sixth word** from the cross and its circumstances: "When he had received the drink, Jesus said, 'It is finished'" (Jn. 19:30). This proclamation consisted of a single Greek word, *tetelestai*, (te-TEL-es-tie) which is literally "it has been finished." The same word occurs in John 19:28 "all was now completed," and together these verses establish the fact of the consummation of God's eternal plan of salvation. The sixth cry has been called the most profound of the seven words, for it is the one with the greatest scope for doctrinal truth.

---

5   Herschel H. Hobbs, *An Exposition of the Gospel of John.* Grand Rapids: Baker Books, 1996, p. 265.

Jesus' earthly ministry was now completed and His hours of suffering were over. His **seventh word** from the cross was His prayer to God: "Father, into your hands I commit my spirit" (Lk. 23:46). These words from Psalm 31:5, were used by some pious Jews as a bedtime prayer. Upon pronouncing them, however, Jesus bowed His head, and His spirit departed. Mankind's Savior had entered the realm of death. He did not die because crucifixion took His life, but because He chose to lay it down.

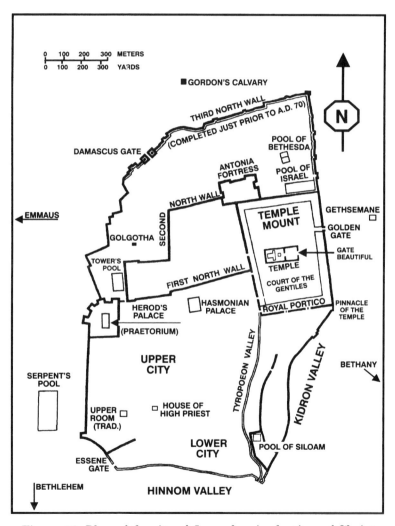

Figure 19: Plan of the city of Jerusalem in the time of Christ. Most of the sites have been established only by tradition, and therefore they are probable but not certain.

A short time later, when the soldiers came to break the legs of the victims on the crosses, they found Jesus already dead. Instead of breaking bones, they settled for a spear thrust into His side, presumably to confirm that He was dead (cf. Jn. 19:34). The prophecy that no bones should be broken links with Psalm 34:20; His pierced side links with Zechariah 12:10. In the past, the discharge of water and blood from the wounded side has been explained as the result of extreme physical suffering, but modern medical opinion appears uncertain about this matter.

Scripture provides the painful details of Christ's death because the account is vitally important. Unless Jesus actually died, Calvary's work would not have been finished, and He could not be our Savior. Notably, the *Qur'an* (*Koran*) denies Jesus' death, and it declares "it only seemed to be so." John anticipated skepticism, and thus he emphasizes the truth of his report. "The man who saw it has given testimony, and his testimony is true" (Jn. 19:35). It appears that this eyewitness was John himself for he is the only disciple identified as being present at the cross (cf. Jn. 19:26). Out of modesty, John avoids specifically designating himself.

5. Events at the Death of Christ (Mt. 27:51-56; Mk. 15:38-41; Lk. 23:47-49)

When Jesus gave up His spirit, "At that moment the curtain of the temple was torn in two from top to bottom" (Mt. 27:51). The curtain would likely have been the one that divided the holy place from the most holy place (holy of holies), though some suggest that an outer doorway curtain would have been more conspicuous. The torn curtain clearly proclaimed the end of the Old Testament pattern of worship. From that time forward every penitent could trust Jesus' sacrifice to qualify him or her to enter God's holy presence. According to Josephus, the temple curtain (veil) that separated the most holy place was a massive weaving as thick as the human palm, and some eighteen meters (sixty feet) high and nine meters (thirty feet) wide.

Matthew tells that when Jesus died there was a violent earthquake that caused even rocks to split. Also, "the tombs broke open and the bodies of many holy people who had died were raised to life" (Mt. 27:52). After Jesus' resurrection, these resurrected holy ones appeared to many people in Jerusalem. Scripture does not have more to say about this resurrection, but it obviously validated the reality of Christ's victory over death. The resurrection of these saints was a foretaste of the end time resurrection of those who sleep in Jesus. Perhaps those who appeared in the city were enjoying a temporary manifestation similar to that of Moses and Elijah at the transfiguration.

The centurion and his soldiers who had carried out the crucifixion were terrified by the earthquake and the accompanying events. They exclaimed, "Surely he was the Son of God" (Mt. 27:54). Luke reports, "The centurion . . . praised God and said,

'Surely this was a righteous man'" (Lk. 23:47). Most scholars feel that the centurion's words exceeded his understanding, and that as a pagan he was declaring that Jesus behaved as a divine hero. The crowd reacted in penitential lamentation and "they beat their breasts" (Lk. 23:48). Now that it was too late, many realized that there had been a tragic and glaring injustice.

Throughout these events, "Many women were there, watching from a distance. They had followed Jesus from Galilee to care

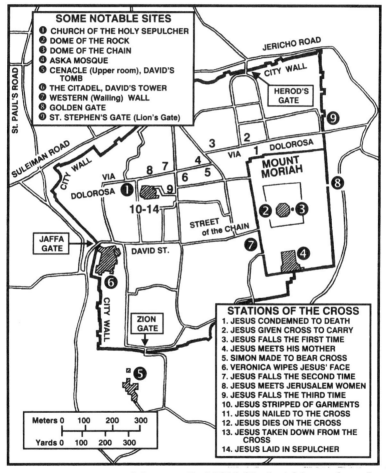

SOME NOTABLE SITES
❶ CHURCH OF THE HOLY SEPULCHER
❷ DOME OF THE ROCK
❸ DOME OF THE CHAIN
❹ ASKA MOSQUE
❺ CENACLE (Upper room), DAVID'S TOMB
❻ THE CITADEL, DAVID'S TOWER
❼ WESTERN (Wailing) WALL
❽ GOLDEN GATE
❾ ST. STEPHEN'S GATE (Lion's Gate)

STATIONS OF THE CROSS
1. JESUS CONDEMNED TO DEATH
2. JESUS GIVEN CROSS TO CARRY
3. JESUS FALLS THE FIRST TIME
4. JESUS MEETS HIS MOTHER
5. SIMON MADE TO BEAR CROSS
6. VERONICA WIPES JESUS' FACE
7. JESUS FALLS THE SECOND TIME
8. JESUS MEETS JERUSALEM WOMEN
9. JESUS FALLS THE THIRD TIME
10. JESUS STRIPPED OF GARMENTS
11. JESUS NAILED TO THE CROSS
12. JESUS DIES ON THE CROSS
13. JESUS TAKEN DOWN FROM THE CROSS
14. JESUS LAID IN SEPULCHER

Figure 20: Features of the so-called "Old City" within modern Jerusalem with the traditional Stations of the Cross. The wall that encloses the old City was last rebuilt by Sultan Suleiman I, in the years 1537-1541, during the era of the Ottoman Turks. Since this wall encloses the site of Calvary, it is evident that modern geographical identifications are not those of Bible times.

for his needs" (Mt. 27:55). These women kept the cross in sight, and displayed sympathy and care by the "ministry of presence." They remained at a distance, perhaps to keep out of harm's way, or because they could not bear to witness Jesus' suffering and shame at close range. The disciples had forsaken Jesus and fled, but these women were positive role models of discipleship.

6. The Entombment of Jesus (Mt. 27:57-61; Mk. 15:42-47; Lk. 23:50-56; Jn. 19:38-42)

The usual chronology assigns Jesus' death to 3:00 o'clock Friday afternoon. John records: "It was the day of Preparation, and the next day was to be a special Sabbath" (Jn. 19:31). The suggested understanding of these words is to see the "day of Preparation" to be the "eve of the Passover," and a "special Sabbath" to be a day in the calendar when the Passover fell on a Sabbath.

Jesus died just three hours before the beginning of the Sabbath at sundown (6:00 p.m.). Although He died under Roman law, Jewish law dictated local attitudes and practices. Judaism decreed that the body of an executed criminal must not be left on a tree overnight, for it would desecrate the land (cf. Deut. 21:22-23). Thus, there were only three hours to do what must be done to remove Jesus' body from the cross and lay it to rest. All work must cease at the beginning of the Sabbath.

If Jesus was to be entombed, it would necessarily be done as an act of charity by His followers; in Roman custom the body of a crucified criminal was cast out as refuse, and there was no provision for burial. The suddenness of Jesus' death, however, had taken everyone by surprise, and without prior planning only a temporary entombment was possible. What was unfinished at sundown would have to be completed after the Sabbath.

The two men who shared in the entombment of Jesus were Joseph of Arimathea and Nicodemus, both of whom had been secret disciples. Leon Morris comments:

> **Whereas the disciples who had openly followed Jesus ran away at the end, the effect of the death of Jesus on these two secret disciples was exactly the opposite. Now, when they had nothing at all to gain by affirming their connection with Jesus, they came right out into the open.**[6]

They were each members of the Council (Sanhedrin) (Mk. 15:43—Joseph; Jn. 3:1—Nicodemus), but they had been unable to prevent the Council's action. Thus, Joseph was "a good and upright man, who had not consented to their [the Council's] decision and action" (Lk. 23:50-51). Joseph forfeited his secret role by boldly requesting and receiving from Pilate the custody of Jesus' body. Releasing the body of one executed for high treason was

---

6   Leon Morris, *The Gospel According to John*. Grand Rapids: Wm. B. Eerdmans Publishing Co., 1971, p. 826.

most unusual for a governor, and particularly to release it to one who was not a relative. Pilate's approval is another evidence that he considered Jesus to be innocent.

As quickly as possible, Joseph, together with Nicodemus, who had brought a generous supply of embalming spices (thirty-four kilograms [seventy-five pounds] cf. Jn. 19:39), proceeded to prepare the body for the tomb. Jewish customs would have required a careful washing of the battered bloodstained corpse. Next, "Taking Jesus' body, the two of them wrapped it, with the spices, in strips of linen . . . in accordance with Jewish burial customs" (Jn. 19:40). The purpose of the spices was to perfume the body rather than to embalm it. The spices were sprinkled generously in the folds of linen cloth in which the body was wrapped.

With the wrapping process completed, Joseph placed the body in his "own new tomb" (Mt. 27:60). John reported, "At the place where Jesus was crucified, there was a garden, and in the garden a new tomb in which no one had ever been laid" (19:41). Golgotha and the tomb were evidently immediately next to one another. Since Joseph's tomb was new, there would be no confusion with the body of another occupant. Also, it precluded any claims that Jesus' resurrection resulted because His body had touched the bones of a prophet (cf. 2 Kings 13:20-21).

A typical tomb of that day would be a cave cut into the rock face of a cliff. It is suggested that Joseph's tomb would have provided an outer room and a smaller inner room reached through a low doorway. The raised shelf upon which the body was placed was in the inner room. The mouth of the cave could be sealed by a stone, like a flat millstone, that rolled in a grove that sloped toward the door. Such a stone could much more easily be rolled into place to close the tomb, than rolled uphill to open it.

After he had placed Jesus' body in the tomb, Joseph used the stone "door" to close the entrance for the Sabbath. Two women, Mary Magdalene and Mary the mother of Joses (Mk. 15:47) had accompanied Jesus' body to this final moment, and they now took note of the tomb's location (cf. Mt. 27:61). They intended to return after the Sabbath with the customary spices and perfumes to complete the care of the body.

As we have noted, the Romans were callously indifferent to the fate of the body of an executed criminal. Had matters taken their usual course, with Jesus' body being abandoned to scavengers, or at best buried in a common grave, the resurrection would have been difficult to establish. Joseph's tomb providentially assured that the authenticity of the resurrection of Jesus could much more readily be demonstrated.

7. The Sealing of the Tomb (Mt. 27:62-66)

The delegation that approached Pilate to request the securing of the tomb consisted of chief priests and Pharisees. They evidently had more faith in the resurrection than the disciples, for they sought to assure that the promise of a resurrection "after three days" (Mt. 27:63) would not be fulfilled. Pilate approved a guard of his own soldiers, and presumably allowed the use of a Roman seal. The sealing involved a cord that passed around the stone, and that was attached to the rock wall by sealing wax that had been impressed with an official seal. The sealing was totally unnecessary to prevent the disciples from stealing Jesus' body, but in God's turnaround the seal became a means to provide positive confirmation of the resurrection's reality. The seal and the guard assured that there could be no deception.

II. THE RESURRECTION OF JESUS

The apostle Paul made the resurrection of Jesus Christ the essential foundation of the message that he preached: "If Christ has not been raised, our preaching is useless and so is your faith" (1 Cor. 15:14). Every believer finds in Christ's resurrection a reassuring validation of His victory over death, and an unswerving hope for life beyond the grave. Christ's resurrection validates all that He claimed, and that He did and taught. The precise chronology of events relating to the resurrection may be debated, but the reality of Christ's resurrection remains an awesome historical fact. Similarly, there may be differences in the accounts of what the various visitors saw in the tomb, but all the accounts agree in reporting that none of the visitors saw the body of Jesus.

1. The Women Prepare to Visit the Tomb (Mt. 28:1; Mk. 16:1)

Before daybreak on the day following the Sabbath, a party of women assembled with the intention of further caring for the body of Jesus. They planned to bring spices to apply to the body, and apparently, they wished to complete the task before the heat of the day. As we have noted, the purpose of the spices was to mask the odors of decay. The use of the word "anoint" (cf. Mk. 16:1) suggests that some of the spices were in liquid form. The party included: Mary Magdalene, Mary the mother of James, Joanna, Salome and others (cf. Lk. 24:10; Mk. 16:1).

The KJV does not clearly designate the actual day of the resurrection: "In the end of the Sabbath, as it began to dawn toward the first day of the week" (Mt. 28:1). Modern versions more precisely reflect the original of this verse. The NIV reads "After the Sabbath, at dawn on the first day of the week," and the Living Bible reads, "Early on Sunday morning, as the new day was dawning." In the NIV John dates events, "Early on the first day of the week, while it was still dark" (Jn. 20:1).

2. The Earthquake and the Descent of the Angel (Mt. 28:2-4)

The dramatic sequence involving the earthquake, the descent of the angel, and the rolling away of the stone took place before the women arrived at the tomb. No doubt at this time the actual resurrection occurred, though the Gospels do not report the process. The guards were at first paralyzed with fear, but when they recovered themselves, they fled. Thus, when the women arrived, probably about at dawn, the guards were no longer there.

All four Gospels speak of the fact that the stone was rolled away. It is frequently pointed out that the tomb was opened, not to let the body of Jesus out, but to let the world see in.

3. The Women Arrive at the Tomb With Their Spices (Mt. 28:5-8; Mk. 16:2-8; Lk. 24:1-8; Jn. 20:1-2)

Apparently the women did not know that the tomb had been sealed and placed under guard. They saw their only problem with the stone to be coping with its weight. The involvement of the women at this time is suggested to have been as follows:

1) **Mary Magdalene arrived first.** She saw that the stone had been rolled away, and ran and told Peter and John (cf. Jn. 20:1-2). Mary had been with the other women, but she had gone on ahead. At this time she focused only on the removal of the stone and neither saw the angel nor heard his message.

2) **One party of women arrived.** They were greeted by an angel seated on the stone, were shown the empty tomb, and were told to share the resurrection message with "his disciples and Peter" (Mk. 16:7). They retreated into shock, however, and "trembling and bewildered, the women went out and . . . said nothing to anyone, because they were afraid" (Mk. 16:8). These women apparently had no part in sharing the news.

3) **Another party of women arrived.** They entered the tomb, and were greeted by two angels as young men in shining white garments. The angels comforted the women and told them to share the message with the disciples (cf. Lk. 24:1-8).

4. The Women Share the News (Lk. 24:9-11)

This second group of women reported to the entire "Eleven and to all the others" (Lk. 24:9). Since Mary Magdalene is named as one of this group, her report to Peter and John was apparently on behalf of the group. In their immediate response, the disciples "did not believe the women, because their words seemed to them like nonsense" (Lk. 24:11). In the culture of the day, a woman's testimony was always considered suspect, and this secular pattern may have colored the disciples' perspective. Peter and John, however, resolved to check matters out for themselves.

5. Peter and John Visit the Empty Tomb (Lk. 24:12; Jn. 20:3-10)

In the race to the tomb John arrived first, but he only looked in. Peter, upon his arrival, boldly entered. The two disciples saw no angels, but they were able to inspect the linen wrappings lying just as Jesus had left them. Following this inspection, they returned to their own homes. It is implied that though John believed, Peter was simply puzzled. The fact that the burial cloth that had been around Jesus' head was folded (or rolled) up by itself (Jn. 20:7) indicated that Jesus had ceased to require burial wrappings, and that in some orderly way He had divested Himself of them. Some see the placement of the wrappings as evidence that in the resurrection-metamorphosis Jesus' body had simply passed through them. Obviously, the orderliness of the tomb established that the body had not been furtively stolen.

6. Mary Magdalene Returns and Sees Two Angels (Jn. 20:11-13)

After Mary had reported to the "Eleven," (cf. Lk. 24:9) and particularly to Peter and John, she returned to the tomb. Peter and John completed inspecting the tomb and left for their homes, but Mary stood outside weeping. At a point, she stooped down and saw the two angels who once again were visible. To the angels' question concerning the reason for her tears, she gave her poignant reply, "They have taken my Lord away . . . and I don't know where they have put him" (Jn. 20:13). Mary apparently did not recognize the persons in the tomb as angels, and thus she showed no surprise. Someone comments, "Mary wept because the tomb was empty; instead she should have rejoiced."

7. Jesus Appears to Mary Magdalene (Mk. 16:9-11; Jn. 20:14-18)

In one of the most tender scenes of Scripture, Mary Magdalene was granted the honor of being the first person to see the resurrected Jesus. As He spoke to her, "Woman . . . why are you crying?" (Jn. 20:15), with her vision blurred by tears, she mistook Him for the gardener. But when He called her by name, she experienced a heart-stopping moment of recognition. Her joyful cry "Rabboni," implied, "My teacher has come back!" Reacting spontaneously, she reached out and apparently grasped Him in an impetuous hug—or she may have fallen down before Him and grasped His feet. Jesus necessarily responded, "Do not hold on to me" (Jn. 20:17). He thus declared that thereafter she must accept His physical absence from the lives of His followers on earth.

Jesus gave as the reason that Mary was not to hold Him: "I have not yet returned [Gk. *anabaino*] to the Father" (Jn. 20:17b). Later, He imposed no such restrictions (cf. Mt. 28:9; Lk. 24:39). The verb *anabaino* (an-a-BUY-no) is translated: go up, ascend, move upward, or climb up. Many suggest that on the morning of resurrection day, after greeting the disciples, Jesus privately ascended to the Father. He promptly returned to earth, however, and followed through with the remainder of the day's activities. Forty days later, when His ministry on earth was completed, He proceeded with His formal and visible ascension.

Jesus instructed Mary, "Go . . . to my brothers and tell them, 'I am returning to my Father'" (Jn. 20:17). On no previous occasion had Jesus called the disciples, "brothers." Some suggest that it is possible that the term "brothers" denoted a wider circle than simply the eleven disciples.

Mary's meeting with Jesus at this time was the **first** of five appearances on the day of His resurrection. During the forty days that He remained on earth, there were five additional appearances, for a total of ten in all. It has been said that though "no man saw Christ rise; many saw the risen Christ."

8. Jesus Appears to the Company of Women (Mt. 28:9-10)

The identity of this group of women is uncertain, but the reported incident is a further experience of one of the groups. As they went forth to share the joyful news of the resurrection, they were suddenly confronted by Jesus Himself. In response to His greeting, they fell in worship before Him, and grasped His feet. He instructed them to tell the disciples to meet Him in Galilee, and once again He called His disciples "brothers." Since all of the surviving disciples were from Galilee, they would naturally return there after the Passover. This appearance was Jesus' **second** on resurrection Sunday.

9. The Guards Report Their Experience (Mt. 28:11-15)

The disappearance of the body of Jesus was a spectacular miracle that baffled the Roman guards. They first took the problem to the Jewish elders rather than to their own commanding officers. The Sanhedrinists seem to have accepted the fact of the resurrection, but their concern was to find ways to deny it. Their scheme to bribe the guards to say that while they slept the body of Jesus had been stolen by the disciples possessed negligible credibility. For a Roman soldier to sleep while on guard duty was normally a capital offense, and if the guards were asleep they could not have witnessed the theft. The "large sum of money" (Mt. 28:12) the Sanhedrin leaders paid in bribing the guards may have been a greater amount than they had given Judas.

10. Jesus Appears to Peter (Lk. 24:34; cf. 1 Cor. 15:5)

There is no direct report of this appearance, but on the evening of resurrection day, the Eleven were talking about it (cf. Lk. 24:34). Later, Paul wrote, "[Jesus] was raised on the third day . . . and . . . He appeared to Peter, and then to the Twelve" (1 Cor. 15:5). Harrison comments:

> **Beyond the fact that the two [Jesus and Peter] met on the first day of the week, we have no information at all. It was a secret affair, too personal and too precious to be made common property, for sin is individual and so is the forgiveness of sin.**[7]

This appearance was the **third** of the five on that day.

---

7   Harrison, op. cit., p. 237.

11. Jesus Appears to the Two on the Road to Emmaus (Mk. 16:12-13; Lk. 24:13-35)

For Cleopas and his companion, the hours required for the ten kilometer (six mile) walk from Jerusalem to Emmaus were an ideal opportunity for an in-depth discussion of the crucifixion and rumored resurrection. They struggled to understand how the one who gave promise of being the Messiah could have been crucified. They felt that since He had died, He could no longer qualify. The unconfirmed reports of the resurrection at this stage had simply added to their confusion.

As they shared their perplexity, Jesus personally joined them and to Cleopas He addressed a leading question: "What things?" (Lk. 24:19). Cleopas responded with a complete rehearsal of events (cf. Lk. 24:19-24). His reply in this passage has been called, "The Gospel according to Cleopas."

At this point, Jesus the prince of expositors began His explanation. He laid down a basic premise: "Did not the Christ have to suffer these things and then enter his glory?" (Lk. 24:26). Calvary was not a human tragedy, nor the vicissitudes of cruel misfortune, but the outworking of the divine will. It was just as the prophets had said. Thus, "Beginning with Moses and all the Prophets, he explained to them what was said in all the Scriptures concerning himself" (Lk. 24:27). A major point of His explanation was that the death of the Messiah was not an unforeseen or disqualifying obstacle to prevent Him from redeeming Israel.

It was not until they had "urged him strongly" (Lk. 24:29), and He sat at their table in their home and blessed and broke the bread, that the two travelers recognized Him. It may have been that as He broke the bread they saw the nail scars in His hands, but also they may have recognized a particular characteristic behavior. At that moment, He disappeared from their sight. Their failure to realize His identity for so long was probably in part because of the unique characteristics of His resurrection body, but also because they believed He was still dead. This event was Jesus' **fourth** appearance on the day of His resurrection.

Traveling after dark increased the risk of robbery and attack, but knowledge of the resurrection was a powerful motivation. Thus, the two disciples excitedly left Emmaus to return to Jerusalem. Back in the city they found the Eleven, and others assembled with them, and they eagerly shared their story of Jesus' appearance to them. Mark reports, "They [the disciples] did not believe them" (16:13). The term "Eleven" was used to designate the company of disciples even though Thomas was absent.

12. Jesus Appears to the Disciples (Mk. 16:14; Lk. 24:36-43; Jn. 20:19-25)

The disciples must have freely discussed the possibility of His resurrection, but when they were confronted by the resurrected

Jesus in their locked meeting room "they were startled and frightened, thinking they saw a ghost" (Lk. 24:37). While they reacted in this fashion He calmly proclaimed "Peace be with you." (cf. Jn. 20:19, 21). The disciples' faith and confidence were restored only when Jesus displayed His scarred hands, feet, and side (cf. Lk. 24:40; Jn. 20:20), and He partook of food. Older versions speak of broiled fish and honeycomb, but newer versions mention only the fish. The food was a snack, not a meal.

At a later time, when Peter spoke in the house of Cornelius, he nostalgically reviewed these events: "God raised [Jesus] from the dead on the third day and caused him to be seen. He was not seen by all the people, but by witnesses whom God had already chosen—by us who ate and drank with him after he rose from the dead" (Acts 10:40-41).

John reports that at this time Jesus "breathed on [the disciples] and said, 'Receive the Holy Spirit'" (Jn. 20:22). This occasion clearly lacked the scope and effects of the later gift of the Spirit on the day of Pentecost (cf. Acts 2:1-4, 41). Most commentators agree, however, that Jesus did bestow something new at this time, and it resulted in a new relationship to the Holy Spirit and a new authority in ministry (cf. Jn. 20:23). It was not that the disciples were given power to absolve sin, but power to preach the gospel which would absolve sin. Man's power is only to forgive the violation of the rules that he has imposed, and not to forgive an encroachment upon God's absolute standards. In this passage, the construction minimizes personal pronouns. What is given is given to the corporate Church rather than to individuals.

At this appearance, which was the **fifth** on the day of His resurrection, the absence of Thomas created a minor complication. The matter of proving the resurrection's reality to Thomas now became a separate project. We speak of "Doubting Thomas," but in fact Thomas was no more a doubter than the other disciples. Because he missed the first appearance of Jesus, he lacked the convincing evidence that they had enjoyed. He was simply asking that he, too, might be shown.

13. Jesus Appears to the Disciples When Thomas is Present (Jn. 20:26-29)

The Greek dates this event "after eight days," but since the Jews included the present day when counting, the NIV and other versions read, "A week later." On this first Sunday following resurrection Sunday, the disciples had again gathered in the same room, but this time Thomas was with them. As Jesus appeared among them, in spite of the locked doors, He particularly singled out Thomas for His personal attention. In an instant Thomas forgot about his intended physical tests, and he responded to Jesus' presence with a fervent and devout testimony: "My Lord and my God! [lit. The Lord of me and the God of me]" (Jn. 20:28).

Thomas' words are not in the vocative case (i.e., form of address), but most commentators interpret them as if they were, for that fits the context. Thomas was thus the first person in the New Testament to confess Jesus as God. His words, affirming both the lordship and deity of Christ, are the most lofty confession to be found in the Gospels. Thomas recognized that only a divine Lord could have risen from the dead. Jesus responded by stating a beatitude for all subsequent believers, "Blessed are those who have not seen and yet have believed" (Jn. 20:29).

14. Jesus Appears to Seven Disciples Beside Galilee (Jn. 21:1-23)

This appearance is not dated, but it was sometime during the forty days prior to the ascension. Only John reports it, and this final chapter is known as "John's epilogue." The group of disciples to whom Jesus appeared included: Peter, Thomas, Nathanael, James, John, and two others who were probably Andrew and Philip since they were from Bethsaida. This meeting perhaps fulfilled Jesus' instructions, "tell my brothers to go to Galilee" (Mt. 28:10), though there was yet to be the final meeting on the mountain in Galilee (cf. Mt. 28:16).

Peter's proposal to go fishing may have been an effort to make good use of their time, but many have seen it to be dangerous. Jesus had trained the disciples for another career, and He had called them to leave their prior vocation. It has been said, "A fisherman can become an apostle, but an apostle cannot become a fisherman." Perhaps as they spent the long night hours without catching any fish they had an extended opportunity to reflect on their actions. Jesus' early morning greeting "Friends, haven't you any fish?" (Jn. 21:5) suggests the warmth of a father, since "friends" might be rendered "boys" or "children."

At this time, just as on the occasion of the original call of the fishermen-disciples, Jesus provided a supernatural catch of fish. His previous strategy had been to make one more cast of the net (cf. Lk. 5:4-5); this time He directed them to cast on the other side of the boat. Notably, the net was not broken even though it contained one hundred and fifty-three large fish. Evidently, the catch was so impressively large that the disciples took time to make a precise count. In a show of his usual impetuousness, Peter jumped into the water to hasten to Jesus, for he could not wait for the fish-laden boat. Before doing so, Peter wrapped his outer garment around him, since apparently he expected to wade to shore in shallow water.

The meal of bread and charcoal-broiled fish is the only breakfast mentioned in the Gospels. That the resurrected Jesus should have provided in this charmingly practical manner affords a heartwarming insight into His person. Though there were already some fish on the fire, Jesus asked them to contribute some of the catch of the one hundred and fifty-three. This occasion of breakfast on the beach with Jesus must have provided a warm and enduring memory for the disciples, and Jesus deliberately gave them opportunity to contribute toward it.

John notes that this occasion was the third time that Jesus had appeared to the disciples (cf. 21:14). Though we have counted five appearances on the day of resurrection, and one a week later, this was indeed His third appearance to the circle of His followers that had been the Twelve (cf. Jn. 20:19; 20:26).

Jesus' question to Peter, "Do you truly love me more than these? (v. 15b) has three possible interpretations. Jesus was asking if Peter loved him more than: 1) fish and fishing gear, or 2) the other disciples (i.e., Was Peter's love for his buddies greater than his love for Christ?), or 3) the other disciples loved (Peter had claimed that his love exceeded theirs [cf. Mk. 14:29].). The exchange between Jesus and Peter that this question precipitated is made more meaningful if the original is rendered by expressions that distinguish the Greek terms. If we take *agapao* to relate to divine love and *phileo* to relate to human love, we can paraphrase the interchange thus:

First Inquiry (v. 15): Do you love (Gk. *agapao*) Me with divine love? I love (Gk. *phileo*) you with human love. Feed (Gk. *bosko*) My sheep (or lambs) (Gk. *arnia* [plural]).

Second Inquiry (v. 16): Do you love (Gk. *agapao*) Me with divine love? I love (Gk. *phileo*) you with human love. Shepherd or tend (Gk. *poimaino*) My lambs (or sheep) (Gk. *probata* [pl.]).

Third Inquiry (v. 17): Do you [really] love (Gk. *phileo*) Me with human love? I love (Gk. phileo) you with human love. Feed (Gk. *bosko*) My lambs (or sheep) (Gk. *probata* [pl.]).

Pronunciations of these terms are as follows: *agapao* (ag-a-PA-oh); *phileo* (fill-EH-oh); *bosko* (BOS-koh); *arnia* (ar-NEE-ah); *poimaino* (poi-MINE-oh); *probata* (PRO-bat-tah); the singular is *probation* (pro-BAT-ee-on).

Expositions based on the Greek terms in this passage should be done with care, and the student should note that current lexicons may not support traditional distinctions.[8] Also, the sharp distinction in the use of verbs to depict divine and human love is not accepted by all scholars; some hold that the use of the two verbs is "merely stylistic." Another approach sees *agapao* associating with love as a motivation or act of will, and *phileo* relating to love that is a feeling or attitude of great affection (cf. p. 212).

---

8 The authoritative *A Greek-English Lexicon of the New Testament* by William F. Arndt and F. Wilbur Gingrich (Chicago: Univ. of Chicago Press, Fourth edition, 1952, p. 107) explains that *arnion* was "no longer felt to be a dim. [diminutive] in N.T. times," and it is translated as either sheep or lamb. The *Lexicon* identifies *probata* with the singular *probation* which it defines as "dim. . . . though it is oft. used without dim. sense = sheep" (p. 709).

Jesus' words to Peter in verse eighteen suggest two possibilities: 1) Peter would live a long life and arrive at a dependent old age; or 2) In old age Peter would be imprisoned and prepared for execution. This second interpretation is supported by verse nineteen which states that Jesus was talking about Peter's death. The phrase "stretch out your hands" in verse eighteen is seen as an allusion to being crucified. Tradition holds that Peter was crucified in Rome during the time of Nero in about A.D. 64.

After hearing this statement about his future, Peter asked what John could expect. In reply, Jesus answered that John's fate was not a matter of Peter's concern. Jesus expressed, however, His right to return within the lifetime of the younger apostle, though He said nothing about His intention.

15. Jesus Appears on the Mountain in Galilee. The Great Commission (Mt. 28:16-20; Mk. 16:15-18; Lk. 24:44-49)

The group who met Jesus on the unnamed mountain in Galilee may have included not only the eleven disciples (Mt. 28:16), but also a large company of others. Thus, it may have been concerning this occasion that Paul reported, "he appeared to more than five hundred of the brothers at the same time" (1 Cor. 15:6). The larger company would explain Matthew's comment, "some doubted" (Mt. 28:16c).

Basically, Jesus' policies limited His post resurrection appearances to His followers only. 1) He no longer was offering Himself to the nation, and He had declared that they would not see Him until His triumphant return (cf. Mt. 23:39). 2) His resurrection appearances reveal a new order of being that was available only to believers. 3) He was now committing to His followers the task of presenting, and as it were, revealing Him to other humans.

Jesus' statement of the Great Commission in Matthew 28:19 sets forth the principle that He intended that believers would be the ones to share the good news with all human beings. The Commission declares the basis upon which converts may be baptized, and it becomes a useful formula-liturgy. The Greek is literally "into the name of." A.W. Argyle commented, "To baptize into the name means to baptize into the possession, protection and blessing of the Godhead, and to establish a living union between the believer and the Father, the Son and the Holy Spirit."[9] The process of making disciples involves two aspects: 1) baptizing converts, 2) conveying teaching that would constitute training in obedience to the commandments of Jesus.

Mark's Gospel, as we have it in our Bibles, has a notable account of the Great Commission. Since the authenticity of Mark 16:9-20 is debated, however, (see "The Epilogue of Mark, p. 13),

---

9 A..W. Argyle, *The Gospel According to Matthew.* Cambridge: Cambridge University Press, 1963, p. 222.

most scholars hesitate to make much use of this material. The preferred approach is to find parallel passages that support similar concepts. Four of the five signs that "will accompany those who believe" (v. 17) are found elsewhere in the New Testament: 1) exorcism (Acts 8:7; 16:18; 19:15-16), 2) tongues (Acts 2:1-12; 10:46; 19:6), 3) coping with serpents (Lk. 10:19; Acts 27:5), and 4) healings (Acts 3:7; 28:8). There are no New Testament instances of immunity from poison, but purification of the poisoned pot of stew (2 Kings 4:39-41) or the "healing" of Jericho's "bad" water (2 Kings 2:19-22) are more or less parallel events.

Luke relates the witnessing ministry of the disciples with a command to remain in Jerusalem while awaiting the Father's promise of the empowering Holy Spirit (cf. Lk. 24:48-49). He reports on the fulfillment of these events in the sequel to his Gospel: the Book of Acts.

Matthew's Gospel ends with Jesus' promise of His presence in the fulfillment of His commission. Since it is the end of the story, Matthew apparently decided that no other conclusion was necessary. The promise of Jesus' presence becomes a powerful incentive for fulfilling the Great Commission. As someone has commented: "[Jesus] would not restrict Himself to occasional behind-the-lines suggestions, but would share the battlefield."

16. Jesus' Final Appearance and His Ascension (Mk. 16:19; Lk. 24:50-51; cf. Acts 1:4-12)

Luke identifies the site of the ascension as in "the vicinity of Bethany" (Lk. 24:50), which would be the eastern slope of the Mount of Olives. Thus, following the great commission, the resurrected Lord and His followers returned from Galilee. Jesus led the company of disciples to the Mount, and after His final words of instruction and comfort, He proceeded to ascend. His last act on behalf of His disciples was to raise His hands in benediction to bestow a parting blessing. The raised hands would have revealed the nail marks that He bore.

Some scholars contest the historicity of Christ's ascension because the texts reporting it (Mk. 16:19; Lk. 24:51) are not in certain ancient manuscripts. Despite these textual disputes, however, the ascension is a Biblical event. It is twice mentioned in Acts (cf. 1:2, 1:9), and four times in the Epistles (cf. Eph. 4:10; 1 Tim. 3:16; Heb. 4:14; 1 Pet. 3:22). The resurrection is seen to have marked the resumption of Jesus' life in heaven as He took His place at His Father's side on behalf of His people.

As the disciples stood watching, "suddenly two men dressed in white stood beside them" (Acts 1:10). These heavenly messengers conveyed God's special promise: "This same Jesus . . . will come back in the same way you have seen him go into heaven" (Acts 1:11). Thus reassured, the disciples "returned to Jerusalem with great joy. And they stayed continually at the temple praising

God" (Lk. 24:52b-53). Though Jesus had left, they could be joyful because they confidently anticipated a future eternal union with Him. In the meantime, they had a personal Friend in heaven!

17. The Conclusion of Mark, Luke, and John (Mk. 16:20; Lk. 24:52-53; Jn. 20:30-31; 21:24-25)

The debate concerning Mark's epilogue has already been discussed, but at this point we can assume the acceptance of the "longer ending" since that is the text in most of our Bibles. In that portion we find a single summary verse (cf. 16:20) in which Mark covers the growth and expansion of the church through the entire Biblical apostolic era.

Luke ends his Gospel with a two-verse account (cf. 24:52-53) of the activities of the disciples following Jesus' ascension. As we have noted, his final words form a bridge to the record of events that he intended to describe in the Book of Acts.

Either one of the two concluding segments in John's Gospel is more than adequate and could have stood alone. In the first he comments that he has preserved a selection of miraculous signs "that you may believe that Jesus is the Christ, the Son of God [i.e., the divine Messiah]" (20:30). In the second he affixed a statement concerning the truthfulness of his record, and he noted in regard to the deeds of Jesus: "If every one of them were written down, I suppose that even the whole world would not have room for the books that would be written" (Jn. 21:25). This concluding comment by John has been called "a pardonable hyperbole."

Appendix One: Issues in Gospels' Studies

Scholar's efforts to understand the Gospels have resulted in the rise and pursuit of distinctive issues and unique study processes. The student of Gospels should be acquainted with at least the more notable of these issues and processes, even though for the present he or she does not become more involved. The material that follows defines and discusses these topics.

It should be noted that those who pursue gospels' issues are often Biblical critics who hold positions not acceptable to the devout student of the Bible. Evangelicals, however, including some committed to the inerrancy of the Scriptures, may see these pursuits as useful tools that can assist the scholar in Biblical understanding and exegesis. The student should make his or her own choices in these matters, while avoiding outlooks or pursuits that become unproductive by-paths, or that overlook or deny the sovereign role of the Holy Spirit in guiding each Biblical author.

The Synoptic Problem

The "Synoptic Problem" involves the question of how it came to be that the three synoptic accounts have so many similarities, and yet so many differences. There is apparently a literary interdependence, but what was its nature—who copied from whom or what? Obviously, the problem is not with the synoptics themselves, but with curious humans who seek a theory to explain the mechanics that functioned in assembling our Gospel accounts.

In the nineteenth century, B.F. Wescott in *An Introduction to the Study of the Gospels* (1860)[1] taught that oral tradition—word-of-mouth stories and reminiscences of the life of Jesus —explained the likenesses in the Gospels. Each writer had gathered these oral traditions and then assembled them in a compilation. These source accounts had been preserved primarily in the sermons of preachers and witnesses. Many personal recollections were involved, and also personal adaptations and applications of the original material. Thus many likenesses could be explained (events remembered accurately and left unchanged), but also many differences (different people remembered differently, and preachers had modified and revised the original version).

In the twentieth century, scholars replaced the oral tradition theory with a theory of literary origins—the gospel writers copied

---

1 In Germany gospel sources theories began with the posthumous publication in 1784 of "New Hypotheses Concerning the Evangelists Regarded as Merely Human Historians" by Gotthold E. Lessing (1719-1781) Others who adopted and expanded Lessing's viewpoint included: J.J. Griesbach (1745-1812), G.C. Storr (1746-1805), J.K.L. Giesler (1792-1854) and Christian H. Weisse (1801-1866).

existing written documents. Notable works setting forth a theory of gospel sources in prior documents included: J.C. Hawkins, *Horae Synopticae* (1899), and W. Sanday (ed.) *Studies in the Synoptic Problem* (1911). According to this theory, each evangelist compiled his book by reference to one or more other documents. Documents were projected that included: the Gospels that we have, an original source document called "Q" for *Quelle* (German for "source"), an earlier form of Luke called "L" or Proto-Luke, and an earlier form of Matthew called "M" or Proto-Matthew. Three differing views have emerged from these assumptions:

1. The Augustinian Hypothesis: The synoptics were written in the order of the Bible canon with Mark drawing on Matthew, and Luke drawing on both.

2. The Griesbach Hypothesis: Matthew was first, Luke drawing on Matthew was second, and Mark using both was last." This view was held by J.J. Griesbach and W.R. Farmer.

3. The Oxford Hypothesis: Mark was first, Matthew was second using Mark and Q, and Luke who also used both Mark and Q was last. Both Matthew and Luke had access to "L" and "M."

What one does with the Synoptic Problem (including ignoring it) has bearing on one's conclusions about dating the Gospels, and his or her attitude toward the study methodologies of: form criticism, redaction criticism, and literary criticism.

Form Criticism

A process that certain scholars use to determine the evangelists' sources is known as form criticism (*Formgeschichte* in German). Form criticism is an attempt to move back beyond the printed page and to discover the form of the Christian tradition when it was only the oral report before it was set down in the Gospels. The principles of form criticism were stated by K.L. Schmidt and Martin Dibelius (1919), and by Rudolph Bultmann (1921). Bultmann's works adopted a critical approach which viewed the Gospels as human literary productions. Others, particularly V. Taylor in *The Formation of the Gospel Tradition* (1968), adapted form criticism "to be palatable to more conservative wings."

Form critics hold that the gospel writers' sources were a collection of disparate oral materials . The evangelists selected from these materials and combined them in order to fulfill their purpose in writing. Their goal was not so much to depict the life of Jesus, but to use the traditions to support their personal viewpoint. Their writings drew from here and there arbitrarily, usually without concern for unity or chronological sequence. Later editors (redactors) revised the manuscripts and added, subtracted, or rearranged. Scribes who made copies introduced errors, explanations and comments that were made part of the text. Thus, as D.F. Strauss characterized the outcome of this view, "Scripture . . . [is seen as] a necklace of pearls of which the string is broken."

B.F. Streeter held his own rather complex theory of gospel sources, but he was critical of those who taught that Scripture is the outcome of the radical revision of the original historical units. He denied that form criticism could achieve its objective of identifying the form of these units within oral tradition. He wrote:

> **If the sources have undergone anything like the amount of amplification, excision, rearrangement and adaptation which the theory postulates, then the critics' pretense that he can unravel the process is grotesque. As well hope to start with a string of sausages and reconstruct the pig.[2]**

As Streeter points out, form criticism holds that the original "oral traditions" concerning Jesus were modified and regulated in the process of being repeated and eventually passed on to the evangelists. Thus, the Gospels are selected reports that were guided by particular points of view. If we are to enter into and understand the actual events in Jesus' life we need to determine the literary form to which they have been accommodated.

Categories in the form critics' catalog of gospels' source material include: **miracle stories** (or tales)—accounts that focus on Jesus' ability to overturn earthly limitations by the powers of the kingdom; **historical stories** (also called legends or myths)—accounts of events in the life of Christ such as His baptism or the triumphal entry; **pronouncements** (also called paradigms)—short sayings of Jesus found in a context that is told for the sake of providing background for the saying; **dominical sayings** (also called sayings or parables)—short sayings of Jesus including those reported without a setting or context (Bultmann stressed this category, but he did not define it sharply); **the passion narrative**—a literary unit (as reflected in Mark 10-16) that was composed anonymously prior to the time of the evangelists.

Form critics invested great effort in categorizing the contents of the Gospels. But many feel that their efforts were a lost cause.

Redaction Criticism

In contrast to form criticism, which focuses on the content of the text, redaction criticism is concerned with the role of the author as a redactor (i.e., editor) in the text's final shaping. This study procedure seeks to discover what the evangelist did to a particular source-tradition upon which his work is founded. Thus, it attempts to determine the redactional (editorial) alterations that the evangelist contributed to the original account. Redaction critics, particularly the more radical, credit the evangelists with literary creativity. Each evangelist may have freely adapted traditions, or even invented new ones if that furthered his goals. The critic seeks to study these alterations in order to deduce how the writer's mind worked.

---

2   B.F. Streeter, *The Four Gospels,* New York: The Macmillan Co., 1925, p. 377.

The objective of redaction critics is to discover the theological motivation behind editorial alterations in order to compose a theology of each evangelist. The evangelist's concerns in regard to a particular church audience are thought to be thus revealed. The redaction critic holds, that to understand the text and determine its meaning, one needs to know not only what Jesus said and did, but how the evangelist has chosen to editorialize that account in order to use it for a particular purpose.

Literary Criticism

This approach to criticism concerns itself with all of the usual techniques of literary study. It speaks of such matters as: plot, linear sequence, geographical movement, and literary devices, and it seeks to discover the author's techniques in using the text as a vehicle of communication. It views the text from a formal standpoint, as a literary or esthetic work, and it attempts analysis on the same terms that other literature is studied.

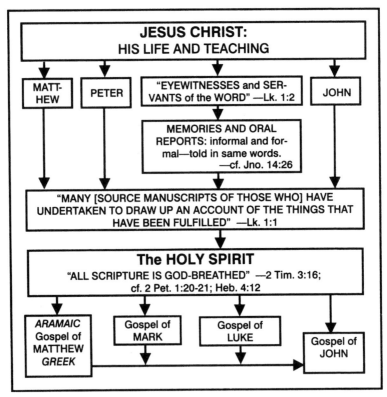

Figure 21: Schema of the transmission and recording as Biblical manuscripts of the facts of the life and teaching of Jesus Christ.

Literary criticism tends to see the Gospels as the creation of skillful human writers on a similar basis to those of other literary masterpieces. This approach is not without its merits, for there is value in applying all of the techniques of literary study to determine the meaning of a gospels' text. Most students of the Gospels, however, hold a much more lofty view of inspiration than most literary critics. Though they appreciate any study that throws light on literary structure, they choose to place their main focus on the interpretation and application of the actual text.

Harmonies and Synopses

Gospel harmonies attempt to merge the four Gospels into a single consistent account of the life and works of Jesus. Obviously, this work is structured on that basis. Published harmonies usually place the individual account of each evangelist beside any parallel accounts in separate columns. As far as possible, similar or identical verses from each gospel appear side-by-side. Typically, the harmony is organized by headings identifying the content of each pericope. The headings are arranged chronologically to follow Christ's life from its pre-incarnate beginnings to the ascension. The Scriptural references include all of the verses that provide a record of the events of that specific pericope.

In general, the gospel account of the life of Christ proceeds smoothly through the years, and the Gospels reinforce one another. There are definite problems, however, in constructing a harmony. The synoptic Gospels do not agree at all points in the order in which they report events. At times, the scholar must decide which evangelist is providing the actual chronological order, and sometimes these decisions are very difficult. Any given harmony (including that used in this book) is certain to have its distracters who hold that there is a better way to report the sequence of events in the life of Jesus.

A gospel synopsis also places parallel texts side-by-side, but its basic purpose is to compare word content rather than primarily to compile a life of Christ. It seeks to serve as a visual tool to reveal the specific verbal differences and similarities among the four Gospels. Study by means of a synopsis particularly appeals to critical scholars. Editions of a gospel synopsis may avoid the controversies of a harmony by printing each Gospel in turn as the "lead gospel" and following its order explicitly. The complete work will have four chapters—one for each Gospel. It is evident that such a detailed word-by-word study would be much more effective in the original Greek rather than in a translation.

A favorite project for seminary students is underlining the words of the Greek gospels in distinctive colors according to the pattern of the occurrence of the words. Usually, only the synoptics are included. A word occurring in all three synoptics might be underlined in blue, a word only in Matthew and Mark in yellow, a word only in Mark and Luke in green, a word in Matthew and

Luke but not in Mark in red. W.R. Farmer's *Synopticon: The Verbal Agreement Between the Greek Texts of Matthew, Mark and Luke Contextually Exhibited* (1969) is a commercially published version of this project.

The Dating of the Synoptics

The dating of the synoptics and the order in which they are thought to have been written are intertwining topics. The prevailing twentieth century view held to the priority of Mark, with late dates for all three synoptics. Because Jesus so accurately described the destruction of Jerusalem, critics assumed that it must have already occurred when the evangelists wrote. Thus, they concluded that the Gospels were written after A.D. 70. Many commentaries, not all of them critical, reflect these views.

As the twentieth century ended, many evangelical voices were calling for a return to traditional views of dating and the priority of the writing of the Gospels. Thus, for instance, John Wenham in his volume *Redating Matthew, Mark & Luke* (1991) defended the following conclusions: 1) Matthew was written around A.D. 40, and it was the first Gospel, 2) Mark's Gospel was probably written about A.D. 45, 3) Luke knew Mark's Gospel, 4) Though there may not be definitive proof, it appears probable that when Luke wrote he made at least limited use of Matthew, 5) Luke's Gospel was well known in the mid-fifties and obviously was written prior to that time.

The Evangelical Perspective

We have suggested that the thoroughgoing evangelical (or at least the inerrantist) would have only limited interest in critical outlooks and methodology in studying the Gospels. Nevertheless, virtually all thoughtful students would likely agree: 1) The Gospels are not simply histories, but selective and interpretative reports, 2) Each Gospel was written primarily as a witness to cultivate faith within a particular circle of readers, 3) The evangelists wrote under the sovereign guidance of the Holy Spirit who uniquely shaped the content of the individual books, 4) Each evangelist came with a body of data out of what he had seen and heard and been taught, 5) Each evangelist would have legitimately used any written materials available to him, including the work of any predecessors.

In addition to the foregoing, two cultural factors of the gospel era should be recognized: 1) Both Roman and Hebrew educative processes involved extensive memorization, and a competent student, which we can assume the evangelists were, would be able to recite lengthy passages word perfect, 2) Bound books (codices) were yet to be developed, and manuscripts were awkward scrolls that effectively discouraged line-by-line research or citation. These conditions help to explain the evangelist's use of the Old Testament that may differ from that of a modern writer.

Appendix Two: Palestine's Political Backgrounds

At the close of the Old Testament, in approximately 400 B.C., Palestine was under the rule of Medo-Persia. This was the era in which the nation experienced revival led by Ezra, Nehemiah, and Malachi. The temple and city of Jerusalem were restored, and to a large measure, national life was revived.

In 333 B.C., at the Battle of Issus, Alexander the Great of Greece defeated King Darius of Medo-Persia, and the Persian Empire collapsed. After conquering and destroying Tyre and Gaza in 332 B.C., Alexander marched on Jerusalem. The ambitious young conqueror chose to look upon the Jews with favor, however, and he spared the city, though he made it his possession.

After Alexander's premature death in 323 B.C., his four generals divided his empire. Palestine was annexed to Egypt under General Ptolemy. For the next century and a quarter, while Ptolemy and his successors ruled, the Jews enjoyed comparative prosperity with minimal foreign interference. The Jewish population in Palestine may have reached one million. Alexandria in North Africa became an important center of Jewish culture, and it was in this era that the Septuagint was produced.

In 198 B.C., Antiochus III, a successor of General Seleucus, overthrew the Ptolemaic empire, and Palestine became part of the Syrian (Seleucid) empire. By 175 B.C., the Seleucid ruler was Antiochus IV, better known as Antiochus Epiphanes—i.e., the illustrious. This ruler was determined to force Greek (or Hellenistic) culture upon the Jews. To achieve this hellenization, he built an altar to *Zeus Olympios* in the Jerusalem temple, and on December 25, 168 B.C., he initiated worship to Zeus by offering a sow upon the altar.

Jewish horror and revulsion toward such events erupted in 167 B.C. in a rebellion against Syrian rule. The Jewish leaders were a native family of priests known as the Maccabees (probably meaning "hammerers") for their exploits, or as Hasmoneans, (or Hasmonaeans) since that was their family name. Four members who became prominent included Mattathias the father, and three sons: Judas, Jonathan, and Simon. Mattathias began the rebellion when he slew an apostate Jewish priest who attempted to offer a heathen sacrifice. By 142 B.C., these leaders had won complete independence for the Jews.

The most notable Hasmonean ruler was John Hyrcanus I (d. 104 B.C.). By capitalizing on the rivalries and weaknesses of the powers of his day, he was able to expand Israel's realm to its greatest extent since the time of Solomon. Hasmonean rule ended in 63 B.C, however, when rival family claimants submitted their dispute to Rome. The Roman authorities resolved the problem by annexing the land in the name of Imperial Rome. Jewish resistance to the loss of independence was crushed when General Pompey occupied Jerusalem and captured the temple.

Under Rome, the Hasmonean, John Hyrcanus II, was appointed priestly leader. Behind the scenes, however, Herod Antipater manipulated various government appointments to favor himself, so that he became the dominant power in Judea. Ethnically, Antipater was an Edomite (Idumean) whose ancestors were migrants who had been incorporated into Israel as proselytes. Julius Caesar greatly admired Antipater, and in 47 B.C. he appointed him procurator (administrator or governor) of Judea.

Herod Antipater proceeded systematically to transfer his power to his son, Herod (later known as Herod the Great), by giving him increasingly important roles in government. Thus, in 40 B.C., the Roman Senate recognized the younger Herod's status by confirming him king of Judea. Three years later, in 37 B.C., he officially assumed his throne. For the next thirty-three years, until 4 B.C., Herod the Great continued to rule as the "loyal friend and ally of Rome." Nevertheless, his rule was harsh and turbulent, and so was his personal life.

In his will, Herod the Great divided Palestine among his three sons. Herod Archelaus received Judea, Samaria, and Idumea. He was given the title "Ethnarch" (ruler of a people or a province). Herod Philip became ruler of the regions north and east of Galilee: Gaulanitis, Trachonitis, Batanea, and Panias. These regions do not figure in the Biblical account. Herod Antipas received Galilee and Perea. These two latter rulers were given the title of "Tetrarch" (ruler of the fourth part of a kingdom). All of the life of Jesus, except for His babyhood, was during the reign of Herod Antipas, and most of His ministry was in Antipas' dominion.

In A.D. 6, Archelaus became so unpopular with the Jews that he was banished. Rome responded by establishing a succession of procurators to rule his territories, and Pontius Pilate was the fifth of these rulers. In Galilee, Herod Antipas continued as tetrarch until A.D. 39. Ordinarily, both the procurator governing Judea, and the Herodian king governing Galilee, lived in Caesarea. At festival time, however, the procurator of Judea took up residence in Jerusalem. One of his powers involved custody of the vestments of the high priest, and he needed to be present to release them for the priest's use during the special ceremonies.

In A.D. 37, Herod Agrippa I became king, and eventually he ruled the land of both Philip and Antipas. In A.D. 44, the kingdom was again broken apart, and procurators were appointed, among them Felix and Festus. Other procurators who served included: Albinus and Florus. The extreme cruelties and excesses of Florus precipitated the final revolt that led to Jerusalem's conquest and destruction by the Roman general Titus in A.D. 70.

Selected Bibliography

Adeney, Walter F., *St. Luke*. Edinburgh: T.C. & E.C. Jack, 1922.

Baker, Charles F., *Understanding the Gospels*. Grand Rapids: Grace Publications Inc., 1978.

Barclay, William, *The Gospel of John* (vol. 1). Edinburgh: Saint Andrew Press, 1955.

—— ,*The Gospel of John* (vol. 2). Toronto: G.R. Welch Co., 1975.

—— , *The Gospel of Luke*. Burlington: Welch Publishing Co., 1975.

—— ,*The Gospel of Mark*. Philadelphia: The Westminster Press, 1956.

—— , *The Gospel of Matthew* (2 vols.). Burlington: Welch Publishing Co., 1975.

—— , *Introduction to the First Three Gospels*. Philadelphia: The Westminster Press, 1975.

Beare, Francis W., *The Gospel According to Matthew*. Peabody (MA): Hendrickson Publishers, 1987 (reprint of edition of 1981).

Beasley-Murray, George R., *John*. Milton Keynes (Eng.): Word Publishing, 1987.

Bentley, Michael, *Saving a fallen world: Luke simply explained*. Durham (Eng.): Evangelical Press, 1992.

Boer, Harry R., *The Four Gospels and Acts*. Grand Rapids: Eerdmans Publishing Co., 1982.

Broadus, John A., *Commentary on Matthew*. Grand Rapids: Kregel Publications, 1990 (Reprint of edition of 1886).

Brooks, James A., *Mark*. Nashville: Broadman Press, 1991.

Browning, Wilfrid R.R., *The Gospel According to St. Luke*. New York: Macmillan, 1960.

Brownson, William C., *Meeting Jesus Through the Good News in Mark*. Grand Rapids: Baker Book House, 1993.

Bruce, F.F., *The Gospel of John*. Grand Rapids: Wm. B. Eerdmans Publishing Co., 1983.

Carter, John Franklin, *A Layman's Harmony of the Gospels*. Nashville: Broadman Press, 1961.

Chadwick, G.A., *The Gospel According to St. Mark*. London: Hodder and Stoughton, nd.

Cole, R. Alan, *The Gospel According to St. Mark*. Grand Rapids: Wm. B. Eerdmans Publishing Co., 1988 (reprint of edition of 1961).

Creed, John M., *The Gospel According to St. Luke*. New York: St. Martin's Press, 1930.

Daniel, Orville E., *A Harmony of the Four Gospels*. Grand Rapids: Baker Books, 1996.

Earle, Ralph, *et al.*, *Exploring the New Testament*. Kansas City: Beacon Hill Press, 1955.

Erdman, Charles R., *The Gospel of John*. Philadelphia: Westminster Press, 1916.

—— , *The Gospel of Luke*. Philadelphia: Westminster Press, 1921.

—— , *The Gospel of Mark*. Philadelphia: Westminster Press, 1917.

—— , The Gospel of Matthew. Philadelphia: Westminster Press, 1920.

Evans, C.F., *Saint Luke*. Philadelphia: Trinity Press International, 1990.

Evans, Craig A., *Luke*. Peabody: Hendrickson Publishers, 1990.

Foster, R.C., *Studies in the Life of Christ*. Joplin: College Press Publishing Co., 1995 (reprint of edition of 1971).

France, R.T., *Matthew: Evangelist and Teacher*. Grand Rapids: Zondervan Publishing House, 1989.

Gangel, Kenneth O., *Matthew 1-14*. Wheaton: Victor Books, 1988.

—— , *Matthew 15-28*. Wheaton: Victor Books, 1988.

Geldenhuys, Norval, *Commentary on the Gospel of Luke*. Grand Rapids: Wm. B. Eerdmans Publishing Co., 1956.

Good, Leland, *An Outlined Commentary on the New Testament*, Vols. 1 and 2: *The Gospels*. (unpublished manuscript).

Gooding, David, *According to Luke*. Grand Rapids: Wm. B. Eerdmans Publishing Co., 1987.

Grant, Frederick C., *The Gospels, Their Origin and Growth*. London: Faber and Faber, 1957.

Hadjiantoniou, George A., *New Testament Introduction*. Chicago: Moody Press, 1957.

Hare, Douglas R.A., *Matthew*. Louisville: John Knox Press, 1993.

Harrison, Everett F., *A Short Life of Christ*. Grand Rapids: Wm. B. Eerdmans Publishing Co., 1968.

Hobbs, Herschel H., *An Exposition of the Four Gospels* (2 vols.). Grand Rapids: Baker Book House, 1996.

Hurtado, Larry W., *Mark*. San Francisco: Harper & Row, 1983.

Ironside, Harry A., *Addresses on the Gospel of John*. New York: Loizeaux Brothers, 1954.

———, *Addresses on the Gospel of Luke*. New York: Loizeaux Brothers, 1947.

Kerr, John. H., *A Harmony of the Gospels*. New York: Fleming H. Revell Co., 1944.

Kistemaker, Simon, *The Parables of Jesus*. Grand Rapids: Baker Book House, 1980.

Killinger, John, *A Devotional Guide to the Gospels*. Waco: Word Books, 1984.

Lane, William L., *The Gospel of Mark*. Grand Rapids: Wm. B. Eerdmans Publishing Co., 1974.

Laney, J. Carl, *Moody Gospel Commentary: John*. Chicago: Moody Press, 1992.

Larson, Bruce, *The Communicator's Commentary: Luke*. Waco: Word Books, 1983.

Lenski, Richard C.H., *The Interpretation of St. Luke's Gospel*. Columbus: The Wartburg Press, 1946.

———, The Interpretation of St. Mark's Gospel. Columbus: The Wartburg Press, 1946.

Liefeld, Walter L., *Luke* (Expositor's Bible Commentary). Grand Rapids: Zondervan Publishing House, 1995.

Linnemann, Eta, *Is There a Synoptic Problem?* Grand Rapids: Baker Book House, 1992.

McCumber, William E., *Matthew*. Kansas City: Beacon Hill Press, 1975.

MacGregor, G.H.C., *The Gospel of John*. London: Hodder and Stoughton, 1928.

Marshall, F., *St. Mark*. London: George Gill and Sons, n.d.

Menzies, William W., *Understanding the Times of Christ*. Springfield: Gospel Publishing House, 1969.

Moorman, John R.H., *The Path to Glory; Studies in the Gospel According to Saint Luke*. Greenwich (CT): Seabury Press, 1960.

Morris, Leon, *The Gospel According to John*. Grand Rapids: Wm. B. Eerdmans Pub. Co., 1971.

———, *The Gospel According to St. Luke*. Grand Rapids: Wm. B. Eerdmans Publishing Co., 1986.

———, *Jesus is the Christ. Studies in the Theology of John*. Grand Rapids: Wm. B. Eerdmans Publishing Co., 1989.

Nineham, D.E., *The Gospel of St. Mark*. New York: The Seabury Press, 1963.

Pate, C. Marvin, *Moody Gospel Commentary: Luke*. Chicago: Moody Press, 1995.

Orchard, John B., *A Synopsis of the Four Gospels*. Edinburgh: T. & T. Clark Limited, 1983.

Pentecost, J. Dwight, *Harmony of the Words and Works of Jesus Christ*. Zondervan Publishing House, 1981.

———, The Words and Works of Jesus Christ. Grand Rapids: Zondervan Publishing House, 1981.

Peters, E.E., *Jerusalem*. Princeton: Princeton University Press, 1985.

Peterson, Robert A., *Getting to Know John's Gospel*. Phillipsburg: Presbyterian and Reformed Publishing Co., 1989.

Plummer, Alfred, *The Gospel According to St. John*. Cambridge: University Press, 1905.

Rattey, Beatrice K., *The Making of the Synoptic Gospels*. London: S.P.C.K. and the National Society, 1957.

Reith, George, *The Gospel According to St. John*. (Parts I and II). Edinburgh: T. & T. Clark, 1889.

Rice, John R., *The King of the Jews: a verse-by-verse commentary on the Gospel according to Matthew*. Grand Rapids: Zondervan Publishing House, (originally published in 1955).

Roney, Charles Patrick, *Commentary on the Harmony of the Gospels*. Grand Rapids: Eerdmans Publishing Co., 1948.

Scroggie, W. Graham, *A Guide to the Gospels*. Old Tappan: Fleming H. Revell Co., n.d.

Shepard, J.W., *The Christ of the Gospels*. Grand Rapids: Eerdmans Publishing Co., 1956.

Sharp, C.J., *The Christ of the Four Gospels*. Cincinnati: The Standard Publishing Co., 1942.

Shroyer, Montgomery J., *The Synoptic Gospels*. New York: Abingdon Press, 1945.

Simpson, A.B., *The Word Made Flesh*. Camp Hill: Christian Publications, 1995 (reprint from Christ in the Bible Commentary).

Stalker, James, *The Life of Jesus Christ*. New York: Fleming H. Revell Co., 1891.

Stein, Robert H., *Difficult Passages in the Gospels*. Grand Rapids: Baker Book House, 1984.

Stock, Eugene, *Talks on St. Luke's Gospel*. Grand Rapids: Baker Book House, 1955.

Streeter, B.F., *The Four Gospels*. New York: The Macmillan Co., 1925.

Swanson, Reuben J., *The Horizontal Line Synopsis of the Gospels* (Revised). Pasadena: William Carey Library, 1984.

Swihart, Stephen D., *Matthew, Mark and Luke* (Logos International Bible Commentary). Plainfield: Logos International, 1981.

Tasker, R.V.G., *The Gospel According to St. John*. Grand Rapids: Wm. B. Eerdmans Publishing Co., 1980.

———, *The Gospel According to St. Matthew*. Grand Rapids: Wm. B. Eerdmans Publishing Co., 1983

Taylor, Vincent, *The Gospel According to St. Mark*. London: Macmillan & Co., 1959.

Tenney, Merrill C., *John: The Gospel of Belief*. Grand Rapids: Wm. B. Eerdmans Publishing Co., 1948.

Thiessen, Henry C., *Introduction to the New Testament*. Grand Rapids: Wm. B. Eerdmans Publishing Co., 1943.

Thomas, David, *The Gospel of St. Matthew*. Grand Rapids: Baker Book House, 1955.

Tinsley, E.J., *The Gospel According to Luke*. Cambridge: Cambridge University Press, 1965.

Towns, Elmer, *The Gospel of John: Believe and Live*. Old Tappan: Fleming H. Revell Co., 1990.

Walvoord, John F., and Roy B. Zuck (eds.) *The Bible Knowledge Commentary*. *New Testament edition*. Wheaton: Victor Books, 1983.

Wenham, John, *Redating Matthew, Mark and Luke*. London: Hodder & Stoughton, 1991.

Wilkins, Chester, *The Four Gospels Arranged as a Single Narrative*. Bartlesville (OK): Wilkins Publications, 1974.

Wilcock, Michael, *The Message of Luke*. Downers Grove: Inter-Varsity Press, 1979.

INDEX

264

Scripture References

MATTHEW

1:I	21	
1:2-17	24	
1:18-25	30	
2:1-12	35	
2:13-18	36	
2:19-23	37	
3:1-6	39	
3:7-10	41	
3:11-12	42	
3:13-17	44	
4:1-11	45	
4:12	59	
4:13-17	62	
4:18-22	63	
4:23-25	67	
5:1-2	79	
5:3-12	80	
5:13-16	81	
5:17-48	81	
6:1-18	83	
6:19-34	84	
7:1-12	85	
7:13-23	86	
7:24-29	86	
8:1-4	68	
8:5-13	87	
8:14-17	65	
8:18	104	
8:19-22	134	
8:23-27	104	
8:28-34	105	
9:1-8	69	
9:9-13	71	
9:14-17	74	

9:18-26	107
9:27-34	108
9:35-38	88
10:1-4	77
10:1-16	90
10:17-39	91
10:40-42	92
11:1	92
11:2-6	92
11:7-19	93
11:20-30	94
12:1-8	75
12:9-14	76
12:15-21	77
12:22-37	97
12:38-45	99
12:46-50	100
13:1-52	100
13:53-58	109
14:1-2	109
14:3-5	59
14:6-12	110
14:13-21	110
14:22-23	112
14:24-36	112
15:1-20	117
15:21-28	119
15:29-31	120
15:32-39	120
16:1-4	121
16:5-12	122
16:13-20	123
16:21-28	125
17:1-8	126
17:9-13	128
17:14-21	128
17:22-23	129
17:24-27	130
18:1-6	130

18:7-11	131
18:12-14	161
18:15-22	133
18:23-35	133
19:1-12	169
19:13-15	170
19:16-30	171
20:1-16	172
20:17-19	173
20:20-28	173
20:29-34	174
21:1-11	178
21:12-16	180
21:17	177
21:18-22	180
21:23-27	181
21:28-45	181
22:1-14	181
22:15-46	183
23:1-39	185
24:1-3	190
24:4-14	190
24:15-26	191
24:27-30	192
24:31-35	193
24:36-44	193
24:45-51	194
25:1-13	194
25:14-30	195
25:31-46	195
26:1-5	197
26:6-13	197
26:14-16	198
26:17-19	199
26:20	200
26:21-25	203
26:26-30	204
26:31-35	206

26:36-46	214
26:47-56	215
26:57, 59-68	217
26:58, 69-75	219
27:1	220
27:2	222
27:3-10	221
27:11-14	222
27:15-30	223
27:31-34	227
27:35	229
27:36-44	230
27:45-50	232
27:51-56	234
27:57-61	236
27:62-66	238
28:1	238
28:2-4	239
28:5-8	239
28:9-10	241
28:11-15	241
28:16-20	246

MARK

1:1	21
1:2-6	39
1:7-8	42
1:9-11	44
1:12-13	45
1:14-15	59
1:16-20	63
1:21-28	64
1:29-34	65
1:35-39	67
1:40-45	68
2:1-12	69
2:13-17	71
2:18-22	74

266